THE CAUSES AND EFFECTS OF ANTI-SEMITISM:
THE DIMENSIONS OF A PREJUDICE

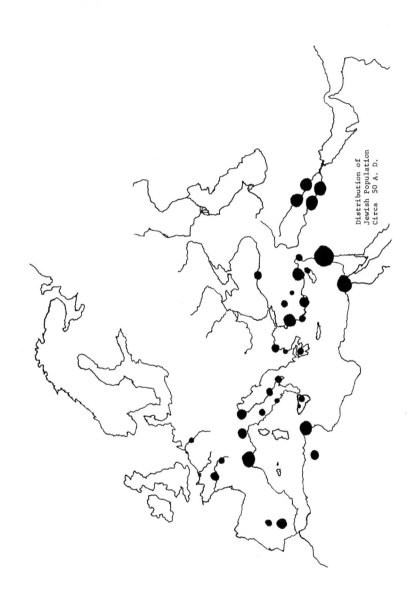

Distribution of
Jewish Population
Circa 50 A. D.

THE CAUSES AND EFFECTS OF ANTI-SEMITISM: THE DIMENSIONS OF A PREJUDICE

AN ANALYSIS AND CHRONOLOGY OF 1900 YEARS OF ANTI-SEMITIC ATTITUDES AND PRACTICES

by
Paul E. Grosser
and
Edwin G. Halperin

PHILOSOPHICAL LIBRARY
NEW YORK

DEDICATION

TO THE VICTIMS OF ANTI-SEMITISM—JEWS AND
CHRISTIANS

FOREWORD

In the early days of World War II, as a war correspondent accompanying the German Army on its sweep through Eastern Europe—from Poland to Hungary, Rumania, Bulgaria, Yugoslavia and Greece—I saw at close hand what the Nazis were doing to Jews. Then came the night when Alex Coler, editor of the leading Rumanian daily newspaper, appeared at my villa on the edge of Bucharest Rumania and asked for sanctuary for himself, his wife and daughter, because, he said, his Christian friend had alerted him that the Rumanian Iron Guard was planning a pogrom that night and that his name was on the list.

After turning over the master bedroom to the Colers I sat all night in the hallway reading a book, with a revolver in my lap. No one came. When the servants announced breakfast I unlocked the bedroom door and Alex went directly to the telephone. He returned trembling with rage.

"While we slept in your bed they went through the Jewish quarter, rounded up three or four hundred Jewish men and women, loaded them into trucks, drove them to the abbatoir on the edge of town, stripped them naked, made them get down on all fours like animals, drove them up the inclined runway, at the top of which a member of the Legion of the Archangel Michael (the official name of the Rumania Fascist Party) cracked each one over the head with a mallet, then others hanged the dripping corpses on hooks around the wall, as if they were the carcasses of animals, and then, as a last macabre touch, they stamped each one with a rubber stamp, 'Kosher.' "

After a moment of chilling silence, Alex Coler apologized for troubling me with such a grim report and suggested we now have breakfast.

Of course no one ate. As we sat in silence staring down at our plates I did more thinking than I had ever done before. My people (for I had been born a Christian) were responsible. Hitler and Mussolini at the time of their death were Catholics in good standing. Protestant chaplains were attached to the German Army. My namesake, St. John the Evangelist, one of the twelve disciples of Christ, had given great aid, comfort and encouragement to anti-Semites by his utterances and his writings.

These people called Jews for twenty centuries had suffered indignities, persecution, terror, catastrophe, which now, in Europe, was coming to a frightful crescendo, inspired by the maniacal rantings of a onetime Austrian Army corporal.

That morning in Bucharest Rumania I also acquired a deep-seated interest in the causes and possible cures of anti-Semitism. During the intervening thirty-five years I have read everything I could find on the subject. And written a bit on the subject, too. Recently I met the authors of this volume and was given the privilege of reading their manuscript. For me they have made the history of anti-Semitism clearer than anything else that has come my way.

This is truly a history of a hatred. The worst hatred that has ever plagued the world. The most persistent hatred. The most virulent hatred. Organized chronologically, it traces a pattern, from the Roman Period, through the Dark Ages, the Crusades, the Inquisition, the Reformation, and the Twentieth Century. By throwing a spotlight, year by year, decade by decade, century by century, on the outbreaks of anti-Semitism, it shows how and where and when the disease has spread, has been temporarily brought under control, and then, suddenly, in some far part of the world, has become endemic again.

The authors have also provided us with a brilliant survey of the causes of this dread disease and in their chapter entitled ''Conclusions'' they theorize as to how Judaism and Jews have been able to survive the thousands of years of malignity and persecution and they express a certain hope for the future.

Scholars and historians will be grateful to Paul Grosser and Edwin Halperin for giving them a reference work that will save them much labor. The average Jew, who has suffered anti-Semitism without, perhaps, knowing its full history, will learn much from this volume. Christians should especially benefit, for among us are many, I know, who, once made acutely aware of the long list of crimes that have been committed in the name of religion, will wish to find ways to atone—or at least to do their part in helping wipe out the dreadful disease.

Robert St. John,
Washington, D.C.
April 2, 1977

PREFACE

For long centuries the rabbis taught: if the gentiles had understood the meaning of the destruction of the Temple, they would have mourned it more than the Jews. Today a parallel interpretation is growing up about another massive event: if the Christians were to understand the meaning of the Holocaust, they would mourn it more than the Jews.

The Holocaust was, of course, the bitter fruit of long centuries of Christian teaching about the Jewish people. From the time of the gentile Church Fathers and the legal establishment of a triumphant ecclesiastical and philosophical control system with Constantine the Great, Christendom treated the Jewish people with contempt and taught contemptuously of them. Precisely, in the statics of a triumphalist power structure called "Christian," the baptized gentiles succumbed to that wrongheadedness against which Paul had warned: they turned in jealousy and envy against the very root that bore them (Rom. 11:18). Until the modern period, throughout the long centuries when ecclesiastical and political power brokers used a monolithic misinterpretation of Christian truth to justify their policies, dissenters were savagely persecuted and the Jewish people maligned, lied about, and consigned to destruction. In the modern period the logic of this false teaching and false position was worked out in Hitler's "final solution to the Jewish problem."

In the shadow of this formative event, a new generation of Christian teachers is arising that is calling co-believers to a right relationship to the Jewish people. During the first great time of testing, the Holocaust, most of the Christian leaders and the masses of the baptized flunked their exams. It remains yet to be seen whether in the second time of testing—the foundation and achieving security of the state of Israel, the Christians will have learned their lessons. In any case, the survival of the Jewish people is the litmus test of authenticity for Christianity.

There were some teachers who did not succumb to the lust for power, expressed in persecution of dissenters and repression and murder of Jews. In the following pages they stand out like flickering lights in a great darkness. If the question is raised, why so many pages of "darkness" should be published, the answer lies in the nature of pathology. Just as every good medical scholar has training in pathology, because the study of sickness and decay gives clues to health, so in looking toward a healthy relationship between Christians and Jews the study of pathological teachings and relationships is imperative. This book makes available valuable material previously inaccessible to most teachers and students, and its authors deserve the warm thanks of all who are trying to straighten out their thoughts and actions to a healthier pattern of human reconciliation and brotherhood.

The survival of the Jewish people, after their recent abandonment by the "civilized" and "Christian" world, is one of the miracles of history. The survival of Christianity, in anything but the most superficial and cosmetic appearance, is now the critical question. This book will make it possible for persons of conscience to see where Christianity went wrong, to perceive where there are clues as to where its teaching may be corrected and developed, and to get the Christian churches back toward a more credible and authentic representation of Biblical truth: the cornerstone of a renewed Christianity must be a more true and healthy relationship to the Jewish people.

Franklin H. Littell
Chairman
Department of Religion
Temple University

CONTENTS

FOREWORD   vii

PREFACE   xi

INTRODUCTION   3

       Purpose
       Definition of Anti-Semitism
       Scope of the Study
       Limits or Qualifications
       Format

PREFACE   15

MIGRATION   21

EXPULSIONS   31

HISTORICAL OVERVIEW
CHART   41

CATALOGUE OF ANTI-SEMITIC INCIDENTS:
   70 A.D.-1970 A.D.

Part I: The Roman Period—70 A.D.-325 A.D.   49
          Background
          Environment
          Incidents
          Continuum

Part II: The Early Christian Period—325 A.D.-500 A.D.   74
    Background
    Environment
    Incidents
    Continuum

Part III: Dark Ages—500 A.D.-1000 A.D.   84
    Background
    Environment
    Incidents
    Continuum

Part IV: The Crusades—1000 A.D.-1348 A.D.   99
    Background
    Environment
    Incidents
    Continuum

Part V: The Black Death—1348 A.D.-1357 A.D.   126
    Background
    Environment
    Incidents
    Continuum

Part VI: The Inquisition—1366 A.D.-1500 A.D.   134
    Background
    Environment
    Incidents
    Continuum

Part VII: The Reformation—1500 A.D.-1599 A.D.   158
    Background
    Environment
    Incidents
    Continuum

Part VIII: The 17th and 18th Centuries—
1600 A.D.-1799 A.D.   174
    Background

Environment
Incidents
Continuum

Part IX: The 19th Century—
1800 A.D.-1899 A.D.   206
    Background
    Environment
    Incidents
    Continuum

Part X: The 20th Century—1900 A.D.-1970 A.D.   237
    Background
    Environment
    Incidents
    Continuum

CAUSES OF ANTI-SEMITISM: WHY THE JEW?   289

Introduction
Causes
    Background and Culture
    Religious Conflict and Attitudes
    Psycho-Christian Demands
    Perpetual Strangers in Conflict Through
        Social, Economic and Religious
        Roles
    Psychological Demands
    Exploitation and Utilization
    Conspicuousness and Vulnerability
    Environment
    Resistance to Solution
    A Life of Its Own
Conclusion to Causes
Notes to Causes

CONCLUSION   337

ISLAM

Introduction to Islam Catalogue   367
The Islamic Catalogue, 600-1970 A.D.   371
    Background
    Incidents
    Continuum
Notes

BIBLIOGRAPHY   393

ACKNOWLEDGMENTS

Many people gave support and encouragement to our efforts at what seemed at times an endless project. We want to acknowledge the help of our careful and dedicated research assistants, Kay Reynolds and Sande Blystone of El Paso and Sally Davis and Jerry Jones of Baton Rouge. Nancy Kohutek's editorial advice forced a clarification of ideas and language. We cannot repay our typists Mrs. Sam P. Mistretta and Miss Jo Scurria who put up with our handwriting and many revisions and stayed with the task in spite of the depressing nature of much of the material.

We also want to thank Profs. Cecil V. Crabb, Rene Williamson and Cecil Eubanks of L.S.U., Prof. Franklin Littell of Temple University, Prof. Nick Hays of U.T., El Paso, Fr. Edward Flannery and Mr. Robert St. John for their criticism, assistance and encouragements. Of course, any errors of fact or interpretation are solely the authors'.

Lastly, our love and thanks to Rachel, Mariamne, Joshua, Rita and Kurt for their understanding and tolerance.

INTRODUCTION

INTRODUCTION

PURPOSE

The purpose of this book is to increase awareness and understanding of anti-Semitism's historical magnitude and continuity, and its deep infection of the Western World.

The book's concept grew from an observation that a communicable historical catalogue of anti-Semitism was non-existent and greatly needed. Many works attempting to evidence the manifestations of anti-Semitism do exist. Some are excellent and most are utilized here (see Bibliography); but they are often uneven—carefully handling some histories and leaving others almost untouched—and, owing to their form, frequently condense periods of anti-Semitism into a general statement and a few dramatic examples.

The extent of anti-Semitism in Western History has never, to say the least, been common knowledge.[1] And today there is a tendency to assume that the problem of Jewish security and the attitudes of Jews toward their survival grow from the experience of the Holocaust alone. The actions of the Nazis and their collaborators are of such a scale and horror as to obscure the long history of anti-Semitism. Often lost in appraisals of anti-Semitism is the fact that the underlying spirit of the Holocaust is almost 2,000 years old. The genocide carried out by a civilized and cultured nation in the mid-twentieth century was an extreme manifestation of this spirit, but not an isolated one.

Three other factors also tend to obscure the history of anti-Semitism. First are the numerous misconceptions that have developed. Various scholars and writers on the subject have focused on particular periods or manifestations of anti-Semitism that are peculiar to a specific historical period without investigating the source or developmental process. This is especially true of works focusing on anti-Semitism in the 19th and 20th centuries that emphasize racial theories.[2] Second are the numerous theories that have also been developed throughout history that have varying degrees of explanatory power. However, none alone is powerful enough or complete enough to adequately account for anti-Semitism's persistence, vitality and complexity. For example, the scapegoat thesis may explain some of Medieval anti-Semitism, such as the persecutions during the Black Death, but has little bearing on anti-Semitism in 19th century America.[3] Third are the distorted images of and beliefs about Jews that have been absorbed by the surrounding culture and transmitted from generation to generation. The pariah status assigned to Jews and Judaism in the first few centuries of the Christian era discouraged curiosity, interest and other efforts to know Jews. This helped to create a cultural ignorance on the topic of Jews and Judaism. This widespread ignorance contributed to a sociological and cultural situation or climate that virtually assured a distorted and perverse view of the Jews, especially as stereotypes. At the same time, many anti-Semitic practices forced some Jews into certain activities and these images were uncritically and unconsciously incorporated by the host culture as stereotypical. As a result they often generated or justified further anti-Semitism by people who were unaware that these stereotypes, besides being selective—and not necessarily condemnable in others or in other times—were products of earlier anti-Semitism. In other words the "objective" observer as well as the anti-Semite helped distorted images grow more prevasive, gain greater uncritical acceptance, perpetuate themselves with finer energy and therefore form an attitudinal base that was even more susceptible to anti-Semitic manipulation.

This study is an aid to overcoming these obstacles to an understanding of anti-Semitism. We have used two devices to bring the subject into clearer focus. One is the concise listing, in chronological order, of anti-Semitic incidents. This allows the reader to appreciate the weight and continuum of anti-Semitism without sorting through a mass of complex and extraneous materials. This catalogue is a new language that, we hope, will cause a greater awareness of the pervasiveness, persistence and effect of anti-Semitism throughout the history of the last nineteen centuries. The other device is a compilation, analysis and synthesis of the causes and theories of anti-Semitism that are apparent from the catalogue, have been developed by various scholars, or are our own contributions based on our experiences and research. The result is a unique treatment that complements the existing literature on the subject and fills an important gap in the study of anti-Semitism.

DEFINITION OF ANTI-SEMITISM

It would require many pages to discuss the various kinds of anti-Semitism (religious, racial, etc.) and their frequently confusing and inconsistent definitions. A definition, however, is required. Therefore we have developed one that is fairly inclusive.

Definition

Anti-Semitism: Attitudes and actions against Jews based on the belief that Jews are uniquely inferior, evil or deserving of condemnation by their very nature or by historical or supernatural dictates.[4]

This definition may or may not apply to attacks against Jews apparently motivated by considerations such as philosophical differences, power struggles and political maneuverings; however, it does apply when culturally-induced, subconscious or surrounding prejudices are consciously or unconsciously utilized.

SCOPE OF THE STUDY

Central Emphasis: The development and growth of anti-Semitism has been traced from the series of Jewish revolts against

Rome and the beginning of Christianity in the first centuries A.D. up to 1970. The study lists incidents and events that are anti-Semitic, by our definition, for a 1900 year time span. The focus of the study is the western world from the Roman Empire to the present. The study covers the Roman World—Western and Byzantine, Europe including Russia—Czarist and Soviet, and the Western Hemisphere—North and South America.

The technique of the catalogue, useful through the Holocaust, is, as other attempts at dealing with post-Nazi anti-Semitism, confounded by the enormity of the Nazi experience. In contrast, much of the anti-Semitic activity since 1945 (and in retrospect much preceding 1933), seems trivial and to dwell extensively with it in a study of this scope would leave the impression of knitpicking. A change of technique was also suggested by one of the positive side effects of the disclosure of the Nazi program of genocide—the increased awareness and sensitivity to anti-Semitism. Since 1945, the reporting of anti-Semitic action has been more systematic and extensive than in the past. Various scholars, organized groups, specialized information agencies, and the world press have provided a comprehensive and extensive record of contemporary anti-Semitism. This record is readily available and accessible. As a result, the continuation of the catalogue of incidents for this period would almost double the length of the study and convey an inaccurate impression of the historic pattern of anti-Semitism. Therefore, the twenty-five year period from 1945 to 1970 is presented in essay form. No attempt is made to be as inclusive as in the rest of the study and the events mentioned are used to illustrate the similarity and continuity of contemporary anti-Semitism with its past.

LIMITS OR QUALIFICATIONS

Pagan Times:

Although some pagan hostility toward Jews does, in a loose sense, conform to our definition of anti-Semitism, it was not responsible for the inception and growth of anti-Semitism in the Christian West.[5] It was not central or unique to Jewish misfortunes and history. It was not the anti-Semitism of Western man. Pagan anti-Semitism did, however, affect that of the West. Because of this it is touched on. (Certainly, much has been written on the role of this variety of anti-Semitism, and we do not mean to dismiss it as unworthy of discussion. It is not, as we see it, central to our analysis.)

The Oriental World: The few Jews residing outside the Western and Islamic worlds fared quite well. They were not an exploited or a "disturbing" factor. There was no anti-Semitism. For example, the Jewish communities in China thrived until recently when they disappeared through assimilation. Some in India still exist today.

The Special Problem of Islam and the Arab-Jewish Experience: Historically, anti-Semitism in the Moslem world was qualitatively and quantitatively distinct from the anti-Semitism of the Christian/Western world. Jewish misfortunes in Islamic countries do not approach in intensity or pervasiveness the Jewish experience in Europe. The Jew in Moslem countries was seldom treated as an alien. There were few large-scale expulsions. He was, for the most part, protected by law from assault almost on a par with his neighbors. The Jews were not the only minority as was usually the case in the Christian West. The Jewish people were not the *central* villains* in the theology of Islam. There was a condition of religious toleration not present under Christianity. Overt violence and anti-Semitic persecution, while not absent, were episodic and unsystematic. There were periods and places of genuinely cordial Islamic/Arab-Jewish interaction.[6] For these reasons, the Islamic/Arab-Jewish relationship is not included in the main body of the study. Properly, it is the topic for a separate indepth study. However, the Arab/Jewish experience is central to the question of Israel. Therefore an Islamic catalogue attempts to bring a focus to this aspect of anti-Semitism.

The Content of the Catalogue: Finally, the catalogue, as it appears, is not an all inclusive or total listing of all anti-Semitic incidents that occurred in the time span covered. Some incidents were omitted in order to keep the catalogue to a manageable size. Certain anti-Semitic actions were so numerous that a representa-

*Jews still played a devil-like role in Islamic theology and myth.

7

tive listing was considered sufficient. Our research was limited to English language sources and as a result incidents not included in these sources were omitted. Lastly, though we were thorough and systematic in our research, cross checked sources and consulted with specialists on various countries and periods, some omissions may have occurred through oversight or error on our part.

FORMAT

The catalogue of anti-Semitic incidents is broken into ten sections. The divisions are based on conventional historical periods such as the Roman Empire, the Dark Ages, the Reformation and specific centuries, or on events or institutions that had particular impacts on the Jewish experience and anti-Semitism such as the Crusades, the Black Death and the Inquisition. To lessen the inherent limitations of the Catalogue, to facilitate the proper placement of co-related factors, and to aid the understanding of the reader who wishes to concentrate on one section, specific forms are consistently used through the Catalogue, each indicating specific types of information. For the same reasons, there is some repetition of facts within these forms:

1. *Background Paper* found preceding historical periods, briefly and generally covers those historical facts and interpretations that will aid in understanding the following anti-Semitic incidents.

2. *Commentary on the Jewish/Christian Environment* follows each background paper and attempts—with the continuum—to communicate the everyday environment of anti-Semitism surrounding both Jew and Christian. The Jewish Environment may note briefly: (a) the general social and political conditions of the Jews brought on by past or present anti-Semitism, (b) the presence of everyday "minor" anti-Semitic incidents and pressures. The Christian Environment may note briefly: (a) the attitudes of the Jews' neighbors and (b) the anti-Semitic religious cultural and political manifestations affecting the Christian community, such as theological tracts and laws, art, plays, books, conventions, secular laws, political and philosophical statements, etc.

3. *Commentary on the Continuum of Anti-Semitism* found at the

end of historical periods: (a) refers to relevant, preceding incidents; (b) points out manifestations that are recurrent in anti-Semitism especially the environmental; (c) expresses relevant anti-Semitic historical facts and patterns; and (d) underlines common, causative denominators.

Naturally, we hope the effort and energy devoted to this project will have some effect on the human problem of bigotry and hatred. The study should, at minimum, contribute to a recognition of the persistence and pervasiveness of anti-Semitism. We believe this will improve the ability and willingness to deal fairly with the problems relevant to anti-Semitism and Jewish affairs in general. But beyond this we hope to have made some contributions to a decline in prejudice and its tragic manifestations.

Finally, we want to express our indebtedness to the hundreds of scholars whose research and analysis made this book possible.

NOTES TO INTRODUCTION

1. Except for historians (whether by profession or avocation), most people know what they know of the past from survey history courses that are part of the required curriculum in secondary schools and colleges. An examination of textbooks used in such courses reveals an absence of any but the most perfunctory mention of anti-Semitism. Most typically, the only mention of anti-Semitism occurs in the section dealing with the Nazi period and World War II. In rarer cases, anti-Semitism is mentioned in conjunction with the Crusades, the Spanish Inquisition and the Dreyfus Affair. The impression from these histories is that anti-Semitism is a rare, episodic, deviant and inexplicable occurrence in Western history.

Cf. Burns, Edward McNoll. *Western Civilization* (3rd ed.). New York: W. W. Norton & Co., Inc., 1949.

Smith, Charles Edward and Lynn M. Cuse. *A Short History of Western Civilization*. Boston: D. C. Heath & Co., 1940.

Stromberg, Ronald N. *A History of Western Civilization*. Homewood, Ill.: Dorsey Press, 1969.

Swain, Joseph Ward. *The Harper History of Civilization*. New York: Harper & Brothers, 1958.

This is only a selected list over a broad time span and of different publishers. The review of most of the general survey history texts found anti-Semitism infrequently mentioned and usually treated in one sentence.

9

2. The writings of the self-proclaimed anti-Semites of the 19th and 20th centuries stress this distinction. They condemn the religiously motivated bigotry of the past and portray their Jew-hatred as more objective, true and worthy. Related arguments making a sharp distinction between modern anti-Semitism and the anti-Judaism of earlier periods have been made by such anti-anti-Semites as Hannah Arendt and Jacques Maretain. Of course, Marxist writers on the subject see all anti-Semitism as growing from economic relations and functions and dismiss the religious factor as inconsequential or merely reflective of the basic materialist source of economic relations.

3. In the formal magical ritualistic victim/sacrifice sense, the scapegoat explanation for anti-Semitic actions has never been accurate. In this magical religious practice the ritual victim took on the sins of the community and the expulsion or killing expiated the people of their sins. This has never been the case with Jewish persecution. Those instances most often explained as scapegoating—the persecutions of the Black Death and the Nazis do not fit the conditions of scapegoat. Blaming Jews for the Black Death and acting on that assertion was not scapegoating. Within the generally superstitious belief system of the 14th century, a belief (and actions based on that belief) that Jews were the cause of the plague was credible and within the context of the times logical and reasonable. The Nazis and other modern anti-Semites who blamed Jews for all misfortunes and portray Jews as despicable beings were more accurately utilizing the psychological mechanism of projection rather than scapegoating. By their standards, Jews were not symbolic or innocent victims but major villains clearly guilty as charged. Even in the most vulgar and popular sense, as when Lt. Calley is portrayed as a scapegoat, the explanation of anti-Semitism as a form of scapegoating involves considerable distorting of events and ignores many factors.

In any event, while the scapegoat thesis is popular and understandable as an explanation of anti-Semitism and even making allowances for redefinition of the original meaning of scapegoat and the distortions required to fit incidents to its conditions, it falls short as an explanation since most historical anti-Semitism does not meet the conditions. Economic factors are equally inadequate as catch all explanations of anti-Semitism. Jewish usury was certainly a reality and those in debt to the money lenders were certainly resentful. However, anti-Semitic incidents and atrocities made no distinction between the Jewish usurer and the Jewish craftsman, woman or child. Jews were at certain times dominant in particular economic activities but not all Jews, not even a majority of Jews. Furthermore, anti-Semitism thrived in regions and countries where there were no Jews or where Jews were kept in a decidedly inferior and subordinate economic and social condition.

10

4. This definition, of course, excludes attitudes and actions that are anti-Jewish, that spring from disagreements with aspects of the Jewish religion, culture or peoplehood—those equivalent to other standard oppositions against philosophies or nations.

5. On this point, in general agreement with Jules Issac, we maintian that anti-Semitic incidents in pagan times were infrequent, localized and sporadic. They were prompted, more often than not, by conflicts with those segments of a people who were stubbornly loyal to their 'strange' (within the cultural context) mono-theistic religion, who were separatist and unassimilable, and therefore visible and distrusted.

Jews at that time constituted an intractable political state that opposed foreign domination, occupied a strategic piece of land and at times constituted unwanted competition in religious proselytizing and economics. Some of these factors appear in Christian anti-Semitism but missing is the major element that made the latter pernicious and durable—the villainous theological role wedded to super-natural damnation and inferiority. To quote Marcel Simon in Isaac's *The Teaching of Contempt*:

"Unlike pagan anti-Semitism, which is more apt to consist of a spontaneous reaction [Christian anti-Semitism] is exceptionally well-directed and organized toward a precise end: to render the Jews hateful," It has moreover, "an official, systematic and unified quality which has always been lacking in the former. It is at the service of theology and is fed by her; it borrows her arguments . . . in a special kind of exegesis of Biblical interpretation . . . for what amounts to a long indictment of the chosen people."

Although there were pagan writings accusing the Jews of possessing ugly racial characteristics, they were too erratic and too of a kind with the rhetoric utilized against other national groups, to justify their being cited as indications of an anti-Semitic period. They were common weapons borne against all those regarded as outsiders—how common can be seen in the fact that pagan libels against the Jews were often transferred intact against the Christians.

The few scholars who have treated anti-Semitism of Christian civilization and pagan anti-Semitism as one phenomena, suggest that the former grew from the latter. This argument which traces Western anti-Semitism's birth to pagan times often seems to be an effort to establish the innocence of the Christian West—with the consequent, if not conscious, implication: an eternal, universal anti-Semitism and the inherent guilt of the Jews.

There is, for all practical purposes, little evidence to support this, and an overwhelming amount to refute it. During pagan times, Jews were often respect-ed, an experience and attitude rare in the Christian/Western world. They were

11

liked by the Greeks, esteemed by the Ptolemies in Egypt and encouraged to flourish under Babylonian and Chaldean rule. In the Roman world Jews were favored by various emperors, enjoyed extraordinary religious privileges (exempted from state religious practices) and had tremendous success in proselytizing. At the time of Christ, Jews constituted approximately 7-10 percent of the population of the Roman Empire. Later, the Jews lived peacefully in India and China.

6. There is general agreement among historians that the golden age of the Islamic Empire was also a golden age for Jews living under Islamic rule. Jewish historians, Arab historians, historians specializing in Jewish or Arabic history and other general historians share this view.

PREFACE

PREFACE

As the study progressed and took shape we periodically experienced some concerns about its form and content. In the interest of honesty this essay shares those doubts and misgivings with the reader.

In addition to the qualifications stated at the beginning of the conclusions, it is obvious that an accurate and complete assessment of anti-Semitism requires an understanding of Jewish history. Much of Jewish life, although often affected by persecutions, fell outside them. Furthermore, the impact of anti-Semitism on Jewish history is only partially revealed by the catalogue of incidents. The total experience created the strong spirituality, peoplehood, culture and accomplishments without which there would be no Jewish entity as we know it. One of the many benefits of our reading and research was such an appreciation. The general reader will probably not have that background. This problem can be overcome by supplementary reading and the bibliography includes many excellent works that would help correct this difficulty.

Our more nagging concerns involved the possible negative effects of the study. There is a danger that a condensation of anti-Semitism indicating its pervasiveness in Western culture might provide the anti-Semite or potential anti-Semite with convenient "proof" of Jewish wickedness. Where before he merely had hearsay "evidence" of the Jew as an enemy of mankind, he now has a black and white list. In his mind the substantial history of persecution may corroborate a belief that the Jew, not the perse-

15

cutor, is guilty. The Jew was persecuted over centuries because he asked for and deserved it. Our research discovered anti-Semites who made this exact claim.

Another danger is that pointing out some of the theological statements behind anti-Semitism will, at the same time, call them to the attention of a public who might read them without the scholarly annotation and reinterpretation now being provided by most Christian theologians and churches and thus regard them as justification for anti-Semitism.

These dangers are not to be lightly dismissed. Our purpose, of course, is to lessen anti-Semitism, not to increase it. But the possibility of the Catalogue and Survey providing some people with what they consider to be anti-Semitic ammunition or attestation, we believe, is insignificant compared to the potential of its objective lessons.

To partially counter these negative effects, it might have been wise to include a list of the achievements and contributions of Jews throughout history so disproportionate to their numbers, and the thousands of great and humble non-Jews who deeply commiserated with, respected and helped the Jew. (Indeed, it is too relevant and ironic not to mention the fact that while they have been persecuted more than most peoples, the Jews, by and large, have been more humanitarian than most cultures. Whether this resulted from their religion and particular culture, or from the fact that by dint of persecution they were made more sensitive to injustice and at the same time not given the power to oppress, can be and has been discussed by others.)

But the inclusion of these materials might merely reinforce the danger, suggest to the anti-Semites that they stand in opposition to the incidents, that on one side are the Jew's contributions and sympathizers, on the other his sins and heroic enemies.

Aside from this, the purpose of this book is not to create respect for Jews or encourage Jewish pride.

Still another danger is that these pages might be stamped by some as merely an outpouring of self-pity, of paranoia, of hysteria, and unhealthy concern for the macabre; a self-piteous, lengthy, repetitious complaining over past grievances—and therefore either a vehicle for keeping bitterness alive or of no use what-

16

soever. But only if there were some reasonable chance that the areas of our concern were confined to the past and did not hold on their soil, seeds to be blown to the future, and only if one refutes that there are lessons to be learned from history, could that opinion be justified.

It is precisely the piteous length, repetition and persistence of anti-Semitism, and its ability to appear in so many situations and ages, that underscores the need to understand and deal with it.

Another order of misgivings concerns the content of the study. Any Catalogue that attempts to digest a phenomena as massive and complex as the almost 2,000-year history of anti-Semitism must suffer from omissions, fractional entries and some error. Some omissions, of course, are the result of error or oversight on our part, a missed source, a misplaced index card, physical or emotional exhaustion.

Some omissions, however, were intentional. These include specific historical incidents that were legion, commonplace or already well documented and researched. Examples would be the many physical and verbal attacks against Jews, all the laws and church and lay writings and sermons directed against Jews and all the anti-Semitic incidents of the Nazi period. We have tried to be representative rather than comprehensive in our treatment of this variety of anti-Semitism.

Another type of omission are environmental incidents including the pressures of anti-Semitism. These include the daily lifestyle of Jews as affected by anti-Semitic attitudes, laws and practices surrounding him, and the anti-Semitic manifestations that permeated the non-Jewish population including social attitudes, unflattering depictions of Jews in the various arts and the anti-Semitic folklore. These are dealt with in the environmental statements. This attempted synthesis of anti-Semitic environmental factors barely touches on its effect, its intensity, and ubiquity. And it is here that synthesis is most inadequate, for without a deep awareness of the impact of anti-Semitic environment, the nature, strength, and durability of historical anti-Semitism cannot be fully appreciated.

The anti-Semitic factors of the social environment sustained a psychological prison whose potential for inflictions, indignities, etc. were a source of fear and oppression to its convicts. Everyday social restrictions, even when not being tested or challenged, constituted a continual burden. Economic and political restrictions, although more obvious and dynamic, were also part of the day, frequently not creating historical incidents as such (when not creating change) but effective nevertheless. In short, anti-Semitism in the Western world was a way of life and, usually, an inherited, mindless or rationalized attitude of the man in the street.

Also omitted are the thousands of unattractive fictional or non-fictional representations of individual Jews that might have either stemmed from anti-Semitic attitudes or selective observations. In either case, they served as a reinforcement to anti-Semitism. They are, however, alluded to in the commentary on environment.

Lastly, there may be errors in the study that stem from our misreading or misinterpreting of particular events or incidents, or that stem from our personalities, psychological make-up, worldview, or point of departure shaped by our experiences and environment. We have tried to guard against this kind of error and hope we were successful.

MIGRATION

MIGRATION

The normal migratory behavior of populations, the refusal of Jews to convert or completely acculturate, outbursts of anti-Semitic violence and the condition of statelessness have combined to make the Jews the most mobile people in history.

Part of this mobility is attributable to the same causes other groups have migrated. As with other people, Jews have voluntarily moved from one area to another motivated by adventure, curiosity, new opportunities, and hope of a better life or a fresh start. As with others, Jews have reluctantly moved from one area to another under the stress of population pressure, military threats, insecurity, failure, natural calamities such as drought and famine, food shortages and hostile environments. In this regard, Jews behaved no differently than did other people in history.

However, the preceding accounts for only a portion of the incredible and almost constant population movement of the Jewish historical experience. Most of this migration was caused by Jews refusing to become non-Jews, their alien status, and anti-Semitism. Many times Jews moved from an area to escape persecution. As outbursts of anti-Semitism occurred in a region or a country, Jews residing there sought refuge in other areas. Another cause of migration was the anti-Semitic practice of expulsion. Local or national, secular or church authorities frequently decreed that Jewish communities within their jurisdiction had to leave. These two factors account for the greatest and most dramatic Jewish migrations. If Jews had possessed a home by right rather than permission, and if anti-Semitism had not been so much a part of Western culture, the massive Jewish migrations would not have occurred.

The following illustrates the scope of Jewish migrations over the period covered by the study.

Extra Empire Diaspora*	Eastern Empire**	Western Empire***	
			100 BC
			BC/AD
			66/70
			100 AD
			113
			132/135

When the Roman Republic collapsed and was replaced by the Empire, the Jewish population was concentrated in the Eastern Mediterranean area and the neighboring empires to the East. There were, however, Jewish settlements and communities throughout the civilized world; as far west as Spain and Southern France and new settlements developed in newly conquered Gaul.

The Judean Revolts against Rome from 70 A.D. to 135 A.D. had two effects. First, on Jewish population patterns, the Roman response through military action and victor's justice decimated the population in the area of Palestine. Many Jews who survived the wars moved to the safety of the neighboring empires and regions, and others were forcibly relocated as captives. Second, the Roman actions destroyed the Jewish state and cast Jews in the role of permanent alien.

*Refers to countries and empires bordering the Roman Empire to the East, e.g., Parthia, Mesopotamia, Arabia, Babylonia, etc. Jewish communities here date from the Babylonia captivity.

**Refers to Roman provinces in the eastern Mediterranean-Egypt, Judea, Syria, Greece, etc.

***Refers to western Roman provinces in North Africa, Spain, Italy, France, etc.

23

Jewish communities outside Judea expanded in number and grew in size as an effect of this first major migration of the Christian era. In the West, Jewish communities expanded in Spain, France and Italy.

As Rome expanded these dislocated Jews moved into the new territories and established new communities. This movement continued after the fall of Rome and during the redefinition of Europe with the barbarian invasions. Jewish settlements developed in Northern Europe, England and Germany.

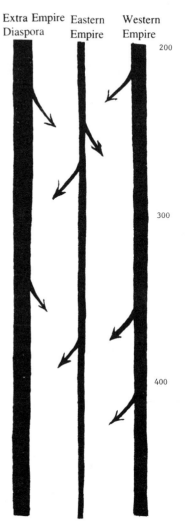

Extra Empire Diaspora   Eastern Empire   Western Empire

200

300

400

In the 7th and 8th centuries two major developments affected Jewish population patterns. First, the rise of Islam as a dominant force from the Eastern Mediterranean to Spain caused Jews to relocate in some areas. The fanaticism of early Islam involved extreme methods of proselytizing. A more tolerant attitude toward infidels (non-Islams) replaced the early militancy when Islamic hegemony was achieved.

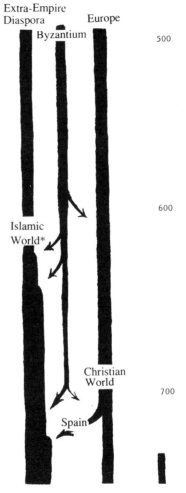

Extra-Empire Diaspora

Europe

Byzantium

500

Islamic World*

600

Christian World

700

Spain

*The Islamic Empire grew with great speed. Arab armies swept out of the Arabian peninsula in the early 7th century and by the early 8th century controlled the Eastern Mediterranean, North Africa and Spain.

Second, the conversion of the Khazars to Judaism and the rise of the Khazar Kingdom created new Jewish settlements in southern Russia and eastern Europe. The break-up of the Khazar Kingdom in the 10th century, as it was overrun by numerous barbarian migrations, created more Jewish settlements in Eastern Europe.

The Norman conquest of England increased the Jewish community there as more Jews came in the wake of the invasion.

Episodic outbreaks of fanaticism especially in the 11th century caused Jews living in the Eastern areas to move to the more remote and tolerant Moorish Spain.

*The Khazar Kingdom converted to Judaism in the 7th century flourished as a trade center and scattered when overrun by migrating tribes from the East.

Islamic World

Christian World

Khazar Kingdom

800

900

East/ 1000
Central
Europe

26

The Crusades forced many Jews in France and Germany to seek a more secure place of residence. The Polish monarchs invited Jews to settle in Poland and granted them considerable privileges. The effort to escape the persecutions of the Crusade period combined with the Khazar dispersion to create major Jewish communities in Eastern Europe and Russia.

Jews were expelled from England in 1290 and resettled in Europe.

The Black Death and the anti-Semitism that followed its wake caused more Jewish migration to the East. Some movement was due to various expulsions; most, however, was to escape the persecutions.

Charles VI of France ordered all Jews living in the crown provinces expelled in 1394.

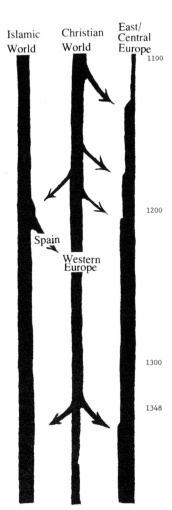

27

Expulsions occurred throughout Germany in the 15th century.

All Jews were expelled from Spain, Sardinia and Sicily in 1492. Some went to the Americas, most to the Moslem empire, some to Italy and Holland.

Jews were expelled from Portugal in 1497. Most relocated in the Americas or Holland.
Considerable Jewish relocation occurred in the 16th and 17th centuries. Frequent expulsions were carried out in Italy and Germany and the war between Poland and Russia plus the Cossack rebellion forced Jews to move. The readmission of Jews to England, and increasing religious tolerance in northern Europe resulted in a rebirth and expansion of the Jewish communities in these areas.

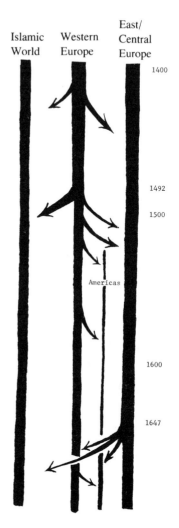

Islamic World | Western Europe | East/ Central Europe

1400

1492

1500

Americas

1600

1647

28

The Pale of Settlement was established in Russia in the 18th century. Jews living under Russian rule were confined to this area. Expulsions were carried out in Moravia, Germany, Bordeaux, Lithuania, Bohemia, Alsace and Poland.

Sweden was opened to Jewish migration.

In the 19th century expulsions and persecutions in Germany, throughout eastern Europe and in Russia resulted in major Jewish migrations to the Western Hemisphere. Most settled in the United States, but Canada, Mexico, Cuba, Brazil, Argentina and Chile also saw an increase in their Jewish population.

In the 20th century Jews from eastern Europe and Russia continued to migrate to the United States and other Western Hemisphere countries. The rise of Zionism, however, brought about another migratory pattern—the return to Palestine. The effort to colonize a Jewish Homeland and the appeal of Zionism affected Jews throughout the world. Between the World Wars, Jewish migrations had two main destinations—the Americas and Palestine.*

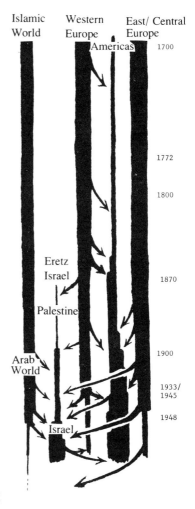

*It should be noted that except for short isolated periods, there has always been a Jewish population since the revolts against Rome.

29

After World War II, the survivors of the Nazi horrors continued this pattern. However, Jews in countries that had not had fascist governments began to increase their migration to Israel.

The Independence of Israel in 1948 followed by the Arab-Israeli war brought a new massive migration of Jews who had previously been living in Arab countries. Anti-Semitic attacks and expulsions saw 700,000 Jews forced from Arab countries. Most of these settled in Israel. After the first Arab-Israeli war, American and European Jews continued to migrate to Israel.

EXPULSIONS

EXPULSIONS

Expulsion is an anti-Semitic tactic clearly based on the condition or status of Jews as permanent aliens. With the destruction of the Judean state, Jews found themselves as a homeless people whose residence was always one of permission or privilege. This condition was not modified until the late 18th century when the concept of citizen changed. Beginning in the 18th and through the 19th centuries, Jews were admitted to full citizenship in various countries. This change of status did not create a permanent security, however, as the Nazi experience and the condition of Soviet Jews indicate. The creation of Israel was the only solution to this problem of statelessness.

In the period between the destruction of Judea and the establishment of Israel, monarchs, noblemen, bishops, town councils and other authorities at various levels expelled Jews from towns, principalities, dioceses, regions and sometimes whole countries and empires. Expulsions have had a variety of motivations—religious, economic, political, psychological and racial. Many times, a combination of motives was the basis for an expulsion.

Devout rulers or churchmen, motivated by the desire to save souls and bring the Jews to the true faith, used expulsion as a form of coercion (convert or leave) with the expectation that Jews would choose conversion over the hardship and suffering of forced migration. Other religiously motivated expulsions were simply efforts to protect the faithful from Jewish influence and to drive the unbeliever from society. Purely religiously motivated expulsions did occur, but often religion combined with economic motives. Many times expulsions were justified on religious grounds but included unstated economic or political motives. With rare exception, expulsions included confiscation of property and wealth in addition to forced migration. The action released wealth and property that could be redistributed as rewards for support or faithful service or to gain support. The newly-available wealth could also be used to lessen pressures for other changes in a system. Expulsions also served to unify a population, to remove a foreign element, to achieve a more homogeneous population, and to reduce conflicts within a political unit.

Expulsions were in some cases thinly veiled extortion. Additional wealth could be gained by expelling Jews and it was more popular than raising taxes. There are instances of expulsions with conditions for return that included payment of moneys as a prerequisite with an annual assessment for continued residence. Other economically motivated expulsions were efforts to remove established economic institutions in order that emerging Christian enterprises could develop; others were aimed at eliminating competition.

Some expulsions were primarily political in motivation. Monarchs or noblemen expelled Jews to gain favor with the Church or to strengthen alliances. Some saw the Jews as a subversive element or disloyal and consequently expelled them. In other cases, expulsions were intended to create a more unified polity. Again, in some cases, the political combined with economic, religious or psychological motives.

Psychologically motivated expulsions served or met some neurotic or psychotic need of the society. Tensions and anxieties, caused by a crisis or dislocation, can be minimized if an outlet for the aggression growing from the anxiety can be found. This is the historical and psychological role of the scapegoat. Anti-Semitism includes this element and Jews have been convenient scapegoats during various historical periods. Psychological motivation is most clearly seen in the expulsions carried out during the Black Death. Other expulsions of this type were manifestations of xenophobia or efforts to remove the stranger or foreign element in a population. Again as with expulsions motivated primarily by other concerns, the psychologically based expulsions also com¹bined other motives.

Racially motivated expulsions are a more modern development. While all expulsions have had some xenophobic dimensions, racial expulsions are more sophisticated and encompassing than the common fear of the outsider. These expulsions grew out of the racial ideologies developed in the 19th century and reached a climax in the Nazi movement. Expulsion and forced migration were part of the effort to make society free of Jews and an integral part of the Final Solution.

Expulsions

Date	Place	Motivation
250	Carthage	Religious
415	Alexandria	Religious
554	Diocese of Clement (France)	Religious
561	Diocese of Uzes (France)	Religious
612	Visigoth Spain	Religious
642	Visigothic Empire	Religious
855	Italy	Religious
876	Sens	Psychological (Scapegoat)
1012	Mayence	Religious
1181	France	Religious-Economic
1290	England	Religious, Psychological, Economic
1306	France	Economic
1348	Switzerland	Psychological
1348	Alsace	Psychological
1349	Hielbronn (Germany)	Psychological & Economic
1349	Hungary	Religious
1388	Strasbourg	Economic
1394	Germany	Economic

1394	France	Religious
1422	Austria	Economic
1424	Fribourg & Zurich	Economic
1426	Cologne	Economic
1432	Savory	Psychological, Economic
1438	Mainz	Economic
1439	Augsburg	Economic
1456	Bavaria	Economic
1453	Franconia	Religious
1453	Breslau	Religious
1454	Wurzburg	Religious
1485	Vincenza (Italy)	Psychological
1492	Spain	Religious, Political, Economic
1495	Lithuania	Economic, Religious
1497	Portugal	Religious, Political, Economic
1499	Germany	Religious, Economic, Political
1514	Strasbourg	Political
1519	Regensburg	Economic
1540	Naples	Political, Religious
1542	Bohemia	Psychological, Political
1550	Genoa	Economic
1551	Bavaria	Economic, Psychological
1555	Pesaro	Political
1559	Austria	Political, Religious
1561	Prague	Religious, Political

1567	Wurzburg	Economic
1569	Papal States	Religious
1571	Brandenburg	Political, Economic
1582	Netherlands	Political, Religious
1593	Brandenburg, Brunswick Austria	Religious
1597	Cremona, Pavia & Lodi	Religious, Economic
1614	Frankfort	Religious, Economic
1615	Worms	Religious, Economic
1619	Kiev	Religious, Political
1649	Ukraine	Political, Religious
1649	Hamburg	Economic
1654	Little Russia	Political, Religious
1656	Lithuania	Political, Religious
1669	Oran (North Africa)	Religious
1670	Vienna	Religious
1712	Sandomir	Religious
1727	Russia	Religious, Political
1738	Wurtemburg	Religious
1740	Little Russia	Religious, Political
1744	Bohemia	Religious
1744	Livonia	Religious
1745	Moravia	Religious
1753	Kovad (Lithuania)	Religious
1761	Bordeaux	Religious
1772	Jews deported to Pale of Settlement (Russia)	Religious

1775	Warsaw (New Jerusalem)	Economic
1789	Alsace	Economic
1804	Villages in Russia	Political
1808	Villages and Countrysides in Russia	Political
1815	Lubeck & Bremen	Political, Economic
1815	Cities in Franconia Swabia and Bavaria	Political, Economic
1820	Bremes	Political, Economic
1843	Russian Border with Austria & Prussia	Political
1862	Area under Gen. Grant's Jurisdiction, U.S.	Political, Economic
1866	Galatz, Romania	Political, Religious
1919	Bavaria (foreign-born Jews)	Political
1938-45	Nazi-Controlled Areas Deported or Relocated as step of Final Solution	Racial
1948	Arab Countries	Political

38

HISTORICAL OVERVIEW

HISTORICAL OVERVIEW

The following is an attempt to present a schematic overview of anti-Semitism from 70 A.D. to 1970. The chart is organized along the same time periods utilized in the catalogue. Anti-Semitic behaviors and practices have been collapsed into thirteen separate categories, ranging from anti-Semitic writings through increasingly severe and physical actions and practices to mass murder. The chart illustrates the historic continuity and progression of anti-Semitism and also shows the correlation between increased anti-Semitism and dislocations or crises in a society.

Categories of the Overview Chart

1. Writings—includes all communications of anti-Semitic nature—religious writings, sermons, plays, fiction, newspapers, broadcasts, folklore, etc.
2. Libels—includes peculiar charges made against Jews—ritual murder, host desecration, conspiracy.
3. Distinctive Dress—includes all requirements that Jews identify themselves with special garments or badges and restrictions on Jewish dress.
4. Special Taxes—includes taxes levied as a license to practice Judaism, exorbitant taxes on Jews, specific taxes on Jewish businesses, residence, products, discriminatory taxes directed at Jews, etc.

5. Religious Restrictions—includes various prohibitions on religious practices and services, limitation on synagogues, requirements to follow non-Jewish practices, etc.
6. Social Restrictions—includes all efforts to minimize or prevent Jewish/non-Jewish interaction or contact.
7. Civil Restrictions—includes all prohibitions or regulations that denied civil or political participation to Jews—bars to public or military office, special court procedures, second-class status, etc.
8. Residential Restrictions—includes all efforts to prevent Jews from residing in the larger community, requirements to live in special areas, forced ghettoization, restrictive real estate practices, etc.
9. Economic Restrictions—includes all practices or regulations that barred Jews from certain enterprises, owning slaves, owning land, employment quotas or that required Jews to perform special economic activities, etc.
10. Forced Conversion—includes all efforts to convert Jews that used coercion or threats—confiscation of property, expulsion, torture, forcible taking of children and raising them in Christian homes or religious institutions, attacks on communities that included choice of conversion or death, etc.
11. Expulsion—includes all forced migration or relocation of Jews.
12. Violent Attacks—includes spontaneous or state-sponsored popular attacks on Jewish communities, businesses, arson, looting, bombing, vandalism, beating, etc.
13. Mass Murder—includes mob attacks that resulted in widespread slaughter, judicial murder as per the Inquisition and the Final Solution of the Nazis.

Period and Place	Anti-Semitic Pattern													Major Historical Events
	1. Writings	2. Libels	3. Distinctive Dress	4. Special Taxes	5. Religious Restrictions	6. Social Restrictions	7. Civil Restrictions	8. Residential Restrictions	9. Economic Restrictions	10. Forced Conversion	11. Expulsion	12. Violent Attacks	13. Mass Murder	
Roman Period														
Eastern Empire	x			x	x		x	x			x		x	Jewish Revolts
Western Empire	x			x	x	x	x				x			Rise of Christianity
Extra-Empire Diaspora	x													
Early Christian Period														
Eastern Empire	x	x		x	x	x		x	x		x	x	x	Christianity became state religion.
Western Empire	x			x	x	x	x		x	x		x	x	Break-up of Roman Empire.
														Barbarian invasions.
Dark Ages														
Europe	x			x	x	x	x	x	x	x	x	x		Barbarian invasions. Collapse of Western Empire. Establishment of feudalism.
Byzantium	x				x		x	x	x	x	x	x	x	
Islamic Empire	x		x	x	x	x		x	x	x	x	x	x	Rise of Islam and establishment of Islamic Empire.

43

Period and Place	Anti-Semitic Pattern													Major Historical Events
	1. Writings	2. Libels	3. Distinctive Dress	4. Special Taxes	5. Religious Restrictions	6. Social Restrictions	7. Civil Restrictions	8. Residential Restrictions	9. Economic Restrictions	10. Forced Conversion	11. Expulsion	12. Violent Attacks	13. Mass Murder	
Crusades														
Western Europe	x	x	x	x		x	x	x	x	x	x	x	x	
East/Central Europe	x		x		x	x	x		x	x		x	x	Crusades
Islamic Empire	x		x	x	x	x	x	x			x	x	x	
Black Death														
Western Europe	x	x	x	x	x	x	x	x	x	x	x	x	x	Bubonic plague.
East/Central Europe	x	x	x		x	x	x		x			x	x	
Islamic Empire	x		x	x	x	x	x	x						
The Inquisition														
Western Europe	x	x	x	x	x	x	x	x	x	x	x	x	x	Break-up of feudalism and rise of the nation-state.
East/Central Europe	x	x	x	x	x	x	x	x	x	x	x	x	x	Widespread heresies threaten unity of Christendom
Islamic World	x		x	x	x	x	x	x						

Period and Place	Anti-Semitic Pattern													Major Historical Events
	1. Writings	2. Libels	3. Distinctive Dress	4. Special Taxes	5. Religious Restrictions	6. Social Restrictions	7. Civil Restrictions	8. Residential Restrictions	9. Economic Restrictions	10. Forced Conversion	11. Expulsion	12. Violent Attacks	13. Mass Murder	
The Reformation														
Western Europe Catholic countries	x	x	x	x	x	x	x	x	x	x	x	x	x	Break-up of Christian unity. Religious wars. Rise of Protestantism. Rise of nationalism. Triumph of the nation-state. Beginning of capitalism.
Protestant countries	x			x	x	x	x	x	x		x	x	x	
East/ Central Europe	x	x	x	x	x	x	x	x	x	x	x	x	x	
Islamic World	x		x	x	x	x	x	x						
17th & 18th Centuries														
Western Europe Catholic countries	x	x	x	x	x	x	x	x	x	x	x	x	x	Triumph of capitalism. Rise of democracy. Emergence of Russia.
Protestant countries	x			x	x	x	x		x					
East/ Central Europe	x	x	x	x	x	x	x	x	x	x	x	x	x	
Islamic World	x		x	x	x	x	x	x			x			

45

Period and Place	Anti-Semitic Pattern													Major Historical Events
	1. Writings	2. Libels	3. Distinctive Dress	4. Special Taxes	5. Religious Restrictions	6. Social Restrictions	7. Civil Restrictions	8. Residential Restrictions	9. Economic Restrictions	10. Forced Conversion	11. Expulsion	12. Violent Attacks	13. Mass Murder	
19th Century														
Western Europe Catholic countries	x	x			x	x	x	x	x	x	x	x	x	Industrial revolution. Imperialism. Socialism. Economic dislocation. Unification of Germany and Italy. Democratic revolutions.
Protestant countries	x	x		x		x			x	x		x	x	
East/Central Europe	x	x		x	x	x	x	x	x	x	x	x	x	
Americas	x	x			x	x	x	x	x			x	x	
Islamic World	x		x	x	x	x	x	x	x					
20th Century														
Western Europe Catholic countries	x	x	x	x	x	x	x	x	x		x	x	x	World War I. Bolshevik Revolution. Nazism. World War II. Arab Nationalism. Establishment of Israel.
Protestant countries	x	x	x	x	x	x	x	x	x		x	x	x	
East/Central Europe	x	x	x	x	x	x	x	x	x		x	x	x	
Americas	x	x				x	x	x	x			x		
Arab World	x	x	x	x	x	x	x	x	x		x	x	x	

46

CATALOGUE OF ANTI-SEMITIC INCIDENTS
70 A.D. - 1970 A.D.

PART I: THE ROMAN PERIOD - 70-325 A.D.

BACKGROUND:

The first section of this study begins with a series of revolts by the Judeans against Rome in the first and second centuries A.D. and continues to the establishment of Christianity as the state religion in the fourth century.

It is important to clarify two points concerning why the chronicle begins at this particular date. First, the decision to begin at 70 A.D. does not imply that anti-Semitism did not exist in the earlier periods. There was some anti-Semitism earlier and indeed the charges and characterizations of ancient writers such as Manetho (3rd Century B.C.) Mnaseas of Patros (2nd Century B.C.) Appolonius Molon (1st Century B.C.) and Apion (1st Century A.D.) were clearly anti-Semitic. These writings reflect a defense of the parochialism and xenophobia of the nations and cultures that produced these writers. The monotheism and universalism of Judaism obviously threatened the conventional world view and political order and had to be discredited. The patent absurdity of these writings is evidence of the credulity of the times. Nevertheless, some of the pagan accusations and stereotypes were incorporated in later anti-Semitic writings and traditions—some survive to the present.

It is erroneous, however, to assume that the anti-Semitism that begins with the destruction of Judea and the rise of Christianity is merely a continuation of pagan resentment and defense against

49

monotheism. Ancient anti-Semitic writings lack the transcendent and universal quality that characterizes anti-Semitism from the First Century to the present. Nor did it constitute an integral part of its religion—the Jew as perennial Christ killer—or attempt in a "well directed and organized" long range if not eternal program to "render the Jews hateful" as it did in Christianity.

Second, the Roman destruction of Jerusalem and the Temple should not be confused with the *Diaspora* (Dispersion) which began six centuries earlier with the Babylonian captivity. By the time of the siege of Jerusalem, Jews made up seven percent of the population of the Roman empire, most of whom lived outside of Judea. (There were over 100,000 Jews living in Alexandria alone.) During this period those living outside Judea strove to maintain their cultural purity and distinctiveness and contributed annually to the upkeep of the Temple. Their strict monotheism, horror of idolatry, and self-imposed separateness in often hostile cultures contributed considerably to pagan anti-Semitism. It is interesting to note that the libels concerning the religious practices of the Jews such as worshiping an ass and ritual murder were also made against the early Christians by their pagan opponents.

In 63 B.C. Pompey occupied Judah and renamed it Judea, as such it became a protectorate of Rome. With the defeat of the Ptolemaic empire in 30 B.C., Rome became the ruler of the "world." Judea was ruled by a series of "kings" imposed by the Romans until Augustus removed Archelaus in 6 A.D. and appointed the first of a series of procurators (governors) to rule the province. With the exception of another "king," Agrippa (41-44), a favorite of Claudius, the province was ruled by Romans until the first revolt broke out in 66 A.D. There were three such major revolts: 66-70, 113-116, and 132-135 A.D.

The cause of these revolts seems to have been the incredible incompetence, stupidity, and venality of the various procurators rather than any inexorable historical force. Political considerations did, however, set the conditions contributing to the savageness of the fighting and the brutality with which the revolts were crushed.

During the early Empire, the Roman tolerance for religious differences seems to have had two major exceptions: (1) Judaism, and (2) early Christianity. Until the end of the First Century, the

Romans made no distinction between Christianity and Judaism. Christianity was seen as a sect or branch of Judaism. Both were subversive to the ideological underpinnings and justification of the Roman state. Both threatened the stability and continuation of a slave-based economy. Both were aggressive in their proselytizing and gained converts throughout the Empire. Roman authority correctly perceived the dangers of the ethical monotheism and concept of brotherhood preached by both faiths and acted accordingly.

In Judea, religious faith was coupled with a national tradition of freedom and this combination was deadly for the Jews. Strong Judean resistance to state religious observances was taken as a personal affront by several emperors, most notably Caligula. This, however, was only a minor indication of the restiveness of the Jews under Roman rule. Rebel organizations and terrorists agitated against Roman occupation. The activities of such groups as the Zealots and their sympathizers, due to Judea's strategic geographic location, threatened the political security if not the actual existence of the Empire. Rome was not a state to take such problems lightly.

The expansion of the Empire under Augustus brought Rome into direct contact with its now neighboring rival for control of the East, Parthia. Judea was a vital link between North Africa and the Eastern provinces and was situated on the Parthian frontier. If Rome lost control of Judea, the Parthians could have swept down the Roman roads through Egypt, Cyrenaica, Africa, Numidia to Mauretania; and north through Syria, Cappadocia, and Cicilia, Bythinia; to Rhodes, Asia, and Greece. To safeguard against this possibility, Judea was heavily garrisoned and kept under tight control by the Romans. The result of this heavy-handedness was the opposite of the intent and a series of very serious revolts occurred which until they were put down posed real threats to the security of the Empire.

The first began in 66 A.D. and was not subdued until Titus besieged Jerusalem, sacked the city and destroyed the Temple in 70 A.D. The second major Jewish rebellion occurred under Trajan's reign from 113-116. This was more widespread than the earlier one and included uprisings by the Jewish populations in Cyprus, Alexandria and Cyrenaica. The last revolt, under Bar

Kochba, in 132-135 was so serious that the rebelling Jews went so far as to perform the sovereign act of issuing coins.

The major effect of the revolts was the destruction of the Judean state, which established one of the primary conditions for the succeeding 1900 years of anti-Semitism. The result of these abortive revolts was to thrust a people with a long dynamic history and a strong religio-cultural tradition into the role of permanent alien. With the destruction of Judea, the Jews became religious, cultural and national aliens wherever they established their communities.

Prior to this development, Jews living outside Judea were foreigners in the country in which they lived but had a homeland, a place of origin and a place to return. The Temple tax paid annually by Jewish communities served to strengthen the national and religious identity of the dispersed Jews. The Temple and the homeland gave a security and national dignity that was destroyed by the Roman response to the Jewish rebellions. Such action against other groups or peoples caused their historical disappearance. The Jews, however, because of the dynamism of Judaism, the strength of the Jewish historical and cultural tradition, and ironically, the terrorism of anti-Semitism, survived and continued to develop. This continued survival with a distinctive identity within a hostile environment—primarily religious—lends a transcendent quality to anti-Semitism from this time to the present.

The second major element at the root of anti-Semitism developed concomitant to the destruction of the Judean state. While the condition of permanent alien is essential to understanding this history, an awareness of the role of Christianity is just as crucial. Before Christianity became the official state religion under the reign of Constantine, it was one of many sects battling for the souls of men. Both Judaism and Christianity actively sought converts. In many cases, converts to Christianity in turn converted to Judaism. The Judaizing tendency or influence was one of the major concerns of the early Christian hierarchy. Since Christianity drew heavily from Judaism, great efforts had to be made to distinguish it from the parent religion and at the same time discredit Judaism. As with civil wars and family quarrels, the struggle between the early

Church and Judaism created mutual intolerance, antagonisms and bitterness.

The generalized failure of Christianity to attract converts among the Jews and the modification of requirements and Hellenization of Christianity by St. Paul in order to make the new religion more palatable to the gentile world further increased the antipathy between the two faiths. The bitter quarrels between the Pauline and Apostolic factions of Christianity show the origin and nature of much of later anti-Semitism. Christian antipathy toward the Jews ultimately obtained divine legitimacy in the New Testament. The Gospels exonerated Rome of any blame for Christ's death and at the same time placed the blame on the Jews as a people. The charge of deicide and the punishment for it transcends the Jews of the time and applies to all Jews at all times since the Crucifixion. Anti-Semitism also gathers support from the many anti-Jewish and anti-Semitic statements and accusations found in the New Testament, especially those found in the writings of St. John.

The anti-Semitism of the sacred writings of Christianity were, of course, elaborated on in the oral tradition and in the writings and devotions of various Church Fathers, Doctors and many of the Saints. It should be noted that these writings as well as the New Testament are ex post facto accounts and elaborations. The anti-Semitism found here is primarily that of Jesus' committed followers working out a *modus vivendi* with the political and social climate of their times.* However, these statements and charges of this early period will later serve as the basis and justification for incredible persecution and suffering.

The religious element and underpinnings of anti-Semitism cannot be over-estimated and are often under-estimated by contemporary observers because of the modern veneer of racial doctrine which tends to give a secular and rationalistic explanation for 18th, 19th, and 20th Century anti-Semitism.

ENVIRONMENT: CHRISTIAN

In the first century A.D., Christianity was considered another Jewish sect by Roman authorities; however, the ruling Sadducee faction in Judea saw it as heresy and blasphemy and persecuted Christian adherents.

As Christianity distinguished itself from Judaism it was declared an illegal religion by Rome and equated with subversion and treason. As such, Christians suffered frequent and terrible persecutions by Roman authorities.

Roman and pagan writers accused Christians of ritual murder, infanticide, sexual perversion, worshipping an ass, and cannibalism.

Christian writers and leaders blamed the Roman persecutions on Jewish instigation.

Christian writers and preachers drew a sharp distinction between Jews. Those of the Old Testament were Hebrews and generally good men. Those of the New Testament and the Christian era were Jews and generally characterized as evil.

Later Christian writers borrowed from the anti-Semitic writings of pagans such as Apion and gave their charges and slanders a Christian respectability.

In the third and fourth centuries A.D., various bishops and councils forbade Christians to have friendly relations with Jews.

The basic doctrinal works of the Christian religion included many statements that were or could be easily interpreted as anti-Semitic. These, of course, were elaborated on by the oral tradition and by many church leaders in various places as they responded to particular events. (See New Testament, Sts. Cyprian, Clement and Eusebius.)

The historical distortion that equates the *Diaspora* (the Dispersion) with the siege of Jerusalem by Titus and with punishment for deicide is first found in the writings of Origen.

ENVIRONMENT: JEWISH

Unlike Christianity during this period, Judaism was a licit religion recognized by Roman authorities and granted exemptions from certain state-religio practices. This status and privilege was, however, periodically revoked and Jews were then persecuted as atheistic and subversive for their failures of emperor worship.

Jews were living throughout the then known world before the

Empire came into existence. Jewish settlements also developed as the Empire expanded in the newly-civilized, i.e., Romanized parts of the world such as Gaul and Germany. (As today, in regards Israel and the world Jewish population, at the time of the Jewish revolts the Jews living outside Judea outnumbered those residing in the homeland.)

Tacitus, Suetonius and Cicero speak of the spiritual and ethical impact of the Jews and some feared Judaism as a subversive force. Anti-Semitism, however, seems to have been restricted to those areas where the Hellenic and the Judaic spirit were in close contact and conflict. Hellenism seemed a corrupt and hollow hedonism and Judaism seemed an unreasonable puritanism. Both however were proselytizing forces and the worst clashes occurred in Alexandria, where both Greeks and Jews were foreigners.

The Judean revolts changed the position and treatment of Jews by the Romans. They now became a homeless nation, a people without a country.

Jewish religious freedom was restricted by imperial decree and proselytizing was punishable by death.

The Roman Emperor Vespasian invented the practice of using Jews as a special revenue source.

Jews were restricted in residence and travel in Palestine.

INCIDENTS:
70 A.D.
Roman legions under the generalship of Titus took Jerusalem, putting an end to the first revolt which had lasted four years. City walls, the Temple and most of the City were destroyed. Emperor Vespasian, however, continued to collect the Temple tax that Jews living in the Empire had been assessed to keep up the Temple. Since the Temple no longer existed the tax now went to the Capitoline Jupiter. Later the tax was diverted to Vespasian's private use and treasury. This action by Vespasian began the practice of the Jew as a special taxpayer and revenue source.[1]

79-81 A.D.
Titus succeeded Vespasian as emperor and continued the Temple tax which was now Fiscus Judaicus. The tax was diverted to the royal treasury and served as a license fee to practice Judaism.[2]

81-96 A.D.

Domitian succeeded Titus as emperor. He continued to collect the Jewish tax but with much greater harshness than Titus or Vespasian. Suetonius recounts his agents going so far as to strip a 90 year old man in court to determine if he were circumcised. Under Domitian, converts to Judaism or those leaning toward Judaism were prosecuted on grounds of irreligion. The punishment included confiscation of property and exile or death. Tacitus relates that executions took place almost continuously. In 95 A.D., Domitian had his cousin, and Consul, Flavius Clemens executed because of his suspected conversion to Judaism. This particular act is said, by Suetonius, to have led to Domitian's assassination.[3]

88-97 A.D.

St. Clement (Pope 88-97) blamed the Jews for Nero's persecution of the Christians.[4]

113-116 A.D.

The second revolt by Jews, this one most widespread, including Jewish communities in Alexandria, Cyrenia, and Cyprus, occurred under Trajan. It was crushed with widespread slaughter by Marcius Turbo and Lucius Quietus. Quietus was rewarded by appointment as governor. His rule was harsh and brutal and in the tradition of his predecessors.[5] (See background to Roman period.)

130 A.D.

Emperor Hadrian announced plans for rebuilding Jerusalem as a pagan city and raising a shrine to Jupiter on the site of the Temple.[6]

131 A.D.

Hadrian, by decree, prohibited circumcision and public instruction in Judaism.[7]

132 A.D.

In response to these actions, the Jews, under the leadership of Rabbi Akiba ben Joseph and Simon bar Kochba, began their third and last revolt against Rome.[8]

56

136 A.D.

The revolt of Bar Kochba was finally crushed. In the process the Romans slaughtered 580,000 men and destroyed 985 towns. After putting down the revolt, Hadrian did, indeed, have Jerusalem rebuilt as a pagan city named Aelia Capitolina. On the Temple mound a column honoring Hadrian and a temple to Jupiter Capitolinus were erected. In addition, Hadrian prohibited not only circumcision but also the observance of the Sabbath and other Jewish holy days and the public performance of any Judaic ritual.[9]

138 A.D.

The successor to Hadrian, Antoninus Pius, restored Jewish religious freedom but to limit the spread of Judaism and to stop Jewish proselytizing retained the restrictions against circumcizing non-Jews under pain of death or banishment.[10]

162 A.D.

Emperor Lucius Verus (co-emperor with Marcus Aurelius) restricted the rights of Jews living in Palestine when he carried out a military campaign against Parthia.[11]

193 A.D.

Co-Emperor Pescennius Niger when petitioned by Jews to lighten their tax burden replied: "You ask me to relieve your lands of their taxes; would that I were able to tax the very air you breathe."[12]

200 A.D.

Emperor Severus promulgated laws forbidding heathens, under penalty of severe punishment, to embrace Judaism.[13]

"We may thus assert in utter confidence that the Jews will not return to their earlier situation, for they have committed the most abominable of crimes, in forming the conspiracy against the Savior of the human race. . . . Hence the city where Jesus suffered was necessarily destroyed, the Jewish nation was driven from its country, and another people was called by God to the blessed election."[14] Origen, Bishop of Alexandria.

250-258 A.D.

St. Cyprian, Bishop of Carthage, demanded that all Jews be expelled from his diocese at the point of the sword.[15]

300 A.D.

Eusebius, Bishop of Ceasaria, in his *Ecclesiastic History*, maintained that Jews in every community crucified a Christian at their Purim festival as a rejection of Jesus. He also stated that during the Roman-Persian war, the Jews purchased 90,000 Christian prisoners merely for the pleasure of killing them. In his writings, he made a sharp distinction between Hebrews who were good men in the Old Testament and Jews whom he characterized as evil. Eusebius here baptizes the ritual murder charge first made by the historian Democritus and popularized by the greatest of the pagan anti-Semites, Apion. (Interestingly, the Romans had made the same charge against the early Christians.)[16]

306 A.D.

Council of Elvira (Spain) banned all community contact between Spanish Christians and the "evil" Hebrews. Especially prohibited was marriage between Christians and Jews.[17]

320 A.D.

Council of Illiberia under Osius, Bishop of Cordova, forbade Christians, under pain of excommunication, to hold friendly intercourse or contract marriages with Jews, or allow Jews to bless the harvest of their fields.[18]

THE NEW TESTAMENT*

The role of Christianity in the developing and sustaining of anti-Semitism is of major importance. In the modern secular world this religious factor is often ignored or minimized. Some have argued that anti-Semitism is really an aberration and a distortion and not part of Christian doctrine or practice. In this view, anti-

*See Note 6 to Causes.

58

Semitism is seen as an ugly accretion brought about by historical situations. In essence the argument holds that anti-Semitism is a perversion that is as anti-Christian as it is anti-Jewish.

A careful reading of the New Testament, the source document of Christianity, leads to the rejection of this argument. The teachings and writings of the Fathers, Doctors and Saints of the Church and the decrees and holdings of Popes, Councils and Canon Law can be explained or minimized, but the New Testament itself cannot be ignored and the anti-Jewish and anti-Semitic statements found there have to be taken into account. It is here, in the fundamental source of Christianity, that the charge of deicide and collective transcendent Jewish responsibility is found. The New Testament began the characterization of the Jews as Satan or in league with the devil.

The following quotations are from the New Testament.[19] They have been grouped into three main categories: (1) the sayings attributed to Jesus; (2) passages that exonerate or minimize the Roman role in the Crucifixion and fix the charge and responsibility for deicide on Jews collectively; and (3) anti-Jewish or anti-Semitic comment not included in the former categories.

PART I

New Testament quotations attributed to Jesus that are anti-Jewish or anti-Semitic in content or *that lend themselves to anti-Semitic interpretation.**

"Amen I say to you, I have not found such great faith in Israel. And I tell you that many will come from the east and from the west, and will feast with Abraham and Isaac and Jacob in the kingdom of

---

*The attribution to Jesus of statements that could be defined as anti-Semitic or as a source of anti-Semitism cannot be disproved. But in the light of the proximate post-messianic conditions surrounding the chroniclers of Jesus' mission, these statements are suspect. This is not to ignore the likelihood that Jesus was strongly critical of the established religion he was trying to reform. But his teachings urging love and forgiveness are at variance with the wholesale condemnation of a people.

heaven, but the children of the kingdom will be put forth into the darkness outside; there will be the weeping and the gnashing of teeth." Matthew 8:10-13

"And whoever does not receive you, or listen to your words— go forth outside that house or town, and shake off the dust from your feet. Amen I say to you, it will be more for the land of Sodom and Gomorrah in the day of judgment than for that town." Matthew 10:14-15.

"Therefore, everyone who acknowledges me before men, I also will acknowledge him before my Father in heaven. But whoever disowns me before men, I in turn will disown him before my Father in heaven." Matthew 10:32-33.

"Jerusalem, Jerusalem! thou who killest the prophets, and stonest those who are sent to thee! How often would I have gathered thy children together, as a hen gathers her young under her wings, but thou wouldst not! Behold, your house is left to you desolate. For I say to you, you shall not see me henceforth until you shall say, 'Blessed is he who comes in the name of the Lord!' " Matthew 23:37-39.

"Do you see all these things? Amen I say to you, there will not be left here one stone upon another that will not be thrown down." Matthew 24:2-3.

"And whoever does not receive you, or listen to you—go forth from there, and shake off the dust from your feet for a witness against them." Mark 6:10-11.

"But be on your guard. For they will deliver you up to councils, and you will be beaten in synagogues, and you will stand before governors and kings for my sake for a witness to them." Mark 13:9-10.

"Go into the whole world and preach the gospel to every creature. He who believes and is baptized shall be saved, but he who does not believe shall be condemned." Mark 16:15-16.

"He who hears you, hears me; and he who rejects you, rejects me; and he who rejects me, rejects him who sent me." Luke 10:16.

"And I say to you, everyone who acknowledges me before men, him will the Son of Man also acknowledge before the angels of God. But whoever disowns me before men will be disowned before the angels of God." Luke 13:8-9.

"And when they bring you before the synagogues and the magistrates and the authorities, do not be anxious how or wherewith you shall defend yourselves, or what you shall say, for the Holy Spirit will teach you in that very hour what you ought to say." Luke 12:11-12.

"Jerusalem, Jerusalem, thou who killest the prophets and stonest those who are sent to thee! How often would I have gathered thy children together, as a hen gathers her young under her wings, but thou wouldst not! Behold your house is left to you. And I say to you, you shall not see me until the time comes when you shall say, 'Blessed is he who comes in the name of the Lord.'" Luke 13:34-35.

"If thou hadst known, in this thy day, even thou, the things that are for thy peace! But now they are hidden from thy eyes. For days will come upon thee when thy enemies will throw up a rampart about thee, and surround thee and shut thee in on every side, and will dash thee to the ground and thy children within thee, and will not leave in thee one stone upon another, because thou hast not known the time of thy visitation." Luke 19:42-44.

"And when you see Jerusalem being surrounded by an army, then know that her desolation is at hand, then let those who are in Judea flee to the mountains; and let those who are in her midst go out, and let those who are in the country not enter her. For these are days of vengeance, that all things that are written may be fulfilled. But woe to those who are with child, or have infants at the breast in those days! For there will be great distress over the land and wrath upon this people. And they will fall by the edge of the sword, and will be led away as captives to all nations. And Jerusalem will be trodden down by the Gentiles, until the times of the nations be fulfilled." Luke 21:20-24.

"Daughters of Jerusalem, do not weep for me, but weep for yourselves and for your children." Luke 25:28.

Jesus therefore said to them, "If God were your Father, you would surely love me. For from God I came forth and have come; for neither have I come of myself, but he sent me. Why do you not understand my speech? Because you cannot listen to my word. The father from whom you are is the devil, and the desires of your father it is your will to do. He was a murderer from the beginning, and has not stood in the truth because there is no truth in him. When he tells a lie he speaks from his very nature, for he is a liar and the father of lies. But because I speak the truth you do not believe me. Which of you can convict me of sin? If I speak the truth, why do you not believe me? He who is of God hears the words of God. The reason why you do not hear is that you are not of God." John 8:42-47.

"He who rejects me, and does not accept my words, has one to condemn him. The word that I have spoken will condemn him on the last day." John 12:48.

"He who hates me hates my Father also. If I had not done among them works such as no one else has done, they would have no sin. But now they have seen, and have hated both me and my Father; but that the word written in their Law may be fulfilled, 'They have hated me without cause.' " John 15:23-25.

"They will expel you from the synagogues. Yes, he hour is coming for every one who kills you to think that he is offering worship to God. And these things they will do because they have not known the Father nor me." John 16:2-3.

"My kingdom is not of this world. If my kingdom were of this world, my followers would have fought that I might not be delivered to the Jews." John 18:36.

PART II

Passages from the New Testament that exonerate or minimize the Roman role in the Crucifixion and place the blame for deicide on the Jews:*

Now at festival time the procurator used to release to the crowd a prisoner, whomever they would. Now he had at that time a notorious prisoner called Barabbas. Therefore, when they had gathered together, Pilate said, "Whom do you wish that I release to you?

*For an historical discussion of Pilate and the Romans see pp 318ff.

they had delivered him up out of envy. Now, as he was sitting on the judgment-seat, his wife sent to him, saying, "Have nothing to do with that just man, for I have suffered many things in a dream today because of him." But the chief priests and the elders persuaded the crowds to ask for Barabbas and to destroy Jesus. But the procurator addressed them, and said to them, "Which of the two do you wish that I release to you?" And they said, "Barabbas." Pilate said to them, "What then am I to do with Jesus who is called Christ?" They all said, "Let him be crucified!" The procurator said to them, "Why, what evil has he done?" But they kept crying out the more saying, "Let him be crucified!"

Now Pilate, seeing that he was doing no good, but rather that a riot was breaking out, took water and washed his hands in sight of the crowd, saying, "I am innocent of the blood of this just man; see to it yourselves." And all the people answered and said, "His blood be on us and on our children." Matthew 27:15-25.

But Pilate addressed them, saying, "Do you wish that I release to you the king of the Jews?" For he knew that the chief priests had delivered him up out of envy. But the chief priests stirred up the crowd to have him release Barabbas for them instead. But Pilate again spoke and said to them, "What then do you want me to do to the king of the Jews?" But they cried out again, "Crucify him!" But Pilate said to them, "Why, what evil has he done?" But they kept crying out the more, "Crucify him!" Mark 15:9-14.

And the whole assemblage rose, and took him before Pilate. And they began to accuse him, saying, "We have found this man perverting our nation, and forbidding the payment of taxes to Caesar, and saying that he is Christ a king." So Pilate asked him, saying, "Art thou the king of the Jews?" And he answered him and said, "Thou sayest it." And Pilate said to the chief priests and to the crowds, "I find no guilt in this man."

But they persisted, saying, "He is stirring up the people, teaching throughout all Judea, and beginning from Galilee even to this place." But Pilate, hearing Galilee, asked whether the man was a Galilean. And learning that he belonged to Herod's jurisdiction, he sent him back to Herod, who likewise was in Jerusalem in those days. Luke 23:1-7.

And Pilate called together the chief priests and the rulers and the people, and said to them, "You have brought before me this man, as one who perverts the people; and behold, I upon examining him in your presence have found no guilt in this man as touching those things of which you accuse him. Neither has Herod; for I sent you back to him, and behold, nothing deserving of death has been committed by him. I will therefore chastise him and release him."

Now at festival time it was necessary for him to release to them one prisoner. But the whole mob cried out together, saying, "Away with this man, and release to us Barabbas!"—one who had been thrown into prison for a certain riot that had occurred in the city, and for murder. But Pilate spoke to them again, wishing to release Jesus. But they kept shouting, saying, "Crucify him! Crucify him!" And he said to them a third time, "Why, what evil has this man done? I find no crime deserving of death in him. I will therefore chastise him and release him."

But they persisted with loud cries, demanding that he should be crucified; and their cries prevailed. And Pilate pronounced sentence that what they asked for should be done. So he released to them him who for murder and riot had been put in prison, for whom they were asking; but Jesus he delivered to their will. Luke 23:13-25.

"If my kingdom were of this world, my followers would have fought that I might not be delivered to the Jews. But, as it is, my kingdom is not from here." Pilate therefore said to him, "Thou art then a king?" Jesus answered, "Thou sayest it; I am a king. This is why I was born, and why I have come into the world, to bear witness to the truth. Everyone who is of the truth hears my voice." Pilate said to him, "What is truth?"

And when he had said this, he went outside to the Jews again, and said to them, "I find no guilt in him. But you have a custom that I should release someone to you at the Passover. Do you wish, therefore, that I release to you the king of the Jews?" They all therefore cried out again, "Not this man, but Barabbas!" Now Barabbas was a robber.

Pilate, then, took Jesus and had him scourged. And the soldiers, plaiting a crown of thorns, put it upon his head, and arrayed him in a purple cloak. And they kept coming to him and saying, "Hail, King of the Jews!" and striking him.

Pilate therefore again went outside and said to them, "Behold I bring him out to you, that you may know that I find no guilt in him." Jesus therefore came forth, wearing the crown of thorns and the purple cloak. And he said to them, "Behold, the man!" When, therefore, the chief priests and the attendants saw him, they cried out, saying, "Crucify him! Crucify him!" Pilate said to them, "Take him yourselves and crucify him, for I find no guilt in him." The Jews answered him, "We have a Law, and according to that Law he must die, because he has made himself Son of God."

Now when Pilate heard this statement, he feared the more. And he again went back into the praetorium, and said to Jesus, "Where art thou from?" But Jesus gave him no answer. Pilate therefore said to him, "Dost thou not speak to me? Does thou not know that I have power to crucify thee, and that I have the power to release thee?" Jesus answered, "Thou wouldst have no power at all over me were it not given thee from above. Therefore, he who betrayed me to thee has the greater sin."

And from then on Pilate was looking for a way to release him. But the Jews cried out, saying, "If thou release this man, thou art no friend of Caesar; for everyone who makes himself king sets himself against Caesar."

Pilate therefore, when he heard these words, brought Jesus outside, and sat down on the judgment-seat, at a place called Lithostrotos, but in Hebrew, Gabbatha. Now it was the Preparation Day for the Passover, about the sixth hour. And he said to the Jews, "Behold, your king!" But they cried out, "Away with him! Away with him! Crucify him!" Pilate said to them, "Shall I crucify your king?" The chief priests answered, "We have no king but Caesar." Then he handed him over to them to be crucified. And so they took Jesus and led him away. John 18:29-40; 19:1-16.

PART III

The following statements from the New Testament have anti-Jewish or anti-Semitic overtones and have been used to stir up hatred and anti-Jewish actions. The passages concerning the passion and death of Jesus have been a constant feature of Easter violence:

Then the high priest tore his garments, saying, "He has blasphemed; what further need have we of witnesses? Behold, now you have heard the blasphemy. What do you think?" And they answered and said, "He is liable to death." Then they spat in his face and buffeted him; while others struck his face with the palms of their hands, saying, "Prophesy to us, O Christ! Who is it that struck thee?" Matthew 26:65-68.

Now while they were going, behold some of the guards came into the city and reported to the chief priests all that had happened. And when they had assembled with the elders and had consulted together, they gave much money to the soldiers, telling them, "Say, 'His disciples came by night and stole him while we were sleeping.' And if the procurator hears of this, we will persuade him and keep you out of trouble." And they took the money, and did as they were instructed; and this story has been spread abroad among the Jews even to the present day. Matthew 28:11-15.

Then the high priest, standing up in their midst, asked Jesus, saying, "Dost thou make no answer to the things that these men prefer against thee?" But he kept silence, and made no answer. Again the high priest began to ask him, and said to him, "Art thou the Christ, the Son of the Blessed One?" And Jesus said to him, "I am. And you shall see the Son of Man sitting at the right hand of the Power and coming with the clouds of heaven."

But the high priest tore his garments and said, "What further need have we of witnesses? You have heard the blasphemy. What do you think?" And they all condemned him as liable to death. And some began to spit on him, and to blindfold him, and to buffet him, and to say to him, "Prophesy." And the attendants struck him with blows of their hands. Mark 14:60-65.

And the passers-by were jeering at him, shaking their heads, and saying, "Aha, thou who destroyest the temple, and in three days buildest it up again; come down from the cross, and save thyself!" In like manner, the chief priests with the Scribes said in mockery to one another, "He saved others, himself he cannot save! Let the Christ, the King of Israel, come down now from the cross, that we may see and believe." And they who were crucified with him reproached him. Mark 15:29-32.

And the men who had him in custody began to mock him and beat him. And they blindfolded him, and kept striking his face and asking him, saying, "Prophesy, who is it that struck thee?" And many other things they kept saying against him, reviling him.

And as soon as day broke, the elders of the people and the chief priests and Scribes gathered together; and they led him away into their Sanhedrin, saying, "If thou art the Christ, tell us." And he said to them, "If I tell you, you will not believe me; and if I question you, you will not answer me, or let me go. But henceforth, the Son of Man will be seated at the right hand of the power of God."

And they all said, "Art thou, then, the Son of God?" He answered, "You yourselves say that I am." And they said, "What further need have we of witness? For we have heard it ourselves from his own mouth." Luke 22:63-71.

And this is why the Jews kept persecuting Jesus, because he did such things on the Sabbath. Jesus, however, answered them, "My father works even until now, and I work." This, then, is why the Jews were the more anxious to put him to death; because he not only broke the Sabbath, but also called God his own Father, making himself equal to God. John 5:16-18.

The Jews therefore murmured about him because he has said, "I am the bread that has come down from heaven." And they kept saying, "Is this not Jesus the son of Joseph, whose father and mother we know? How, then, does he say, "I have come down from heaven?" John 6:41-42.

Now after those things Jesus went about in Galilee, for he did not wish to go about in Judea because the Jews were seeking to put him to death. John 7:1.

The Jews therefore were looking for him at the feast, and were saying, "Where is he?" And there was much whispered comment among the crowd concerning him. For some were saying, "He is a good man." But others were saying, "No, rather he seduces the crowd." Yet for fear of the Jews no one spoke openly of him. John 7:11-13.

The Jews therefore took up stones to stone him. Jesus answered them, "Many good works have I shown you from my Father. For which of these works do you stone me?" The Jews answered him, "Not for a good work do we stone thee, but for blasphemy, and because thou, being a man, makest thyself God." John 10:31-33.

Jesus therefore no longer went about openly among the Jews, but withdrew to the district near the desert, to a town called Ephrem; and there he stayed with his disciples.

Now the Passover of the Jews was at hand; and many from the country went up to Jerusalem before the Passover, in order to purify themselves. And they were looking for Jesus. And as they stood in the temple they were saying to one another, "What do you think, that he is not coming to the feast?" But the chief priests and Pharisees had given orders that, if anyone knew where he was, he should report it, so that they might seize him. John 11:54-56.

Now the great crowd of the Jews learned that he was there; and they came, not only because of Jesus, but that they might see Lazarus, whom he had raised from the dead. But the chief priests planned to put Lazarus to death also. For on his account many of the Jews began to leave them and to believe in Jesus. John 12:9-11.

Therefore, let all the house of Israel know most assuredly that God has made both Lord and Christ, this Jesus whom you crucified. Acts 2:36.

But when Peter saw it, he said to the people: "Men of Israel, why do you marvel of this, or why do you stare at us, as though by any power or holiness of our own we had made this man walk? The God of Abraham and the God of Isaac and the God of Jacob, the God of our fathers, has glorified his Son Jesus, whom you indeed delivered up and disowned before the face of Pilate, when he had decided he should be released. But you disowned the Holy and Just One, and asked that a murdered should be granted to you; but the author of life you killed. . . . Repent therefore and be converted, that your sins may be blotted out. . . . Acts 3:12-20.

Stiff-necked and uncircumcised in heart and ear, you always oppose the Holy Spirit; as your fathers did, so you do also. Which of the prophets have not your fathers persecuted? And they killed those who foretold the coming of the Just One, of whom you have now been the betrayers and murderers, you who received the Law as an ordinance of angels and did not keep it. St. Stephen—Acts 7:51-53.

But Peter began, and said, ''Now I really understand that God is not a respecter of persons, but in every nation he who fears him and does what is right is acceptable to him. He sent his word to the children of Israel, preaching peace through Jesus Christ (who is Lord of all). You know what took place throughout Judea; for he began in Galilee after the baptism preached by John: how God anointed Jesus of Nazareth with the Holy Spirit and with power, and he went about doing good and healing all who were in the power of the devil; for God was with him. And we are witnesses of all that he did in the country of the Jews and in Jerusalem; and yet they killed him, hanging him on a tree. Acts 10:34-40.

. . . But on seeing the crowds, the Jews were filled with jealousy and contradicted what was said by Paul, and blasphemed. Then Paul and Barnabas spoke out plainly: ''It was necessary that the word of God should be spoken to you first, but since you reject it and judge yourselves unworthy of eternal life, behold, we now turn to the Gentiles. For so the Lord has commanded us,

I have set thee for a light to the Gentiles, to be a means of salvation to the very ends of the earth.

On hearing this the Gentiles were delighted, and glorified the word of the Lord, and all who were destined for eternal life believed. And the word of the Lord spread throughout the whole country. But the Jews incited the worshipping women of rank and the chief men of the city, and stirred up a persecution against Paul and Barnabas and drove them from their district. . . . Acts 13:45-51.

And they also, if they do not continue in unbelief, will be grafted in; for God is able to graft them back. . . . For I would not, brethren, have you ignorant of this mystery, lest you should be wise in your own conceits, that a partial blindness only has befallen Israel, until the full number of Gentiles should enter, and thus all Israel should be saved, as it is written. Paul to Romans 11:23-26.

Now I exhort you, brethren, through our Lord Jesus Christ, and through the charity of the Spirit, that you help me by your prayers to God for me, that I may be delivered from the unbelievers in Judea. Paul to Romans 15:30-31.

We are Jews by birth, and not sinners from among the Gentiles. But we know that man is not justified by the works of the Law, but by the faith of Jesus Christ. Hence we also believe in Christ Jesus, that we may be justified by the faith of Christ, and not by the works of the Law; because by the works of the Law no man will be justified. . . . For I through the Law have died to the Law that I may live to God. With Christ I am nailed to the cross. It is no longer I that live, but Christ lives in me. And the life that I now live in the flesh, I live in the faith of the Son of God, who loved me and gave himself up for me. I do not cast away the grace of God. For if justice is by the Law, then Christ died in vain. Paul to Gallatians 2:15-21.

Stand fast, and do not be caught again under the yolk of slavery. Behold, I, Paul, tell you that if you be circumcised, Christ will be of no advantage to you. And I testify again to every man who has himself circumcised, that he is bound to observe the whole Law. You who would be justified by the Law are estranged from Christ; you have fallen from grace. Paul to Gallatians 5:1-4.

For there are many disobedient, vain babblers and deceivers, especially those of the circumcision. These must be rebuked for they upset whole households, teaching things that they ought not, for the sake of base gain. One of themselves, a prophet of their own, said "Cretans, always liars, evil beasts, lazy gluttons." This statement is true. Hence rebuke them sharply that they may be sound in faith, and may not listen to Jewish fables and the commandments of men who turn away from the truth. Paul to Titus 1:10-14.

For you, brethren, have become imitators of the churches of God which are in Judea in Christ Jesus, in that you also have suffered the same things from your own countrymen as they have from the Jews, who both killed the Lord Jesus and the prophets, and have persecuted us. They are displeasing to God, and are hostile to all men, because they hinder us from speaking to the Gentiles, that they may be saved. Thus they are always filling up the measure of their sins, for the wrath of God has come upon them to the utmost. First Epistle of Paul to the Thessalonians 2:14-16.

Who is the liar but he who denies that Jesus is the Christ? He is the Antichrist who denies the Father and the Son. No one who disowns the Son has the Father. 1 John 2:22-23.

. . . and that thou art slandered by those who say they are Jews and are not, but are a synagogue of Satan. . . . Apocalypse 2:9-10.

. . . Behold I will bring some of the synagogue of Satan who say they are Jews, and are not, but are lying—behold, I will make them come and worship before thy feet. . . . Apocalypse 3:9.

CONTINUUM:

Two aspects of the Roman period are important for this study. The one concerns the anti-Semitic practices of the state; the other involves the Christian justification of anti-Semitism. Both transcend their origins and have become constant features of anti-Semitism to the present day.

For a variety of reasons, including reaction to the Jewish revolts, the refusal of Jews to observe emperor worship, and the appeal Judaism had for Roman nobility, Judaism was often seen as a threat to the security and stability of the Roman Empire. In an effort to eliminate this perceived threat, Roman authorities used various techniques that continue to be used by governments with a policy of anti-Semitism. Various emperors made Jewish proselytizing or conversion to Judaism capital offenses. Some prohibited Jewish religious observances or practices or required payment of a tax as a license to practice Judaism. Jews were sometimes subjected to expulsion, confiscation of property and restrictions on movement. The Romans also invented the fiscal policy of using the Jews as a specialized revenue source.

It should be noted that persecutions of Jews under the Roman Empire were not a constant feature of state policy. Judaism had the status of a legal religion. Some emperors were pro-Jewish and many were quite cordial to Jews and Judaism.

Christianity in its various forms created the intellectual, emotional, and religious justification for anti-Semitism that survived the decline of Rome and the disappearance of Paganism. The preaching, pastoral letters, theological writings, and decrees of bishops, saints and church councils, and passages of the New Testament as well as the oral tradition of this new religion as it strove to distinguish itself from the parent religion, contain many rationales for anti-Semitism. This base has been added to and elaborated on by Christian churchmen throughout Western history.

Christianity incorporated and baptized pagan anti-Semitic charges of ritual murder and lewdness. More important, however, are the specifically Christian contributions. The keystone is the charge of deicide and the collective and transcendent Jewish responsibility, guilt and punishment for the crucifixion of Jesus. From this charge, grows the myth that persists today that the scattering of the Jews, The *Diaspora*, coincided with the Roman seige of Jerusalem in 70 A.D. and was a punishment for the crime of deicide.

In addition, the continued refusal of Jews to accept Jesus as the Messiah had to be explained. Since the truth of Christianity was so obvious to the adherents of the faith, the refusal to accept Christ had to have demonic assistance. Therefore, Jews became, in the Christian view, handmaids of Satan—evil and perverse.

These ideas had immediate consequences. As Christianity became more powerful, it attempted, through decrees and actions by its councils, to protect the faithful from Jewish influence and contamination. This period dates the beginning of efforts at forcible ghettoization of the Jews.

PART 1. ROMAN PERIOD

1. Heinrich Graetz, *History of the Jews* (Philadelphia: The Jewish Publication Society of America, 1898), II, 305-16.

2. Ibid., p. 316.

3. Ibid., pp. 288-91.

4. Edward H. Flannery, *The Anguish of the Jews: Thirty-three Centuries of Anti-Semitism* (New York: The Macmillan Company, 1965), p. 27.

5. Graetz, op. cit., p. 316.

6. Ibid., pp. 406-407.

7. Flannery, op. cit., p. 18.

8. Graetz, op. cit., p. 409.

9. Ibid., pp. 407-19.

10. Leon Poliakov, *The History of Anti-Semitism* (New York: The Vanguard Press, 1965), p. 22.

11. Graetz, op. cit., p. 447.

12. Ibid., pp. 463-64.

13. Ibid., p. 464.

14. Origen, *Against Celsus*, Poliakov, op. cit., p. 23.

15. Dagobert Runes, *The Jew and the Cross* (New York: Philosophical Library, 1966), p. 41.

16. Flannery, op. cit., p. 46; Runes, op. cit., p. 39.

17. Flannery, op. cit., p. 52.

18. Graetz, op. cit., p. 650.

19. *The New Testament of Our Lord and Savior Jesus Christ* (New Jersey: St. Anthony Guild Press, 1941), Trans. from the Latin Vulgate, A Revision of the Challoner—Rheims Version.

PART II: THE EARLY CHRISTIAN PERIOD—325-500

BACKGROUND:

This period is one of considerable upheaval, unrest, and political and social dislocation. The decline of the Western Roman Empire was a time of invasion and massive migrations of barbaric but more dynamic peoples. The Vandals, Huns, Goths, Visigoths and Franks possessed a robust ferocity but aside from war and plunder, sought the mantle of Roman legitimacy and sophistication.

The accession of Christianity with the triumph of Constantine and the Edict of Milan must have had a hollowness at the time that is lost in retrospect. The Christian success was to preside over a collapsing political order. The situation was further complicated by the internal problems of youthful Christianity: heresy, and the fear of being overwhelmed by Judaism. More secure or stable times may have seen a greater degree of tolerance, but given the precariousness of the period, order and stability were the paramount concern and threats had to be eliminated.

A significant step in the solution of theological conflict was Christianity's emergence as the official state religion in 391. Christianity perceived its role to be the salvation of mankind. As an essentially monotheistic religion, despite trinitarianism and the absorption of hellenic philosophy and eclectic incorporation of some elements of paganism, rivals, whether in the form of divergent interpretations within the church or in the form of other religions, had no right because they were in error. (If there is only one God it is obvious there is only one religion—all others are false and therefore cannot be tolerated.) The mission of saving mankind plus the intolerance of monotheistic religions coupled with the fanaticism common to religious movements in their formative phase was now armed with the power of the state: a condition that made life altogether unpleasant for the heretic and the non-Christian.

The social and political dominance of Christianity and the statelessness or alien status of the "condemned" Jew are the dual sources of anti-Semitism for the next sixteen centuries. The writings and sermons of the Fathers and Doctors of the Church, St. Ambrose, St. Jerome, St. Augustine and many other saints are products of this period. They reflect the beleaguered and threatened condition of the Church as it fought against heresy, error and the Judaizing tendency. The anti-Jewish and anti-Semitic statements in these writings and sermons cited by themselves are shocking enough but in the hands of lesser men with often venal motives (even in the context of the times) were causes of many outrages and atrocities. The fact, however, that they were made by great intellects and leading figures of the Church give the words more weight than would be the case of the ravings of fanatical monks. The prestige and importance of these men in the development of Christianity lend an overwhelming authority and a transcendent timelessness to their comments on the Jews. Just as their more profound and appropriate theological and devotional works are drawn on over time, so too, their anti-Semitic utterances are cloaked with the same aura and are used to the present by the Jew-hater to lend his position the authority it cannot maintain on its own. As silly as they seem today, and as historically unjustified as they are and indeed were at the time, the teachings contain the seeds of much of historical anti-Semitism. They did not remain historical documents but became timeless documents incorporated into the dogma, theology and tradition of the Church.

In addition, during this period of Christian expansion, the conversion of the barbarians, Goths, Visigoths, Franks, etc., usually was accompanied by anti-Jewish measures and adoption of Church policy as state policy. This was sometimes based on simple cynical opportunism to further or insure political power and sometimes on sincere religious fervor. Regardless of motivation, a sure way to win favor with Rome was to attack the Jews.

ENVIRONMENT: CHRISTIAN

With the exception of the short reign of Julian the Apostate, Christianity was not only legal but had become the official state religion. Paganism was outlawed and Judaism and Jews cast in the role of pariah.

Christianity further disassociated itself from Judaism and discredited Judaism.

Christians were forbidden to interact with Jews.

Conversion to Judaism was punishable by confiscation of all property.

Church hymns, conciliar decrees, pastoral teachings, and theological writings heaped contempt and derision on Jews and Judaism.

State policy restricting the political and civil rights of Jews furthered the image of the Jew as a "second class" citizen.

Leading churchmen rebutted lay authorities who tried to protect the rights or property of Jews.

Hating the Jews was taught to be a Christian duty.

ENVIRONMENT: JEWISH

The alien status of the Jew (a people without a country) was intensified when Christianity became the official state religion and Church teachings and regulations about Jews became state policy and law.

Jews and Judaism were vilified and ridiculed.

Religious practice was curtailed. The number of synagogues allowed was prescribed by law. Proselytizing was forbidden and punishable by death.

There were isolated outbursts of violent anti-Semitic behavior instigated by high church officials. These included forced expulsion, coerced baptism, confiscation of property, mob attacks and burnings of Jewish communities and synagogues.

Jews were barred from public and military office.

State policy began to force Jews out of agriculture by laws that forbade Jewish ownership of Christian slaves and prohibited circumcision or conversion of Christian slaves to Judaism.

The Jewish tax to maintain the Patriarch was diverted to the state treasury and the practice of using Jews as a special revenue source was continued by the Christian state.

INCIDENTS:
324 A.D.
After becoming sole emperor Constantine declared himself a Christian and urged his subjects to convert to Christianity.[1]

325 A.D.
Constantine reenacted Hadrian's law forbidding Jews to live in Jerusalem. Jews were also forbidden to convert slaves or engage in any proselytizing activity.[2]

The Council of Nicaea, called by Constantine to settle the controversy of Arianism, continued efforts of early Church to disassociate Christianity from Judaism by deciding that Easter would no longer be determined by or celebrated during Passover.[3]

"For it is unbecoming beyond measure that on this holiest of festivals we should follow the customs of the Jews. Henceforth let us have nothing in common with this odious people. . . ."[4]

330 A.D.
Emperor Constantius decreed that Jews forfeited any slaves converted to Judaism and that the circumcision of a Christian slave carried with it the death penalty and confiscation of all property.[6]

337 A.D.
The Emperor Constantine was baptized on his death bed and succeeded by Constantius. On becoming emperor, Constantius declared: "Let my will be religion and the law of the Church!" One of his first acts was to prohibit marriage between a Jew and a Christian woman. Such marriages were punishable by death.[5]

351 A.D.
Ursicinus, legate of Co-emperor Gallus while carrying out a military campaign against Persia required Jews to violate the Sabbath and Passover and publicly burned a scroll of the Law.[7]

357 A.D.
Emperor Constantius passed a law that confiscated all the property of any Christian who converted to Judaism.[8]

367 A.D.
St. Hilary of Poitiers in sermons and writings characterized the Jews as a perverse people forever accursed by God.[9]

376 A.D.
Hymns written by St. Ephroem refer to synagogues as whorehouses.[10]

379-395 A.D.
(Emperor Theodosius the Great protected Jews from the Church's persecution of heretics.) St. John Chrysostom and St. Ambrose of Milan were the leading Churchmen who advocated Jewish persecution.[11]

"The Jews are the most worthless of all men. They are lecherous, greedy, rapacious. They are perfidious murderers of Christ. They worship the devil, their religion is a sickness. The Jews are the odious assassins of Christ and for killing God there is no expiation possible, no indulgence or pardon. Christians may never cease vengeance, and the Jew must live in servitude forever. God always hated the Jews. It is incombent upon all Christians to hate the Jews."

> St. John Chrysostom—Patriarch
> of Constantinople, "Bishop with
> the Golden Tongue."[12]

St. Ambrose of Milan, Bishop and Doctor of the Church, reprimanded Theodosius for ordering the rebuilding of the synagogue and offered to burn the synagogue in Milan himself.[13]

"I hereby declare, that it was I who set fire to the synagogue; indeed, I gave the orders for it to be done so that there should no longer be any place where Christ is denied.''[14] Ambrose to Emperor Theodosius

St. Gregory of Nyssa in sermons and writings characterized Jews as assassins of the prophets, companions of the devil, a race of vipers, a sanhedrin of demons, enemies of all that is beautiful, hogs and goats in their lewd grossness.[15]

Council of Laodicia forbade Christians to respect the Jewish Sabbath.[16]

395-408 A.D.

The Byzantine Emperor Arcadius commanded resistance to Christian fanatacism and destruction of synagogues but also reenacted Emperor Constantius' decrees prohibiting proselytizing by the Jews. (See 329 A.D. Emperor Constantius.)[17]

Dishonesty and indolence cited as typical Jewish characteristics by St. Epiphonius in his history of heresies.[18]

408-450 A.D.

Emperor Theodosius II prohibited Jews from building new synagogues and owning Christian slaves.[19]

415 A.D.

St. Cyril, Bishop of Alexandria, incited a Christian mob against the Jews and had them expel the Jews from Alexandria. The Bishop distributed Jewish property to the mob. The civil authorities under Prefect Orestes were unable to stop the expulsion.[20]

Bishop Severus burned the synagogue in the village of Magona and had the Jews attacked and harassed in the streets. The effect was that many Jews converted to Christianity to avoid persecution.[21]

''The true image of the Hebrew is Judas Iscariot, who sells the Lord for silver. The Jew can never understand the Scriptures and forever will bear the guilt for the death of Jesus.''[22]

St. Augustine, Bishop
of Hippo, Father of the
Church

''The Jews held him; the Jews insulted him, the Jews bound him, they crowned him with thorns, dishonoured him by spitting upon him, they scourged him, they heaped abuse upon him, they hung him upon a tree, they pierced him with a lance."[23] St. Augustine

The Jews of the Syrian village of Imnester were accused of ritual murder during their celebration of the feast of Purim. The accused were punished by Emperor Theosodius II. Christians in Alexandria in revenge for the "ritual murder" forcibly occupied the synagogues in Alexandria.[24]

The Christians of Antioch also avenged the "ritual murder" by confiscating synagogues in Antioch. The imperial prefect protested to the emperor who ordered that the synagogues be returned. This imperial edict was rescinded when Simon Stylite protested and reprimanded the emperor for being unfaithful to the Church.[25]

418 A.D.

Severus, Bishop of Majorca, carried out forced conversion of Jews on the island of Minorca. Violent street fighting broke out between Christians incited by the bishop and Jews in the town of Magona, resulting in the burning of the synagogue. Jews encouraged one another to remember the Maccabeans and die for the Divine Law. Some Jews attempted to escape by sea but failed. Finally the leadership of the community yielded and 540 Jews were converted on Minorca.[26]

"Jews are congenital liars who lure Christians to heresy. They should therefore be punished until they confess."

> St. Jerome (translator
> of the Vulgate Bible),
> Tract Against the Jews[27]

"If you call it a brothel, a den of vice, the Devil's refuge, Satan's fortress, a place to deprave the soul, an abyss of every conceivable disaster or whatever you will, you are still saying less than it deserves."[28] St. Jerome on the synagogue.

Note:

The writings of Sts. Jerome, Ambrose and Augustine are of special significance. These are not obscure bishops and fanatical obsessed monks or mendicant preachers, they are the Fathers and

Doctors of the Church as important to the growth of Christianity as the Apostles and St. Paul. Their anti-Semitism just as their other writings had widespread profound and lasting impact. They bestowed a sanctity and respectability on anti-Semitism that survived the struggle between Judaism and Christianity of their times.

429 A.D.

Honorius, the Western Emperor, ordered taxes collected for the Patriarch forfeited to the imperial treasury. He also barred Jews from public and military office.[29]

465 A.D.

Council of Vannes forbade clergy to take part in Jewish banquets.[30]

489 A.D.

A Christian mob attacked the Jewish quarter in Antioch, set fire to synagogues and threw the bodies of slain Jews into the fire. When informed of the incident, Emperor Zeno asked why live Jews were not burned as well.[31]

Note:

In Persia under Emperor Jezdijird III (440-457) and Emperor Firiz (469-70) persecution of Jews occurred. Emperor Jezdijird prohibited the observance of the Sabbath and Firiz executed half the Jewish population of Ipahan after the Jews were accused of murdering two Maji. Jewish children were taken from their families and raised in the Temple of Howan, the Persian fire god.[32]

CONTINUUM:

The early Christian period coincided with the end of the Western Roman Empire, and was a period of great social dislocations, invasions and migrations. As is clear throughout this chronicle, such conditions tend to be associated with outbursts of particularly vicious anti-Semitic activity.

The Jews of the period were subject to the older persecution tactics of discriminatory taxation, prohibition of religious practice and proselytizing, expulsion and ghettoization. In addition, new techniques were added to the anti-Semitic arsenal including forced baptism, destruction of synagogues, confiscation of goods and property, forced sequestering during Eastertide, and denial of civil rights.

These persecutions were justified and glorified by the great Catholic thinkers and theologians such as Sts. Augustine, Jerome and Ambrose as well as lesser saints as St. John Chrysostrom and St. Cyril. The Saints, Bishops, Doctors and Fathers of the Church in their writings and sermons further legitimized and added to the ideology of anti-Semitism. They enhanced the older charges of Christ-killer, handmaid of Satan and ritual murder and added the charges that Jews were on the whole indolent and dishonest and prone to gross sexual perversions and license.

Church councils, synods and various popes and bishops constantly exhorted the faithful to refrain from contacts with Jews. During this period the power of the state was added to Church policy. Under Constantine and his successor, imperial law included bars to Christian-Jewish relations and restrictions on Jewish participation in various sectors of the society. When the Western empire collapsed under the force of the barbarian invasions, the Church still found secular allies among the various monarchs of the period who adopted and enforced Church law as state policy. From this time on, anti-Semitism has enjoyed the support of state enforcement and became a constant factor in the political and cultural life of the West.

There were some notable exceptions of monarchs giving protection and sometimes privilege to Jews within their domains. Some lay authorities attempted to minimize Church or religious-based persecutions of Jews, but these were exceptions to the general pattern of Church and state cooperation in perpetuating and carrying out anti-Semitic policies.

These charges against the Jews and the tactics of persecution will be used again and again as it becomes a Christian duty to hate the Jew.

PART II. EARLY CHRISTIAN PERIOD

1. Will Durant, *The Story of Civilization: Part III Caesar and Christ* (New York: Simon & Schuster, 1944), p. 655.

2. Graetz, p. 564.

3. Ibid., p. 563.

4. Ibid., pp. 563-64.

5. Ibid., pp. 566-67.

6. Ibid., p. 567.

7. Ibid., pp. 568-69.

8. Ibid., p. 572.

9. Dagobert Runes, *War Against the Jews* (New York: Philosophical Library, 1968), p. 91.

10. Ibid., p. 67.

11. Friedrich Heer, *God's First Love* (New York: Weybright and Talley, 1967), pp. 35-39; Graetz, op. cit., pp. 612-13.

12. Runes, *The Jew and the Cross*, pp. 61-62.

13. Flannery, op. cit., pp. 57-58.

14. Runes, *War Against the Jews*, p. 113.

15. Flannery, op. cit., p. 47.

16. Ibid., p. 53.

17. Graetz, op. cit., p. 616.

18. Runes, *War Against the Jews*, p. 67; Flannery, op. cit., pp. 46-47.

19. Graetz, op. cit., p. 617.

20. Ibid., pp. 618-19.

21. Ibid., pp. 619-20.

22. Runes, *War Against the Jews*, p. 58.

23. Jules Isaac, *The Teaching of Contempt Christian Roots of Anti-Semitism* (New York: McGraw Hill Book Company, 1965), p. 111.

24. Graetz, op. cit., p. 622.

25. Flannery, op. cit., p. 58.

26. Yitzhak Baer, *History of the Jews in Christian Spain*, I (Philadelphia: The Jewish Publication Society of America, 1961), 17.

27. Runes, *War Against the Jews*, p. 96.

28. Heer, op. cit., p. 37.

29. Graetz, op. cit., p. 622.

30. Heinrich Graetz, *History of the Jews, III* (Philadelphia: The Jewish Publication Society of America, 1898), 36.

31. Flannery, op. cit., p. 77.

32. Graetz, op. cit., II, pp. 627-29.

PART III: DARK AGES—500-1000

BACKGROUND:

The connotative impact of the historical term "The Dark Ages" is quite misleading. The apparent anarchy of this period is usually contrasted with the stability, order and harmony of Roman rule of the empire's golden age. But Pax Romana and this heroic image of the empire had disappeared centuries earlier. Certainly the period was one of great social and political upheaval but there were also many positive developments, often overlooked or minimized, that belie the connotation of the term.

Among the positive features of this period are: the development and spread of the great monastic orders that preserved literacy and learning amid the political instability; the emergence of the papacy as a dominant religious and political force; the development of the feudal system; the rise of the Germanic tribes; the further expansion of Christianity; the spread of Islam; and dramatic incidents of adventure and heroism. It is clear that while troubled, chaotic and unstable, this period was not one of stagnation.

Political stability was a rare condition. The invasions and migrations of the "barbarians" saw the collapse of the Western empire and the disappearance of the administrative and political unity of the West. The brief revival of the unified Roman Empire under Justinian collapsed. The defeat of the Ostrogoths was a pyrrhic victory; the wars so weakened the Empire that the invasions by the Lombards, Persians, Arabs and Avars overwhelmed both the

Western and Eastern Empire. Civil war, wars of succession, the Islamic conquest of Spain, political and religious rivalries and migrations all contributed to the political anarchy and social chaos that understandably most readily springs to mind and popularly typifies this historical epoch.

The major unifying and stabilizing force was the Church and the tensions of the period were also present here. Church unity was not certain, the Papacy and Roman dominance at the beginning of the Dark Ages rested on a confederation of regional synods and councils. The Church was wracked with heresy and unsure of its authority. Pope Gregory the Great, a very martial and political pope, aided by the decline of Constantinople established the primacy of Rome. Spiritual and temporal interests were mutually reinforcing as Pope and monarch used each other to solidify their positions.

Within this environment of political and spiritual chaos the Jews existed and suffered from the instability. Jewish settlements existed throughout the Empire in virtually every province and city. There was movement between these settlements which served to link the communities. With a common and distinctive religious and cultural tradition now held together by the completion of the Talmud, the Jewish communities exhibited an increasing vitality.

Some Church and state authorities saw the Jews as a rival force for stability and unity (within a social and political milieu torn by centrifugal tendencies) and a potential challenge to their positions. Others saw in the Jewish presence a tool for creating unity by casting the Jew in the role of villain and enemy. Still others adopted and implemented anti-Semitic policies out of sincere religious belief and conviction. In any case, whatever the motivation, anti-Jewish and anti-Semitic policies were a fairly constant feature of the period.

Competing monarchs and warriors curried favor with the Church to gain the added legitimacy of spiritual anointment by dealing severely with the Jews in their realms. Struggles for succession were marked by persecution of the Jews. In this period the link between societal instability and anti-Semitism is clearly discernible. Periods of peace and prosperity are marked by an absence or abatement of anti-Semitism. Exceptions to the general pattern of elite anti-Semitism, Charlemagne, Charles the Bold and the Arian nobility of Visigothic Spain, saw the Jews as a positive force contributing to their realms. These leaders not only resisted pressure to persecute but instead, gave active protection to Jews within their jurisdiction.

Anti-Semitism manifested itself in the technique of forced baptism, expulsion and restriction. There is little recorded mob or popular anti-Semitism. Anti-Semitism at this time still seems to be an elitist phenomena linked to political and religious intrigues at the higher levels of society. Some have interpreted the anti-Semitic decrees and prohibitions in Spain as part of the struggle by the Crown and Church to achieve hegemony over feudal lords and Arianism. The absence of popular anti-Semitic feelings is documented by the almost constant and repetitive royal and Church decrees commanding the faithful and lower clergy to refrain from interacting and maintaining friendly relations with Jews. This indicates that the common people of the time (1) did not take Church decrees too seriously; (2) did not perceive Jews as dangerous; and (3) were on friendly terms with the Jewish communities.

ENVIRONMENT: CHRISTIAN

The teaching of contempt for Jews and Judaism continued to be part of the Christian message. Preachers, bishops, popes, saints and church councils all added to the growing tradition of anti-Semitism within the Christian belief system.

The Theodosian and Justianian codes included church policy that required a subordinate position for Jews vis-à-vis Christians. The ''second class'' status of Jews based on the charge of deicide had the full force of state law.

Anti-Semitic civil code and conciliar decrees were continuously adopted and enforced by the new monarchs of the invading peoples of the period.

Church councils and leaders repeatedly urged Christians to refrain from interacting with Jews.

Jews were declared enemies of the state for refusing to convert to Christianity.

In various places, Christians were urged to attack the Jewish communitie in revenge for crucifying Jesus.

A whole tradition of community anti-Semitic activities during Easter week grew from this time.

Jewish physicians were blamed for the deaths of various monarchs. They were accused of poisoning them. This belief became part of anti-Semitic folklore and similar charges recur throughout history.

Jews were frequently blamed for natural disasters, invasions or military defeats.

Pope Gregory The Great furthered the myth that the *Diaspora* was punishment for the crucifixion of Jesus and dated from the destruction of Jerusalem and the Temple by Titus.

Religious art depicting the crucifixion of Jesus in livid detail began and was to become a constant feature of the daily Christian experience and a constant reminder of the role assigned the Jew in Church teaching.

ENVIRONMENT: JEWISH

The civil, political and religious liberties of Jews were severely restricted by state and church policy.

Jews were expelled from various regions and jurisdictions by church and lay authorities.

Strenuous and continuous efforts to convert Jews to Christianity were a fairly constant feature of the Jewish experience.

Conversion was made very attractive and resistance to conversion had many penalties ranging from increased taxation through confiscation of property and expulsion to execution.

Jews were barred from various economic activities. Owning land and engaging in agricultural production was particularly difficult.

Land owned by Jews was frequently confiscated and given to Christians.

Sometimes Jewish children were removed from parental control, baptized and raised by Christian families or in monasteries. Jews were required to stay indoors during the Easter week.

In addition to episodic expulsions, Jews were subjected to annual attacks and insults during the Easter season.

INCIDENTS:

500 A.D.

Theodosian Code governed Italian Jews and gave autonomy in the management of the internal affairs of the community but forbade building of new synagogues, assumption of judicial office or military rank, and possession of Christian slaves.[1]

506 A.D.

Lex Romana Visigothum, the law governing Spain and the Jewish community of Spain, incorporated provisions of the Theodosian Code which curtailed Jewish rights in accordance with Christian teachings. The Jews were forbidden to hold public office, intermarry with Christians, build new synagogues, own Christian slaves, or to prosecute apostates.[2]

Spanish Jews were concentrated in the culturally advanced areas, Toledo and the Mediterranean coast (present day Andalusia and Catalonia). Spanish Jews were required to pay a special tax and in large cities had to live in separate communities.[3]

A Christian mob celebrating the results of the chariot races attacked the synagogue at Daphne near Antioch. The synagogue was destroyed, holy items were desecrated and the congregation was slaughtered.[4]

516 A.D.

King Sigismund of Burgundy, when he converted to Christianity, introduced oppression of Arians and Jews as state policy.[6]

517 A.D.

The Council of Epaone, presided over by Avitus (Bishop of Averna), extended the ban on attending Jewish banquets to laymen. (Cf. Council of Vannes— 465.) King Sigismund confirmed this conciliar decree and gave it the force of state law by enforcing it.[7]

519 A.D.

Christian population of Ravenna attacked the Jewish population and burned the synagogue.[8]

528 A.D.

The Emperor Justinian began the work of systematizing and codifying Roman Law that came to be known as *Corpus iuris civilis* or Body of Civil Law—the Justinian Code. It includes the *Codex Constitutionuum* (529), the *Digesta* (533), the *Institutiones* (533), and after Justinian's death, his additions to the *Codex* were published as *Novellae*. As with the Theodosian Code earlier, the Code of Justinian made Church Law and doctrine state policy. The Justinian Code included provisions which limited the civil and religious liberties of Jews. Jews were absolutely forbidden to have Christian slaves; they were not permitted to testify against Christians; and were not permitted to celebrate Passover before Easter. The Code also prescribed which versions of Scripture was to be used in Jewish services and prohibited certain prayers that were seen as anti-Trinitarian.[9]

535 A.D.

The Council of Clermont restated the provision of the Theodosian Code barring Jews from any positions of authority over Christians.[10]

538 & 545 A.D.

Third and Fourth Councils of Orleans commanded Christians not to take part in Jewish banquets. Jews were also forbidden to proselytize or appear in public during the Easter period.[11]

554 A.D.

King Childebert I of Paris made the clerical ban on Jewish public appearance during Eastertide state policy when he incorporated this decree of the Council of Orleans in the constitution for his kingdom.[12]

Bishop Avitus of Averna again and again exhorted the Jews of Clermont to convert but with no result. He then incited the Christian populace to attack the synagogues and raze them. The Jews were then told to choose between baptism or expulsion. One Jew submitted and during the procession was sprinkled with rancid oil by a Jew. The enraged mob attacked the Jewish quarter and killed many. To avoid further destruction and violence 500 Jews submitted to baptism. The rest fled to Marseilles.[13]

561 A.D.
St. Ferrial, Bishop of Uzes (France), gave the Jews in his See the choice of Baptism or expulsion.[14]

581 A.D.
Council of Macon reenacted ban on public appearance by Jews during Eastertide and also denied the judicial and tax collecting posts to Jews for fear that Christians would appear to be subject to them.[15]

582 A.D.
The Merovingian king Chilperic ordered all Jews in his kingdom to convert to Christianity or have their eyes torn out.[16]

John of Ephesus occupied seven Jewish temples and turned them into churches.[17]

589 A.D.
King Reccared of Visigoth Spain converted from Arianism to Christianity. He then enforced the decrees of the Council of Toledo which prohibited Jews from contracting marriage with Christians owning Christian slaves or holding public office. Children born of mixed marriages were to be forcibly baptized.[18]

Pope Gregory I (the Great) declared Judaism a superstitious, perfidious, depraved belief. He also praised King Reccared for the severity of his anti-Jewish policy.[19]

"The Apostles had scarcely set foot on the land of exile when Judea fell to Titus, her people, driven forth, were scattered all over the Earth."[20] Pope Gregory the Great; Homilies XXXIX.

612 A.D.
King Sisebut issued a decree which began the full-scale persecution of Jews in Spain. He ordered all Christians freed from all

relationships that made them dependent upon Jews. Jews were required to give up Christian slaves, servants and tenants together with the land the latter held in lease. The Jews either had to transfer them to Christian control or set them free. A Jew who converted a Christian to Judaism was liable to the death penalty and confiscation of property. Later Sisebut ordered Jews to accept Christianity or leave his kingdom.[21]

615 A.D.

The Frankish king Clotaire II upheld the Council of Paris which forbade Jews to hold magisterial power or enter military service.[22]

628 A.D.

The Byzantine Emperor Heraclius, who still controlled part of Spain after his victory over Persians and Jews in Palestine, ordered conversion by force of all Jews throughout the provinces of his empire and renewed the Hadrian and Constantine edicts which barred Jews from Jerusalem and its environs.[23]

629 A.D.

The Merovingian king Dagobert followed Heraclius' example and ordered the forced conversion of Jews in his kingdom or they would be treated as enemies and put to death.[24]

633 A.D.

The Third Council of Toledo was called by King Sisenand and presided over by Isidore, Bishop of Hispalis (Seville). This Council decreed that Jews should not be converted by force but rather by persuasion. However, Jews forcibly converted in the past could not revert to Judaism. Therefore they were to be forcibly constrained from practicing the tenants of Judaism and removed from the Jewish community. Children of both sexes were forcibly taken from their parents and raised in monasteries. Any convert discovered practicing Judaism was to be sold into slavery of orthodox Christians chosen by the king. Converts as well as Jews were excluded from public office.[25]

638 A.D.
The Fourth Council of Toledo forbade all non-Catholics to live in Spain. Converts were placed under strict episcopal supervision and were not permitted to travel within the country without a permit signed by local Church authorities. Every Jew was required to take an oath that he had given up Jewish law and practice. The penalty for falsely swearing or lapsing varied from religious penance to flogging, loss of limb, confiscation of property to burning at the stake.[26]

"Polemical tracts against Judaism were written by Isidore, Bishop of Seville and Julian, Bishop of Toledo."[27]

638-642 A.D.
King Chintila decreed no one was permitted in the Visigothic empire who was not a Catholic; Jews were required to emigrate.[28]

652 A.D.
King Recceswith of Spain reapplied the orders of the Fourth Council of Toledo but imposed severe penalties on those who attempted to leave the country.[29]

653 A.D.
Recceswith appeared before the eighth Council of Toledo. He characterized Judaism as a pollution of the realm and called for more anti-Jewish actions. The Council and Crown jointly agreed that the country should be rid of all unbelievers and blasphemers.[30]

653 A.D.
King Recceswith decreed a body of law that stripped Judaism of all rights and required Jews to sign an oath (*placitum*) that made the practice of Judaism virtually impossible. Jews who violated the oath were subject to the death penalty by burning or stoning.[31]

655 A.D.
The ninth Council of Toledo ruled that baptized Jews were required to spend all Jewish and Christian holy days in the presence of a bishop.[32]

681 A.D.

Spanish King Erwig attempted to enforce existing anti-Jewish legislation and added new restrictions. Practicing Jews were forbidden to enter seaports. Converts were exempted from taxes and their share added to taxes of the remaining Jewish community. All land and slaves owned by Jews were taken by the state at a fixed price. All Jews in the realm were ordered to accept baptism. Jewish converts were required to listen to Christian sermons and forbidden to make dietary distinctions.[33]

The twelfth Council of Toledo affirmed the measures of King Erwig.[34]

692 A.D.

The Trullan Council (Quinisext) an ecumenical council in the Eastern Empire decreed that clergymen and laymen were forbidden to attend Jewish feasts, have friendly relations with Jews, be attended by Jewish physicians, or to bathe with Jews in the public baths. These restrictions were backed with the penalty of excommunication.[35]

693-694 A.D.

The Sixteenth and Seventeenth Councils of Toledo under the leadership of King Egica and Felix, Bishop of Toledo (successor of St. Julian) attacked economic power of some Jews. Jews were required to turn over to the royal treasury all slaves, buildings, and agricultural and other property ever acquired from Christian owners. Jews were also forbidden to engage in export or import business and were permitted to trade only among themselves. They were charged with undermining the Church and plotting with the Moors and North African co-religionists to seize the crown, massacre Catholics and destroy the country. Therefore the Seventeenth Council declared all Jews slaves, confiscated their property and turned it over to former Christian slaves for cultivation. Jewish children were forcibly removed from parental control and raised in Christian houses or monasteries and were later to be married to persons of non-Jewish descent.[36]

93

722 A.D.

The Byzantine Emperor Leo III outlawed Judaism and required all Jews within his realm to be baptized. Some converted but others burned to death in their synagogues to avoid baptism.[37]

740 A.D.

In England, Egbert, Archbishop of York, forbade Christians to attend Jewish festivals.[38]

829 A.D.

Epistles of St. Agobard, Archbishop of Lyon, "proved" Jews were born slaves, were stealing Christian children and selling them to the Arabs, are accursed by God and should be so regarded by all Christians.[39]

845 A.D.

Agobard's successor, Bishop Amulo, Hinkmar, the Bishop of Rheims, the Archbishops of Sens and Bourges called the Council of Meaux, which reenacted old canonical laws and anti-Jewish restrictions, with the purpose of Emperor Charles the Bald making them state policy. The Jews were not to hold public office, be seen in public during Easter week, etc. (Charles refused and dissolved the Council.)[40]

846 A.D.

(Charles summoned the Council of Paris [same clergymen as Council of Meaux] under his supervision and three-fourths of the eighty decrees passed at Meaux were omitted, including the anti-Semitic ones.)[41]

848 A.D.

When Norman pirates sacked Bordeaux, Bishop Prudentius of Troye blamed the Jews despite the fact that they had suffered as severely as the Christians from the raid.[42]

855 A.D.

When Louis II, the son of Lothaire, became ruler of Italy he decreed that all Jews must leave. No Jew was to show his face after October 1, 855.[43]

The successive bishops of Beziers in sermons during the Easter season encouraged the townspeople to stone the Jews in revenge for their crucifying Jesus, a tradition that lasted for centuries.[44]

The Counts of Toulouse had the privilege of publicly boxing the ears of the president of the Jewish community every year on Good Friday. Once this ritual was carried out with such zeal that it killed the recipient. Later the box on the ears was changed to an annual payment by the Jews.[45]

Another Easter custom that survives to the present developed in Catalonia. Special clappers and mallets are distributed to the Congregation on Maundy Thursday and at the end of the services the priest gives a sign and those in attendance beat the clappers to signify killing the Jews.[46]

876 A.D.

When a Norman band approached the City of Sens, Ansegis the Archbishop banished the Jews from the community.[47]

877 A.D.

The death of Charles the Bald was blamed on his Jewish physician Sedekias who was accused of poisoning him.[48]

897 A.D.

Charles the Simple gave all lands and vineyards owned by the Jews in the Duchy of Narbonne to the Church.[49]

945 A.D.

The Senate of Venice issued a decree forbidding sea captains from taking Jews or other merchants on board.[50]

981 A.D.

Otto II, Emperor of Germany, gave the Jews of Merseburg to the bishop as a present.[51]

996 A.D.

When the French king Hugh Capet died, his Jewish physician was accused of murdering him. This was widely believed and accepted as fact by the chroniclers of the time.[52]

CONTINUUM:

The Dark Ages added three new techniques to anti-Semitic practices. One that had great historical impact is the designation of those who refused to submit to forced baptism as enemies of the state and therefore liable for the death penalty. The second, while having less of an historical effect seems more horrible in its immediate impact, was the forcible taking of Jewish children and raising them in Christian homes or monasteries. The third was the establishment of local annual public insults of the Jewish population usually during the Easter season.

These new additions became a permanent feature of anti-Semitism until the rise of modern anti-Semitism in the 19th century. They expand the already existing repertoire that continued to make Jewish life a common daily nightmare. Forced baptism, destruction of synagogues, denial of civil rights and freedom of movement and residence, expulsion, discriminatory taxation, prohibition of religious practices and proselytizing continue to be used by Church and civil authorities.

Two future developments were also foreshadowed during this period. One was the suspicion that Jews who converted to Christianity were not sincere. The other was isolated outbursts of mass or mob anti-Semitism.

As in the Roman and Early Christian periods, some secular and church leaders defended Jews against anti-Semitic attacks by granting protection or recommending less harsh treatment. Some rulers actively encouraged Jews to settle and granted them privileges. Such action, however, was increasingly rare.

The anti-Semitism of this period with a few exceptions was still an elite phenomena. The commoners during this period as in the earlier periods appear to have generally ignored the urgings of Church officials and the Crown to shun the Jews.

PART III. DARK AGES

1. Graetz, op. cit., II, 628-29; Flannery, op. cit., pp. 53-56.
2. Baer, op. cit., pp. 18-19.

3. Ibid., pp. 17-21.

4. Graetz, op. cit., III, 10-11.

6. Graetz, op. cit., III, 37.

7. Ibid.

8. Cecil Roth, *Venice* (Philadelphia: The Jewish Publication Society of America, 1930), p. 3.

9. Graetz, op. cit., III, 12-16.

10. Cecil Roth (ed.), *The World History of the Jewish People*, Vol. 2, *The Dark Ages* (New Brunswick, N.J.: Rutgers University Press, 1961), pp. 75-76; Ernest L. Abel, *The Roots of Anti-Semitism* (Cranberry, N.J.: Associated University Press, Inc., 1975), p. 239.

11. Graetz, op. cit., III, 31.

12. Ibid., p. 37.

13. Ibid., pp. 38-39.

14. Runes, *War Against the Jews*, p. 72.

15. Graetz, op. cit., III, 39.

16. Baer, op. cit., p. 19.

17. Runes, *War Against the Jews*, p. 105.

18. Graetz, op. cit., III, 46.

19. Runes, *War Against the Jews*, p. 85.

20. Jules Isaac, op. cit., p. 45.

21. Baer, op. cit., pp. 19-20.

22. Graetz, op. cit., p. 40.

23. Baer, op. cit., p. 19.

24. Graetz, op. cit., p. 40.

25. Baer, op. cit., pp. 20-21; Graetz, op. cit., pp. 49-50.

26. Baer, op. cit., p. 21.

27. Ibid.

28. Graetz, op. cit., p. 51.

29. Ibid., pp. 102-104.

30. Flannery, op. cit., pp. 74-75.

31. Ibid., p. 75.

32. Ibid.

33. Baer, op. cit., pp. 21-22.

34. Flannery, op. cit., p. 75.

35. *The Jewish Encyclopedia*, Vol. IV (New York: Funk & Wagnallis Company, 1903), p. 78.

36. Baer, op. cit., p. 22.

37. Will Durant, *The Age of Faith* (New York: Simon and Schuster, 1950), p. 389.

38. A. M. Hyamson, *A History of the Jews in England* (London: Chatto and Windus, 1908), p. 5.

39. Runes, op. cit., pp. 1-2.

40. Flannery, op. cit., pp. 83-84.

41. Ibid., p. 84.

42. Ibid., p. 85.

43. Graetz, op. cit., III, 174.

44. Ibid., pp. 173-74.

45. Ibid., p. 174.

46. Flannery, op. cit., p. 85.

47. Flannery, op. cit., p. 86.

48. Ibid., p. 81.

49. Ibid., p. 85.

50. Roth, op. cit., p. 8.

51. Graetz, op. cit., III, 243.

52. Flannery, op. cit., p. 81.

PART IV: THE CRUSADES—1000-1348

BACKGROUND:

This was a period of revitalization and expansion. Europe was no longer threatened by invasion or subjected to population migrations. Feudalism with its layered loyalties and obligations was the political and economic order of the day. All of Europe with the exception of Moorish Spain was Catholic. The papacy and the Church was at the height of its spiritual and temporal power. This was an age of faith in which the most primitive motivation and the basest act had the flavor of religion. Despite Manicheanism, the sacred and profane were still united. Sex, greed, power, hatred, sadism and masochism had not yet been secularized. Murder, torture, robbery, rape plunder and pillage were frequently great acts of faith and never simple acts of selfishness. Great deeds, sacrifices and adventures were carried out for the faith. Cathedrals, universities, art, wars and pilgrimages were under the mantel of God and more specifically Roman Catholicism. No act, no event, no thought was without religious interpretation or significance. God and the devil were actively engaged in the life and history of man.

Catholicism claimed to be, and its claims were accepted, the only way to salvation. It was the one true faith. The saving of man's immortal soul was the paramount concern of the times. The Church's organization, dogma and ritual dominated all of society. Political power was by Grace of God. Defeat or victory was by divine intervention. Droughts, floods, earthquakes were God's punishment or God's test. Sin was the work of the devil and mental illness was possession by the devil. (The Church exorcised both.) There was no psychology. Visions, miracles, cures, voices made God real and present. Misfortune and suffering was a test of faith or a purge of evil. And the gatekeeper to everlasting life and happiness in the hereafter was the Church. It was within this general social framework that the Crusades occurred.

Pilgrims to the Holy Land returned home with stories of Moslem desecration of the holy places. These descriptions inflamed the religious fervor and passions of the Europeans to the point that they felt compelled to embark on crusades to free the Holy Land from the infidels. The Crusades brought Europe direct contact with Islamic civilization, a rediscovery of Greek philosophy and Roman law, and a revitalization of science and math. As a result learning came out of the monasteries and the great universities were established. In addition, the Crusades broke the insularity of the feudal manor and by reopening the East to Western trading interests helped to displace the manor with the city. The feudal economy came under the assault of the expanding merchant capitalism. The political order of feudalism also came under attack as the political rivalries expressed and intensified by the Crusades began the centralization that led to the birth of the nation-state. It has to be emphasized that this growth, vitalism and change occurred within the framework of Christian piety.

Beneath the surface piety, however, lurked interest in the rich trade of the East, opportunity for plunder, the possibility of extending the baronial holdings of the participants—indeed, the establishment of new baronies—and in later Crusades cancellation of debts. The Crusades and Crusaders were a mixed bag. Some Crusaders were indeed disciplined and spiritually motivated soldiers of the Cross, exhibiting the highest ideals of knighthood. But whenever mass movements occur and populations are mobilized with emotional fervor, things tend to get out of hand. The Crusades also unleashed undisciplined mobs and outright gangsters. Religion, here, served to cloak the brigand and freebooter with respectability.

The attack on the infidel was not confined to the Holy Land. If slaughter, pillage and plunder were God's will against the infidel in the Holy Land, the question arose—"Why not all infidels—those at home as well as in the Holy Land?" Logic prevailed and the Crusaders slaughtered and plundered or forcibly baptised the Jewish communities they encountered on the way to the Holy Land. The logic was extended to include Crusades against heretics in Europe, specifically the Albigensian Crusade which slaughtered the Jewish communities as well. The reconquest of Spain also became part of the Crusader's agenda. And the Church established the Inquisition in the 13th century to safeguard the faith at home.

The 13th century also produced one of the staggering intellects of Christianity—if not all of history. The philosophical and theological writings of St. Thomas Aquinas, the Angelic Doctor, set the tone of western philosophy until Descartes. Even today, Thomism is still the dominant and base line philosophy of Catholicism; this indicates the power and scope of his intellect. However, because of his influence, St. Thomas legitimized and perpetuated two concepts that have had painful effect on Jews living within Christendom. One was the rationale for perpetual servitude of the Jews for their crime of deicide; the other was the lending of credence to demonology. St. Thomas embraced the medieval superstition of the real and physical presence of the devil. It is a short step, once credible, to see the God-killing Jew as devil incarnate, particularly when the idea of a corporeal devil has the endorsement of a Doctor of the Church.

During the 13th century there were also sporadic outbreaks of forced baptism. There were distinctions made by various Church leaders as to what constituted force. Generally, economic coercion, confiscation of property or exile were not considered force. As to physical coercion, Pope Innocent III ruled that it made no difference what the threat (death, torture, etc.), if the person did not cry out against baptism during the act he was not unwilling. Only if there was a struggle or show of resistance during the actual baptism was a person considered unwilling. Therefore, any Jew who submitted to baptism to avoid torture or death and tried later to revert to Judaism was subject to be burned as a heretic.

101

ENVIRONMENT: CHRISTIAN

Religion permeated and shaped every aspect of life. Religious services and observances were more frequent and clergy were more available. The regular preachings of mendicant friars brought the anti-Semitic teachings of the Church elite to the common man.

The power and influence of the Papacy and the Church was at its zenith and dominated both the secular and sacred aspects of life, indeed there was little distinction between the two.

Crusaders attacked, extorted and slaughtered Jewish communities under the cloak of "God's Will" and with the apparent approval (with some exceptions) of the lay and ecclesiastical authorities.

Religious and secular leaders treated Jews with contempt. Confiscation of Jewish property, extortion and expulsion of Jews became common practice. Church and civil law clearly defined Jews as inferior and odious.

The Fourth Lateran Council made the position of the Jew in Christian society visible to all by requiring the "Jew badge."

Church and lay authorities publicly burned Jewish Holy Books and other writings.

Christians were rebuked and punished for friendly relations with Jews.

Folktales of ritual murder and host desecration by Jews were widespread.

Jews were routinely blamed for natural or man-made disasters.

Sermons, fairs, art, plays, songs and poems popularized anti-Semitic stereotypes and justified anti-Semitic acts.

ENVIRONMENT: JEWISH

Jewish existence was one of almost continuous terror. Jews throughout Europe regularly experienced attacks, slaughter, extortion, expulsion, kidnap, ransom, forced baptism and confiscation of property by the Church, the state and mobs.

Jews and Judaism were subjected daily to ridicule and indignities required and sanctioned by Canon and civil law.

Jews were barred from almost all contact with Christian population and society and restricted in the practice of their religion.

More and more occupations were closed to Jews through the development of guilds and the rise of Christians in particular fields, who then had Jews excluded. Jews became concentrated in occupations and economic roles that were unpopular or contemptuous, and reduced to chattel status in many areas.

Jews were required to observe Christian religious practices.

Jews were frequently blamed and punished for natural or manmade disasters.

Folklore portrayed Jews as inferior, evil and devils.

Entire Jewish communities were reduced to poverty to pay assessments or meet taxes; debts, credits and contracts were subject to fiat.

INCIDENTS:

1009 A.D.

When Moslems destroyed the Holy Sepulcher, the Jews of Orleans were accused of collusion and attacked by mobs.[1]

1012 A.D.

The first persecution in Germany occurred under Emperor Henry II. When Jews refused to accept baptism they were expelled from Mayence (Mainz).[2]

News of the desecration of the Holy Sepulcher touched off massacres and forced baptism of Jewish communities in Rouen, Limoges and Rome.[3]

1021 A.D.

An earthquake followed by a hurricane struck Rome on Good Friday. Pope Benedict VIII arrested a number of Jews who allegedly had put a nail through a host on Holy Thursday as the probable cause of the calamity. They confessed* and were burned.[4]

*Note: The reader should remember that torture was the accepted method of interrogation and prosecution. It is not surprising that throughout history Jews and others as well have confessed to impossible and monstrous acts.[6]

103

1063 A.D.

In the war to oust the Saracen from Spain, Christian soldiers on the march often attacked the Jews. Pope Alexander II warned the French knights not to attack the Jews.[5]

1078 A.D.

Pope Gregory VII barred Jews from any office in Christendom or any supremacy over Christians.[7]

1081 A.D.

Alfonso VI of Toledo was reprimanded by Pope Gregory VII for appointing Jews to court and diplomatic positions.[8]

1095 A.D.

Godfrey Bouillon, Duke of Lorraine, in gathering an army for the Crusade, spread the rumor that he was avenging the death of Christ with the blood of the Jews before he left. The Jews of the Rhineland paid him 500 pieces of silver if he would not. Emperor Henry IV ordered him not to attack the Jews. Godfrey, his blackmail a success, complied.[9]

Crusaders massacred Jews of Rouen and other cities in Lorraine who refused to be baptized.[10]

Jewish communities in France warned German co-religionists of the Crusades. Rumors of the massacre at Rouen alarmed German Jews enough for them to comply with Peter the Hermit's request to supply his army.[11]

1096 A.D.

From January to July, it is estimated that 10,000 Jews were murdered in Northern France and Germany ([1/4 to [1/3 of the Jewish population of the area at that time).[12]

1096 A.D.

In April, Volkmar (Folkmar) gathered 10,000 men to join Peter the Hermit in the East. They arrived in Hungary in July and attacked the Jewish community of Prague. Bishop Cosmos and lay authorities protested vehemently but had no effect. From Prague they went to Nitra and attempted to do the same, but the Hungarians resisted, attacked and scattered the Crusaders.[13]

Gottschalk (a disciple of Peter) followed the route taken by Peter with a larger force than Volkmar. They massacred the Jewish population of Ratisbon.[14]

Count Emich of Leisinger gathered a larger force than Gottschalk. He ignored the order of Henry IV forbidding the molesting of Jews and immediately began a campaign of terror against them. At Speir he killed twelve Jews. (The Bishop of Speir gave the rest of the community protection, captured some of the murderers and cut off their hands as punishment.)[15]

Emich's band moved on to Worms; the Bishop was unable to protect the Jews and 500 were massacred after they had paid Emich for protection.[16]

Archbishop Rothard had closed the gates of Mainz [Mayence] to Emich and with the Chief Lay Protector of the city gave sanctuary and protection to Jews. Emich's troops forced the gates and in two days of slaughter killed 1,000 Jews.[17]

1096 A.D.

The synagogue of Cologne was burned and since the Jews had fled before the Crusaders reached the city, only two were killed. Later, Jews of Cologne were discovered, and in the sweep down the Rhenish valley through Neuss, Wevelinghafen, Ellen, Mehr, Kerpen, Geldern, Eller and Xanten, 12,000 Jews are said to have been slaughtered.[18]

Part of Emich's band broke off and headed down the Moselle Valley killing Jews as they passed. The community of Treves was given protection by the Bishop on condition of converting. The Elders of the community urged conversion. Others committed suicide to avoid execution by the Crusaders of William the Carpenter.[19]

1099 A.D.

After Godfrey of Bouillon took Jerusalem and massacred the Mohammedans he drove the Jews, Rabbanites and Karaites into a synagogue and burned it and all inside.[20]

105

1100 A.D.

Early in the twelfth century the Jews of Kiev experienced their first pogrom. From the time that Vladimir Monomakh was offered the throne of Kiev until he entered the city, several riots broke out and after looting the homes of high officials the mob plundered the Jewish section.[21]

1130 A.D.

Jews of London were accused of killing a sick man who had come to one of them for treatment. The community was fined £2000. The fine cancelled claims of Jewish financiers and put the Jewish community in debt to the Crown.[22]

1140 A.D.

Rudulf (Radulf), a Cistercian monk, began preaching a Crusade in Northern France and Germany. His sermons attacked the Jews and urged people to attack them. Massacres occurred in Cologne, Mainz, Worms, Spier and Strassbourg. (Archbishops of Mainz and Cologne complained to St. Bernard of Clairvaux. Bernard wrote letters reprimanding Rudulf and charging the populace not to molest Jews. These letters had no effect. Bernard went to Germany and, in direct confrontation with Rudulf, ordered him back to the monastery.)[23]

Ironically, St. Bernard of Clairvaux was a major force behind the calling of the Second Crusade. While he did oppose the killing of the Jews, in his sermons he characterized them as bestial, descendants of the Devil and murderers from the beginning of time.[24]

1144 A.D.

First recorded instance of ritual murder charge in the Christian era. On Easter Eve the body of a young skinner's apprentice named William was found in the woods near Norwich, England. It was rumored that Jews had enticed him into the synagogue and crucified him in mockery of the passion of Jesus. The Sheriff gave refuge in the Castle and denied the request that the Jews be turned over to the Bishop's court for trial. Despite protection by civil authorities the community's leaders were murdered by followers of a knight who was in debt.[25] (See Continuum paper for discussion of ritual murders.)

"Peter the Venerable of Cluny believed Jews should be punished and that they should finance the Crusades. They shouldn't be killed but rather made to suffer torment and have an existence worse than death. He attempted to turn Louis VII of France against the Jews."[26]

1146 A.D.

Despite protection of Conrad III in Germany, the agitation by Rudulf caused the murder of Simon the Pious of Treves and a woman in Speir when they refused to accept baptism.[27]

Pope Eugenius III who called for the New Crusade suggested to the princes that crusaders be absolved of debts to Jews as incentive to participate.[28]

The preaching of the monk Rudulf encouraged mob attacks, forced baptism and massacres of Jews in Mayence, Cologne and other communities in the Rhine Valley. These attacks occurred in spite of the efforts of bishops and noblemen to protect the Jews.[29]

1147 A.D.

Crusaders murdered 20 members of the Jewish community of Wurzburg on the basis of a rumor that they had murdered a Christian. In Belitz, Germany, all Jews were burned on the basis of a ritual murder charge. Crusaders murdered 150 Jews in Bohemia.[30]

In France, Crusaders attacked the Jewish communities of Carenton, Ramenu and Sully.[31]

1168 A.D.

Ritual murder charge at Gloucester.[32]

1171 A.D.

Ritual murder charge in Blois. Count Theobald of Chartres commanded all Jews of Blois thrown into prison. After trial by water the entire community was burned at the stake. Thirty-four men and 17 women were burned.[33]

1179 A.D.

Third Lateran Council decreed that Jews and Christians should live separately.[34]

1180 A.D.

Philip Augustus of France ordered all Jews living on the estates of the crown imprisoned on charge of ritual murder. They were ransomed for 1,500 marks of silver, a case of simple extortion.[35]

1181 A.D.

Ritual murder charge at Bury St. Edmund in England.[36]

Philip Augustus commanded all Jews in his provinces to leave. They were allowed to sell moveable property, but real property became property of the crown and synagogues were made into churches.[37]

1183 A.D.

Ritual murder accusation at Bristol.[38]

1188 A.D.

The coronation of Richard I was followed by mob attacks on the Jewish communities of London and York. (Richard punished the rioters and permitted those who had converted to avoid death to return to their faith.)[39]

1190 A.D.

Richard's protection proved effective only while he was in the country. When he crossed the Channel to gather forces for a new Crusade, the Crusaders assembled in England attacked English Jews.[40]

The Jewish section of the Port of Lynn in Norfolk was put to the torch and the inhabitants either slaughtered or perished in the flames. Norwich Jews were saved from a similar fate by taking refuge in the royal castle. At York 1,500 Jews were slaughtered and crusaders burned credit records. The Jewish community of Stanford was pillaged, and those who did not make it to the royal castle were put to the sword. Pillaging and looting occurred in other towns of England as well.[41]

1191 A.D.
French king surrounded the town of Bray and gave Jews the choice of baptism or death. The community decided on suicide but Philip still had 100 burned. The only ones spared were children under 13.[42]

1192 A.D.
Ritual murder charge at Winchester.[43]

1194 A.D.
The Jews of London were assessed 5,000 marks to help pay the ransom of Richard I. This was three times the amount assessed the Christian burghers of London.[44]

1195-98 A.D.
A fiery preacher, Fulk of Neuilly, carried his message of reform and attack against usury throughout France. He did not incite people against Jews but urged usurers to give back their "unclean" wealth and distribute it to the poor. In many places mobs attacked and mistreated Jews, and barons used his preachings as an excuse to expel Jews and confiscate their holdings.[45]

1205 A.D.
Pope Innocent III censured Philip for being too lenient with Jews and threatened Alfonso, King of Castille, with excommunication if he continued to treat Jews leniently.[46]

1208 A.D.
"The Jews, like the fratricide Cain, are doomed to wander about the earth as fugitives and vagabonds, and their faces must be covered with shame. They are under no circumstances to be protected by Christian princes, but, on the contrary to be condemned to serfdom. . . ." Letter of Pope Innocent III to Count Nevers.[47]

1209 A.D.
In the Crusade against the Albigensian heresy the city of Beziers was stormed and the inhabitants massacred. Twenty thousand people perished including the city's Jewish population of 200.[48]

109

1212 A.D.
The Council of Paris decreed that Christian midwives were not to attend Jewish women in labor. Those who helped bring "the brood of the Devil" into the world would be expelled from the Holy Church.[49]

1215 A.D.
The Fourth Lateran Council presided over by Pope Innocent III passed four decrees covering Jews: Christian princes were to keep close watch over their usury and tithes from property that passed to their hands were to be paid to the Church; baptized Jews were forbidden to practice Jewish customs; Jews were forbidden to appear in public at Easter time and were barred from public office; they were to wear a distinguishing badge. This was the first time distinctive clothing was required in the West.[50] (Cf. Code of Omar in Appendix I—Islam & Judaism.)

Alice of Montmorency, the wife of Simon de Montfort, ordered all Jews of Toulouse, France, arrested and offered the choice of baptism or death. (Simon intervened and freed the captives.)[51]

1218 A.D.
King Henry III by Royal Decree required all Jews in England to wear, at all times, a badge on their outer garment that they might be distinguished from Christians. This is an instance of secular enforcement of a Conciliar decree.[52] (Cf. 1215, Fourth Lateran Council.)

1222 A.D.
The Council of Canterbury affirmed anti-Jewish regulations of the Fourth Lateran Conference for English Jews (cf. 1215) and added prohibitions against Jews employing Christians, building new synagogues, and entering or storing valuables in churches. (In order to safeguard valuables and records from mob and Crusaders' destruction, Jews often utilized facilities provided by various friendly clergy.)[53]

The Bishops of Norwich and Lincoln threatened excommunication of those who dealt with Jews, even proscribing basic provisions. (In response to this, the Justician Hubert de Burgh issued an order forbidding the king's subjects, under pain of imprisonment, to refuse to provide Jews with the necessities of life.)[54]

1228 A.D.

James I of Aragon, at the urging of clerical advisors, issued a series of laws forbidding Jews to hold public office of authority over Christians. These laws were seldom enforced and appear to have been designed to satisfy the Church in a symbolic manner.[55]

1231 A.D.

Pope Gregory IX officially established the Inquisition under papal authority.[55a*]

1232 A.D.

Exorbitant taxes were levied against the Jews of England.[56]

1233 A.D.

Pope Gregory IX complained to the bishops of Germany that the Jews in Germany were living too well. God had condemned them to utter wretchedness. He chided the overfriendly relations be-

---

*NOTE: The dynamism and vitality associated with the rebirth of Europe in the 11th and 12th centuries infected religion and theology as well as the more secular areas of politics and economics. Heresies sprang up and lured many from orthodoxy and challenged the authority of the Roman Church. The lay and ecclesiastical officials recognized that Crusades were effective against widespread heresies, as the Albigensians and Waldensians learned, but believed it more prudent to check heresy early to prevent its spread. If heresies could be stopped before they attracted large numbers of adherents, the large-scale bloodlettings and massacres associated with the Crusades could be avoided.

The instrument devised to root out heresy was the Inquisition. Tribunals, usually composed of the mendicant orders—Dominicans or Franciscans—were established either at a major city in a district or on a roving basis. These tribunals were charged to search out and put an end to heresy and punish unrepentant heretics. Church and Crown cooperated in this endeavor. The Inquisition served as police, prosecution, judge and jury but secular authorities carried out the execution of unrepentant heretics. The Inquisitors were to avoid the shedding of blood so as a subterfuge the mode of execution associated with the Inquisition was burning at the stake.

tween Christians and Jews and forbade all conversation between them.[57] (See Introduction.)

1236 A.D.

Crusaders attacked the Jewish communities of Anjou, Poitou, Bordeaux, and Angouleme. Jews were given the choice of baptism or death. Five hundred chose baptism. But over three thousand, including children and pregnant women, were brutally murdered. Many were simply trampled to death by the Crusaders' horses. Sacred books were destroyed, houses were burned and property was pillaged. Pope Gregory IX, who had called this Crusade, was so appalled by this outrage that he wrote to the clergy of these communities admonishing them for not preventing it.[58]

1239 A.D.

A bloody riot started in London when a Jew was accused of murder. A number of Jews were imprisoned, several were put to death and 1/3 of the entire community's property was confiscated as punishment.[59]

1239 A.D.

Pope Gregory IX ordered all copies of the Talmud confiscated in France, England, Castile, Aragon and Portugal. The seizure was to take place on Saturday, March 3, 1240, when all Jews would be in their synagogues. The books were to be turned over to the Dominicans and Franciscans for examination.[60]

1240 A.D.

King Louis IX (St. Louis) of France carried out papal order for confiscation of Talmud.[61]

All Jewish books were seized in England and the Talmud was burned in accordance with papal decree. It is not clear that this actually occurred. Most historians only single out France as carrying out the decree in 1240.[62] (See Poliakov and Graetz.)

In Spain the Dominicans and Franciscans conducted an intensive missionary campaign. Jews were compelled to attend conversion sermons.[63]

1242 A.D.
Twenty-four cartloads of copies of the Talmud were burned in Paris. Copies of the Talmud were burned on numerous occasions in various places. Pope Innocent IV finally stopped the destruction and ordered the remaining copies returned after objectionable passages were expunged.[64]

1244 A.D.
Oxford students sacked the Jewish quarter.[65]

1244 A.D.
Ritual murder accusation in London. The Jewish community of the realm was assessed 60,000 marks as punishment.[66]

1247 A.D.
The ritual murder libel had become so widespread and caused so many atrocities that Pope Innocent IV conducted an investigation and completely exonerated Jews of the charge.[67]

1251 A.D.
English Jews were forbidden to eat meat on Friday or during Lent.[68]

1254 A.D.
King Louis IX expelled Jews from France. Landed property, synagogues and cemeteries were confiscated by the crown.[69]

1255 A.D.
Ritual murder charge in Lincoln (Little St. Hugh of Lincoln.) The corpse of Hugh was discovered in a cesspool near the house of Copin, a Jew. Copin was seized and tortured. He confessed that Hugh had been murdered for ritual purposes. Henry III ordered Copin hanged immediately after he was dragged through the streets tied to a horse. One hundred Jews implicated were brought to London for trial. Eighteen requested mixed jury of Jews and Christians. Their request was seen as an admission of guilt and they were hanged immediately. Seventy-nine others were duly

113

convicted and sentenced. Only three of the hundred escaped death. One was acquitted; two were pardoned.[70]

1261 A.D.

Canterbury students, with priests and monks participating, attacked the Jewish quarter.[71]

1262 A.D.

Anti-Jewish riots occurred in London. The Jewish quarter of London was sacked.[72]

1263 A.D.

Disputation was held at Barcelona. Rabbi Moses ben Naleman defended the Talmud against Pablo Christiani's (a converted Jew) attempt to prove the validity of Christianity from the Talmud. The case was heard before King James I, bishops, leading Franciscans and Dominicans, and nobility.[73]

As a result of the disputation James ordered the Jews to erase all blasphemous references to Jesus and Mary which Pablo Christiani and the Dominicans discovered. Failure would be punished by a heavy fine and burning of the Talmud.[74]

1264 A.D.

London's Jewish quarter was sacked. The synagogue was looted and defiled.[75]

1267 A.D.

Council of Vienna decreed that all Jews were to wear horned hats (pileum cornutum) to show they were offspring of the devil. In popular lore the hat was believed to actually be a covering for real horns growing out of the Jew's head.[76]

1270 A.D.

After the death of Frederick II massacres of Jewish communities occurred in Weissenberg, Magdeburg, Armstadt, Coblenz, Sinzig, Erfurt and other cities. In Sinzig the community was locked in the synagogue on a Sabbath and burned alive.[77]

1272 A.D.

The principal London synagogue was confiscated on the grounds that the chanting disturbed the devotions of the neighboring monks. Jewish devotions were then held in private homes but the Bishop of London forbade this and permitted services to be held in only one home.[78]

1275 A.D.

A number of English Christians were excommunicated for attending a Jewish wedding.[79]

King Edward I of England in Common Council of the Realm passed the Statutum Judeismo. This law forbade Jews to charge interest on loans, but for the first time Jews were allowed to lease land for tillage and farming. This law also granted the right to become merchants and artisans. However, the law also included residential restrictions and extended the Jewish badge to all persons of either sex above the age of seven and required those above twelve to pay a poll tax of three pence annually at Eastertide.[80]

1276 A.D.

Ritual murder accusation occurred in London.[81]

1278 A.D.

Anti-Jewish outburst occurred at Genoa, Spain during the Easter season. Priests and servants hurled stones from the church steeple into neighboring Jewish quarter causing considerable damage. (Pedro III sent letter threatening punishment of the bishop if attacks were not stopped.)[82]

Pope Nicholas III issued a papal bull ordering preachers to be sent out all over Europe to convert the Jews. The Jews were to be compelled to attend these conversion sermons.[83]

Edward I ordered Jews throughout England arrested and a house-to-house search conducted for evidence of coin clipping. Six hundred and eighty were imprisoned in the Tower of London. A large number were hanged and their property seized by the crown.[84]

1279 A.D.
The Jews of Poland were locked in their houses during Church processions. They were not permitted to have Christian servants, wetnurses, or mistresses, and social intercourse with Christians was forbidden. Only one synagogue was permitted in each city. The Jewish badge included a peculiarly shaped hat and a ring of red cloth sewn on the upper left side of the outer garment. [85]

1279 A.D.
The policy of Poland reflected the presence and interest of the Roman Church. The state originally attempted to attract Jews by establishing Jewish life on rational civic foundations. The Church, however, insisted on isolating the Jews from the general life of the country. [86]

Church Synod of Buda under the direction of the papal legate for Hungary, Poland, Dalmatia, Croatia, Slavonia, Ladomeria and Galicia excluded Jews from public service and tax farming, proscribed interactions between Jews and Christians and introduced the Jewish badge in this area. [87]

Abraham fil Deulecresse was burned for blasphemy at Norwich, England. [88]

Ritual murder accusation at Northampton. [89]

Alfonso X (The Wise) of Castille was rebuked by Pope Nicholas III for continuing to employ Jews in official capacities. In response, Alfonso imprisoned all Jewish tax farmers. [90]

Pedro III ordered all officials in his realm to compel Jews to attend conversion sermons by friars in their synagogues. Fanatical mobs attacked Jews but Pedro tried to prevent these popular excesses. [91]

1281 A.D.
All Spanish Jews were arrested in their synagogues on a Sabbath in January. They were released on promise to pay ransom of 4,380,000 gold maravedis. [92]

1282 A.D.
Archbishop of Canterbury closed all synagogues in his diocese. [93]

1283 A.D.

Ritual murder charge in Mayence; ten Jews were murdered by mob.[94]

Ritual murder charge at Bacharach resulted in murder of twenty-six Jews.[95]

Spanish Jews were barred from judicial or executive authority over Christians and removed as tax collectors by royal decree.[96]

1285 A.D.

Forty Jews were murdered at Oberwellel on charge of ritual murder.[97]

Ritual murder charge in Munich resulted in a mob burning 180 Jews alive in the synagogue.[98]

1290 A.D.

Edward I in Council on July 18 ordered all Jews to be out of England by the first of November (All Saints Day). Those that remained behind were subject to the death penalty.[99]

An outburst of persecution in Naples resulted in a large proportion of the Jewish community being forcibly baptized.[100]

1293 A.D.

Sancho IV in Spain forbade Jews to purchase land from Christians and ordered previously acquired land, except dwellings, sold. This order also applied to Moslems in Sancho's realm.[101]

1294 A.D.

A Christian girl disappeared in Biel, a village in Aragon. All local Jews were arrested on ritual murder suspicion.[102]

1298 A.D.

A report of host desecration in the town of Rottingen (accompanied by the miraculous bleeding of the host) launched one of the most severe persecutions through Franconia, Bavaria and Austria. Rindfleisch, a German nobleman, put together a small army that took the name *Judenschächter* (Jew slaughterers), and proceeded to massacre all Jewish communities in his path. The entire Jewish

117

population of Rottingen was burned alive. The Jewish populations of Wurzburg, Nurenberg, Ratisbon, Augsburg, Heilbroun and many other towns were slaughtered. Over 140 communities were destroyed and an estimated 100,000 Jews were slain. This persecution lasted approximately six months.[103]

1302 A.D.
Ferdinand IV recalled Jews to royal service.[104]

1306 A.D.
On January 21, Philip IV issued a secret order to the higher and lower officials throughout his kingdom to put all the Jews of France under arrest on one and the same day without warning of any kind. They were imprisoned on July 22. They were told that they had to leave the country within one month and were to leave behind all goods and debts owed them. Those who remained were liable to the death penalty. One hundred thousand in all were banished; they were allowed to take only the clothes on their backs and provisions for one day. Jewelry and money were directly confiscated by the crown; other property was sold in auction. Philip's feud with the Pope and the war against the Flemish had exhausted the royal treasury; the Jewish property seized after expulsion was to help replenish the crown.[105]

Seats at Universities vacated by the expulsion of Jews were sold to the highest bidders. Philip gave a synagogue as a gift to his coachman. In Orleans alone the sale of Jewish property brought the royal treasury 337,000 francs.[106]

Eleazar ben Joseph of Chinon, a learned scholar, and his two brothers who remained behind but refused to convert to Christianity were burned at the stake simply because they were Jews.[107]

1308 A.D.
John of Dirpheim, Bishop of Strasburg, demanded and received from Henry VII of Germany the Jews of Rufach and Sulzmatt. They were charged with desecrating a host and most were burned alive.[108]

118

1311 A.D.

The property of certain Jews in Tarragona and Montblanch was confiscated and they were banished for life.[109]

1313 A.D.

The Jewish communities of Tarragona and Montblanch were assessed heavy fines, and the synagogue in Tarragona was converted into a Church. The synagogue of Montblanch was destroyed.[110]

1315 A.D.

The property of the Jewish community of Majorca was confiscated and privileges were rescinded.[111]

King Louis X recalled Jews to France. They agreed to return if he accepted the following conditions: (1) return to former place of residence; (2) drop charges of former transgressions; (3) return synagogues, cemeteries , and books; (4) right to collect debts. Louis agreed with proviso that $^2/_3$ of moneys collected went to royal treasury and that they wear the Jewish badge.[112]

1320 A.D.

Pope John XXII authorized the inquisition of Toulouse. Bernard Gui, the Inquisitor, placed the Talmud on trial. The Talmud was burned in Toulouse and Perpignon.[113] (See 1240, Paris.)

The Shepards Crusade (Pastorelli) was organized despite Pope John XII's discouragement. Forty thousand shepards and peasants marched from Agen to Toulouse and killed any Jew along the path of march who would not submit to baptism. At Verdun, 500 Jews besieged in a tower committed suicide rather than submit. The lone surviving adult was killed when he asked for baptism, and the surviving children were baptized. The Jews of Toulouse, Bordeaux, Gascogne, and Albi were slaughtered. In total 120 communities in southern France and nothern Spain were massacred during this Crusade.[114]

1321 A.D.

In the Aragon village of Teruel two Jews were accused of poisoning a well and were executed.[115]

1328 A.D.

A Christian mob, inflamed by the anti-Jewish preaching of a mendicant friar, attacked the Jewish community of Estella and burned their houses. Five thousand Jews perished in this massacre.[116]

1336 A.D.

Alfonso XI at the urging of his counsel imprisoned and tortured high court Jews; many died as a result.[117]

1338 A.D.

Bishop of Strasburg caused a group of Jews to be massacred on the anniversary of the Conversion of St. Paul.[118] (See 1308, John of Dirpheim.)

1348 A.D.

A series of reform laws were passed by Alfonso XI of Spain. These measures prohibited Jews from lending money at interest. Government officials were not allowed to collect debts owed to Jews. The Church was called upon to assist the enforcement of the decrees with its power of excommunication.[119]

CONTINUUM:

The Crusades opened a new era of anti-Semitism. In the period up to the Crusades, anti-Semitism was for the most part an elitist phenomena. Church Fathers, Doctors, Popes, Saints, Bishops and Council, secular rulers and noblemen were constantly repeating strictures against the Jews and exhorting the people to shun the Jews. This indicates the populace did not take the restrictions very seriously. The situation changed dramatically in the 11th century. The anti-Semitic and anti-Jewish doctrines and preaching had seeped down into the consciousness of the people and the atrocities committed against the Jews that followed sprang from the people. The Church and state elites in the 11th and 12th centuries frequently found themselves in the role of restraining this mass anti-Semitism and protecting the Jews from popular attack.

The 13th century marked an apparent change in elite attitude toward the Jews. The period of the Crusades saw many instances of intervention on behalf of the Jews by Church and state hierarchies against the mob outrages. But now a combination of elite and mass anti-Semitism began to emerge.

To the earlier practices of compulsory baptism, expulsion, restriction and extortion, the techniques of mass torture and slaughter were added to the anti-Semitic repertoire. The history of the Jews in the Middle Ages reflects a side of Christian society not found in most accounts of this romantic, idealistic, pious and chivalrous age. Ignorance, cruelty and superstition are an integral part of Medieval life. It was a time when devils roamed the earth and miraculous happenings occurred. The Jews played an important role in this incredible demonology and this role continues to the present day where it takes on more secular forms.

In a superstitious age the explanation was the Devil, the Devil incarnate, the Jew, already the villain of Christian theology and Christian social history and the only non-Christian in Christian Europe. He was the natural suspect. This universal Jew hatred isolated the Jew. There is no cushion of popular apathy against elite attacks nor elite protection against the mob. This development must have had severe day-to-day repercussions in Jewish life. It certainly created an existence of total insecurity and instability. Since the 13th century, anti-Semitism has been a continuous and all pervasive feature of Western society.

Two of the more curious and bewildering developments of this period, which probably made sense in the context of that cultural milieu were the reintroduction of the charge of ritual murder, and the charge of host desecration. These libels became part of the stock in trade of the anti-Semites—and continued to be into the 20th century.

The ritual murder libel was cast back and forth in the ancient world and was used by Pagan critics against both Judaism and Christianity. It was dusted off in the 12th century and has two versions. One concerns a misinterpretation of the Feast of Purim which includes in its celebration the hanging in effigy of Haman, a Persian enemy of the Jews. This was interpreted as a mockery of the crucifixion and the dummy became, in the minds of the Christians a Christian victim. The other version which has been more prevalent and horrible in its effect is the assertion that the matzoh (bread) for the Passover Seder requires the blood of a Christian. Most ritual murder charges have occurred at Eastertime when religious fervor and indignation over deicide are highest.

The host desecration libel charged that Jews obtained consecrated hosts and then variously (1) recrucified Jesus by stabbing the host; (2) tore it, spat and walked on it to show their contempt for the Savior; (3) burned it; (4) mixed it with excrement and other vile substances; and (5) used it for making poisons and magic potions. The stories and legends involving host desecration often contain "miraculous" events. For example: when stabbed, the host bled; when torn, it became whole again; when thrown in a fire, the host did not burn or char. Those tormenting the host were often: (1) struck down by heavenly powers; or (2) converted to the true faith—Christianity. (The Catholic doctrine of transubstantiation that holds a consecrated host is really the body and blood of Jesus explains the unnatural behavior of the host in these stories.)

Both libels were taken seriously and produced saints, relics, shrines, art and cults and, in their wake, incredible suffering for the Jews.

PART IV. THE CRUSADES

1. Flannery, op. cit., p. 90.
2. Graetz, op. cit., III, 245-56.
3. Poliakov, op. cit., p. 36.
4. Runes, *War Against the Jews*, p. 18.
5. Flannery, op. cit., p. 90; Baer, op. cit., p. 47.
6. The Soviet purge trials, the Nazi Peoples Courts, and various prisoner of war experiences are contemporary examples of the effectiveness of torture (physical or psychological) to evoke the desired confession.
7. Graetz, op. cit., III, 293.
8. Baer, op. cit., p. 50.
9. Steve Runciman, *A History of the Crusades: The First Crusade* (London: Cambridge University Press, 1953), Vol. I, 138-41.
10. Flannery, op. cit., p. 90.
11. Runciman, op. cit., pp. 138-41.

12. Flannery, op. cit., p. 90.

13. Runciman, op. cit., pp. 140-41.

14. Ibid.

15. Ibid.

16. Ibid.

17. Ibid.

18. Flannery, op. cit., p. 90; Runciman, op. cit., pp. 140-41.

19. Runciman, op. cit., pp. 134-41; Graetz, op. cit., III, 299-300.

20. Louis Browne, *Stranger Than Fiction* (New York: MacMillan Co., 1927), pp. 217-20; Graetz, op. cit., III, 308.

21. S. M. Dubnow, *History of the Jews in Russia and Poland* (Philadelphia: The Jewish Publication Society of America, 1920), Trans. I. Friedlander, pp. 31-32.

22. Cecil Roth, *A History of the Jews in England* (Oxford: Clarendon Press, 1964), p. 8.

23. Runciman, op. cit., II, 254; Flannery, op. cit., pp. 92-94.

24. Edward A. Synan, *The Popes and the Jews in the Middle Ages* (New York: The MacMillan Company, 1965), pp. 74-78; Heer, op. cit., p. 67.

25. Roth, *History of the Jews in England*, p. 9; Flannery, op. cit., pp. 98-101; Poliakov, op. cit., pp. 56-64.

26. Flannery, op. cit., pp. 92-94.

27. Graetz, op. cit., III, 351-52.

28. Flannery, op. cit., pp. 92-94.

29. Poliakov, op. cit., pp. 48-49; Flannery, op. cit., p. 93.

30. Graetz, op. cit., III, 354-56.

31. Flannery, op. cit., p. 93.

32. Roth, *History of the Jews in England*, p. 13.

33. Graetz, op. cit., III, 379-81.

34. Roth, *Venice*, p. 52.

35. Graetz, op. cit., III, 402.

36. Roth, *History of the Jews in England*, p. 13.

37. Graetz, op. cit., III, 402.

38. Roth, *History of the Jews in England*, p. 13.

39. Runciman, op. cit., pp. 7-8.

40. Roth, *History of the Jews in England*, p. 21.

41. Ibid.

42. Graetz, op. cit., III, 404.

43. Roth, *History of the Jews in England*, p. 21.

44. Ibid., p. 27.

45. Graetz, op. cit., III, 405.

46. Ibid., p. 499.

123

47. Ibid., p. 500.

48. Ibid., pp. 502-503.

49. Runes, *War Against the Jews*, p. 47.

50. Flannery, op. cit., pp. 120-108; Graetz, op. cit., III, 510-11; Roth, *History of the Jews in England*, p. 40; Poliakov, op. cit., pp. 64-67.

51. Graetz, op. cit., III, 514.

52. Roth, *History of the Jews in England*, p. 40.

53. Ibid., p. 42.

54. Ibid.

55. Baer, op. cit., p. 144.

55a. Durant, op. cit., pp. 779-84.

56. Roth, *History of the Jews in England*, pp. 43-67.

57. Synan, op. cit., p. 108.

58. Graetz, op. cit., III, 570; Synan, op. cit., pp. 110-11.

59. Roth, *History of the Jews in England*, p. 55.

60. Baer, op. cit., pp. 150-51.

61. Graetz, op. cit., III, 575-76.

62. Roth, *History of the Jews in England*, p. 55.

63. Baer, op. cit., pp. 151-52.

64. Graetz, op. cit., III, 579; Synan, op. cit., pp. 110-11; Heer, op. cit., pp. 86-87.

65. Roth, *History of the Jews in England*, p. 59.

66. Ibid., p. 55.

67. Graetz, op. cit., p. 596.

68. Roth, *History of the Jews in England*, p. 55.

69. Graetz, op. cit., p. 585.

70. Roth, *History of the Jews in England*, pp. 56-57.

71. Ibid., p. 59.

72. Ibid., p. 61.

73. Baer, op. cit., pp. 152-53.

74. Ibid., p. 155.

75. Roth, *History of the Jews in England*, p. 61.

76. Runes, *War Against the Jews*, p. 92.

77. Graetz, op. cit., III, 611.

78. Roth, *History of the Jews in England*, p. 77.

79. Ibid.

80. Ibid., pp. 70-71.

81. Ibid.

82. Baer, op. cit., p. 167.

83. Ibid.; Runes, op. cit., p. 132.

84. Roth, *History of the Jews in England*, p. 75.

85. Dubnow, op. cit., pp. 47-49.
86. Ibid.
87. Graetz, op. cit., III, 614.
88. Roth, *History of the Jews in England*, p. 78.
89. Ibid.
90. Baer, op. cit., p. 130.
91. Ibid., p. 168.
92. Ibid., p. 130.
93. Runes, *War Against the Jews*, p. 27.
94. Graetz, op. cit., III, 636.
95. Ibid.
96. Baer, op. cit., p. 172.
97. Graetz, op. cit., III, 637.
98. Ibid.
99. Roth, *History of the Jews in England*, p. 85.
100. Cecil Roth, *The Jews in the Renaissance* (Philadelphia: The Jewish Publication Society of America, 1959), p. 5.
101. Baer, op. cit., p. 136.
102. Baer, *History of the Jews in Christian Spain*. Vol. II (Philadelphia: The Jewish Publication Society of America, 1961), 19.
103. Flannery, op. cit., pp. 106-107; Poliakov, op. cit., pp. 99-100.
104. Baer, op. cit., I, 308.
105. Graetz, op. cit., IV, 46-48.
106. Ibid., p. 47.
107. Ibid., p. 49.
108. Runes, *War Against the Jews*, p. 105.
109. Baer, op. cit., II, 11.
110. Ibid.
111. Ibid., p. 10.
112. Graetz, op. cit., IV, 53-54.
113. Baer, op. cit., II, 16.
114. Graetz, op. cit., IV, 56; Baer, op. cit., II, 15.
115. Baer, op. cit., II, 16.
116. Graetz, op. cit., IV, 77-78.
117. Baer, op. cit., I, 354-60.
118. Runes, *War Against the Jews*, p. 105.
119. Baer, op. cit., I, 360-61.

PART V: THE BLACK DEATH—1348-1354

BACKGROUND:

Europe in the 14th century was a religious society. God and Satan and their agents were clearly evident in the experiences of medieval man. It was also a period of political struggle between the aristocracy and unifying monarchs. Representative assemblies and royal taxation were methods used by the crown to unify the realm and break down the fragmented loyalties of feudalism. These political changes, however, did not happen without resistance; and the Hundred Year War, in addition to making a mockery of chivalry created considerable political chaos. The increasing needs for money and the rise of the Christian merchant states also added to the general ferment of the period. It is into this kind of a civilization that the Black Death brought its horror.

Between 1347 and 1350 the Black Death spread throughout Europe. Historians estimate as many as 1/3 of the population was exterminated by the plague. The Jews were seen by much of the populace as the perpetrators of the plague which they were accused of bringing about by poisoning wells. It is impossible to estimate the total casualties suffered by European Jewry in this fanatical outburst of anti-Semitism. Hundreds of Jewish communities were completely destroyed. Massacres of Jews occurred in every major city in Germany. While the superstition and fear accompanying the plague were no doubt the major causes of these massacres, the economic factors cannot be overlooked. Many of the massacres were accompanied by the destruction of debt records, pillaging and looting.

It is significant that only in Christian countries did the charge of Jewish conspiracy and responsibility for the plague occur. The Arabs made no such charge against the Jews living under their rule during the plague.

ENVIRONMENT: CHRISTIAN

The plague terrorized Europe. The suffering and death that accompanied it were on an almost unbelievable scale.

The population afflicted by the plague was woefully ignorant, credulous and superstitious within a cultural setting that was dominated by a religion that used fear and terror as one of its methods of control.

Bizarre and sado-masochistic religious cults emerged to fight the plague, which was seen as a punishment for sin or the work of the Devil.

The image of the Jew, cultivated over centuries, as odious, Christ-killing, evil, Satanic and poisoner, fit the need for an explanation of the plague. This image made the Jew a credible scapegoat.

Within the mind-set of the time with its incredible (by modern standards) beliefs—witches, incubi, succubi, apparitions, miracles, and a real Devil—believing that the Jews were in conspiracy to kill all Christians with the plague by poisoning wells was not particularly incredible.

ENVIRONMENT: JEWISH

Jews suffered and died as did Christians as the plague spread through Europe.

In addition to the ravages of the disease the Jews found themselves further victims of the plague as they were blamed for it and persecuted and slaughtered.

The anti-Semitic attitudes and beliefs that had developed over

127

the centuries found a new form of expression and in turn added a new dimension to the anti-Semitic tradition. The role of international conspirator was added to the catalogue of slurs already incorporated in the Western culture heritage.

In the purest sense, the Jewish persecution of the Black Death period represents the role of scapegoat.

In addition to slaughter, Jews were further affected by actions that expelled or barred Jews from residing in certain areas or principalities. For example, after burning those Jews who refused baptism, Strasbourg decreed that Jews were barred from residence for 100 years.

In other instances, Jews found themselves treated as property by various authorities. Jews were donated, transferred and had their property seized and redistributed as though they were cattle or any other transferable commodity.

Some Jewish communities set examples of great heroism, courage and martyrdom, that became part of the Jewish tradition.

INCIDENTS:

1348 A.D.

Spanish Jews were charged with the diabolical scheme of sending out messengers with the poison and threatening excommunication to their co-religionists to coerce them into the plan. The supposed poison was concocted from the flesh of a basilisk or from spiders, frogs and lizards or from the hearts of Christians and the dough of the consecrated wafer.[1]

In May, 1348, a Jewish congregation in southern France including men, women and children together with their holy writings were burned.[2]

The outburst in southern France was followed in June by massacres in Catalonia and Aragon in Spain. Twenty Jews were slaughtered by a mob which plundered Jewish houses in Barcelona. A few days later the community in Cervera was attacked. Eighteen were killed and the rest forced to flee.[3]

In September, Duke Amadeus of Savoy commanded the arrest of several Jews suspected of poisoning in two small towns, Chillon and Chatel, on Lake Geneva. Under torture they confessed. As a consequence all Jews in the region of Lake Geneva and Savoy were burned at the stake.[4]

The Consul of Berne sent for the proceedings of the Savoy Trial. Certain Jews of Berne were put to torture to extract confessions and the entire community was burned. The same fate struck the community of Zafingen.[5]

1348 A.D.

In Zurich, the charge of poisoning wells was raised along with that of murder of a Christian child. Those who were suspected were burned at the stake; the rest of the congregation was expelled from the town. A law was passed forbidding Jews to ever return to Zurich.[6]

The Consul of Berne sent letters to Basle, Strasburg, Freiburg and Cologne announcing Jews had been found guilty of poisoning wells. A Jew in chains was sent to Cologne in order to convince everyone of the diabolical plans of the Jews.[7]

At a meeting of the Council of the towns of Alsace presided over by Bishop Berthold of Strasburg to consider the charges against the Jews, the Bishop demanded that they be exterminated.[8]

Jews in the cities around Lake Constance—St. Gall, Ueberlingen, Schaffhausen, Constance and Lindau—were burned alive, put to the wheel, expelled or forcibly baptized.[9]

In September, Clement VI issued another papal bull which declared the Jews innocent of the charge of causing the plague and attempted to show the absurdity of the charge. He admonished the clergy to give protection to the Jews and excommunicated accusers and murderers.[10]

In Poland the royal protection given the Jews by King Casimir prevented widespread slaughters, but despite the king's efforts Christian mobs slaughtered 10,000 Jews in cities near the border with Germany.[11]

1348 A.D.

In Strasburg the burgomaster Conrad of Wintertur, the sheriff Gosse Sturm and master workman Peter Swaber made great efforts to prove Jews innocent and defended them against mob attacks and the bishop's demand for extermination. The authorities of Basle, Freiburg and Cologne followed similar courses.[12]

In Basle the guilds and a mob rebelled against the Council and demanded the banishment of the Jews.[13]

A council was held in Benfelden (Alsace) near the close of 1348 representing the cities of the upper Rhine. It decreed the banishment of Jews from Alsace. They were declared outlaws and either expelled or burned.[14]

1349 A.D.

In January, the Jewish community of Basle was burned to death in a house especially constructed for that purpose on an island in the Rhine. A decree prohibited Jewish settlement in Basle for 200 years.[15]

At approximately the same time, all the Jews in Freiburg were burned at the stake with the exception of twelve men who were permitted to live in order to discover the names of their creditors. This indicates the underlying economic motive in the massacres.[16]

A mob attacked the community of Speyer and killed several persons. Some Jews burned themselves or converted to Christianity to avoid the mob. The council confiscated the property and estates of the Jews.[17]

1349 A.D.

In February, the entire Jewish community of Strasburg was imprisoned. On the following Sabbath they were dragged to the burial ground and burned at the stake. Two thousand perished and the only survivors were those who submitted to baptism. The Council decreed Jews prohibited for 100 years.[18]

Emperor Charles IV gave the citizens of Worms the Jews as reward for their services so that "the city and the burghers of Worms might do unto the Jews and Judaism as they wished, might act as with their own property." The Council of Worms decreed that the Jews should be burned. The victims anticipated their death and set fire to their own homes. More than 400 persons were burned to death.[19]

The Jews of Oppenheim burned themselves to death rather than submit to torture and burning; the same pattern was followed by the Jewish community of Frankfort.[20]

In Mayence, 6,000 Jews were burned to death when a mob attacked the community and set fire to their houses.[21]

The entire community of Erfurt, over 3,000, were slaughtered. Similarly the community in Breslau was completely exterminated.[22]

On the advice of their Rabbi, the Vienna congregation committed suicide to avoid persecution.[23]

In Bavaria and Swabia, the communities of Augsburg, Wurzburg and Munich were destroyed.[24]

1349 A.D.

The Jewish community of Heilbronn was expelled and all property was confiscated.[25]

Emperor Charles IV freed the Council of Nuremburg of any responsibility for the Jewish community there. Strong anti-Jewish sentiment had long existed because of the economic success of the community. Those who had not emigrated were dragged to a pyre and burned to death on a spot since known as *Judenbühl* (Jew's hill).[26]

Margrave Louis of Brandenburg ordered all the Jews of Konigsberg burned and their property confiscated.[27]

King Louis of Hungary expelled the Jews from his realm not on the charge of poisoning but as infidels since they had refused his scheme of conversion. This action seems to have been wholly motivated by religious fervor.[28]

A mob attacked the community in Brussels and slaughtered all. Approximately 500 died in this massacre.[29]

1354 A.D.

During the civil war in Castile (Spain), forces in opposition to Don Pedro slaughtered 12,000 Jews, men, women and children in Toledo.[30]

1354 A.D.

Jews of Seville, Spain, were attacked by a mob; they were rumored to have desecrated a host.[31]

1357 A.D.

The plague struck again in Franconia. As earlier, it was blamed on the Jews, who were again accused of causing the plague with poison.[32]

CONTINUUM:

The period of the Black Death is extremely important to the history and development of anti-Semitism. As the plague killed thousands, an explanation for it developed that has had repercussions for the Jews down to the present. A myth was invented that said an international Jewish conspiracy aimed at the extermination of Christians was the cause of the plague. The Jewish leadership in Spain allegedly directed Jewish communities throughout Europe to poison wells and caused the sickness and death. This myth was attacked again and again by more responsible Christian leaders but it captured the imagination of the masses and was believed in the face of evidence to the contrary and its patent absurdity.

It is true that Jews had been charged with conspiracy in the past, in Spain as the Moors invaded, in Jerusalem and in the Crusade against the Albigensian heresy, but these had been restricted to specific groups or communities. The earlier charges of conspiracy did not include every Jew wherever he lived nor did they assert that his overriding mission was the extermination of all Christians. The myth of the international Jewish conspiracy originated in the confused reaction to the Black Death and still persists today. The experience of the Jews during the plague was a precursor of the modern scapegoat role and the secular *Protocols of the Elders of Zion*.

This period also saw a continuation of the older anti-Semitic rhetoric and techniques. Charges of ritual murder and host desecration were made and Jews were victims of expulsion, oppressive taxation, expropriation and confiscation of property, residential and civil restrictions, restrictions on religious activity, forced Baptism, torture, plunder and mass slaughter.

132

PART V. BLACK DEATH

1. Graetz, op. cit., IV, 101-102.
2. Ibid., p. 102.
3. Ibid., pp. 102-104.
4. Ibid., pp. 103-104.
5. Ibid., pp. 104-105.
6. Ibid., p. 105.
7. Ibid.
8. Runes, *War Against the Jews*, p. 19.
9. Graetz, op. cit., IV, 105.
10. Ibid.
11. Ibid., pp. 111-12.
12. Ibid., p. 106.
13. Ibid., p. 107.
14. Ibid.
15. Ibid.
16. Ibid.
17. Ibid., pp. 107-108.
18. Ibid., p. 108.
19. Ibid., pp. 108-109.
20. Ibid., p. 109.
21. Ibid.
22. Ibid.
23. Ibid., p. 110.
24. Ibid.
25. Cecil Roth (ed.), *The Standard Jewish Encyclopedia* (Garden City, N. Y.: Doubleday & Co., Inc., 1959), p. 882.
26. Graetz, op. cit., IV, 110.
27. Ibid., pp. 110-11.
28. Ibid., p. 111.
29. Ibid., p. 112.
30. Ibid., p. 118.
31. Baer, op. cit., I, 362.
32. Joshua Trachtenberg, *The Devil and The Jews* (New Haven: Yale University Press, 1943), p. 107.

PART VI: THE INQUISITION—1366-1500

BACKGROUND:

The Inquisition had its roots in the Crusades and the struggle for political and economic supremacy between Christianity and Islam. The elimination of Moorish (Islamic) domination in Spain in the 14th century was accompanied by the slaughter of Jewish communities paralleling the Jewish experience in the rest of Europe during the Crusades. The Christian reconquest of Spain was part of the general battle between Christianity and the infidel but the arena was Europe rather than the Middle East. The power struggle following the destruction of Moorish control was a period of incredible social instability; nobility and commoner exchanged roles frequently as indicated by Cervantes in *Don Quixote*. The unification of Spain under the Catholic monarchs Ferdinand and Isabella led to the establishment and consolidation of the power of the lay and ecclesiastic nobility represented by and supporting those monarchs. The major instrument of this consolidation was the Inquisition. On the religious level the Inquisition, in an age of Catholic absolutism, had the legitimate purpose of preserving the purity of the faith. Many Jews had been forcibly converted or converted to escape persecution or extermination but continued covertly true to Judaism. One aim of the Inquisition was to destroy this practice. A secondary and often overlooked purpose of the Inquisition was the consolidation of the power of the lay nobility and elimination of any serious rivalry. The incipient capitalism represented by the Jewish community was destroyed with that community in Spain and, in part, this explains the rapid collapse of Spanish hegemony in the following centuries. To attempt to explain the Inquisition in terms of the cross alone is to misread history. Spanish history has always been a deadly mixture of the cross and gold, faith and greed. This is true of the Inquisition just as it was true of the Spanish adventure in the New World.

The twin motivations of the cross and gold were also operative in the experience of the Jews in the rest of Europe and when focusing on the Inquisition there is a tendency to assume that it was a strictly Spanish phenomena. In Spain it was simply more systematic and of longer duration, but the Inquisition was a European experience, a futile effort of Catholicism to retain monopoly in the salvation of souls as it battled the various heresies that were springing up throughout Europe and culminated in the Reformation. One of the effects of the Inquisition and the expulsion was the further development of the Polish-Jewish community. Poland in the 15th and 16th centuries became a haven and refuge for Jews escaping the persecutions of the Inquisition in Western Europe just as it had been a refuge to the German Jews who fled the Crusaders.

ENVIRONMENT: CHRISTIAN

Europe was still Catholic but serious strains were developing in the social, political, economic and religious order. The Inquisition, founded in the thirteenth century to safeguard the purity of the faith and root out heresy in its early stages, was expanded and intensified as an instrument for protecting the political and religious status quo.

Challenges to the conventional wisdom and orthodoxy of the time grew from scientific discoveries, explorations, the emergence of capitalism, the intellectual ferment in the great universities and the beginnings of the nation state.

Church authority was no longer unquestioned. The Great Schism, Erasmus, Savonarola, Hus and Wycliffe foreshadowed the Reformation. The Inquisition tried to root out these dangerous forces. Heresy, free thinking and insincerity were the targets.

But traditional conventional attitudes, sermons, the arts, education etc. continued to nurture and sustain anti-Semitism.

Jews who had converted to Christianity (Conversos-Marranos—the New Christians) were suspected of secretly practicing Judaism. In many cases the suspicion was correct. There were Conversos who accepted baptism to avoid persecution but continued true to Judaism.

One of the side effects of the Inquisition was the increase in people who acted as spies and informers. This created an atmosphere of distrust and caution, added to the terror of the Inquisition, and furthered its objectives.

Ritual murder and host desecration stories were part of the folk wisdom and gossip.

The Inquisition especially in its actions against Jews who were accused of converting to Christianity but secretly practicing Judaism added to the image of the Jew as cheat, sneak and untrustworthy. This in turn created greater distrust and suspicion of Jews by the Christians and was applied to other activities.

ENVIRONMENT: JEWISH

Jews who had converted to Christianity (Conversos-Marranos—the New Christians) were a special target of the Inquisition.

St. John Capistrano who conducted the Inquisition in Poland included all Jews. He is known as the "Scourge of the Jews" and held that the Catholic had a duty not a choice to fight the Jew.

Expulsion occurred frequently and in many places in Europe.

Mob attacks on Jewish communities often accompanied the Inquisition.

The Talmud and other sacred writings were seized or banned in certain areas.

Jewish leaders were compelled to defend Judaism against various charges in Disputations organized by the Church or the state.

Ritual murder and host desecration charges were usually accompanied by mob attacks and slaughter.

Constant pressures were put on Jews to convert, but conversion was no longer an escape from persecution. Those who did convert to escape persecution, torture or slaughter were still suspect and subjected to many indignities, loss of privacy and insecurity.

INCIDENTS:

1360 A.D.

When Don Henry de Trastamara captured Burgos, the capital of Castile, he cancelled all debts by Christians to Jews and levied a fine of 50,000 doubloons on the Jewish community. The community was forced to sell all property and chattel even sacred ornaments to meet this obligation. Many were sold into slavery.[1]

King John (in captivity), at the urging of the ruling dauphin Charles, signed a decree allowing Jews to return to France for a twenty-year period on payment of an entry fee and an annual Jewish tax.[2]

1366 A.D.

During the Spanish Civil War between King Pedro and Henry of Trastamora both sides employed mercenaries. Henry's French mercenaries massacred the Jewish community of Briviesca. Two hundred perished. When Henry captured the city of Burgos he demanded 1,000,000 maravedis from the Jewish community. Those who could not pay their share were sold into slavery.[3]

The Prince of Wales (the Black Prince) came to the aid of Pedro, and the Jewish communities of Villadiego and Aguilar de Compo were slaughtered by the English troops.[4]

When Henry recaptured Valladolid the inhabitants destroyed eight synagogues, looted the Jewish quarter and tore up sacred writings.[5]

1367 A.D.

In Barcelona Jews were accused of stealing a host. The entire community was imprisoned in the synagogue. The charges were later dropped.[6]

1368 A.D.

Eight thousand Jews were slain in Henry's siege of Toledo.[7]

Pedro permitted his Moslem allies in Granada to sell the Jews of Jaen into slavery. Three hundred families were involved.[8]

137

1369 A.D.

When Pedro was finally defeated he was greeted by Henry with the following words: "Where is the Jew, the son of a harlot, who calls himself king of Castille?"[9]

"The Church must rejoice at the death of such a tyrant, a rebel against the Church, and a favorer of Jews and Saracens. The righteous exult in retribution."[10]

Statement of Pope Urban V on hearing the news of Pedro's defeat and execution

1370 A.D.

There were recurrent mob attacks on the Jews of Majorca, Penignon and Barcelona.[11]

1377 A.D.

Charged with desecrating a host, the Jews of Huesca, Spain were tortured and burned at the stake.[12] (See background paper for discussion of Host Desecration Charges.)

1377 A.D.

The Cortes of Burgos forbade Jews to accept any kind of obligation from Christians. It also revoked the law providing a collective fine as the penalty for the murder of a Jew.[13]

1380 A.D.

The Cortes of Lorca passed more anti-Jewish legislation. Jews were ordered to delete benedictions concerning heretics from their prayerbook. Jewish communities were no longer permitted to try criminal or civil cases. They were also forbidden to circumcize Tartar and Moslem slaves.[14]

At the urging of the nobility, a mob in Paris attacked the Jewish community, robbed, pillaged and destroyed debt records. A number of Jews were killed and children were taken from their mothers and forcibly baptized.[15]

1381 A.D.

Mobs attacked, plundered and murdered Jews in Paris and in other provinces in France during the Maillotin uprising.[16]

1384 A.D.
A mob invited by the clergy attacked and murdered the entire Jewish community—men, women and children—in Nördlingen.[17]

The Jewish community of Augsburg was imprisoned until a 20,000 florin ransom was paid.[18]

1384 A.D.
Jews in Nürnberg and surrounding communities were imprisoned and held for ransom.[19]

1388 A.D.
The Jews in Strasbourg were expelled.[20]

1389 A.D.
A mob attack on the Jewish community of Prague lasted a day and a night. Thousands were murdered, many committed suicide to avoid forced baptism. The synagogue was burned, and sacred books, scrolls, and the Jewish cemetery were desecrated.[21]

1390 A.D.
Emperor Wenceslaus cancelled all debts owed to the Jews of Germany.[22]

1391 A.D.
Castille synagogues were converted to churches. The Jewish quarter was destroyed. Those who were not forcibly converted were slaughtered or sold as slaves to Moslems.[23]

In Toledo, the family of Rabbi Judah and his students were slaughtered. The Toledo synagogues were either destroyed or converted to churches.[24]

Those of the community of Madrid who did not convert were slaughtered. The same fate befell the congregations of Seville, Cordova and Cuenca. In Seville, 4,000 were murdered and the women and children were sold as slaves to the Arabs. Two of the three Seville synagogues were converted to churches.[25]

In Valencia, 250 members of the Jewish community were murdered; the rest were forcibly converted.[26]

In Majorca, 300 Jews were killed.[27]

1391 A.D.

A Christian mob attacked the Jewish community of Barcelona; over three hundred were killed or committed suicide. Eleven thousand were forcibly baptized. No Jew remained in Barcelona after this event.[28]

1392 A.D.

In Spain, the king declared all debts to Jews cancelled. Conversos were forbidden to carry arms or to travel to Moslem lands. The outbursts in Spain were largely peasant and lower class inspired. The king tried unsuccessfully to prevent them. This action seems to have been an appeasing gesture to the masses.[29]

Widespread attacks on the Jews occurred throughout Spain. In Barcelona 500 were killed; 78 in Lerida; 40 in Gerona. Whole communities in Catalonia were exterminated. Hundreds were forcibly baptized throughout Spain. This outburst was accompanied by widespread looting and vandalism. The Jewish quarter at Jaca was destroyed by fire.[30]

1392 A.D.

In France, the news of the Spanish persecutions was followed by mob attacks on the Jewish communities throughout Provence.[31]

The Venetian Senate refused to renew the agreement that permitted Jewish bankers in the city. The following economic crisis produced a new agreement, with the exiles permitted to return for periods of fifteen days to conduct business. The new agreement also required the Jews to wear the yellow badge for the first time.[32]

1394 A.D.

Jews were expelled from the Palatinate district.[33]

1394 A.D.

King Charles VI expelled all Jews from France. In contrast to the earlier expulsion by Philip the Fair, they were permitted to take movable property and chattel and were given time to collect debts. (The banishment did not apply to provinces not directly under the French crown.)[34]

1399 A.D.

The Jews of Posen, Poland, were charged with bribing a Christian woman to steal hosts from a local church. Supposedly these hosts were stabbed and thrown into a pit. Legend has it that blood spurted from the pierced hosts (confirming Eucharistic dogma). The Archbishop of Posen learned of the blasphemy and instituted proceedings against the Jews. The Rabbi, thirteen elders and the woman were tied to pillars and roasted alive over a slow fire.[35]

1399 A.D.

A number of Jews in Prague were arrested on charges made by a convert to Christianity, Pessach-Peter. He accused Jews of blasphemous statements and anti-Christian prayers.[36]

1400 A.D.

After Emperor Wenceslaus was deposed, eighty of the Jews arrested in Prague on the charges of Pessach-Peter were burned at the stake.[37]

1407 A.D.

In a sermon during the Easter season a priest named Budek charged: "The Jews living in Cracow killed a Christian boy last night and made sport over his blood; moreover, they threw stones at a priest who was going to visit a sick man and was carrying a crucifix in his hands." The mob rushed out and began to loot the Jewish quarter. Royal authorities stopped the riots momentarily, but they resumed later and began killing in addition. Many houses were set on fire. Some Jews found refuge in the Tower of St. Anne which the mob set on fire. Those who survived and did not convert were slaughtered. Children of the victims were baptized.[38]

In Spain, the preaching of the fanatical reformer and monk, Vincent Ferrer (later Sainted), in his attacks on corruption fanned anti-Jewish sentiment and created popular demand for action against the Jews. These actions took the form of more oppressive legislation and mob attacks on Jews.[39]

141

1408 A.D.

New anti-Jewish laws were introduced in Castile after the death of Don Henry III. These laws prohibited Jews from holding any political or official office. Penalties were applicable to the Jew who held the office or performed the function and to the person who made the appointment.[40]

In Segovia, a number of Jews, among them chief rabbi of Castile, Don Meir Alguades, were arrested on charges of host desecration. They were tortured and executed after they confessed.[41]

1412 A.D.

In Castile, Aragon, and Majorca, Jews were confined to separate quarters in all cities and villages. All contact with Christians was barred. Legislation also specified dress and hair styles. The use of Christian names and the title of Don were also forbidden.[42]

1413-1415 A.D.

Pope Benedict XIII authorized Don Ferdinand of Aragon to convene a religious disputation at Tortosa. The purpose was to aid the conversion of Jews to Christianity. The leading Jews of Aragon were summoned to dispute with Geronimo de Sante Fe, a newly-baptized Jew who sought to prove that the Talmud proved Jesus was the Messiah. The disputation lasted one year and nine months. At its conclusion Pope Benedict XIII in a papal bull forbade Jews to study or teach the Talmud or Talmudic literature. All copies of the Talmud were to be confiscated. All anti-Christian literature was banned. Each Jewish community was to be limited to one synagogue. All contact between Jews and Christians was forbidden.[43]

1414 A.D.

Forced conversions were carried out in Aragon. Jews who refused baptism were arrested. Whole communities were destroyed. These actions are attributed to the turmoil caused by the preaching of Vincent Ferrer. Ferrer is credited with over 20,000 forced baptisms in Castile and Aragon.[44]

1415 A.D.

The schismatic Pope, Benedict XIII, ordered the confiscation of the Talmud and decreed that all Jews were to attend sermons for their conversion. The penalty for refusing was death.[45]

1419 A.D.

Pope Martin V and the Spanish kings abolished a series of earlier anti-Jewish edicts. The Talmud and synagogues were returned to the Jews and the remaining anti-Jewish laws were not enforced.[46]

1420 A.D.

Jews expelled from Mainz.[47]

1422 A.D.

The Crusade against the Hussite heresy had the same consequences for the Jews as the Crusades against Islam and the Waldensian heresy. The Dominicans preaching the Crusade included the Jews in their fierce denunciations of the Hussites. They were accused of secretly supplying money and arms, and the old charges of host desecration and ritual murder were again made. As a result the people and princes alike attacked Jews and Hussites.[48]

Archduke Albert of Austria ordered all Jews in the realm imprisoned. The poorer Jews were immediately banished. The wealthier were detained in prisons; their property was confiscated and their children were taken and raised as Christians. In March, 1421, the Jews were burned. In Vienna, over a hundred were burned in a field near the Danube. Albert then issued a decree banning Jews from Austria.[49]

The German Emperor Sigismund with his imperial army and Dutch mercenaries on march against Prague slaughtered Jewish communities along the Rhine in Thuringen and Bavaria. The same rationale used by the 12th century Crusaders was used to justify these atrocities. ''We are afar to avenge our insulted God shall those who slew him be spared?''[50]

143

1423 A.D.
Jews were forbidden to own land in Venice. The Ghetto Nuovo was put under perpetual lease at rental one-third higher than previously charged.[51]

1424 A.D.
Jews were expelled from Fribourg and Zurich.[52]

1426 A.D.
Jews were expelled from Cologne.[53]

1427 A.D.
Pope Martin V issued bull forbidding Italian sea captains to transport Jews to holy land under pain of excommunication.[54]

1429 A.D.
Martin V issued another bull urging the protection of the Jewish community and establishing rights of community, including the right to attend the university.[55]

1431 A.D.
A ritual murder accusation in southern Germany resulted in the communities of Ravensburg, Ueiberlingen and Lindau being burned alive.[56]

1432 A.D.
Jews were expelled from Saxony.[57]

1434 A.D.
The Council of Basle called by Martin V but presided over by Pope Eugenius IV reenacted old restrictions and also decreed that Jews should (1) live in separate sections of cities, (2) attend compulsory conversion sermons, (3) not be permitted to study at the universities.[58]

1434 A.D.
Jews in Augsburg were required to wear a yellow wheel on their clothing.[59]

1438 A.D.
City council of Mainz expelled Jews.[60]

1439 A.D.
Emperor Albert II of Germany, who succeeded Sigismund as German Emperor (cf. 1420), consented to the town council of Augsburg's expulsion of its Jewish community. After expulsion, Jewish gravemarkers were used to repair the walls of the city.[61]

1442 A.D.
Pope Eugenius IV in a bull for Castile repealed privileges and protections granted by Pope Martin V and restored the anti-Jewish legislation. Christians were forbidden to eat, drink, bathe or live with Jews or to use medicine of any kind prescribed by them. Jews were ineligible for any office or honor. No new synagogues were to be built and in repairing existing ones ornamentation was prohibited. Once again Jews were required to remain indoors during Easter. The testimony of Jews against Christians was declared invalid. And Jews were to be distinguished from Christians by special dress and special quarters.[62]

1443 A.D.
Jews in Venice were required to wear the yellow badge. Physicians were often exempted from the requirement.[63] (See Fourth Lateran Council, 1215.)

1447 A.D.
Pope Nicholas V followed the policy of Eugenius IV and in a bull for Italy withdrew the privileges previously granted Italian Jews. (Provisions of this bull were virtually the same as Eugenius' bull for Castile.) John of Capistrano was commissioned to see the bull enforced.[64]

1449 A.D.
In Toledo, several conversos under torture admitted to practicing Judaism. An edict was promulgated declaring conversos untrustworthy in matters of religion. A number were burned at the

stake. Conversos were consequently barred from holding public office.[65]

1450 A.D.
Louis the Rich, Duke of Landshilt, Bavaria, had all Jews in this country arrested. The men were thrown into prison and the women were shut up in the synagogues. Their property and jewelry were confiscated. After four weeks they were permitted to ransom themselves for 30,000 gulden; then penniless and nearly naked, they were expelled from the country.[66]

1451 A.D.
Pope Nicholas V issued a new bull confirming old exclusions from Christian society and all honorable walks of life and abolished all privileges of Italian and Spanish Jews.[67]

Cardinal Nicholas de Cusa, who was appointed to carry out reforms in the German church, instituted the Jewish badge in the province of Bamberg. Men were required to wear round pieces of red cloth on their chests; women were to wear blue strips on their headdress.[68]

St. John of Capistrano ("The Scourge of the Jews") was appointed by Pope Nicholas V to lead the Inquisition of the Jews and enforce canonical restrictions in northern countries.[69]

"To fight the Jew is a duty of the Catholic, not a choice."[70]

St. John Capistrano

1453 A.D.
Godfrey, Bishop and Duke of Franconia, at urging of Capistrano, decreed the banishment of Jews from Franconia.[71]

Capistrano's sermons included charges of ritual murder and host desecration. Following his preaching in Breslau the Jewish community there, men, women and children, were imprisoned, and their property and lands were confiscated. In addition, 318 Jews living around Breslau were brought to trial. One was burned; the rabbi committed suicide and the rest were banished from Breslau. Children under seven were forcibly baptized and given to Christian families to raise.[72]

146

King Ladislau of Silesia decreed that from that time forward no Jew would be permitted to settle in Breslau, Olmitz and Brumm.[73]

In Passau, Germany, Jews were accused of profaning a host. The bishop had great numbers put to death, some mercifully by the sword, but most by burning alive or by red hot pincers.[74]

1454 A.D.

John of Capistrano visited Cracow at the invitation of Bishop Zbigniew Olesnicki. The Bishop was outraged at the privileges and royal protection extended to Jews in Poland. Capistrano in preaching stirred up the clergy and populace against the Jews. This coincided with the rout of the Polish armies by the Teutonic Order and the Prussians. The clergy claimed that the defeat was God's punishment for the royal lenience toward the Jews.[75]

Jews were expelled from Würzburg.[76]

Under pressure from the clergy the king promulgated the Statute of Nyesheeva which rescinded Jewish privileges as being equally opposed to Divine right and earthly laws. In several towns throughout Poland mobs attacked the Jewish communities.[77]

1457 A.D.

Archbishop Diether of Mayence required all Jews in Frankfort to wear distinctive markings on their clothing.[78]

1463 A.D.

Polish troops en route to the Crusade against the Turks attacked the Jews of Cracow, looted their houses and killed about thirty people.[79]

1473 A.D.

In Andalusia armed conflict between old Christians and conversos resulted in widespread looting, pillage and slaughter.[80]

1475 A.D.

The Jews of Ratisbon were charged with ritual murder and imprisoned by the bishop. (Emperor Frederick III ordered them freed.)[81]

147

A wave of anti-Jewish sentiment swept Italy. In the city of Trent, Fr. Bernadina de Feltre preached Lenten sermons full of anti-Jewish hysteria and predicted a ritual murder. A three year old boy was found drowned in the river. All members of the Jewish community were arrested and under torture confessed to ritual murder. The leaders were executed and the rest banished from Trent.[82]

Cult of Little Simon of Trent spread throughout Europe. (See Discussion of Ritual Murder in Background to Part IV.) Authorities in Venice gave protection to Jews and prohibited inflammatory sermons. Jews in Swabia were expelled as a consequence of accusations in regard to the ritual murder in Trent.[83]

1478 A.D.
Papal Bull empowered Ferdinand and Isabella to establish an Inquisition in Castile.[84]

1480 A.D.
Spanish laws separating Jews from Christians were reenacted and the Catholic Monarchs appointed two Dominican friars as Inquisitors for the realm.[85]

The community of Portoboffole was charged with ritual murder. Three who confessed under torture were burned alive in Venice. Survivors were banished from Venetian territories forever.[86]

1481 A.D.
The Inquisition began in Seville and many conversos fled to Andalusia. Seven were burned at the stake in Seville. In order to avoid the plague the Inquisition moved from Seville to Aracena where twenty-two conversos were burned at the stake. In Seville over the period from 1481 to 1483, 750 conversos, both men and women, were burned at the stake and over 5,000 were brought back to Christianity after meeting penalties.[87]

1482 A.D.
Pope Sixtus IV tried to intervene on behalf of conversos. He called for the dismissal of overly zealous inquisitors and ordered the Inquisition to submit to the authority of the bishops, to conduct

148

trials in proper legal manner and to permit appeals to the Papal Court. Ferdinand was indignant at this attempted papal interference. He rebuked the Pope and ordered the arrest of the conversos who petitioned the Pope.[88]

1483 A.D.

Despite the protest of the Spanish Monarch, Pope Sixtus IV sent letters of absolution to the accused conversos.[89]

The Inquisition issued an edict expelling all Jews in the archbishoprics of Seville and Cordova, i.e., the entire province of Andalusia. Thereafter Jews had to have special permits from the Inquisition to enter the area.[90]

Thomas de Torquemada was appointed Inquisitor General by Pope Sixtus IV for all the territories under the rule of Ferdinand and Isabella. He had been an inquisitor since 1482 and probably one of the proponents of the expulsion of Jews from Andalusia. As Inquisitor General he presided over the Consijo de la Suprema y General Inquisicion (Supreme Council of the Inquisition). In addition to appointing Torquemada the Pope revoked all earlier papal edicts which favored or gave protection to the conversos.[91]

1484 A.D.

In Cuidad Real (Villareal), thirty-four Jews were burned alive.[92]

In Guadalupe, fifty-two conversos were burned at the stake for continuing to practice Judaism; forty-eight conversos' corpses were exhumed from the grave and burned at the stake, and twenty-five conversos who had fled were burned in effigy.[93]

In Saragossa, two conversos were burned alive and a woman's corpse was exhumed and burned.[94]

In Teruel, thirty conversos were sent to the stake.[95]

1485 A.D.

In Saragossa on September 15th the inquisitor Pedro de Arbues Maestrede Epila was murdered at prayer in the Cathedral. The news caused a mob to attack the Jewish and Moslem quarters. The outburst was stopped by municipal authorities.[96]

In December, two conversos were burned at Saragossa.[97]

When the Inquisition moved to Toledo the conversos there

149

planned a revolt which was to include the assassination of the Inquisitor and the entire Christian community during the Corpus Christi procession. The revolt failed to materialize but several conversos were arrested and ordered hanged by order of the Mayor.[98]

1485 A.D.

The Inquisitors compelled the rabbis to announce in the synagogues that all Jews who were aware of Jewish practices by conversos were duty bound under pain of excommunication and the ban to testify before the Court of the Inquisition. This proved a successful method for obtaining evidence against conversos.[99]

A Dominican friar, Antonio de la Pena, stirred mob hatred for Jews in Segovia by violent anti-Jewish sermons.[100]

A ritual murder charge in Vicenza, Italy, resulted in expulsion of Jews from the community.[101]

1486 A.D.

In Toledo, 750 men and women conversos were led in procession through the streets, sentenced to various penances and fined 1/5 of their fortunes. The fines were to go to the fund for prosecuting the war with Granada. In April, a similar procession of 900 penitents occurred and in June, 750 penitents were in procession.[102]

In August, twenty-seven conversos were burned in Toledo.[103]
The Inquisition burned twenty-three conversos in Toledo.[104]

1488 A.D.

Forty conversos were burned in Toledo.[105]

1490 A.D.

Twenty-two conversos were burned in Toledo.[106]

Between 1486 and 1490, 4,850 conversos were reconciled to the Church in the Province of Toledo. In the twelve years of the Inquisition from 1478 to 1489, 13,000 conversos were found to have remained attached to Judaism and the Jewish people.[107]

The royal physician to the court of Grand Duke Ivan III, Master

Leon, a learned Jew from Venice, was executed in a public square in Moscow for failing to cure the oldest son of the Grand Duke.[108]

1491 A.D.
A ritual murder and host desecration charge combined in the case of "the holy child of La Guardia." The Jewish community of the city of Astorga was brought before the Inquisition and tortured.[109]

1492 A.D.
In the city of Granada, Ferdinand and Isabella signed the edict expelling Jews from all territories under the crowns of Castile and Aragon. The reason was to prevent Jews from inflicting further injuries on the Christian religion.[110]

The edict enumerated the steps taken in the past twelve years to prevent Jews from influencing conversos and to purify the Christian faith. The segregation of Jews in separate quarters, the Inquisition, and the expulsion of Jews from Andalusia had failed. Therefore, expulsion was the only course left.[111]

The expulsion of Jews from Spain began in May. They were given three months to leave and during this time were afforded royal protection and permitted to sell property and collect debts. Although some extortion occurred it was a relatively humane expulsion. It is estimated that between 100,000 and 120,000 moved to Portugal, and an estimated 50,000 moved to North Africa, Italy or Eastern Europe.[112]

1492 A.D.
The refugees to Portugal were expelled in eight months. Those who remained were sold as slaves to the Portugese nobility. The children between the ages of 3 and 10 of those sold into slavery were baptized and sent to the island of St. Thomas to be raised as Christians.[113]

1494 A.D.
The sons of the Polish King Casimir IV, King John Albert of Poland and the Lithuanian Grand Duke Alexander Yaghello, re-

versed the generally favorable Jewish policy in Poland. A large part of the city of Cracow was destroyed by fire, and the mobs, taking advantage of the general disorder, plundered Jewish households. The Jews who had lived scattered throughout the city were ordered by King John Albert to move to Kazimieth, a suburb of Cracow, to live apart from Christians. This established the first ghetto in Poland.[114]

1494 A.D.

During these years the fanatical Franciscan friar, Bernardino de Feltre, traveled throughout Italy as protector of Christian children "whom Jews want to steal and crucify." His preaching incited Italian peasants and servants to attack the Jews especially during Holy Week. This monk spread and gave credibility to the ritual murder libel. A story is told of an old Jewish man trying to help a crying child who was lost from his parents. He was stoned to death by a hysterical mob who suspected he was trying to lure the child away for ritual murder purposes. This story indicates the kind of popular hysteria that abounded in this period and the precarious quality of life entailed in being a Jew.[115]

1495 A.D.

Alexander Yaghello, Grand Duke of Lithuania, ordered the expulsion of the Jews from Lithuania. He confiscated the immovable property of the expelled Jews in the districts of Grodno, Brest, Lutzk, and Trochi and distributed it to the local Christians. The Jews were permitted to return to Lithuania in 1501 and some of their property was returned.[116]

1496 A.D.

A regulation was passed prohibiting any Jew from staying in the city of Venice for more than a fortnight each year, and after this limit was reached a twelve-month interval had to elapse before any further visit was permitted.[117]

1497 A.D.

King Manuel of Portugal issued a secret command that all Jewish children under the age of fourteen were to be taken from their parents and baptized on Easter Sunday. Later the same year he expelled all Jews from Portugal.[118]

The German Emperor Maximilian granted Nuremberg the privilege of being exempt from receiving Jews within its walls.[119]

The townsmen of Nuremberg expelled the city's Jewish community.[120]

Similar expulsions took place at Ulm, Nordingen, Colmar and Magdeburg.[121]

The only Jewish communities remaining in Germany were in Ratisbon, Frankfort on Main and Worms. These were under constant threat of expulsion and daily harassment.[122]

In Ratisbon, millers and bakers refused to sell to Jews. The clergy threatened tradesmen with excommunication should they trade with the Jews. Jews could shop in the market only on certain days during specified hours.[123]

CONTINUUM:

During the latter part of the 14th and throughout the 15th century no new techniques were added to the practice of anti-Semitism. The Jews were subjected to the now well established practices of confiscation of property, expulsion, forced conversion, ghettoization, restrictions on religious practices, travel and occupation, denial of civil rights, torture and massacre and charges of ritual murder and host desecration.

The Inquisition added nothing to the techniques of anti-Semitism except increased cooperation between clergy and crown and a more thorough and systematic application of the older techniques. Torquemada and Spain leap to mind when the Inquisition is mentioned but it is important to remember that the Inquisition occurred throughout Europe as the Roman Church fought to maintain its control and monopoly of the salvation of men's souls and as various ruling groups used the Inquisition to protect the social and political status quo.

What is unique about the Inquisition and makes it important for an understanding of anti-Semitism is that, from this period, conversion by Jews to Christianity was no longer sufficient as a means of escaping persecution. For while Jews as Jews suffered under the Inquisition, in Spain, its main targets were those Jews who converted to Christianity but were suspected of insincerity or secretly practising Judaism. Any Jewish convert to Christianity whether sincere or cynical in his new faith became suspect.

The Inquisitorial mentality expanded the scope of future anti-Semitism. As a result of the Inquisition, hatred and persecution of the Jews was no longer restrained or restricted by outward appearances. Jewish efforts to become less conspicuous by conversion, which removed their religious distinctiveness or assimilation which removed their cultural or life style distinctiveness, were no longer a guarantee against prejudice and persecution. The Jewish taint survived and contaminated. In this sense, the Inquisition may be interpreted as the intellectual and historical precursor of the racial anti-Semitism of the 19th and 20th centuries epitomized by Nazism.

PART VI: THE INQUISITION

1. Graetz, op. cit., IV, 123-24.
2. Ibid., pp. 128-32.
3. Baer, op. cit., I, 364-66.
4. Ibid., p. 366.
5. Ibid.
6. Baer, op. cit., II, 38-39.
7. Ibid., I, 367.
8. Ibid., p. 366.
9. Graetz, op. cit., IV, 126.
10. Ibid.
11. Baer, op. cit., II, 86.
12. Ibid., p. 89.
13. Ibid., I, 375.
14. Ibid., pp. 375-76.

15. Graetz, op. cit., IV, 150-52.
16. Ibid., pp. 152-52.
17. Ibid., p. 163.
18. Ibid.
19. Poliakov, op. cit., p. 118.
20. Ibid., p. 119.
21. Graetz, op. cit., IV, 164-65.
22. Roth, *Venice*, p. 25.
23. Baer, op. cit., II, 96.
24. Ibid., p. 97.
25. Ibid.
26. Ibid., p. 100.
27. Ibid., p. 102.
28. Graetz, op. cit., IV, 171.
29. Baer, op. cit., II, 102-103.
30. Ibid., pp. 104-12.
31. Graetz, op. cit., IV, 173.
32. Roth, *Venice*, p. 20.
33. Poliakov, op. cit., p. 119.
34. Graetz, op. cit., IV, 175-77.
35. Dubnow, op. cit., pp. 56-57.
36. Graetz, op. cit., IV, 177-78.
37. Ibid., p. 178.
38. Dubnow, op. cit., pp. 56-57.
39. Baer, op. cit., II, 167.
40. Graetz, op. cit., IV, 193-95.
41. Ibid., pp. 195-96.
42. Baer, op. cit., II, 167-68.
43. Graetz, op. cit., IV, 207-16.
44. Baer, op. cit., II, 230.
45. Runes, op. cit., p. 18.
46. Baer, op. cit., II, 245.
47. Poliakov, op. cit., p. 119.
48. Graetz, op. cit., IV, 222-23.
49. Ibid., pp. 223-24.
50. Ibid., p. 225.
51. Roth, *Venice*, p. 54.
52. Poliakov, op. cit., p. 119.
53. Graetz, op. cit., IV, 227.
54. Roth, *Jews in the Renaissance*, pp. 30-31.
55. Ibid., p. 37.

155

56. Graetz, op. cit., IV, 227.
57. Poliakov, op. cit., p. 119.
58. Runes, op. cit., p. 47.
59. *Anti-Semitism*, Israel Pocket Library (Jerusalem: Ketter Publishing House Jerusalem Ltd., 1974), p. 91.
60. Poliakov, op. cit., p. 119.
61. Graetz, op. cit., IV, 244.
62. Ibid., p. 250.
63. Roth, *Venice*, p. 29.
64. Graetz, op. cit., IV, 253.
65. Baer, op. cit., II, 274-80.
66. Graetz, op. cit., IV, 253-54.
67. Ibid., p. 254.
68. Ibid., p. 255.
69. Ibid., p. 258.
70. Runes, op. cit., p. 28.
71. Graetz, op. cit., IV, 259-60.
72. Ibid., pp. 261-62.
73. Ibid., pp. 262-63.
74. Ibid., p. 306.
75. Dubrow, op. cit., p. 63; Graetz, op. cit., IV, 265-66.
76. Graetz, op. cit., IV, 259-60.
77. Dubrow, op. cit., p. 63.
78. Baron, Sala, *A Social and Religious History of the Jews*, IX, p. 172.
79. Dubrow, op. cit., pp. 63-64.
80. Baer, op. cit., II, 306-309.
81. Graetz, op. cit., IV, 299-307.
82. Roth, *Venice*, pp. 32-33.
83. Graetz, op. cit., IV, 307; Roth, *Venice*, pp. 33-34.
84. Baer, op. cit., II, 325.
85. Ibid.
86. Roth, *Venice*, p. 34.
87. Baer, op. cit., II, 325-27.
88. Ibid., pp. 327-29.
89. Ibid., p. 329.
90. Ibid., pp. 330-31.
91. Ibid., p. 331.
92. Ibid., p. 336.
93. Ibid., p. 337.
94. Ibid., p. 363.

95. Ibid., p. 366.
96. Ibid., pp. 367-68.
97. Ibid., p. 368.
98. Ibid., p. 339.
99. Ibid., pp. 339-40.
100. Ibid., pp. 340-41.
101. Roth, *Venice*, p. 35.
102. Baer, op. cit., II, 343.
103. Ibid.
104. Ibid.
105. Ibid.
106. Ibid.
107. Ibid., pp. 343-44.
108. Dubnow, op. cit., p. 37.
109. Baer, op. cit., II, 398-423.
110. Ibid., p. 423.
111. Ibid.
112. Ibid., p. 438.
113. Graetz, op. cit., IV, 371.
114. Dubnow, op. cit., p. 64.
115. Runes, op. cit., p. 19; Roth, *Venice*, p. 48.
116. Dubnow, op. cit., p. 65.
117. Roth, *Venice*, pp. 20-21.
118. Graetz, op. cit., IV, 375.
119. Ibid., p. 416.
120. Ibid.
121. Ibid.
122. Ibid., pp. 416-17.
123. Ibid.

PART VII: THE REFORMATION, 1500-1599

BACKGROUND:

The Reformation was similar to the Dark Ages in the degree and extent of instability that affected European society. It was a time of revolutionary change. The unity of the preceding centuries represented by the Roman Church and feudalism was shattered. It is true, this unity was never as complete as some writers depict it and there is ample evidence of the centrifugal forces that were present. The Church's constant battle with heresy, the power struggles between the papacy and various monarchs, the wars of nationalism, the struggle to define and defend orthodoxy, the scientific break-through of Galileo and Kepler, and the secular tendencies of the Rennaisance and Humanism, illustrate the tenuous and fragile nature of the unity of Medieval society. These earlier developments were the basis for the Revolutionary changes of the Reformation.

It is difficult to assign degrees of importance to these changes because they complement and re-enforce each other and all contribute to the change in world view and philosophical makeup of European civilization. But, the decline of the papacy and the fragmentation of Christianity caused by the Protestant Reformation are of major importance. The world would never again be Catholic and the universal quality of the faith disappeared. The decline of the Roman Church coincided with the rise of the modern nation state. The development of national and parochial loyalties and the ideology of nationalism combined with the Protestant revolt. Hence Luther aided German nationalism, Calvin and Zwingli Swiss nationalism, and Anglicanism was a manifestation of English nationalism. (Strictly speaking, Anglicanism is not Protestant, but it still represented the influence of nationalism on religion and the fragmentation of Christian unity.)

During this period, Catholic Europe was at war with itself as Spanish, French and Austrian nationalism undercut the Holy Roman Empire. Italy was one of the battlegrounds of this struggle and the Italian city states became client states of the larger warring nations. The Dutch revolted against Spain. Civil war occurred in France between the Huguenots and Catholics. German princes withdrew from the Empire. Peasant revolts reflecting left-wing Protestantism such as the Anabaptists alarmed Protestant and Catholic alike. The wars of the Catholic countries worked to the advantage of the Protestant reformers. The Church could not effectively respond to the Protestant challenge until a semblance of peace and order was restored to her allies. By the time the Council of Trent was called to deal with the problem, Protestantism was well established.

The response of the Roman Church to the Protestant Reformation aggravated the split in the faith. Instead of a policy of reconciliation and compromise, the Church took a hard unyielding line. The Council of Trent, the Jesuits, the Index of Forbidden Books, the reestablishment of the Inquisition that make up the Counter Reformation resulted in a long series of bloody religious wars between Protestants and Catholics, wars that were also expressions of nationalism. The most dramatic example is the war between England and Spain and the defeat of the Armada.

The Jewish experience during the Reformation varied with location. Generally the Protestant countries reflected a previously unknown religious tolerance. Holland became a refuge for Jews fleeing persecution in the Catholic countries. Part of this stems from the Protestant emphasis on the Old Testament and interest in Hebrew. The Jewish suffering during these religious wars was impersonal in the sense that they were not the target but simply a people caught between opposing forces.

Because Catholicism was under attack and on the defensive, the

159

Jews living in the solidly Catholic countries were the hardest hit. Jews were expelled from Catholic countries and principalities; the ghetto was formally established in Venice. The Talmud was seized and burned by papal order. Poland increased its persecutions and became the center of major anti-Semitic attacks.

While most anti-Semitism of the period was Catholic in origin, an important anti-Semitic development occurred in Protestant Germany. Luther, who epitomizes the Reformation, was, in his early career, a champion of the Jews against Catholic persecution. Luther and other Protestant leaders first hoped the Jews would convert to their faith. If this had happened, Catholicism would have been dealt a serious blow. The Jews, however, resisted Protestant efforts to convert them. In his disappointment, Luther turned in fury on the Jews. Luther's anti-Semitic writings were utilized by later anti-Semites, and Luther's prominence gave credibility and weight to lesser and venal men.

ENVIRONMENT: CHRISTIAN

The Reformation helped to break the universally negative view of Jews and Judaism that typified the Medieval Catholic mind. The intellectual curiosity and tolerance of earlier Humanism found some refuge in Protestant and Reformation thinkers and writers. No great emphasis should be placed on the tolerance of the period, but Protestant interest in the Old Testament and early Christianity that required a knowledge of Hebrew resulted in a more balanced image of the Jew. This was reflected in greater religious freedom enjoyed by Jews living in Protestant Europe in contrast to those living under Catholic rule. There were also instances of intellectual and elite defense and protection of Jews.

The new attitudes of tolerance and the more favorable image of the Jew was within, or veneered over, an environment that for 1200 years had preached and practiced hatred and intolerance. It had preserved them in histories, treatises, educational institutions, folklore, and the arts. From father to son over generations passed an image of the Jew that was evil, odious and deserving of contempt and hatred.

Those living in Catholic countries not exposed to the Reformation lived in an environment of intensified anti-Semitism. Anti-Semitic provisions of Canon law were enforced with renewed vigor. The term and the meaning of ghetto have their origins in this period. In the Catholic view there was little to recommend the Jew. The image was completely negative. The anti-Semitic acts of the Church and Catholic rulers reflect this attitude.

ENVIRONMENT: JEWISH

The Jewish environment was, as the Christian, dependent on whether Protestantism or Catholicism was dominant. In Protestant areas, Jews found greater tolerance and fewer restrictions on their religious, political and economic life. This contributed to a more dynamic and vital Jewish culture.

The experience under Catholic rule was the reverse. To an intensified anti-Semitism of expulsions, confiscations, attacks and slaughter, the ghetto was added. Residence restrictions had existed previously but were never enforced with the thoroughness and severity typified by the ghetto. One effect of this intensification of the anti-Semitism in Catholic countries was a stifling of the Jewish culture, that created a new stereotype—the ghetto Jew.

INCIDENTS:
1506 A.D.

In Lisbon, a mob stirred by the preachings of Dominicans murdered between 2,000 to 4,000 new converts (conversos). Men, women and children were victims. A witness tells of women and children thrown from windows and caught on the spears of the street mobs. The slaughter was accompanied by widespread rape of women and girls.[1]

1509 A.D.

John Pefferkorn, a Jew who converted to Christianity, began his anti-Semitic career. After publishing a number of anti-Jewish pamphlets, he received permission from Emperor Maximilian to examine all Jewish books for the purpose of destroying all that were blasphemous or hostile to Christianity. Frankfort was the first target of this fanatic, and all prayerbooks found in synagogues or in a house-to-house search of the Jewish quarter were confiscated. Over fifteen hundred manuscripts were seized.[2]

1510 A.D.
In the Mark of Brandenburg, Jews were accused of host desecration and ritual murder. They were brought to Berlin for trial. Joachim I, Elector of Brandenburg, had them tortured and ordered thirty to be burned alive.[3]

1511 A.D.
A proclamation was issued, at the instigation of Friar Rufin Lovato, requiring Jewish refugees to leave Venice within a month. This decree was never enforced.[4]

1514-1515 A.D.
Imperial decrees banished Jews from Strasbourg. These remained in effect until the end of the 18th century.[5]

1515 A.D.
"Anti-Jewish feeling increased in Venice. Easter sermons, especially those of Friar Giovanni Maria de'Arezzo, were very inflammatory."[6]

In Poland, the economic strength of the Jewish community agitated Christian merchants. Business competition occasionally resulted in physical violence and street riots. Anti-Jewish riots occurred in Posen and Bret-Kuyaush. The king responded by limiting the extent of trade and commodities which Jewish merchants could handle and severely warned Christians against violence to the Jews.[7]

1516 A.D.
All Jews in Venice were required to move to the Ghe to Nuovo.[8]

1519 A.D.
After a number of attempts that had been frustrated by the intercession of Emperor Frederick III, the municipality of Regensburg (Ratisbon) expelled its Jewish community. (This community had existed in Regensburg since before the birth of Christ.)[9]

162

1520 A.D.
The agreement permitting Jews to remain in Venice was renewed but a 10,000 ducat/year assessment was added.[10]

1521 A.D.
Emperor Charles V granted a pardon to the City Council of Regensburg for their expulsion of the Jewish community.[11]

1531 A.D.
Inquisition against Marranos was instituted in Portugal under King Joao. Laws were passed forbidding sea captains to give passage to those who sought to escape. Many were burned by the Inquisition.[12]

1536 A.D.
Pope Paul III under pressure from Emperor Charles V reinstituted the Inquisition in Portugal.[13]

1537 A.D.
Jews were forbidden to enter the city of Florence.[14]

1539 A.D.
In Cracow, Catherine Zaleshouska, a Catholic and wife of an official, was convicted of denying the fundamental dogma of Christianity and adhering secretly to Jewish doctrines. The Bishop of Cracow, Peter Gamrut, failing to bring her back to the church, condemned her to death. She was burned at the stake in the market place.[15]

There were many rumors that Christians were converting to Judaism and going to the greater safety of Lithuania. The Polish king sent two commissioners to Lithuania to conduct a strict investigation. Jewish homes were raided and travelers were arrested. Cross examination failed to discover the alleged proselytizing.[16]

In Portugal, the Inquisition burned ten to forty Marranos a year between 1539 and 1548. Hundreds more were imprisoned.[17]

163

1540 A.D.

Charles V, on his return from a victorious expedition to Africa, ordered the Jews of Naples to wear the badge or leave the city. (See Fourth Lateran Council—1215.) They chose voluntary exile. This was changed into banishment and any Jew who tried to enter Naples was subject to severe penalties.[18]

Levantine (Morrocan) Jews living in Venice, who were not previously required to live in segregated quarters, were forced to move into the area known as the Ghetto Vecchio (the old cannon foundry).[19]

The disappearance and death of a four-year-old boy in the Duchy of Neuberg in Bavaria brought ritual murder charges against the Jews. The Bishop of Eichstadt had a number arrested and brought before him for trial. He also urged the neighboring princes to imprison the Jews. The Inquiry did not prove the charges and Duke Otto Henry of Neuberg came to their defense. He refused the request of the bishop to banish the Jews and urged the publication of a pamphlet, "Little Book About the Jews," which was designed to disprove the ritual murder libel.[20]

1541 A.D.

The Bishop of Eichstadt commissioned Dr. John Eck to write an answer to the "Little Book About the Jews." Eck's pamphlet was to prove "the evil and wickedness brought about by kingdoms."[21]

1542 A.D.

Luther turned against the Jews. In his early career of Reformation Luther had been very solicitous of and a defender of the Jews. In 1542 his attitude changed completely. He published a pamphlet, "Concerning the Jews and Their Lies." He urged the emperor and the princes to expel the Jews from the country without delay and drive them back to their own land. If the nobility did not, it was the duty of the robber knights, the clergy and the people.[22]

"Because the Christians, for more than a thousand years had robbed them of all the rights of man, had treated them as evil beasts, had trodden underfoot, lacerated and slain them, in a word, because they had fallen into distress through the harshness of

164

Christians, therefore, they must be rejected, and the Savior of the world must have appeared." Martin Luther, "Concerning the Jews and Their Lies."[23]

There were a number of fires in the towns of Bohemia and the Jews were accused of setting them. In addition they were also charged with betraying to the Sultan the secret preparations for the war against the Turks. They were expelled along with their possessions. Most went to Poland and Turkey. Those who settled along the borders of Bohemia were later readmitted after paying a tax of 300 schock groschen and agreeing to wear the yellow badge.[24]

1548 A.D.
Pope Paul III issued a general absolution for Marranos. Eighteen hundred were released from prison in Portugal.[25]

1550 A.D.
The Venetian Senate decreed on July 8 that all Marranos were to leave Venice by September that year.[26]

Jews were banished from Genoa. A proclamation was issued prohibiting Jews from returning to the city.[27]

1551 A.D.
Jews were expelled from all of Bavaria. In return for the release of four imprisoned Jews, the Jewish leaders promised never again to set foot in Upper or Lower Bavaria.[28]

1553 A.D.
Pope Julius III approved and signed a decree presented by the Inquisitor General that ordered the seizure of the Talmud. On September 9, 1553 (Jewish New Year), all copies of the Talmud and compilations from it in Rome were burned. The same occurred in Romagna, Ferrara, Mantua, Padua, Venice and Candia. Other Hebrew books, including the bible, were also seized and burned.[29]

1553 A.D.
A Bavarian Land Ordinance characterized Jews as "pernicious elements."[30]

165

1554 A.D.

Pope Julius III issued a papal bull that compelled Jews under threat of corporal punishment to surrender all copies of the Talmud. Other Hebrew books were specifically exempted and bailiffs were ordered not to harass the Jews when collecting the Talmud. In the future all other Hebrew books were to be inspected before publication.[31]

1555 A.D.

Pope Paul IV, in a bull for the papal states, renewed enforcement of canonical laws pertaining to Jews. Segregation in ghettos was continued; all synagogues except one were destroyed; all male Jews were required to wear a green cap and Jewesses were to wear a green veil. Jews were barred from professions and forbidden to own real estate. Those who owned real estate were compelled to sell it within six months. Christians were not to be employed by Jews in any capacity. Jewish physicians were forbidden to treat Christians under heavy penalties.[32]

Jews of Rome were conscripted into slave labor to repair walls of Rome.[33]

Pope Paul IV issued a secret decree that ordered all Marranos in Ancona imprisoned in the dungeons of the Inquisition. A trial was instituted and all property was seized. Between twenty-four and sixty Marranos were burned alive by this Inquisition at Ancona.[34]

1556 A.D.

An Inquisition was established in Poland by the Papal Nuncio Lippomano, who had been sent from Rome to combat all forms of non-Catholic belief.[35]

Dorothy Laxhentzka, a woman in the Polish town of Sokhachev, was accused of selling to the Jews of the town the holy wafer she had received during communion. They were accused of stabbing the wafer until it bled. On the order of the Bishop of Khelm three Jews and the woman were put on the rack and finally sentenced to death. The king attempted to stop the execution but the sentence was hastily carried out. They were burned at the stake protesting their innocence. The executioners stopped "the mouths of the criminals with burning torches."[36]

166

1558 A.D.
Duke Guido Aboldo expelled Marranos from Pesaro.[37]

1559 A.D.
At the urging of the Dominicans, the governor of Milan burned between 10,000 and 12,000 copies of the Talmud.[38]

All Jewish books in Prague were confiscated and sent to Vienna.[39]

1559 A.D.
A fire in the Jewish quarter of Prague destroyed many houses. A Christian mob roamed into the section and threw many women and children into the flames as they plundered the quarter.[40]

The Austrian Emperor Ferdinand I began a campaign to expel Jews from Bohemia and Prague. He first imposed internal passes for Austrian Jews. Those traveling from place to place within the Empire had to have a passport and on arrival in a community had to inform the local marshal of the nature of their business and the duration of their stay.[41]

Ferdinand decreed the expulsion of all Jews from lower Austria in 1559; it was accomplished in 1561.[42]

1561 A.D.
Ferdinand ordered second expulsion of Jews from Prague. The exiles were attacked and plundered by robber knights.[43]

(The nobility of Prague petitioned Ferdinand to recall the Jews. He refused on the grounds that to do so would be to break an oath. Pope Pius IV absolved Ferdinand of his oath and the Jews were recalled under the special protection of Ferdinand's son, Maximilian.)[44]

1562 A.D.
The Polish Diet confirmed previous anti-Jewish legislation. Jews were required to dress differently from Christians, prohibited from owning Christian serfs or domestics and from holding public office.[45]

1562 A.D.
(Pope Pius IV suspended many of the anti-Jewish edicts of Pope Paul IV.)[46]

1563 A.D.
Ivan the Terrible viewed Jews as evil influences and corrupters of Christians. When Russian troops occupied the Polish border city of Polotzk the Czar gave orders that all local Jews were to be converted to the Greek Orthodox faith. Those who refused baptism were drowned in the Dvina River.[47]

1564 A.D.
Strong anti-Jewish sentiment existed in Lithuania. A Jew in Bielek was accused of killing a Christian girl and was executed though loudly proclaiming his innocence from the scaffold. Similar trials occurred in other Lithuanian towns.[48]

1566 A.D.
The Lithuanian Statute promulgated the same restrictions passed by the Polish Diet.[49]

Pope Pius V reinstated disabilities and restrictive edicts of Pope Paul IV.[50]

1567 A.D.
The Council of Avignon decreed the cessation of all intercourse between Christians and Jews. Christians were forbidden to employ Jewish physicians, enter Jewish homes, participate in Jewish festivals, seek employment by Jews, or to serve as their masons or barbers.[51]

1567 A.D.
Emperor Ferdinand II gave permission to expel Jews from Würzburg.[52]

1569 A.D.
Pope Pius V issued a papal bull that ordered all Jews out of the Papal States except Rome and Ancona within 3 months. Those

who remained behind would be sold into slavery. (Bull Hebraeorum gens.)[53]

1571 A.D.
The Senate of Venice thanked God for the defeat of the Turks by agreeing to expel the Jews when the agreement expired in 1573. (This action was revoked in 1573.)[54]

The death of Joachim II, Elector of Brandenburg was followed by the arrest of Munzmeister Lippold on charges of embezzlement. Lippold had served Joachim as mint master, financier, treasurer and confidant. Under torture Lippold confessed to all manner of crimes including sorcery and poisoning. He was accused of murdering Joachim by poison. The confession was recanted at his trial but under further torture he again confessed. He was executed in Berlin and the Jewish community in the Electorate was attacked by roving mobs. Their property was confiscated and they were expelled.[55]

1577 A.D.
King Stephen of Poland enacted pro-Jewish legislation and cautioned the magistrates to safeguard the life and property of the Jews. A Christian mob attacked the Jewish quarter of Posen, looted property and killed a number of Jews.[56]

Pope Gregory XIII decreed that all Roman Jews, under pain of death, must listen attentively to the compulsory Catholic conversion sermon given in the synagogues after their Sabbath services.[57]

1578 A.D.
Pope Gregory XIII required the Jews of Rome to maintain a house of Conversion.[58]

1581 A.D.
Pope Gregory decreed that Jewish physicians were not permitted to treat Christian patients and confiscated all sacred literature from the Jews of Rome.[59]

169

1582 A.D.

The Duke of Alba prohibited the printing of Hebrew books in the Netherlands.[60]

The Netherlands had been a haven to Jews escaping the Inquisition. They established thriving communities in Brussels, Antwerp and Ghent. However, when the Netherlands came under the rule of Charles V of Spain he had them expelled.[61]

1592 A.D.

King Sigismund of Poland decreed that the Jews had to receive the permission of the Catholic clergy before they could build any new synagogues.[62]

1592 A.D.

In Vilna, the Christian burghers demolished the synagogue and sacked the Jewish residences in the city.[63]

In Posen, mob attacks on the Jewish quarter were a regular occurrence.[64]

1593 A.D.

Jews of Berlin and the province of Brandenburg were given the choice of baptism or expulsion.[65]

Duke Henry Julius of Brunswick expelled the Jews from his realm.[66]

Emperor Rudolph II expelled Jews from the archduchy of Austria.[67]

1596 A.D.

Marrano refugees in Amsterdam were suspected of being papists by the Protestant authorities and on the Feast of Atonement were imprisoned. The mixup was clarified and they were released from prison and in 1598 given permission to build a synagogue.[68]

1597 A.D.

Jews were expelled from the Italian cities of Cremona, Pavia and Lodi.[69]

1598 A.D.

The Tribunal of Lublin sentenced three Jews to death on ritual murder charges. Execution by quartering was carried out. The body of the boy was transferred to a local church by the Jesuits where he was venerated as a martyr. Similar trials occurred throughout Poland.[70]

CONTINUUM:

The insecurity of the Roman Church that created the Inquisition continued throughout the Reformation. Here the frontal assaults by Luther and Calvin on the Church contributed to the backlash in Catholic countries against the Jews. Instability, tension and political and religious ferment again found the Jew a handy target for release.

During the period of the Reformation, the standard techniques developed earlier were used in attacking the Jews. Forced Baptism, expropriation of property, expulsion, imprisonment, torture, execution, mob attacks including arson, pillage and slaughter, discriminatory taxation, confiscation and burning of sacred writings, forced labor, prohibition of religious practice and proselytizing, restrictions on occupation, movement and residence, prescribed clothing, and ritual murder and host desecration charges were the anti-Semitic practices of the time. No new techniques were added and most of the anti-Semitic actions took place in the countries and principalities that were faithful to the Roman Church. There were not many instances of anti-Semitic outbursts in the Protestant countries. However, the writings of Luther, especially his later writings on the Jews, added to the intellectual heritage of anti-Semitism and provided ammunition for later anti-Semites, especially in Germany.

PART VII: THE REFORMATION

1. Graetz, op. cit., IV, 486-87.
2. Ibid., pp. 422-29.

3. Ibid., pp. 439-40.
4. Roth, *Venice*, p. 44.
5. Baron, op. cit., IX, 188-89.
6. Roth, *Venice*, p. 48.
7. Dubnow, op. cit., pp. 75-76.
8. Roth, *Jews in the Renaissance*, p. 13; *Venice*, pp. 48-50.
9. Poliakov, op. cit., p. 120; Durant, Will, *The Story of Civilization, Part VI, The Reformation*. (New York: Simon & Schuster, 1953), pp. 731-32.
10. Roth, Venice, p. 57.
11. Baron, op. cit., IX, 233-34.
12. Gratez, op. cit., IV, 488-90.
13. Ibid., pp. 517-18.
14. Roth, *Jews in the Renaissance*, p. 27.
15. Dubnow, op. cit., p. 79.
16. Ibid., p. 80.
17. Graetz, op. cit., IV, 520-27.
18. Ibid., pp. 534-44.
19. Roth, *Venice*, p. 61.
20. Graetz, op. cit., IV, 545.
21. Ibid., pp. 546-47.
22. Ibid., pp. 549-52; Heer, op. cit., pp. 128-34.
23. Graetz, op. cit., IV, 549.
24. Ibid., pp. 544-45.
25. Ibid., p. 527.
26. Roth, *Venice*, p. 64.
27. Graetz, op. cit., IV, 554.
28. *Anti-Semitism*, Israel Pocket Library, p. 207.
29. Graetz, op. cit., IV, 565.
30. Baron, op. cit., IX, 209.
31. Graetz, op. cit., IV, 565-66.
32. Ibid., pp. 566-67.
33. Ibid., p. 567.
34. Ibid., p. 568.
35. Dubnow, op. cit., p. 86.
36. Ibid.
37. Graetz, op. cit., IV, 580.
38. Ibid., p. 583.
39. Ibid., p. 584.
40. Ibid., p. 585.
41. Ibid.

42. Ibid.
43. Ibid., p. 586.
44. Ibid., pp. 586-87.
45. Dubnow, op. cit., p. 87.
46. Graetz, op. cit., IV, 588.
47. Dubnow, op. cit., p. 243.
48. Ibid., p. 87.
49. Ibid.
50. Graetz, op. cit., IV, 588.
51. Runes, op. cit., p. 12.
52. Roth, Cecil (ed.), *The Standard Jewish Encyclopedia* (Garden City, New York: Doubleday & Company, Inc., 1959), col. 1932.
53. Graetz, op. cit., IV, 591; Runes, op. cit., p. 143.
54. Roth, *Venice*, pp. 89-90.
55. Graetz, op. cit., IV, 652.
56. Dubnow, op. cit., p. 90.
57. Runes, op. cit., p. 45.
58. Ibid., pp. 85-86.
59. Roth, *Jews in the Renaissance*, p. 38; Runes, op. cit., pp. 85-86.
60. Runes, op. cit., p. 2.
61. Graetz, op. cit., IV, 661-62.
62. Ibid., p. 643.
63. Dubnow, op. cit., pp. 94-95.
64. Ibid.
65. Graetz, op. cit., IV, 652.
66. Ibid.
67. Ibid.
68. Ibid., pp. 666-67.
69. Ibid., p. 660.
70. Dubnow, op. cit., p. 96.

PART VIII: THE 17TH AND 18TH CENTURIES—1600-1799

BACKGROUND

The Treaty of Westphalia in 1648 brought an end to the Religious wars of the Reformation. Western Europe then entered a new period of growth and expansion. The dramatic political, economic, social and religious changes of the preceeding 200 years were formalized and institutionalized and the shape of the modern age was clearly defined.

The nation state and capitalism replaced the feudal political and economic order. Exploration and colonization to increase political power and economic wealth preoccupied the nations of Western Europe. Technological innovations in agriculture broke the manor economy. Cash replaced service or barter exchange and freed large numbers of peasants from bondage to the manor. Many moved to the cities and became the labor supply for the developing manufacturing and industrial sectors.

Protestantism, nationalism and capitalism combined to create a new concept of man, the idea of individualism and secularism. In Protestant countries where these forces were strongest, individualism led to a broadening of the concept of freedom and responsibility. The natural consequence was development of the idea of citizen and a greater degree of tolerance which culminated in the democratic revolutions. This occurred, however, near the end of this period.

The immediate consequence of the Treaty of Westphalia was the establishment of the territorial state. No longer would the change of monarch be accompanied by a change in borders or population. Whatever changes along these lines that would occur would now result from war or treaty. With the exception of England, where revolution and civil war were still settling the question of the Crown's prerogative, all of Europe came under the political system of absolute monarchy. The last vestiges of power based on feudal politics were broken.

Sweden, Spain and Portugal declined as major powers and England, Holland and France became the great powers. The sleeping giant of Russia began to awaken and broke Polish expansion into and dominance of eastern Europe. The colonization of the Americas, and the economics of trade and merchant capitalism were reflected in the new power arrangements. The bourgeoisie and non-titled gentry came into prominence and political power.

While absolutism dominated the political scene, its survival was doomed almost from the start. The ideological justifications— "divine right" and religious legitimation of political power— were undercut by the Reformation and the writings of the great thinkers produced by this period. Hobbes, Locke, Descartes and Bacon dealt hammer blows to an already crumbling concept of man and world view that had its roots in Catholic Medieval Europe and influenced even the great revolutionaries of the Reformation. Later Kant, Rousseau, Hume and the French philosophes would finish the job.

In the west, and particularly the Protestant west, the Jewish experience was a great improvement over earlier centuries. Religious tolerance, the talents of the Jews and the progressive vitality of early capitalism worked to the benefit of Jewish communities and a dramatic decline in anti-Semitism in the Protestant countries.

In the Catholic West and East Europe, whether Roman or Orthodox, Jews were subjected to incredible persecutions. This is particularly true in the East. The wars between Poland, Russia and Sweden, and the Cossack Rebellions focused much of their fury on the Jews. Jewish suffering during this period dwarfed the persecutions and slaughter inflicted during the period of the Crusades.

175

ENVIRONMENT: CHRISTIAN

Christian attitudes and actions toward the Jews reflected the Catholic/Protestant split in the faith.

In Protestant areas, Christians were much more tolerant and less antagonistic. Rulers and communities welcomed Jewish migration and granted religious freedom and relaxed other restrictions that had been based on Canon law.

Anti-Semitic attitudes of the earlier period still survived and hostility and suspicion can be seen in the resistance of England to the readmission of the Jews and in the restrictions that were coupled with the readmission.

(The preservation and perpetuation of these attitudes continued to be borne by the artists, historians, teachers, preachers etc. and by the works of their predecessors.)

On balance, though, Protestant Europe was much less anti-Semitic than Catholic Europe.

Catholic Europe continued the extreme anti-Semitism that accompanied the Papacy's response to the Reformation. The ghetto system was applied in a methodic manner throughout the Roman Catholic countries, expulsions were frequent, host desecration and ritual murder charges were common and the economic and social restriction of Canon law were systematically enforced.

The political conflict between Poland and Russia, which was also a conflict between Roman Catholicism and Orthodox Catholicism, was accompanied by the most extreme anti-Semitism of the period.

ENVIRONMENT: JEWISH

While anti-Semitic attitudes and beliefs continued to survive, Jews living in Protes ant Europe lived in relative safety. In addition, new religious and political, social, and economic freedoms were granted by various countries.

The experience of Jews in Catholic and Orthodox countries was in sharp contrast. Systematic application of anti-Semitic provisions of Canon law in the Catholic countries was also accompanied by expulsions, ritual murder and host desecration charges and outbursts of mob violence.

176

In Orthodox Russia, anti-Semitism took its most extreme and brutal forms during the Cossack Rebellions. Unbelievable torture and slaughter of Jews went hand in hand with the war between Russia and Poland.

The Russian victory over Poland brought many Jews under Russian authority for the first time. The response to this new population was either to convert them to the Orthodox faith or eliminate them. Neither slaughter nor elimination proved effective and a stop-gap measure, the Russian equivalent to the ghetto, was adopted. Jews were restricted to an area known as the Pale of Settlement.

Jews under Russian rule were under constant pressure to convert to the Orthodox faith and were severely restricted in religious, economic and social activities. Travel beyond the Pale was made almost impossible.

INCIDENTS:

1604 A.D.

One hundred and fifty Marranos imprisoned in Lisbon refused to return to Catholicism. They promised to release Philip III from the royal debt and in addition gave him a gift of 1,200,000 crusados ($700,000) and persuaded Pope Clement VIII to grant them absolution. They were freed after a symbolic confession of guilt and penance but were deprived of all civil rights.[1]

In Amsterdam, Jewish funeral processions had to pay a tax to churches which they passed en route to the cemetery.[2]

1610 A.D.

The Jews in Mantua were required to live in a walled ghetto. The ghetto gates were locked at sunset and unlocked at dawn.[3]

1612 A.D.

The Senate of Hamburg granted Portuguese Jews free residence in the city for an annual protection fee of 1,000 marks. They were not allowed a synagogue or to conduct religious services privately or circumcision. They were, however, permitted to bury their dead in their own cemetery at Altona.[4]

1613 A.D.
Frankfort on Main permitted Jewish settlement under severe restrictions of canon law. The council of Frankfort reserved the right to expel the community at any time.[5]

1614 A.D.
A mob under the leadership of Vincent Fettmilch attacked the community of Frankfort. Two days and a night of plundering, desecration and destruction resulted in the murder of 2,920 Jews. The rest of the community was permitted to leave the city but without property of any kind.[6]

1615 A.D.
The community of Worms was expelled at the instigation of the lawyer, Dr. Chemnitz—after which the synagogue and cemetery were destroyed.[7]

1616 A.D.
The Jews were readmitted to Worms.[8]
The Jews of Frankfort were led back to the city in triumphal procession. Vincent Fettmilch was hanged and quartered and the city fined 175,919 florins by the emperor as compensation for the losses suffered by the Jews.[9]

1617 A.D.
Emperor Matthias abolished the permissive residence of Jews in Worms and Frankfort. They were now under the protection of the emperor, and the council no longer had the right to banish them. However, regulations concerning dress, occupation and movement were retained and in addition the community of Frankfort was limited to 500.[10]

1619 A.D.
The Amsterdam city council decreed that intercourse between Jews and Christians, even prostitution, was strictly forbidden. However, Jews were permitted to practice religion freely.[11]
The Jews were expelled from Kiev.[12]

1622 A.D.
King Christian IV of Denmark, the Duke of Savoy and the Duke of Moderna invited Jews to settle in their lands with the right to worship and extensive privileges. These were rare respites from the hardships of the Thirty Years War that wracked Europe at the time.[13]

1630 A.D.
Jews in Vienna were required to attend conversion sermons every Saturday.[14]

1635 A.D.
Anti-Jewish riot took place in Vilna.[15]

1636 A.D.
The Jews of Lublin were charged with ritual murder when a Christian child disappeared. The Crown Tribunal acquitted the Jews of the charge. However, the local clergy brought new charges, this time with the necessary "evidence." A Carmelite monk claimed that the Jews lured him into a house and had him bled by a German surgeon. They poured his blood into a vessel and murmured mysterious incantations over it. The Tribunal accepted this testimony as evidence and sentenced one Jew to death.[16]

1637 A.D.
In Cracow, Peter Yurkevich, a Pole, was convicted of having stolen some church vessels. Under cross examination on the rack, he testified that a Jewish tailor, Jacob Gzheslik, had persuaded him to steal a host. Since the Jew could not be found, Yurkevich was burned alive. Just before he died he claimed that the confession was false and was forced by torture, but he was still executed. The Jewish quarter was attacked by mobs, and forty Jews from the ghetto were taken to be thrown into the river. Thirty-three saved themselves by accepting baptism; the other seven were drowned.[17]

The Cossack leader, Panluk, appeared in the Province of Poltara. He incited the peasants to attack the Jews. Several synagogues in Lubny and surrounding towns were destroyed and about 200 Jews were killed.[18]

179

1638 A.D.
The ghetto system was introduced in the Italian city of Modena.[19]

1639 A.D.
Two elders of the community of Lenchitza were sentenced to death by the Crown Tribunal on the charge of ritual murder of a boy from the neighboring village. The bodies of the executed Jews were cut into pieces and hung from poles at the crossroads. The Bernardine monks placed the remains of the supposedly martyred boy in their church along with a painting depicting in great detail the alleged murder.[20]

1641 A.D.
Civil and economic restrictions were applied to the Jewish community in Worms.[21]

1647 A.D.
The Marrano Isaac de Castro Tortos, a Dutch citizen, was burned by the Inquisition in Lisbon.[22]

1648 A.D.
In April the Polish army was defeated by the alliance of Cossacks and Tartars. This served as the signal for the region east of the Dnieper River to rise in rebellion. The Russian peasants and town dwellers in roving bands attacked and sacked the estates of the Polish aristocracy, slaughtering as they went. A particular target were those Jews who served the aristocracy as stewards and tax farmers, and the Jews in general.[23]

In the towns of Peregaslav, Piryatin, Lolchvitz, Lubny and the surrounding country, thousands of Jews were savagely murdered and their property destroyed or pillaged. The roving bands of rebels allowed only those who converted to the Greek Orthodox faith to survive. Jews living in the Kiev area fled to the Tartar camps and surrendered. (As a rule the Tartars refrained from killing them but rather sold them into slavery in Turkey where there was an excellent chance of being purchased by their Turkish coreligionists.)[24]

Bands of Cossacks and Russian peasants under the leadership of the Zaporozhian Cossacks began the indiscriminate extermination of the Poles and Jews in the Ukraine. In May, King Vladislav IV died; the rebellion expanded and Cossack terrorism increased. The whole of the Ukraine as well as Volhynia and Podolia were now in rebellion.

"Killing was accompanied by barbarous tortures; the victims were flayed alive, split asunder, clubbed to death, roasted on coals, or scalded with boiling water. Even infants at the breast were not spared. The most terrible cruelty was shown toward the Jews. They were destined to utter annihilation and the slightest pity shown them was looked upon as treason. Scrolls of the Law were taken out of the synagogues by the Cossacks who danced on them while drinking whiskey. After this Jews were laid upon them and butchered without mercy. Thousands of Jewish infants were thrown into wells or buried alive. Contemporary Jewish chroniclers paint a vivid picture of the brutality and suffering of this period. Victims of massacres were purposely allowed to live longer in order to torture them; hands and feet were cut off; children were split asunder fish like or roasted on a fire; the bellies of women were split open and live cats sewed up in them while they were alive."[25]

1648 A.D.
Several thousand Jews took refuge in the fortified city of Niemirov. A detachment of Cossacks under the command of Zaporozhian Gania tried but failed to take the city by storm. They later approached the city carrying Polish banners. The defenders thought it was the Polish army coming to their aid and opened the gates. The Cossacks then proceeded to massacre the Jews. The women and girls were raped before being murdered. Six thousand Jews were slaughtered in Niemirov. Those who escaped fled to the fortified city of Tulchyn.[26]

1648 A.D.
Cossacks and peasants laid siege to the city of Tulchyn which contained several hundred Poles and 1,500 Jews. The Poles and

181

the Jews took an oath not to betray one another and to defend the city to their last breath. After a long and unsuccessful siege the Cossacks persuaded the Poles to betray the Jews in return for their lives. When the Jews learned of this they thought of attacking the Poles but were dissuaded by Rabbi Aaron who said that such an act would bring the hatred of the Poles down on the Jews throughout the Empire. "Let us rather perish as did our brethren in Niemirov. . . ." They turned over to Count Chelventinski, the Polish leader, their property and asked him to offer it to the Cossacks for their lives. When the Cossacks entered the city they took the ransom and then drove the Jews into a garden where they offered them their lives if they converted to Orthodoxy. The rabbi exhorted them to accept martyrdom and the 1,500 were murdered in a savage manner. The Polish Catholics were later slaughtered by the Cossacks.[27]

The Cossack rebellion spread in the Province of Volhynia and the massacres continued through the summer and fall of 1648. In the town of Polonnoye, 10,000 Jews were eliminated. Those not slaughtered by the Cossacks were taken into slavery by the Tartars. Three hundred Jews led by the Cabalist Samson of Ostropol, who were offering prayers in the synagogue, were murdered one by one.[28]

Massacres occurred by Zasloz, Ostrog, Chernigov, Constantinov, Bratzlau, Narol, Kamenetz, Kremenetz, Bar and many other cities. The Ukraine, Volhynia and Podolia were one big slaughterhouse for the Jews.[29]

Cossacks massacred 600 Jewish families in the Ukranian town of Belaya Tsorkov.[30]

From the Ukraine the rebellious peasants and Cossacks penetrated White Russia and Lithuania. After the Jewish inhabitants of Chernigov, Brest-Litovsk, Minsk, Pinsk and Starodub were exterminated or scattered, the hordes moved toward the city of Kowel. The rebels bribed the city authority to surrender the Jews who were then given the choice of conversion to the Greek Orthodox faith or death. An eye witness stated that: "The Rosh-Yeshibah was the first to offer himself as a martyr. Young and old saw the tortures, sufferings, and wounds of the teacher who did not cease exhorting them to accept martyrdom in the name of God. The victims were killed with spears in order that they would die more slowly. Husbands, wives and children fell in heaps. They were not buried and dogs and swine fed on the bodies.''[31]

In September, the Cossacks, under the leadership of Khmelnitzki, set siege to Lwow (Lemberg) the capital of Red Russia. After pillaging the suburbs, the Cossacks were unable to penetrate the fortified center of the city. (The magistracy of Lemberg refused to surrender the Jews but did pay the rebels a large ransom [most of which had been contributed by the Jews] and the Cossacks then withdrew.)[32]

1649 A.D.

Peace negotiations were being conducted between the Cossacks and the new Polish king, John Casimir. In the spring, civil war broke out again and many more Jewish communities were destroyed by the Cossacks. In August, a peace treaty was finally accepted. The treaty forbade Jews to reside in the portion of the Ukraine inhabited by Cossacks, the regions of Chernigov, Poltava, Kiev and parts of Poldolia.[33]

The Jewish community was expelled from Hamburg.[34]

1650 A.D.

In the writings of those who advocated the return of the Jews to England, most authors stipulated codes of special dress regulations, restrictions from public office, and restrictions upon their interactions—social and otherwise—with Christians.[35]

1652 A.D.

The Marrano, Manuel Fernando de Villa Real, who conducted consular affairs for Portugal, was burned at the stake in Lisbon.[36]

1654 A.D.

In Cuenca, fifty-seven Marranos were brought before the Inquisition. Ten were burned and the others were given corporal punishment and their property was confiscated.[37]

The Inquisition burned twelve Marranos in Granada.[38]

1654 A.D.
The Colonies in the New World were not free from anti-Semitic literature. Peter Stuyvesant sent the following letter on September 22, to the West India Company:

"The Jews who have arrived would nearly all like to remain here, but learning that they (with their customary usury and deceitful trading with the Christians) were very repugnant to the inferior magistrates, as also to the people having the most affection for you . . . we have, for the benefit of this weak and newly developing place and the land in general, deemed it useful to require them in a friendly way to depart; praying also most seriously in this connection, for ourselves as also for the general community of your worships, that the deceitful race— such hateful enemies and blasphemers of the name of Christ— be not allowed further to infect and trouble this new colony, to the detraction of your worships and the dissatisfaction of your worships' most affectionate subjects."[39]

When Little Russia was annexed by Czar Alexis Michaelovich the Russians encountered masses of Jews for the first time. Jews had not been allowed to live or travel in Russia. In Vilna and Moghilev, cities in the occupied provinces of Poland, the Jews were murdered as matter of course. Those who survived were expelled; in Vitebisk, the Jews were made prisoners of war; in other cities, assaulted, plundered and murdered.[40]

1654-1656 A.D.
The alliance of the Cossacks with the rulers of Muscovy resulted in great hardships for Jews living in Lithuania. The capture of the principal cities such as Minsk, by the combined armies of the Cossacks and Muscovites was accompanied by the extermination or expulsion of the Jewish population.[41]

1655 A.D.
At the approach of the Polish army the surviving Jewish community in Moghilev was ordered expelled by the commander of the

Russian garrison, Colonel Poklovski. As they were leaving the city, virtually all the men, women and children were killed.[42]

A Marrano youth was burned at the stake in Granada.[43]

Abraham Nunez Bernal, a Marrano, was burned in Cordova.[44]

In Vitebisk, the Jews played an active role in the defense of the city against the besieging Russian army. When the city was taken the Jews were completely robbed by the Zaporozhian Cossacks. Many were taken prisoner; others were forcibly baptized or exiled to Pakov, Novgorod or Kazan.[45]

When Sweden invaded Poland in 1655, some Poles and Jews offered assistance in the hope of removing the Russians. The Poles later turned on the Jews for their lack of patriotism.[46]

1656 A.D.

William Prynne in *A Short Demurrer to the Jews* . . . stated that the readmission of the Jews to England was against law and public welfare. Prynne also declared that the Jews were the enemies of Christ, usurers, coin clippers, murderers, and crucifiers of children, "not fit for our land nor yet for our dung-hills."[47]

Troops of Polish irregulars that had organized in 1655 to combat the Swedish invasion ruthlessly attacked the Jewish population as the Swedes withdrew. The Poles had learned well the lessons taught by the Cossacks on the art of exterminating Jews. Except for the community in the city of Posen, the Jewish settlements in the provinces of Posen, Kalish, Cracow and Piotrkov were destroyed. The irregulars under the command of Charnetzki tortured and murdered the rabbis, raped girls and women, and killed all those who did not convert to Catholicism. Between 16,000 and 20,000 Jews were murdered and 30 settlements were destroyed, many burned to the ground.[48]

1657 A.D.

In the Lithuanian town of Ruzkany, the local Christians placed a dead child's body in the yard of a Jew and charged the whole community with ritual murder. The trial lasted three years and ended with the execution of two representatives of the community, Rabbi Israel and Rabbi Tobias.[49]

185

The extent of the tragedy for the Polish Jews of the decade of 1648-1658 was incredible. The contemporary chroniclers number the Jewish victims of the massacres between 100,000 and 500,000. Some seven hundred communities in Poland were pillaged and massacred. In the Ukrainian cities on the left bank of the Dnieper, the region of the Cossacks, the provinces of Chernigov, Poltava, and Kiev, the Jewish communities had disappeared almost completely. On the right side of the Dnieper, Volhynia, Podolia and the Polish Ukraine, only about 1/10 of the Jewish population survived. The rest had either been killed by the hordes of Khmelnitzki, captured by the Tartars or had emigrated west.[50]

1660 A.D.

In Poland, two rabbis were executed on charges of ritual murder.[51]

In Seville, the Inquisition burned 60 Marranos in an auto da fe.[52]

A ghetto was established in Genoa for the Jewish residents of the city.[53]

1663 A.D.

In Cracow, a Jewish apothecary, Mattathiah Calabona, argued with a local priest about religious topics. The priest invited him to a disputation in his cloister but he declined and promised to put his views in writing. Later the priest found in the church a statement written in German that contained a violent attack on the cult of the Virgin. Charges of blasphemy were brought against the Jew who pleaded innocent and claimed ignorance of German. After torture he still refused to confess. He was sentenced to death. The execution was carried out in the following manner: First his lips were cut off, next his hand, then his tongue; he was then burned at the stake and the ashes were shot into the air from a cannon. This execution was followed by mob attacks on the Jewish community.[54]

1664 A.D.

Students of the Cathedral school and the Jesuit Academy of Lemberg organized an attack on the Jewish quarter. They were met by a group of armed Jewish youths. The students were aided by a mob, and the riot turned into a massacre. About a hundred Jews were killed, much of the quarter was demolished and the synagogues were desecrated.[55]

For protection against such attacks the Jewish communities paid an annual tax to the rectors of the local Catholic schools. This tax was called the kozubales and was recognized in common law.[56]

1667 A.D.

By the Peace of Andrusovo, captive Jews were allowed to remain in Muscovy; however, a special permit ("red ticket") was needed for them to visit the capitol Moscow.[57]

1669 A.D.

Jews were banished from the Province of Oran (North Africa) by the dowager Regent Maria Anna of Austria.[58]

1670 A.D.

A Jewish peddler, Raphael Levi, was accused of ritual murder in the city of Metz. He was condemned by the Metz Parliament and put to death by torture. (When Louis XIV learned of the case he ordered that in the future, criminal charges against Jews were to be brought before the King's council.)[59]

Jews were readmitted to Brandenburg, Landsberg and Frankfort on the Oder.[60]

Emperor Leopold of Austria banished Jews from Vienna. Violation of the ban was punishable by death. The Jewish quarter of Vienna was purchased from the Emperor by the magistrate and named Leopoldstat in his honor. The Talmud school was converted to a church, and a church was built on the former site of the synagogue. Later the same year the Jews were expelled from the rest of Austria.[61]

The Diet of Poland passed laws restricting Jewish trade and interactions with Christians.[62]

Street attacks on Jews by Christian college students became an everyday event in the cities of Poland. This involved not only insults and assaults on Jewish passers-by on the street but often invasions of the Jewish quarters where pillage and physical attack were the rule of the day. Most of the attacks were led by the students at the Academy of Cracow and the Jesuit schools in Posen, Lemberg, Vilna and Brest.[63]

1671 A.D.
The Jewish community of Minsk was attacked by a mob of townspeople.[64]

1676 A.D.
Jews were forbidden to live in Little Russia or to enter the city of Moscow.[65]

1679 A.D.
The ghetto system was established in the Italian city of Turin.[66]

1681 A.D.
The Jews were persuaded by the officials of Vilna to go outside the town for the municipal census. Once outside the walls the members of the trade unions and other Christians began to shoot at them and rob them of their clothes and valuables. (The community would have been annihilated had not the students of the local Jesuit college taken pity and rescued them from the mob.) The city officials looked on the attack with "great satisfaction."[67]

1682 A.D.
The Jewish community of Cracow was attacked by a band of students and townspeople.[68]

1685 A.D.
The Black Code, a body of law to regulate slavery in the French West Indies, was promulgated. Article I ordered the expulsion of all Jews. Article III prohibited any religion except Roman Catholicism.[69]

1687 A.D.
Christian students attacked the Jewish quarter in Posen. For three days a pitched battle raged in the Jewish quarter of the city.[70]

1689 A.D.
The House of Commons assessed the Jewish community £100,000 in addition to the £10 tax assessed due to their status as merchant strangers.[71]

The Jewish community in Worms was massacred by the army of Louis XIV.[72]

1690 A.D.
The tax assessed the Jews in England as merchant strangers was increased to £20, while non-Jewish merchant strangers were still assessed the £10 tax.[73]

1693 A.D.
The ghetto system was established in the city of Trieste.[74]

1698 A.D.
Parliament passed a bill suppressing blasphemy and profaneness which exempted persons of the Jewish faith. For the first time, the practice of Judaism received parliamentary sanction in addition to royal protection.[75]

A ritual murder trial was held in Copenhagen.[76]

1699 A.D.
Anti-Semitism was brought to colonial America along with the rest of the cultural tradition the European settlers carried with them. In the New England colonies, born of the struggle for religious freedom, there was little toleration for the dissenter or the non-Christian. The Puritans while admiring and respecting the Hebrew (the Old Testament) had contempt and pity for the Jew (the rejector of Jesus). Leading Puritans such as Cotton Mather required the study of Hebrew in the colleges but saw the Christian mission to be the conversion of Jews to Christianity. Jews were characterized as rebellious and backsliding and rejected by the Messiah.[77]

Jews were expelled from Lubeck.[78]

189

Early 1700 A.D.

In Rome, pontifical plays known as Guidate, which mocked Jewish life and customs, were a large part of the traditional dramas acted on oxcarts around the streets during the carnival season.[84]

1702 A.D.

The English Parliament required Jewish parents to make adequate provision for their children who converted to Protestantism.[79]

1702 A.D.

In Poland, special government posts were created to protect the Jews (Starosta). Frequently they became their most relentless oppressors. The Jewish communities were often blackmailed with threats of imprisonment to enrich the local Starosta. "In the Polish Ukraine the Starosta of Kaniev entertained himself by ordering Jewish women to climb an apple tree and call like cuckoos. He would shoot at them with small shot and watch them fall wounded from the trees. He, then, laughing would throw gold coins among them."[80]

In Poland, the meetings of the local Diets and the conferences of the Shlakhta (court tribunals), became fixed occasions for attacking the local Jews and invading their synagogues and houses.[81]

1709 A.D.

In Italy, the mock funeral of a rabbi was the hit of the Fisherman's Guild burlesques during the carnival season. (This anti-Semitic play was repeated at his special request before Prince Alexander Sobieski of Poland.)[82]

1710 A.D.

In the town of Sandomir, Poland, a Christian woman threw the dead body of her illegitimate child into the yard of a community elder. Ritual murder charges were brought against the Jews and the fanatical priest, Stephen Zhakhaskia, brought two additional

190

charges against them. He also published a book full of tales of horror committed by Jews. The case ended with the acquittal of the Jews but Zhakhaskia succeeded in getting a new trial. The Tribunal of Lublin, acting as the Inquisition, sentenced the elder to death.[83]

1712 A.D.
King Augustus ordered the expulsion of all Jews from Sandomir and converted the synagogue into a Catholic chapel. The Catholic clergy placed a gory painting in the church depicting an alleged ritual murder.[85]

1717 A.D.
The Polish Diet protested against attacks on the Jews and threatened rioters with severe fines. The custom, however, remained quite popular.[86]

1718 A.D.
Charles XIII of Sweden opened Sweden to Jewish immigration with the right of religious freedom. This royal permission had to be renewed from time to time. Freedom of movement, however, was greatly restricted and there were also economic restrictions.[87]

1724 A.D.
The Jews of Posen were obliged to furnish the Carmelites with two pails of oil annually to supply the burning lamp in front of the three hosts in the church.[88] (See 1399—Host Desecration.)

The Black Code governing slavery in the French West Indies (see 1685) was applied to Louisiana.[89]

1725 A.D.
Danish Jews were forbidden to have Christian servants.[90]

1727 A.D.
Russian inhabitants of the Jewish area violently protested the presence of the Jews. When a tax farmer, Borukh Leibov, built a synagogue for the Jews of the village of Zveronich, the many

protests caused Catherine I to issue an ukase through the Supreme Secret Council that removed Borukh and his associates from their offices and ordered that they "be deported immediately from Russia beyond the border."[91]

The Empress, Catherine I, promulgated a strict ukase which affected all Jews in the border provinces, particularly those residing in Little Russia. ". . . the Jews, both of the male and female sex, who have settled in the Ukraine and in other Russian cities be deported immediately from Russia beyond the border, and in no circumstances be admitted into Russia. . . ."[92]

1734 A.D.

Fugitive peasants and itinerant Zaporozhians, organized and led by Cossack commanders, devastated many Jewish villages in the Province of Kiev, Volhynia, and Podolia. The brutality of the slaughterers matched that of the seventeenth century.[93] (See 1648 ff.)

1736 A.D.

A ritual murder charge in Posen resulted in the arrest of several of the community leaders. Two did not survive the torture of cross-examination. The darshan (preacher), Arie Leib Calahara, had his bones broken while roasting over a fire. An elder, Jacob Perkosevich, was compelled to hold a lamp in his hands to give light to the torturers. The two were taken to their homes covered with wounds and blood and in great pain. They died shortly after. The case was then transferred to a special commission. The remaining persons were sentenced to be burned alive together with the bodies of the preacher and the elder which were to be exhumed for this purpose. (The Polish king intervened and prevented the executions; the prisoners were freed in 1740.)[94]

1738 A.D.

Borukh Leibov (See 1727) who had been banished by Catherine I continued to travel into Russia; in 1738 he converted a retired naval captain. The captain was circumcized and his conversion became known and both were arrested. After prolonged torture they were burned alive on July 15.[95]

The Jewish community of Wurttenberg was expelled.[96]

1739 A.D.

The Russian Senate ordered the expulsion of the Jews who had taken up residence in Little Russia despite the restrictions on them. The war with Turkey postponed this expulsion.[97]

1740 A.D.

Empress Anna of Russia ordered the expulsion of 292 males and 281 female Jews who resided on 130 manorial estates in Little Russia.[98]

1741 A.D.

The Russians wanted to either convert the Jews or expel them. The threat of expulsion was thought of as an incentive for the Jews to embrace the Greek Orthodox faith. Elizabeth Petrovna issued a ukase acknowledging that some Jews were living in the Empire under false pretenses. These were ordered expelled with their property immediately and never permitted to reenter under any circumstances.[99]

1744 A.D.

Empress Maria Theresa banished the Jews from the royal province of Bohemia.[100]

Empress Elizabeth Petrovna issued another ukase demanding immediate steps be taken to detect Jews in Little Russia and Livonia and to expel all except those willing to be baptized.[101]

1745 A.D.

Empress Maria Theresa banished the Jews from the royal province of Moravia.[102]

1747 A.D.

Pope Benedict XIV issued a papal bull that asserted that Jewish children over the age of seven could be baptized against the will of their parents.[103]

193

The discovery of the body of a Christian during the spring thaw in a nearby village was the base of a ritual murder trial in the town of Zaslav in Volhynia. A peasant informed the authorities that the Jews of Zaslav had been praying and feasting the whole night. The Bernardine monks decided that they were celebrating the murder. (In reality, they were celebrating the circumcision of a new-born baby.) The community elders were charged and, under torture, one confessed. The leaders were then executed. Some were impaled on iron poles, others were skinned alive, some had their hearts cut out while alive and others had their hands and feet cut off and nailed to the gallows. An uninterrupted string of ritual murder charges followed the Zaslav case; for the next fifteen years they were an annual occurrence.[104]

1748 A.D.
A ritual murder trial was held in the town of Dinaigrod in Podolia.[105]

1750 A.D.
Cossack irregulars again devastated the towns and villages of Kiev, Volhynia and Podolia. Jews were the special target of the slaughter and pillage.[106] (See 1734.)

1753 A.D.
Twenty-four Jews were arrested for the murder of the peasant boy, Studzienski, in Zlytrovia, Poland. Under torture they confessed to the crime. Eleven were skinned alive and thirteen accepted baptism to avoid execution.[107]

An image of the alleged martyr Studzienski in vivid detail (he was portrayed as covered with pins) was passed through the region by the clergy to intensify the popular hatred against Jews.[108]

Jews were expelled from Kovad, Lithuania.[109]

By 1753, the banishment of Jews from Russia under the impetus of Empress Elizabeth Petrovna had resulted in the expulsion of some 35,000.[110]

A bill to naturalize the Jews of England passed Parliament, but the public outrage and opposition to it caused its repeal.[111]

1757 A.D.
Bishop Nicholas Dembowski of Kamenetz commanded a dispu-

tation between the Frankists and the Talmudists. The Bishop decided for the Frankists and ordered all copies of the Talmud in his diocese brought to Kamenetz and burned. Nearly 1,000 copies were burned.[112]

1759 A.D.

The Canon de Mikulski called a second disputation between the Frankists and the Talmudists in Lemberg. Following the disputation there was a mass baptism of the Frankists.[113]

[The Frankists were a mystical cult growing out of the Sabbatean sect. Sabbatai Zwevi was a major messiah produced by the kabalistic branch of 17th century Judaism. The kabalist movement was a mystical approach to Judaism that downplayed the Torah and Talmud and instead insisted that tradition and the mystical occultist Zohar were the primary source of Judaism. That is, Judaism preceded and produced the Torah and Talmud. Jacob Frank, the founder of the Frankist cult, went the kabalist and Sabbatean movement one better. His mystical and ecstatic services included sexual orgies. Frank maintained that salvation through purity was easy—the real challenge lie in salvation through impurity. The Talmudists, in contrast, were the protectors of the orthodoxy, the codifiers, the learned rabbis. Frank and his followers were excommunicated by the Jewish community in Poland for heresy and licentiousness. The excommunication was prompted largely by the sexual excess of the cult.[114]]

Jews of Lvov (Lemberg) were forced to live in ghettos.[115]

In the town of Voislavitza near Lublin, the community was accused of the murder of a Christian boy for the purpose of mixing his blood in the matzoh flour. Five elders were brought to trial. The rabbi committed suicide while in jail; the other four leaders were sentenced to death by quartering. Before execution, they were offered leniency if they converted to Christianity. The leniency offered turned out to be a change in the method of execution; they were beheaded instead of quartered.[116]

1761 A.D.

Duc de Richelieu ordered all foreign Jews banished from the province of Bordeaux.[117]

In Poland, Jews were expelled from Lublin.[118]

1762 A.D.

During the first year of her reign, Empress Catherine II of Russia issued a manifesto that permitted the immigration of all foreigners except Jews.[119]

1764 A.D.

The Polish Diet, which formulated the new constitution for the reign of King Stanislav Augustus, increased the tax for Jews and modified the method of assessment. Previously, the Jewish communities were assessed a lump sum annually which they apportioned. The new constitution levied a head tax of two gulden on "every Jewish soul" and each community's leaders were held responsible for the accurate collection from each of its members.[120]

The Patriarch of Jerusalem on a visit to Bucharest ordered Prince Alexander Glinka to demolish the synagogue. It was done.[121]

1768 A.D.

A new Cossack rebellion under the leadership of the Zaporozhian Cossack Zheleznyak began in April with the district of Kiev. Again Jews were the special target of the barbarism, and the communities of Lysyanka, Belaya, Tserkov, and Tetyev were brutally massacred.[122]

Later the rebels moved towards Uman where tens of thousands of Poles and Jews had fled. On the first day of the siege, the Poles and Jews fought side by side against the Cossacks. On the second day Mladanovich negotiated with Zheleznyak and exchanged the lives of the Jews for the lives of the Poles. The rebels entered the city and the Jews were murdered in Cossack fashion; the women were first raped before being trampled to death by horses. A crowd of 3,000 were slaughtered one by one in the synagogue. After the Jews were killed, the Cossacks attacked and slaughtered the Poles. In all, over twenty thousand Jews and Poles were killed in the Uman massacre.[123]

While the Uman massacre was taking place, smaller detachments of the rebels were exterminating the Jews in other parts of the Ukraine and Podolia.[124]

1772 A.D.

In 1767 Empress Catherine II, the Great, had established a protectorate over Poland through armed force. In 1772, the Czarina was forced to end the protectorate, and Poland-Lithuania was divided between Russia and the Hohenzollerns and Hapsburg empires. Of this first partition of Poland, Russia acquired only part of Lithuania but, in the process, two thousand Jews. The Czarina issued a manifesto to the new territories on August 16, 1772, which distinguished the Jewish and non-Jewish subjects and specifically limited the territory in which Jews could live. This is regarded as the official establishment of the Jewish Pale of Settlement.[125]

Note:

Prior to the Russian victory over Poland, Russia proper did not have a large Jewish population. Even so, the Russian and Orthodox goal for the Jew was elimination either by conversion or expulsion. Tolerance of separate Jewish communities has never been, to this day, a Russian characteristic. The defeat of Poland and Russia's expansion confronted the Russian rulers with a large and established Jewish community inside Russian borders. In reaction, Czarina Catherine the Great established a territory called the Pale of Settlement. The purpose was to restrict the Jewish population to this area and confine the impact of the Jewish population on Russian society. It was a relatively arid and unproductive area that also served as a buffer zone between Greater Russia and the West. Jews were required to have special permits to travel beyond the Pale.[126]

1773 A.D.

Voltaire, in a letter concerning Spanish-Portuguese Jews in the English colonies, stated the following:

"I know that there are some Jews in the English colonies. These marranos go wherever there is money to be made. . . . But that these circumcised Jews who sell old clothes to the savages claim that they are of the tribe of Naphtali or Isachar is not of the slightest importance. They are, nonetheless, the greatest scoundrels who have ever sullied the face of the globe."[127]

1775 A.D.

A new Polish Constitution was adopted and established a supreme administrative body, the Permanent Council. The constitution also increased the Jewish per capita tax from two to three gulden levied on both male and female and including the new born. In addition, restrictions were placed on Jewish marriages but these provisions were never enforced.[128]

The Jews had traditionally been forbidden to reside in Warsaw and other specific towns in Poland, but some aristocrats permitted Jews, for a fee, to live on their estates just outside the city. Jews who entered the city had to purchase tickets for the privilege. The sale of these tickets brought an annual revenue of 200,000 gulden to the city's treasury. The Jewish settlement outside Warsaw was known as New Jerusalem. On January 22, 1775, the Jews were expelled from around Warsaw and New Jerusalem was demolished. All goods and valuables were confiscated and later sold at public auction.[129]

Pope Pius VI, in a papal bull for the papal states, decreed that Jews living there must listen to conversion sermons to be delivered in the synagogues following the Sabbath services.[130]

1780 A.D.

The Jews living in Russia were driven from the occupations of brewers, distillers and innkeepers which had been three of the few occupations open to them in Russia. In addition, new restrictions were announced affecting trade, handicraft and other professions.[131]

1783 A.D.

Jews were again expelled from Lublin.[132]

1789 A.D.

Mobs attacked the Jews living in Alsace, destroying houses, property and forcing them to flee half naked from the province.[133]

1790 A.D.

The French National Assembly excluded the Jews of France from electoral participation.[134]

In March a crowd of artisans surrounded the town hall in Warsaw and threatened to murder all Jews unless the magistracy expelled them from the city. The Council expelled the Jewish artisans and street venders but allowed Jewish merchants who had stores or warehouses to remain.[135]

1791 A.D.

Catherine the Great decreed that Jews were to enjoy the privilege of citizens and burghers in White Russia only. They could not register as merchants in the towns and seaports of the rest of the Empire. Within the Pale, Jews were taxed double that of Christians.[136]

The French National Assembly abrogated all anti-Jewish laws and in November, Louis XVI proclaimed full equality for the Jews.[137]

1793 A.D.

In France, the revolutionary government declared: "The Catholic faith is annulled and replaced by the worship of reason." In Nancy, the holy writings of the Jews were burned, and services in the synagogue were forbidden. In Strasbourg and Troyes the observance of the Sabbath was forbidden.[138]

1794 A.D.

An Imperial ukase further limited the area of Jewish residence in the Russian Empire and increased the taxation. Jews who refused to remain in the cities were fined a double tax for three years and expelled from the Empire. Jews were forbidden to serve in the military but had to pay a special tax for this privilege.[139]

The first play written by an American and produced in America with a Jewish character was Susanna Haswell Rowsom's *Slaves in Algiers: or a Struggle for Freedom*. The Jew in the play was portrayed as a scoundrel who changed his faith to Mohammedanism when it offered him monetary advantage. He also described

199

himself as a forger and a crook, one who cheated the Gentiles because it was demanded by Moses.[140]

1796 A.D.
Holland granted full equality and citizenship to Jews.[141]

1797 A.D.
In Rome, Jews were required to wear a distinctive badge on their clothing.[142]

1798 A.D.
The first appointment of a Jew to public office in modern Europe occurred in Holland.[143]

CONTINUUM:

The 17th and 18th centuries were periods of decline of massive anti-Semitic outbreaks in Western Europe. There are few incidents of outright slaughter in the West. There were periodic expulsions and the less violent techniques of anti-Semitism were in use and the Inquisition in Spain and Portugal continued to persecute Marranos. The real tragedies, however, occurred in the East—Poland, Lithuania and Russia. The Jews who, fleeing persecution in Western Europe during the Crusade and the Inquisition, had found protection and refuge in the East now were the victims of particularly terrible persecutions and wholesale slaughter. The incredible atrocities of the Cossack and Tartar massacres of Jews are in addition to the tactics and techniques of the past; religious and civil restrictions, discriminatory taxation, economic limitations, confiscation, expulsion, forced conversion, charges of ritual murder and blasphemy, confiscation and distribution of holy writings and scapegoating.

This period did, however, have some positive aspects; in some of the Western countries Jews were granted full equality and rights of citizenship. And as secularism and the democratic and scientific revolutions became the order of the day, it appeared that anti-Semitism might be a dying part of Western tradition. The virulent anti-Semitism of this period does indeed occur in those countries either unaffected by or resisting modernism. And its characterization as a part of the dying feudal and clerical order seems at this time to be in order. This is especially true when the progress toward full citizenship by Jews is most apparent in the most modernized countries. The 19th century, however, destroyed this optimism.

PART VIII: THE 17TH AND 18TH CENTURIES

1. Graetz, op. cit., IV, 670-71.
2. Ibid., p. 673.
3. Durant, W. A. *The Story of Civilization Part VIII, The Age of Louis XIV* (New York: Simon & Schuster, 1963), p. 456.
4. Graetz, op. cit., IV, 688.
5. Ibid., pp. 695-96.
6. Ibid., pp. 697-98.
7. Ibid., p. 699.
8. Ibid.
9. Ibid., pp. 699-700.
10. Ibid., p. 700.
11. Ibid., p. 674.
12. Roth, *The Standard Jewish Encyclopedia*, col. 1128-29.
13. Graetz, op. cit., IV, 675.
14. Ibid., pp. 702-706.
15. Weinryb, Bernard D. *The Jews of Poland* (Philadelphia: Jewish Publication Society of America, 1972), p. 153.
16. Dubnow, op. cit., p. 100.
17. Ibid., pp. 101-102.
18. Ibid., pp. 143-44.
19. Roth, *Standard Jewish Encyclopedia*, col. 1337.
20. Dubnow, op. cit., pp. 100-101.
21. Roth, *Standard Jewish Encyclopedia*, cols. 1929-30.
22. Graetz, op. cit., V, 52.
23. Dubnow, op. cit., p. 145.
24. Ibid.
25. Ibid., pp. 146-47.
26. Ibid.
27. Ibid., pp. 147-48.

28. Ibid., pp. 148-49.
29. Ibid., p. 149.
30. Roth, *Standard Jewish Encyclopedia*, col. 257.
31. Dubnow, op. cit., pp. 149-50.
32. Ibid., pp. 150-51.
33. Ibid., p. 151.
34. Roth, *Standard Jewish Encyclopedia*, cols. 831-32.
35. Glassman, Bernard, *Anti-Semitic Stereotypes Without Jews* (Detroit: Wayne State University Press, 1975), pp. 106-33.
36. Graetz, op. cit., V, 91.
37. Ibid.
38. Ibid., p. 92.
39. Selzer, Michael (ed.), "*Kike!*" (New York: World Publishing, 1972), p. 10.
40. Dubnow, op. cit., pp. 244-45.
41. Ibid., p. 153.
42. Ibid., pp. 153-54.
43. Graetz, op. cit., V, 92.
44. Ibid.
45. Dubnow, op. cit., p. 154.
46. Ibid., p. 155.
47. Roth, *History of the Jew in England*, p. 166; Graetz, op. cit., V, 45-46.
48. Dubnow, op. cit., p. 156.
49. Ibid., p. 162.
50. Ibid., pp. 156-57.
51. Dubnow, op. cit., I, 162-64.
52. Graetz, op. cit., V, 111.
53. Roth, *Standard Jewish Encyclopedia*, col. 737.
54. Dubnow, op. cit., pp. 164-65.
55. Ibid., pp. 161-62.
56. Ibid.
57. Ibid., pp. 245-46.
58. Graetz, op. cit., V, 169.
59. Ibid., pp. 174-76.
60. Ibid., pp. 173-74.
61. Ibid., pp. 169-71.
62. Dubnow, op. cit., pp. 160-61.
63. Ibid.
64. Roth, *Standard Jewish Encyclopedia*, col. 1327.
65. Dubnow, op. cit., pp. 245-46.

66. Roth, *Standard Jewish Encyclopedia,* cols. 1844-45.

67. Dubnow, op. cit., p. 166.

68. Wienryb, op. cit., p. 153.

69. Roth, *The Standard Jewish Encyclopedia*, col. 321; Sachar, op. cit., p. 1.

70. Dubnow, op. cit., p. 166.

71. Roth, *History of the Jews in England*, p. 187.

72. Roth, *Standard Jewish Encyclopedia*, cols. 1929-30.

73. Roth, *History of the Jews in England*, p. 187.

74. Roth, *Standard Jewish Encyclopedia*, col. 1840.

75. Roth, *History of the Jews in England*, p. 188.

76. Max Raisin, *A History of the Jews in Modern Times* (New York: Hebrew Publishing Co., 1949), p. 9.

77. See Solomon Liptzin, *The Jews in American Literature*, (New York: Block Publishing Company, 1966).

78. Roth, *Standard Jewish Encyclopedia*, col. 1226-27.

79. Roth, *History of the Jews in England*, p. 192.

80. Dubnow, op. cit., pp. 169-70.

81. Ibid., pp. 170-71.

82. Roth, Cecil, *History of the Jews in Italy*, p. 386.

83. Dubnow, op. cit., pp. 172-73.

84. Roth, *History of the Jews in Italy*, p. 386.

85. Dubnow, op. cit., pp. 172-73.

86. Ibid., pp. 170-71.

87. Raisin, op. cit., pp. 2-3.

88. Dubnow, op. cit., p. 249.

89. Roth, *The Standard Jewish Encyclopedia*, col. 321.

90. Raisin, op. cit., p. 5.

91. Dubnow, op. cit., p. 249.

92. Ibid., pp. 249-50.

93. Ibid., pp. 182-83.

94. Ibid., pp. 175-76.

95. Ibid., pp. 251-53.

96. Roth, *Standard Jewish Encyclopedia*, col. 1972.

97. Dubnow, op. cit., pp. 253-54.

98. Ibid.

99. Ibid., p. 255.

100. Graetz, op. cit., V, 251-52.

101. Dubnow, op. cit., p. 257.

102. Graetz, op. cit., V, 252.

103. Runes, op. cit., p. 18.

104. Dubnow, op. cit., p. 177.

105. Ibid., p. 178.

106. Ibid., pp. 182-83.

107. Ibid., p. 178.

108. Ibid.

109. Roth, *Standard Jewish Encyclo*|*edia*, col. 1150.

110. Dubnow, op. cit., p. 258.

111. Roth, *History of the Jews in England,* pp. 216-23.

112. Graetz, op. cit., V, 280-82.

113. Ibid., pp. 284-87.

114. Dimont, Max, *The Indestructable Jews* (New York: New American Library, 1971), pp. 299-302; Graetz, op. cit., V, 272-290.

115. Roth, *Standard Jewish Encyclopedia*, col. 1233.

116. Dubnow, op. cit., pp. 178-79.

117. Graetz, op. cit., V, 343.

118. Roth, *Standard Jewish Encyclopedia*, col. 1227.

119. Louis Greenberg, *The Jews in Russia* (London: H. Milford, Oxford University Press, 1944), p. 4.

120. Dubnow, op. cit., p. 181.

121. Runes, op. cit., p. 67.

122. Dubnow, op. cit., pp. 183-84.

123. Ibid., pp. 184-85.

124. Ibid., p. 185.

125. Ibid., p. 307.

126. Manners, Ande, *Poor Cousins* (Greenwich, Conn.: Fawcett Publications, Inc., 1972), pp. 25-26.

127. Hertzberg, Arthur, *The French Enlightenment and the Jews* (New York: Columbia University Press, 1968), pp. 284-85.

128. Dubnow, op. cit., p. 267.

129. Ibid., pp. 268-69.

130. Runes, op. cit., p. 130.

131. Dubnow, op. cit., p. 130.

132. Roth, *Standard Jewish Encyclopedia*, col. 1227.

133. Graetz, op. cit., V, 437.

134. Ibid., p. 442.

135. Dubnow, op. cit., pp. 285-86.

136. Greenberg, op. cit., pp. 8-9.

137. Graetz, op. cit., V, 456.

138. Ibid., pp. 451-52.

139. Dubnow, op. cit., p. 318.

140. Schappes, Morris U. *The Jews in the United States* (New York: Citadel Press, 1958), pp. 44-46.
141. Graetz, op. cit., V, 456.
142. Roth, *Standard Jewish Encyclopedia*, col. 215.
143. Graetz, op. cit., V, 458.

PART IX: THE 19TH CENTURY—1800-1899

BACKGROUND:

In the 19th century, the Industrial Revolution was completed and finance capitalism, European dominance and imperialism were established as the new order. It was a century of significant social, political, economic and technological change. Science, progress and nationalism were the ideological driving forces of this epoch. The forces of superstition and reaction were routed in one confrontation after another. Urbanization replaced rural life. The factory replaced the field; machines replaced muscles. The steam engine, railroad, telegraph, steamship, rifle and howitzer drastically changed the nature of work, the size of the world and the power relationship within and between nations. The 19th century was the European century. Europe owned the world.

The century opened with the Napoleonic Wars which changed the map and politics of Europe. In the wake of Napoleon's rise and fall, popular revolutions occurred in Italy, Spain, Russia, Belgium, Poland, Germany and France during the 1820's and 1830's. A similar flurry of revolutionary activity took place between 1848 and 1850. While many of the revolutions were aborted, they were successful in bringing about the adoption of many reforms.

The 1840's also produced the national unification movements in Germany and Italy. These movements succeeded in the emergence of Italy and Germany as unified countries in the 1870's.

In the course of the century much of Asia, India, Africa and the

Middle-East became colonies of Europe. The politics of this period were dominated by Napoleon, Metternich, Victoria, Gladstone, Disraeli, Bismarck, Mazzini, Garibaldi, Pius IX and Nicholas I. The intellectual and ideological movements influenced and reflected the politics.

Capitalism, democracy and liberalism fought the old order as the middle-class—the bourgeoisie—gained political power either by expanding the old order or by overthrowing it. Privilege and birth fought rear guard actions against the rights of man. Social Darwinism legitimized the barbarism of early capitalism. Socialism developed as a critique and challenge to capitalism. Racial theories of history were developed to explain and justify the white man's burden. Philosophical systems rationalized the order of the world. Spencer, Sumner, Darwin, Marx, Hegel, Gobineau, Comte, DeTocqueville, Carlisle and Gibbon dominated the intellectual life of the period.

During the 19th century, the spread of democratic ideals brought citizenship and full equality to Jews throughout Western Europe. Anti-Jewish legislation and restrictions were repealed in country after country. The major holdout and exception to this trend was Russia.

For a time, during the first half of the century, it seemed that anti-Semitism would disappear as nations became more secular and the last vestiges of feudalism and privilege fell to political liberalism and scientific and economic progress. This optimism was mistaken. Hating the Jew was too much an integral part of western culture and tradition and was not to be exorcised.

The new models for ordering and making sense of the world still needed an explanatory devil. Writers of such divergent persuasions as social Darwinism, capitalism, socialism, conservatism and philosophy of history in turn embraced the old Devil of Christianity—the Jew. A new term, a new justification for hating and persecuting Jews developed in the scientific and secular age of the 19th century—anti-Semitism. The term anti-Semitism was coined by the German, Wilhelm Marr in the 1870's to label anti-Jewish attitudes and behaviors based on racial and pseudo-scientific theories of history and economics.

Anti-Semitic movements and political parties developed and prospered. This was not, however, a dramatic break with the past. The continuous and persistent hatred of the Jew that has existed in Western civilization since the beginning of the Christian era and had been primarily justified on religious or theological grounds, was in a secular, nonreligious age given intellectual respectability compatible with the secular and scientific mindset.

The 19th century bridged both traditions of anti-Semitism. The Mortara Incident (See 1858) was a carry-over of Jew hatred from the age of religious absolutism and the Inquisition. The Dreyfus Affair (see 1894-99) foreshadowed the Jew hatred of anti-Semitism in the 20th century.

ENVIRONMENT: CHRISTIAN

Jewish successes following their emancipation caused resentment on the part of many Christians.

The emancipation of the Jews which gave them full citizenship in many countries did not include the elimination of anti-Semitic attitudes or beliefs.

Religious teachings and beliefs and especially Canon Law still contained and continued the teaching of contempt.

Anti-Semitic stereotypes and images were present in the works of such great writers and thinkers as Voltaire, Fichte, Goethe, Marx, von Treitsche, Engels, Feuerbach, and Twain.

Every means of communication—drama, poetry, fiction, satire, paintings, sculpture, caricature, cartoons, newspapers, pamphlets, essays, folktales, fairytales even nursery rhymes and the wisdom passed from generation to generation as parents shape the mind of the child—include anti-Semitic portraits of Jews, stereotypes and attitudes.

Increased literacy and inexpensive communication allowed spread of anti-Semitism. Religious and "scientific" anti-Semitism combined to pervade all aspects and segments of 19th century life. Whether a person was revolutionary or reactionary, modernist or traditionalist, clerical or anti-clerical, capitalist or socialist, aristocrat or republican, religious or irreligious, the Jew—as a villain, troublemaker, evil, conspirator, culture destroyer, usurer, or subhuman—was available to explain reality that did not fit his expectations.

The scientific age and mindset gave anti-Semitism a new respectability. As religion lost ground to science, anti-Semitism became in part scientific. No longer based solely on religious belief, this new version of anti-Semitism became respectable and acceptable to the modernist.

ENVIRONMENT: JEWISH

Political emancipation freed talents and abilities long repressed. Success created resentment and reaction in form of discrimination and quotas.

Jews who assimilated or converted, became secular or modern still found no acceptance as anti-Semitism added a racial and cultural dimension to its religious base.

Just as a Jewish convert was suspected of insincerity, now his loyalty and patriotism were questioned.

Russia recreated conditions of anxiety and terror similar to the Crusades. Pogroms resulted in attacks, slaughter, pillage and looting with the approval of secular and church authorities.

Contempt, ridicule and indignities could be experienced daily by Jews wherever they lived in the second half of the 19th century. Political emancipation and personal achievement were no defense against modern anti-Semitism.

For the Jew, it had reached a point that no matter what he did, how he behaved, what he believed, anti-Semitism could be a feature of his existence.

INCIDENTS:

1800

"The Jew in the Bush," a story from Grimm's German *Fairy Tales,* had as its main character a cheating, thieving Jew who winds up on the gallows.[1]

Even nursery rhymes turned out to be anti-Semitic. One "Mother Goose" set of verses went as follows:

"Jack sold his egg to a rogue of a Jew,
Who cheated him out of half his due."[2]

German Jews were still required to pay a poll tax when traveling within Germany. This tax was not required in the rest of Western Europe.[3]

In the United States, Jews were barred from holding state and local political offices by provisions in most state constitutions that required office holders to believe in the divinity of Jesus.[4]

1801

In Bucharest, a mob killed 128 Jews and destroyed much of the Jewish quarter. The authorities ordered the synagogues closed and severely restricted Jewish activity.[5]

1804

Czar Alexander I, with the avowed purpose of breaking down the isolation of the Jews and integrating them into the economic and political fabric of the empire, passed a law whose affects were disastrous for the Jews. The provisions of the law pertaining to educational and agricultural opportunities were more liberal than any previous legislation concerning the Russian Jews. But, Article 34 ordered that within three to four years Jews should be prohibited from leasing or managing taverns or inns in villages or thorough-fares or even to reside in the villages. Sixty thousand families (about half a million people) were affected by this provision. This law made no provisions for the absorption of the evicted population and many starved or died of exposure since it was implemented in the middle of winter.[6]

1808

After the Peace of Tilsit established an entente cordiale between Napoleon and Alexander I, the Czar issued an ukase for the expulsion of the Jews from the villages and countryside. It was to be spread over a three-year period: 1/3 in 1808, 1/3 in 1809, and 1/3 in 1810. They were driven like cattle into the cities and left in the open squares. Approximately a half million Jews were affected until disease broke out among the displaced and fear of an epidemic caused the ukase to be canceled in late 1808.[7]

Napoleon issued an imperial decree limiting Jewish economic activities and freedom of movement and abrogated previous privileges some Jewish communities had been granted before his conquest.[8]

1809

Jews were ordered to remove their businesses from the main street of Warsaw within six months. Exception was made for some, such as bankers.[9]

1811

Duchy of Frankfort passed legislation granting equality of citizenship to Jews in return for a payment of 440,000 florins.[10]

1812

During the War of 1812 in Poland, Jews were often more loyal to Russia than Poland. Many Jews who sheltered or aided the Russians were shot or hanged by the French forces.[11]

1814

Denmark granted almost complete emancipation to its Jewish population.[12]

Following Napoleon's defeat, the cities of Lubeck, Bremen, Hanover, Hildeshein, Brunswick and Hesse repealed laws granting rights to the Jews.[13]

1815

Lubeck and Bremen ordered Jewish families to leave.[15]

A German history professor, Friedrick Ruhs, explained Germany's decline and occupation by foreign troops as the result of allowing the Jews to prosper.[15]

Emperor Francis I and Metternick required Jews of Austria to return to the ghettoes.[16]

Pope Pius VII returned to Rome and reinstituted the Inquisition. Jews in the papal states were driven back into ghettoes and stripped of civil rights, liberties and positions granted by the city republics. Conversion sermons were again required and a tradition of forcing the Jews to run the gauntlet among the Corso during the Roman Carnival was established.[17]

211

1819

Imperial ukase ordered that all farm leases were to be taken away from the Jews in Russia.[18]

Anti-Jewish riots, the HEP! HEP! Riots (from the Crusaders—Hierosolyma est Perdita—Jerusalem is lost), occurred in Frankfort, Darmstadt, Bayreuth, Karlsruhe, Dusseldorf, Heidelberg, Wurzburg.[19]

The city of Wurzburg expelled the Jewish community. Similar expulsions occurred throughout the provinces of Franconia, Swabia and Bavaria.[20]

The HEP! HEP! Riots spread to Copenhagen where a mob tore up cobblestones and attacked Jewish houses.[21]

1820

The Russian Duma issued an ukase officially forbidding Jews to have Christian servants.[22]

The Jewish community in Bremen was expelled.[23]

1821

During the Greek War for Liberation, the Turkish janizaries, who were putting down the revolt, killed the Patriarch Gregory. They forced several Jews to throw the Patriarch's body into the sea. The Greeks blamed the Jews for this outrage and in Morea massacred them almost to the last man. The anti-Jewish excesses led to the emigration of thousands from Greece.[24]

Czar Alexander I forbade Jews to enter the interior of Russia even for business purposes.[25]

A mob of townspeople attacked the Jewish community in Odessa. Similar attacks were made against the Odessa Jews in 1859, 1871 and 1881.[26]

1823

Pope Leo XII reestablished the ghetto in Rome, which had been opened by the Napoleonic armies during the occupation of Italy, and ordered the revival of forced conversion sermons on the Sabbath.[27]

In an ukase in April, the Czar forbade the Jews in the provinces of Maghilev and Vitebsk to hold land leases, keep public houses, inns, or saloons. All contracts to the contrary were null and void. He further decreed that Jews were to be removed from the villages and countryside and resettled in the towns and cities by January 1, 1825.[28]

The rise of the Sabbatarian sect* in Russia and its success in attracting converts from Christianity caused considerable alarm in the government and Greek Orthodox hierarchy. The Committee of Ministers, on discovering the existence of the Sabbatarians in the provinces of Vononyezh, Sanator and Tula (where, ironically, there were no Jews), decreed that the preachers of the "Judaizing" sect were to be drafted into military service. Those unfit for service were exiled to Siberia. All Jews were to be expelled from districts where the sect had followers.[29]

1824

The 1823 ukase of Alexander I brought ruin to the Jews. Local authorities enforced the order with enthusiasm and by January over 20,000 Jews had been driven from the villages of the provinces of Maghilev and Vitebsk into the overcrowded towns.[30]

1825

The Czar declared the provinces of Astrokhor and the Caucusus (open to Jews since 1804) closed to the Jews. In addition to the prohibition of residence in the province of Volhynia with a radius of fifty verst from the border was extended to all border areas.[31]

1827

Czar Nicholas I decreed that Jews had a military obligation of twenty-five years. This was to have a Christianizing influence. (The Russian army of the time was not a citizen army; merchants, university graduates and the nobility had no obligation.) Normally military service began at 18 but Jewish boys of 12 and even 9 were impressed into service. Time toward the 25-year obligation did not

---

*Note: The Sabbatarian Sect was a non-Jewish religious movement that incorporated many Jewish religious practices, especially the rigid observance of the Sabbath. It was a puritanical and ascetic sect.[32]

213

count until the youth turned 18. There were some instances where boys as young as five were taken. The children were taken as far from the Pale as possible to minimize desertion. The military guards, in order to pocket the money alloted for transportation, forced the children to make the journey, often lasting 6 months to a year, on foot. There are many accounts of torture and beatings with the aim of converting them to Russian Orthodoxy. Not surprisingly, the conversion rate was high and suicide was not a rarity.[33]

The Czar ordered Jews driven out of the villages in the province of Grodno.[34]

1829
The Jews were forced to move from the villages along the Baltic and Black seas.[35]

1840
Another ritual murder charge was made in Rhodes. A ten-year-old boy hanged himself, and the Christians blamed the Jews. Two Greek women accused a Jew who was arrested and tortured. Red hot coals were placed on his head and a heavy stone on his chest. Finally, he confessed and named several others. They were arrested and tortured but denied the charges. The ghetto was ordered closed and no food was allowed to go in for three days. Widespread mob violence against the Jews followed the accusation.[36]

In the town of Julich in Rhenish Prussia, a nine-year-old girl claimed that a Jew had stabbed her. Her six-year-old brother confirmed her charge. A Jewish family traveling through Julich at the time was charged with the crime and the additional murder of an old Christian. The judicial inquiry found the supposedly murdered Christian to be still alive, the stab wound to be merely smeared blood and the statements to be lies. (The Jews were acquitted, and two Christians were charged with inducing the children to make the accusation.)[37]

1841
Czar Nicholas I ordered the establishment of special Jewish schools. The education of these schools was to weaken the influ-

ence of the Talmud by teaching secular subjects and Jewish religion according to Russian Orthodox interpretation. The covert purpose was to convert the Jews to Russian Orthodoxy. The ukase in addition prohibited attendance at other schools.[38]

1843

An ukase was issued that evicted all Jews from the towns and villages in the frontier along the Prussian and Austrian borders. Thousands of families were displaced.[39]

1844

Karl Marx published *Zur Judenfrage* (On the Jewish Question), an economic and cultural criticism of Jews and Judaism.[40]

"The chimerical nationality of the Jew is the nationality of the merchant, of the moneyed man generally. . . . What is the secular basis of Judaism? Practical need, self-interest. What is the worldly cult of the Jews? Huckstering. What is his worldly god? Money.
. . . Out of its entrails bourgeois society continually creates Jews. . . . Emancipation from huckstering and from money, and consequently from practical, real Judaism, would be the self-emancipation of our era."[41]

1845

Alphonse Toussenel, a French socialist, published *Les Juifs Rois de l'époque* (The Jews Kings of the Time), an anti-Semitic attack on the economic role of the Jews.[42]

1846

Parliament passed legislation removing all disabilities except political exclusion from English Jews.[43]

1848

The revolution in Austria served as a cover for mob attacks on Jewish property in Presburg and Pest. The synagogue in Steinamanger was vandalized and the sacred scrolls were torn and thrown into the river.[44]

In April, during the revolution, the gates of the Roman ghetto were torn down and the Jews liberated. The liberation was short

215

lived however, because Pius IX with the help of French troops reestablished the ghetto and punished the Jews for participating in the revolution.[45]

1850
During the revolution in Hungary, the Jews suffered attacks from both sides. The Slovaks and Serbs attacked the communities under the cover of the revolution, and the Austrians, in their reconquest, assessed the Hungarian community 2,300,000 florins.[46]

Czar Nicholas I abolished state Jewish schools because the purpose of conversion was not being achieved. At the same time he issued a ukase forbidding Jewish form of dress and ritual adornment. The customary dress of the Russian-Jew—the long, black caftan was banned and the earlocks were cut by bands of police armed with scissors.[47]

In New York City, a rumor of ritual murder brought together a crowd of 500 led by three Irish policemen who broke into a synagogue, beat the congregation and wrecked the building.[48]

1851
The revised constitutions of Prussia and Austria included anti-Semitic provisions, that effectively undid the steps toward the emancipation of Jews that were part of the 1848 revolutions.[49]

1855
Comte de Gobineau published his *Essai sur l'inéqalité des Races humaines (Essay on Inequality)* which held that human races were unequal, the Nordic race being most superior. Modern anti-Semitism drew heavily from this racist thesis.[50]

Mobs of townspeople attacked Jewish community in Odessa.[51]

Ernest Renan in his study of Semitic languages states that "science and philosophy were almost foreign to the Semites" and "the Semitic race, compared to the Indo-European, represents in reality an inferior composition of human nature."[52]

1857

A ritual murder trial was conducted in the Russian town of Saratov.[53]

1858

The Edward Mortara incident occurred in the Papal States. In 1852 a Christian servant had baptized the infant Edward Mortara during an illness. When priests learned of this, a military detachment was sent to the Mortara household to take the child from his parents to be raised as a Catholic. The widespread outcry against this action throughout Europe and the United States had no effect on the Pope who threatened the leaders of the Jewish community with retaliatory action.[54]

Romania declared Jews to be native aliens. This meant they were denied the right of citizenship and at the same time were not able to appeal to the protection of any foreign power.[55]

1862

During the Civil War in America, the following order was issued by Ulysses S. Grant's Command Headquarters:

"General Orders,
    No. 11

The Jews, as a class violating every regulation of trade established by the Treasury Department and also department orders, are hereby expelled from the department within twenty-four hours from the receipt of this order.

Post commanders will see that all of this class of people be furnished passes and required to leave, and any one returning after such notification will be arrested and held in confinement until an opportunity occurs of sending them out as prisoners, unless furnished with permit from headquarters.

No passes will be given these people to visit headquarters for the purpose of making personal applications for trade permits.

By order of Maj.-Gen. U. S. Grant.

Jno. A. Rawlins,
Assistant Adjutant-General"[56]

1866

In the city of Galatz in Roumania, city officials designated certain Jews as vagabonds and forced them into a boat for delivery to Turkey across the Danube. The Turks sent them back. They were ferried back and forth until the Romanians ordered "Out with the Jews into the heathen land of the Turks—or else into the water with them!" The Turks sent them back and they were thrown into the river. The Turks rescued them but not before two had drowned.[57]

In Bucharest a mob gathered to prevent the granting of equal citizenship to Jews. Synagogues and sacred writings were desecrated and destroyed.[58]

1867

In Romania, a law was passed forbidding Jews to live in villages or to own inns or taverns.[59]

1868

Hermann Goedsche writing under the pseudonym Sir John Ratcliffe published the novel *Biarritz*. A chapter titled "In the Jewish Cemetery in Prague" described a secret midnight meeting of representatives of the 12 tribes of Israel who received directions from the Devil for the Jewish world domination. Such meetings occurred ostensibly every hundred years.[60]

1869

In Germany, the final emancipation law was passed and Jews received equal citizenship status.[61]

1870

Despite the opposition of Pope Pius IX, the Roman ghetto was formally and finally abolished and Jews were granted equal rights in the kingdom of Italy.[62]

1871

The vicious anti-Semitic pamphlet *Der Talmudjude* (*The Talmud Jew,*) written by Father August Rohling of Prague, one of the

218

founders of modern anti-Semitism, was published. It was widely reprinted and circulated in the Catholic press.[63]

The Jewish community of Odessa was attacked by a mob of townspeople.[64]

1872

The chapter "In the Jewish Cemetery in Prague" was published as a pamphlet in St. Petersburg. The pamphlet included the statement that though the story was fiction it was based on fact. It was reprinted later in Moscow, Odessa, and Prague.[65]

In order to divert attention from the anti-clerical attacks and sentiment of the period, Pope Pius IX made a series of anti-Jewish pronouncements. In the Catholic countries the response to the Pope's action was widespread attacks against the Jews. In France, Jews holding government office were summarily dismissed. In Italy, there was widespread demand that the Jews be disenfranchised. The Catholic press throughout Europe carried on concerted attacks against the Jews.[66]

1873

The term "anti-Semite" was first used. It was coined by Wilhelm Marr. It marked a shift in focus of anti-Jewish thinking. The religious factors were downplayed and the emphasis became one of race and ideology. Marr's pamphlet *Der Sieg des Judentums uber das Germanentum (Jewry's Victory over Teutonism)* published this year set forth the major points of modern anti-Semitism. The pamphlet did not attack Judaism, indeed, it declared that it was idiotic to blame the Jews for the crucifixion. Marr committed himself to the unconditional defense of the Jews against all religious persecution.[67]

Marr saw the Jews as highly gifted and talented, a tough people with endurance and resilience. Their economic function was forced on them by the Church, legal restrictions, and their desire to survive. They were revolutionaries in 1789 and 1848 because they were an oppressed group. However, he saw the German state as dissipated and judaized. The Jews had corrupted all standards, destroyed idealism; they dominated commerce, the state services,

219

the theater and the press. He went on to caution against hating individual Jews. They were a racially determined group and could not change or be changed. To live with them on equal footing, however, was impossible because of their superior qualities.

Marr projected a last desperate counterattack against the Jews, possibly led by Russia. Since popular indignation was rising against the "Semitic-aliens" and the "judaizing of society," the general pogrom was unavoidable and uncontrollable.[68]

1874

A literary magazine, *Die Gartenlaube*, published a series of articles by Otto Glagau on "The Stock Exchange and Speculation Fraud in Berlin." The articles blamed Jewish legislators for passing laws that favored trade, the stock exchange and big business at the expense of farmers and artisans. "Jewry is applied Manchesterism in the extreme. It knows nothing anymore but trade, and of that merely haggling and usury. It does not work but makes others work for it, it haggles and speculates with the manual and mental products of others. Its center is the stock exchange. . . . As an alien tribe it fastens itself on the German people and sucks their marrow. The social question is essentially the Jewish question; everything else is swindle."[69]

1875

The *Kreuzzeitung*, a newspaper identified as the voice of Prussian conservatism and Protestantism, charged that Germany's economic problems were the product of Bismarck's financial adviser and were nothing but a banker's policies made for and by Jews. The article further stated that the Semitic race dominated the National Liberals and therefore the legislature as well as the liberal press. The position of the Jews would not change until the Christian German people recognized the nature of the "Jew policy" carried out by the politically dominant groups.[70]

Germania, the house organ of the Catholic Center Party, picked up and reinforced *Kreuzzeitung*'s charges. It reprinted a speech against Jewish emancipation made by Bismarck in the Prussian Diet in 1847 and used anti-Jewish statements from Goethe, Kant, Herder and Fichte. Attention was called to the underrepresentation

220

of Jews in "productive" occupations and overrepresentation in lucrative businesses and their heavy enrollment, in relation to the population, in higher education. The Kulturkampf (Bismarck's campaign against the Catholic Church) was interpreted by *Germania* as a program of Jewish revenge against Rome for the 1800 years of persecution and as a smokescreen for swindling and exploiting the German people. Christian economic unity was necessary, therefore, to emancipate the Christians from the Jews. "Don't buy from Jews! Don't borrow from Jews!"[71]

1877
Joseph Seligmann, a well-known and respected Jewish businessman, and his family were refused lodging at the Grand Union Hotel in Saratoga Springs, N. Y. solely on the basis of "race."[72]

1877
A Jew was blackballed by the New York City Bar Association, solely because of "race."[73]

1878
A ritual murder trial was conducted in the Russian town of Kutais.[74]

Adolph Stoecker founded the Christian Socialist Workers Party in Germany. It was intended to undermine the support of the Social Democrats. Its appeals included social reformism, state socialism and anti-Semitism.[75]

Despite provisions of the Congress of Berlin which granted Jews equal rights, the Romanian government passed and enforced discriminatory laws. Two hundred laws were passed barring Jews from various trades and professions. They were prohibited from living in the villages and were required to move to the urban ghettos. The terror of possible starvation caused some 125,000 to emigrate to the United States.[76]

1879
Professor Heinrich von Treitschke, the world famous historian at the University of Berlin, attacked the Jews in Germany as disloyal and dangerous to the German civilization.[77]

221

In his collection of essays *Ein Wort uber unser Judentum* (*A Word on Our Jewry*), von Treitschke stated that anti-Semitism was "a natural reaction of the German national feeling against a foreign element which had usurped too large a place in our life."[78]

1880

A new anti-Semitic campaign was launched by the Berlin Movement. Bernhard Forster, Max Liebermann von Sonnenberg, and Ernst Henrici collected signatures for "The Anti-Semites Petition." The petition called for the emancipation of the German people from Jewish domination; a restriction of the civil rights of Jews; limitations on Jewish immigration; exclusion of all Jews from government jobs, especially the judiciary; exclusion of Jews from teaching positions in the primary schools; restrictions on employment of Jews in higher education and the reestablishment of the special census of the Jewish population. The petition, with approximately 250,000 signatures, was submitted to Bismarck in 1881.[79]

By the end of 1880, the dominant theme of public affairs in Berlin was anti-Semitism. "A whole press sprang up which fed it. Anti-Semitic leaflets and libels against everything Jewish or suspect of Jewish sympathies were spread on a large scale; they advocated social and economic ostracism of the Jews and this ostracism was occasionally carried out in a most insulting manner."[80]

In Dresden, the German Reform Party was founded. Its program was borrowed from the Berlin Movement.[81]

1881

Czar Alexander III, who came to the throne after the assassination of Alexander II, instituted policies of reaction and repression. There were enough Jews associated with the liberal and radical movement in Russia that the government made all Jewry its major target of the anti-revolutionary program. The Czar's chief adviser, Pobedonostsev, had a special formula for solving the "Jewish problem": one-third was to emigrate, one-third was to die, and one-third was to disappear (i.e. convert to orthodoxy).[82]

* * *

222

Pobedonostsev was aided in carrying out his pogrom by the *Sacred League,* a secret society of 300 army officers who performed intelligence and agent provocateur activities against the Jews. They were instrumental in organizing the pogroms.[83]

Easter of 1881 marked the beginning of the first great pogrom which spread through southern Russia. A hundred Jewish settlements were attacked; thousands were maimed, murdered and impoverished under the benevolent eyes of the police. The attacks occurred simultaneously and followed a general pattern. The peasants believed they were carrying out the will of the Czar and the government placed the blame on Jewish exploitation of the peasants. Other pogroms occurred throughout the year. The most vicious took place in Warsaw (it was condemned by Polish civic and religious leaders).[84]

The terror and suffering caused by the pogroms resulted in one of the major emigrations of Jewish history.[85]

Jews were permitted to settle in Cuba but were forbidden to hold public worship or build synagogues.[86]

1881

"The origin of the general contempt felt for the Jewish race lies in its absolute inferiority in all intellectual fields. Jews show a lack of any scientific spirit, a feeble grasp of philosophy, an inability to create in mathematics, art, and even music. Fidelity and reverence with respect to anything great and noble are alien to them. Therefore, the race is inferior and depraved. . . . The duty of the Nordic peoples is to exterminate such parasitic races as we exterminate snakes and beasts of prey."

Eugen Duhring
*Die Judenfrage als Rossen-
Setten-, undt Culturfrage*
The Jewish Question as a
problem of Race, Customs
and Culture).[87]

In the town of Neu-Stettin in Germany the synagogue was burned and Jewish stores stoned and looted by the Protestant population.[88]

Bismarck was quoted in a newspaper as saying: "The Jews do all they can to make an anti-Semite out of me."[89]

Bismarck told his Minister of Agriculture: "While he was opposed to anti-Semitic agitation he had done nothing against it because of its courageous stand against the Progressives."[90]

After Berlin Movement rallies, organized bands of anti-Semites roamed the streets shouting "Judenraus," attacked Jews or Jewish-looking people on the streets, and smashed windows of Jewish homes and businesses.[91]

1881

Appearing in a town without a single Jew in it, *L'Anti-Semite de Mindidier* was one of the earliest anti-Semitic French newspapers that helped to prepare the atmosphere that led to the Dreyfus Affair.[92]

1882

In Russia, the Temporary Rules of 1882 (May Laws) provided that: (1) no new Jewish settlements were permitted outside the Shtetlach of the Pale; (2) no Jews were to buy, lease or manage real estate or farms outside the cities of the Pale; and (3) no Jew was to transact business on Sunday or other Christian holiday. (These temporary rules were in effect for thirty-five years.)[93]

At the International Congress of Anti-Semites held in Dresden, Ernst Henrici urged the expulsion of all Jews from Germany.[94]

Ritual murder charges were brought against the entire Jewish community of Tisza-Eslar in Hungary. News of the charges caused bloody riots directed against the Jewish communities in Pressburg and Budapest.[95]

Father E. A. Chabauty published his anti-Semitic *Les Juifs, nos maîtres!* (*The Jews, our Masters!*) held that Christianity and Christian nations were being attacked by a secret Jewish conspiracy whose objective was Jewish rule of the world. This work forecasts the 20th century anti-Semitic hoax, *The Protocols of the Learned Elders of Zion.*[96]

1883

The Austro-Hungarian Reicherath passed legislation that required public school principals to be of the same religion professed by a majority of the pupils in the school. The effect and purpose was to bar Jews from these administrative positions.[97]

1886

The German Anti-Semitic Alliance (Deutsche Anti-semitische Vereinigung) was formed with the unification of the German Reform Party in Leipzig led by Theodor Fritsch and the branch in Kassel led by Otto Boeckel with the remnants of the Berlin Movement. The Alliance worked for the repeal of the emancipation law and urged special legislation that would change the status of German Jews to that of alien.[98]

Edouard-Adolphe Drumont published his *La France Juive*, a violently anti-Semitic work. It gained widespread circulation and contributed to the growth of anti-Semitism in France. Drumont became a leading figure in modern anti-Semitism.[99]

1887

Otto Boechel (see 1886) was elected to the Reichstag on the slogan "Peasants! Free yourself from the Jewish middlemen!" He was the first anti-Semite deputy not to enroll in the Conservative Party. He founded an autonomous anti-Semitic Reichstag group that became a permanent feature of the German Parliament.[100]

Anti-Semitic riots occurred in Slovakia. Jewish communities were attacked by mobs.[101]

1887

Karl Lueger, a leftist politician, made his public conversion to anti-Semitism. In the future, he became the anti-Semitic Lord Mayer of Vienna and a major leader of Austrian anti-Semitism. In *Mein Kampf,* Hitler attributes his anti-Semitism to the influence of Lueger.[102]

1888

A viciously anti-Semitic book, *An American Jew,* was published anonymously in New York.[103]

1889

Max Lieberman von Sonnenberg, a leader of the now defunct Berlin Movement, founded the German Social Anti-Semitic Party

(Deutschsozial Anti-semitische Partei) in Bochun, Westphalia, because he was unable to work out a unified program with Boechel who organized the Anti-Semitic People's Party (Antisemitische Volkspartei).[104]

In Russia, legislation was passed attempting to bar Jews from almost every profession. One law made the admission of a Jew to the bar dependent upon the special permission of the Minister of Justice. During the period between 1889 and 1899 only one Jew was granted this permission. (It should be noted that he had already been a judge for twenty-five years.) A result was that hundreds of young Jews who had completed their legal education at universities or who had acted as assistants to practicing attorneys were prevented from practicing law.[105]

1889

In Austria, a number of ritual murder cases occurred in the provinces of Bohemia and Slovakia. These charges were accompanied by mob attacks on the Jewish communities.[106]

The first Hungarian anti-Semitic newspaper was founded in Pressburg.[107]

1890

Hermann Ahlwardt published his pamphlet *Der Verzweiflungskampf der Arischen Volker mit dem Judentum* (*The Aryan Peoples' Battle of Despair Against Jewry.*) In it he depicted the Jewish monster octopus controlling every phase of German life, army, government, business, education, agriculture. The attempts on the Kaiser's life in 1878 were explained as part of the Jewish conspiracy. This alleged conspiracy had supposedly financially enslaved the ruling class and exploited, abused, and undermined the German nation's health and stability.[108]

Leipzig became the major publication center for anti-Semitic propaganda. It was the headquarters for the German Anti-Semitic Alliance under the leadership of Theodor Fritsch.[109]

In the 1890 elections in Germany, Anti-Semitic parties gathered 48,000 votes and won fives seats in the Reichstag.[110]

1891

A ritual murder charge was made in the town of Xanten in the Rhineland.[111]

1892

The German Conservative Party's platform contained the following statements:

"State and Church are institutions decreed by God; their cooperation is necessary as a prerequisite of our peoples' moral health.

"We consider the denominational Christian grammar school the basis of public education and the most important safeguard against the growing brutalization of the masses and the advancing disintegration of all social life.

"We fight the multifarious and obstrusive Jewish influence that decomposes our people's life. . . ."[112]

Ahlwardt published the pamphlet *Judenflinten* (Jewish Rifle,) which accused the firm of Ludwig Loive of supplying faulty rifles to the Army. It was not a matter of profiteering it stated, but was a plot hatched by the *Alliance Isrealite Universelle,* and high German officials were criminally involved. The public outrage that followed the publication caused an investigation by the German War Ministry. (The investigation concluded that the charges were a figment of Ahlwardt's imagination. The technical deficiencies in the army weapons were not in the Loive rifles which met all specifications.)[113]

1892

Edouard Drumont, the prominent French anti-Semite, founded his newspaper *La Libre Parole,* which he used to continue to popularize anti-Semitism. The paper played an important role in the Dreyfus Affair.[114]

1893

The Bund der Landwirte (Agrarian League) was organized as the political arm of the German peasants. Its program was anti-liberal, anti-Semitic, and anti-labor. It became the most important mass movement on the right and served as a link between the junker and peasant classes. It formed close liaison with the Conservative party.[115]

The 1893 elections in Germany saw the anti-Semitic parties increase their vote to 263,000 votes and capture 16 seats in the Reichstag.[116]

The League of Anti-Semites founded by Wilhelm Marr and the Social Reich Party of Ernst Henrici attempted to build a political organization and movement around anti-Semitism as the single and exclusive principle for political action and the one solution for national problems.[117]

The German Federation of Salaried Commercial Employees (Deutscher Hardlungsgehilfen Verbund) was founded in Hamburg. It was organized to fight the "brutal force" of the Social Democrats who were attempting to unionize the white-collar employees. It accepted only German gentiles and barred from membership the "agents of decomposition, the Jews."[118]

1893

Theodor Fritsch published the *Antisemitem Katchismus (Anti-Semitic Catechism)*; in it the list of charges against the Jews included: (1) usurious dealings with peasants and artisans; (2) unfair business practices that were ruining honest businessmen: (3) destructing handicraft industries and creating wage slaves; (4) forcing wages and prices down to the point that revolution was a constant threat; (5) monopolizing the press and deceiving the people by attacking legitimate authority; (6) degrading national culture with sensationalism and obscenity; (7) committing fraud during financial crash; (8) dominating legislatures; (9) commercializing all values and running the white slave trade; (10) luring and bribing prominent persons; those who resisted were slandered in the Jewish press; (11) through financial operations, dominating all states; "no individual state can dare to take steps against the Jews without being set upon by neighboring states."[119]

1894

In Russia, Alexander III placed the liquor trade under government control at the urging of Witte, the Minister of Finance. The "purpose" was to eliminate "Jewish exploitation." As a result tens of thousands of Jewish families engaged in the liquor trade or operating inns and hostelries were driven out of business.[120]

1894

The French Intelligence acquired by accident the *bordereau,* a secret military document sent by a French officer to the military attaché of the German embassy in Paris. With the sole evidence being only a certain similarity of handwriting, Alfred Dreyfus was arrested on the charge of treason and court-martialed. The trial was a sham. Testimonies were insufficiently verified; secret military documents (some forged) were illegally placed before the tribunal by the ministry of war and Dreyfus' attorney was not informed of this action. Dreyfus was unanimously found guilty of treason and sentenced to life imprisonment.[121]

1895

In Romania, an anti-Semitic League was formed and organized economic boycotts against the Jews.[122]

Karl Lueger, a "Democrat" turned anti-Semite was elected Lord Mayor of Vienna.[123]

1896-1897

Left-wing Senator Auguste Scheurer-Kestner, announced in the Senate that Dreyfus was innocent and Esterhazy guilty. F. J. Méline, the prime minister, tried to prevent action against Esterhazy. The Dreyfus case increasingly became the focus for political and ethnic struggles in French society. Esterhazy was tried and acquitted.[124]

1897

Sporadic pogroms occurred in Russia. In the town of Kantakuzenka the Christian inhabitants wrecked all Jewish stores, destroyed the goods, vandalized houses and attacked the Jews. (Troops were eventually sent and arrested many rioters after the rioting was over. More than 60 peasants were sentenced to prison terms of 8 to 14 months.) A peasant who was sentenced voiced his surprise: "They told us we had permission to beat the Jews, and now it appears that it is all a lie."[125]

As a result of various restrictions on Jewish employment in certain cities of the Pale, the number of Jews without occupations amounted to 50 per cent or more. Destitute Jews who applied for help before the Passover festival in Odessa, Vilna, Korvo, and Mirsh ranged to 40 and even 50 per cent of the total Jewish population.[126]

Anti-Jewish riots occurred in Prague.[127]

1898

Novelist Emile Zola published "J'accuse!" an open letter to the president of the republic, in Georges Clemenceau's newspaper *L'Aurore*. The letter proclaimed Dreyfus' innocence and accused his denouncers of malicious and deliberate libel. Zola instead was found guilty of libel for writing the article.[128]

Anti-Semitic riots broke out in different areas of France. Jews were beaten on the streets and their homes and shops were vandalized and, throughout the riots, defending the Jews was equated with defending Dreyfus.[129]

1898

When Victor Basch took up the Dreyfus cause and demanded a retrial, his house at Rennes was stormed by a mob under the leadership of three priests; Dominican Father Didion called on the students of the College D'Aarcueil to "draw the sword, terrorize, cut off heads . . . run amok."[130]

Officers of the French general staff threatened to resign if Dreyfus was acquitted.[131]

Because of the growing protestations, the new war minister, Cavaignac, reopened the case and re-investigated the documents. Henry's forgeries were discovered and he later committed suicide in a prison cell. The government requested a retrial for Dreyfus.[132]

1899

Houston Stewart Chamberlain published *The Foundations of the Nineteenth Century.* This work carried Gobineau's racial theory to its logical conclusion. It proclaimed Germans the master race and urged a crusade against all Jews, who are portrayed as vicious, and culture destroyers. This work had a major influence on Nazi anti-Semitism.[133]

1899
A pogrom occurred in the city of Nicholayev during the Easter festival and lasted three days. Several thousand rioters attacked the Jewish quarter, beating Jews, looting, pillaging, and destroying the stores and houses. Police and Cossack proved "powerless" to stop the rioting.[134]

Ritual murder charges occurred in Polna in Bohemia; the trial was accompanied by mob attacks on Jewish communities.[135]

1899
The second court-martial decided by a majority that Dreyfus had committed treason, but because of what was termed "extenuating circumstances" he was given a ten-year imprisonment sentence. Anti-Semites saw the verdict as a justification of their positions, while a difference of opinion developed in the pro-Dreyfus group. Many felt that principle was involved and an appeal should be filed. Dreyfus and his family were only concerned with his release; an arrangement was worked out whereby he dropped his appeal and was granted a "pardon" by the president of the republic.[136]

CONTINUUM:

The 19th century was one of considerable progress toward equality and full citizenship for Jews. This tendency was most evident in northern and Protestant Europe. The persecution of Jews during this period was less systematic, pervasive and constant than in previous centuries. Religious pluralism and the rise of religious tolerance in this increasingly secular age is generally given credit for the mildness and decline of persecutions.

While in balance, the 19th century was not as gruesome as others; it should not be seen as representing a new era of brotherly love. The Jews still suffered, particularly in Catholic southern and

231

Orthodox eastern Europe. Here the techniques of religious, social, economic and political restriction, discriminatory taxation, forced conversion, expulsion, ghettoization, plunder and slaughter contributed to a generalized existence of terror goaded by episodic charges of host desecration and ritual murder.

Two of the most infamous cases of anti-Semitism, one representing the past, the Mortara incident, and the other representing the wave of the future, the Dreyfus affair, are products of the 19th century. This period of impressive technological, scientific, political and economic innovation and progress also created the theory of modern or racial anti-Semitism, a theory that makes traditional persecution and hatred of Jews acceptable and respectable to modern and secular man. Whereas previous persecutions and hatred had been legitimized solely by theology, modern persecution and hatred is legitimized by pseudo science and ideology as well.

The racial theories of history first begun by Gobineau and elaborated on by others, defined nations and peoples as racial groups rather than as religious or cultural groups. The logical conclusion of course meant that conversion or assimilation had no affect. This was foreshadowed in the Inquisition's attack on the Spanish and Portuguese Conversos and the future consequence is the Nazi.

PART IX—THE 19TH CENTURY

1. Runes, *War Against the Jews,* pp. 66-67.
2. Ibid.
3. Graetz, op. cit., V, 464.
4. Flannery, op. cit., pp. 248-51.
5. Nathan Ausubel, *Pictorial History of the Jewish Peeple* (New York: Crown Publishing Co., 1953), p. 204.
6. Dubnow, op. cit., p. 346; Greenbery, op. cit., p. 29.
7. Dubnow, op. cit., pp. 346-51.
8. Graetz, op. cit., V, 498-99.
9. Dubnow, op. cit., p. 300.
10. Graetz, op. cit., V, 595.
11. Dubnow, op. cit., pp. 357-58.

12. Raisin, op. cit., p. 5.

13. Graetz, op. cit., V, 511-12.

14. Ibid., p. 520.

15. Ibid.

16. Graetz, op. cit., V, 523.

17. Runes, op. cit., p. 144; Ausubel, op. cit., pp. 198-99.

18. Dubnow, op. cit., pp. 404-405.

19. Graetz, op. cit., V, 529-31.

20. Ibid.

21. Ibid., p. 531.

22. Dubnow, op. cit., p. 404.

23. Roth, *Standard Jewish Encyclopedia,* cols. 353-54.

24. Ausubel, op. cit., p. 208.

25. Greenberg, op. cit., p. 30.

26. Elbogen, Ismar. *A Century of Jewish Life* (Philadelphia: Jewish Publication Society of America, 1954), p. 63.

27. Runes, op. cit., p. 45.

28. Dubnow, op. cit., p. 406.

29. Ibid., p. 402.

30. Ibid., p. 406.

31. Greenberg, op. cit., p. 30.

32. Dubnow, op. cit., I, 401-403.

33. Greenberg, op. cit., pp. 48-51.

34. Ausubel, op. cit., p. 231.

35. Ibid.

36. Graetz, op. cit., V, 641-42.

37. Ibid.

38. Greenberg, op. cit., p. 37.

39. Ibid.

40. Though Marx was not an anti-Semite, his writings can and have been interpreted as anti-Semitic. His writings have been used by genuine anti-Semites to add weight to their position.

41. Bottomore, T. B. (trans. & ed.) *Karl Marx: Early Writings.* (New York: McGraw-Hill Book Company, 1964), pp. 1-40.

42. Flannery, op. cit., p. 176.

43. Roth, *History of the Jews in England,* p. 256.

44. Ismar Elbogen, *A Century of Jewish Life* (trans. Moses Hudes; Philadelphia: Jewish Publication Society of America, 1945), p. 25.

45. Ibid., pp. 29-31.

46. Ibid, pp. 26-27.

47. Manners, op. cit., p. 18.

233

48. Selzer, op. cit., pp. 18-19.

49. Adler, H. G., *The Jews in Germany.* (Notre Dame: Notre Dame University Press, 1961) pp. 67-68.

50. Sachar, Howard Morley, *The Course of Modern Jewish History* (New York: Dell Publishing Co., Inc. 1958), p. 253.

51. Roth, *Standard Jewish Encyclopedia,* cols. 1444-45.

52. Israel Pocket Library, *Anti-Semitism.* p. 181.

53. Flannery, op. cit., p. 172.

54. Graetz, op. cit., V, 701-702.

55. Elbogen, op. cit., p. 69.

56. Selzer, op. cit., pp. 25-26.

57. Ausubal, op. cit., pp. 204-205.

58. Elbogen, op. cit., pp. 69-70.

59. Ibid., p. 70.

60. Norman Cohn, *Warrant for Genocide* (New York: Harper & Row Publishers, 1966), pp. 33-36.

61. Paul W. Massing, *Rehearsal for Destruction* (New York: Harper Brothers, 1949), p. 3.

62. Runes, op. cit., p. 144.

63. Raisin, op. cit., pp. 38-39.

64. Elbogen, op. cit., p. 63.

65. Cohn, op. cit., p. 36.

66. Ibid., p. 39.

67. Massing, op. cit., pp. 6-9.

68. Ibid., pp. 6-8.

69. Ibid., pp. 10-11.

70. Ibid., p. 14.

71. Ibid., pp. 14-15.

72. Flannery, op. cit., p. 252.

73. McWilliams, op. cit., p. 4.

74. Israel Pocket Library, *Anti-Semitism,* p. 82.

75. Massing, op. cit., pp. 29-30.

76. Ausubel, op. cit., p. 205.

77. Raisin, op. cit., p. 44.

78. McWilliams, op. cit., p. 104; Massing, op. cit., pp. 75-77.

79. Massing, op. cit., pp. 39-40.

80. Ibid., p. 40.

81. Ibid., p. 87.

82. Flannery, op. cit., pp. 189-90.

83. Manners, op. cit., pp. 23-24.

84. Flannery, op. cit., 189-90.

234

85. Ibid.

86. Ausubel, op. cit., p. 213.

87. "Anti-Semitic Political Parties and Organizations," *Encyclopaedia Judaica* (New York: Macmillan Company, 1971), col. 84.

88. Massing, op. cit., p. 108.

89. Ibid., p. 42.

90. Ibid.

91. Ibid., p. 40.

92. Cohn, op. cit., p. 50.

93. Dubnow, op. cit., pp. 24-25.

94. Massing, op. cit., p. 107.

95. Raisin, op. cit., p. 53.

96. Cohn, op. cit., p. 45-47.

97. Raisin, op. cit., p. 51.

98. Massing, op. cit., p. 87.

99. Cohn, op. cit., p. 51.

100. Massing, op. cit., p. 88.

101. Roth, *Standard Jewish Encyclopedia,* col. 1731.

102. Pulzer, Peter G. *The Rise of Political Anti-Semitism in Germany.* (New York: John Wiley & Sons, Inc., 1964) pp. 168-69; 341.

103. Selzer, op. cit., pp. 45-113.

104. Massing, op. cit., p. 91.

105. Dubnow, op. cit., pp. 26-27.

106. Ausubel, op. cit., p. 177.

107. Roth, *Standard Jewish Encyclopedia,* col. 1731.

108. Massing, op. cit., pp. 92-93.

109. Ibid., p. 91.

110. Ibid., pp. 71; 91.

111. Massing, op. cit., p. 108.

112. Ibid., p. 66.

113. Ibid., pp. 93-94.

114. Flannery, op. cit., pp. 183-89.

115. Massing, op. cit., pp. 67-68.

116. Ibid., p. 71.

117. Ibid., p. 85.

118. Ibid., pp. 137-38.

119. Ibid., pp. 77-78.

120. Dubnow, op. cit., pp. 22-23.

121. Hannah Arendt, *The Origins of Totalitarianism* (New York: Harcourt, Brace & World, Inc., 1966), pp. 89-123; Flannery, op. cit., pp. 183-89; Elbogen, op. cit., pp. 181-90.

235

122. Flannery, op. cit., p. 193.

123. Elbogen, op. cit., pp. 170-71.

124. Howard Morley Sachar, *The Course of Modern Jewish History* (New York: Dell Publishing Co., Inc., 1958), pp. 230-33.

125. Dubnow, op. cit., III, 33-34.

126. Ibid., pp. 23-24.

127. Raisin, op. cit., p. 52.

128. Flannery, op. cit., pp. 184-85.

129. Elbogen, op. cit., pp. 181-90; Arendt, op. cit., pp. 106-13.

130. Arendt, op. cit., p. 102.

131. Israel Pocket Library, *Anti-Semitism.* p. 193.

132. Elbogen, op. cit., pp. 188-89.

133. Ibid. p. 167.

134. Raisin, op. cit., pp. 52-53.

135. Chapman, Guy. *The Dreyfus Case.* (New York: Reynal and Company, 1955.), pp. 300-320.

PART X: THE TWENTIETH CENTURY—1900-1970

BACKGROUND:

The 20th century is, more than any other, the century of anti-Semitism. The historical patterns are quite clear; anti-Semitism correlates in its incidents and savagery with social dislocation, tension and change. In the 20th century change swept and wrecked the economic, social and political patterns of the whole world. The old order under attack since the 17th century was swept away.

The traditional institutions that had provided some underlying stability for change in the past were themselves under attack. Some were destroyed by the attack; others collapsed from internal decay. The crown, the church and the family were replaced by nationalism, science and psychology. In the 20th century the work of Freud, Darwin, Marx and Einstein supplemented by Ford, Edison, Lenin, Nietzche and von Braun undercut virtually all that had previously passed as natural, the truth or civilization.

This century has correctly been tagged as the century of nationalism and the century of total war; the two labels are symbiotic. Both feed off and nourish the other. The two world wars drew and redrew the political geography of the globe. Nationalism continues the job of cartography.

Economic progress and chaos in league with technological advance and complexity created and destroyed fortunes and whole

237

classes and continues in this enterprise. Capitalism triumphed and was challenged by socialism. Bolshevism checked both. Fascism, in turn, threatened everything during its brief moment.

The racism and reactionary developments of the latter 19th century coupled with the nationalist fervor of the 20th. Chauvinism and xenophobia are exaggerations of nationalism. The white man's burden, white supremacy and anti-Semitism usually appear wrapped in a flag. Mystical nationalism based on blood and soil myths once again cast the Jews in the role of alien.

The political, economic, and social dislocations that typify this century demanded an explanation. In 1903, a publication appeared that provided that explanation—*The Protocols of the Learned Elders of Zion.* This forgery was devised by the Czarist secret police to justify their pogroms against the Jews. It had effect far beyond the Czarist pogroms. This is basically the old myth of the international Jewish conspiracy of the period of the Black Death in modern secular form. It has been characterized as the *Warrant for Genocide.* It was part of the gospel of Nazism and became a best seller. The *Protocols* was and is widely believed despite its patent absurdity.

The readjustments and changes that followed World War I created tremendous insecurity and anxiety. One of the attractions of fascism is its promise of order and stability within a revolutionary framework. Fascist movements thrived and succeeded during this period and its most insane manifestation, Nazism, came to dominate as the Nazis gained control of Germany and later most of Europe either by alliance or conquest. While all fascism includes romantic blood and soil and racial myths, for Nazism this was the dominant feature. The concept of the Aryan uber mensche was complimented by the Semitic unter mensche. Nazi anti-Semitism combined pell-mell the religious and racial varieties and came to overshadow all other features, policies and goals of the Third Reich. This is evidenced by the sacrifice of rational military needs, while losing a major war, to the requirements of the Final Solution.

The twelve-year period of Nazi power, especially the last six years of their regime, was the most precarious period in Jewish history. In contrast to other periods of anti-Semitic excesses, such

238

as the Crusades and the Black Death, no havens were available and virtually no escape was possible for Jews under Nazi control. The very survival of Jews was never more seriously threatened than during this period. If the Axis powers had been successful in their push for world domination, as appeared quite likely in 1942, the Final Solution would have been more final and horrible than it was. Given the single-minded anti-Semitism of the Nazis and Nazi domination of the Axis (seen in the adoption of Nazi anti-Semitic policy by the Italian Fascists) had the Allies lost World War II, there is no doubt that the world today would be Judenrein.

An effect of both world wars and nationalism was the establishment of the state of Israel. It was a hope that this event would at last bring an end to anti-Semitism. This did not occur. Instead anti-Semitism became virulent in the Islamic world. Arab nationalism and resentment turned on Israel and a people *relatively* free of anti-Semitism throughout history began to match the Nazis in anti-Semitic rhetoric and behavior.* Anti-Semitism as state policy also continued in Communist bloc countries. And while Western countries no longer had it as state policy, private anti-Semitism and anti-Semitic movements continue to exist to the present. Jewish communities periodically experience worldwide waves of swastika daubings, synagogue and cemetery desecrations and bombings. Anti-Semitic beliefs, myths and stereotypes continue to persist and be held by many.

ENVIRONMENT: CHRISTIAN

Anti-Semitism permeated the Western world. The anti-Semitic cultural tradition perpetuated over centuries by religious teachings and beliefs—Catholic, Orthodox and Protestant—expanded in scope by the racial anti-Semitism of the 19th century had its greatest impact in the 20th century.

The reputation of the Jew as one holding unappealing and

---

*See pp. 367-387 for a fuller discussion of anti-Semitism in the Islamic/Arab world, and pp. 350-363 for an analysis of Israel as a necessary refuge from and counter to anti-Semitism.

unacceptable characteristics remained vital and secure in, and was easily perpetuated by, much of the Western mind. It was supported in no small measure by its reflection in the arts, social sciences, secular and religious education, conventional attitudes, language, the media, etc.—transmitting agencies that had often (sometimes unconsciously) inherited and absorbed, and received justification of, the reputation, from their own related traditions and from the traditions of the communities in which they had participated.

The *Protocols of the Learned Elders of Zion* were a major contributor to the widespread anti-Semitism of this century. This popularized the myth of the international Jewish conspiracy and blamed Jewish machinations for every evil.

The Dreyfus affair of the preceding century was followed by the Beilis case in Russia (see 1911) and the Leo Frank case in the United States (see 1915).

Anti-Semitic and fascist movements gained political power in some countries and exerted considerable influence in others such as the Ku Klux Klan in the United States.

Anti-Semitic beliefs, attitudes, myths and stereotypes were widely shared. Hating the Jew was never more popular or pervasive.

The speed with which the *Protocols of the Learned Elders of Zion* became a best seller and widely accepted as truth indicates the predisposition to anti-Semitism in the culture of the West.

ENVIRONMENT: JEWISH

Anti-Semitism was so pervasive that Jews living anywhere outside the Far East were affected by it.

Mob attacks, pogroms, expulsions, economic and political restrictions, pillage and slaughter plus the minor indignities of discrimination, social ostracism, insults and racial slurs combined to shape the experience of Jews in this century.

This intensive anti-Semitism increased Jewish support for the Zionist movement.

The disclosure of the Holocaust, the systematic murder of nearly 6 million Jews that culminated the Nazi Reign of Terror created non-Jewish support for the establishment of a Jewish state.

Anti-Semitism survived the defeat of the Nazis but Israel provides a homeland and assures the survival of the Jewish cultural tradition. The existence of Israel removes the one condition associated with anti-Semitism and part of the Jewish experience since 70 A.D.; the Jew is no longer a permanent alien. With Israel he has a homeland and if persecuted a haven by right rather than privilege.

INCIDENTS:

1900

Charges of ritual murder in Konitz, West Prussia, caused a riot. The Prussian government declared martial law and sent troops to restore order.[1]

In Vilna, a Polish servant girl accused her employer, David Blondes, who was a barber, of wounding her and trying to use her blood for the Passover Matzoh. A Christian crowd seized Blondes, beat him and threw him into prison. The anti-Semitic press launched a campaign to influence the trial. The court found Blondes guilty of assault but denied any murderous intent and sentenced him to four months in prison. *The case was ordered retried on appeal and the District Court of Vilna returned a verdict of not guilty and Blondes was freed.*[2]

Four thousand Jews emigrated from Romania to escape that country's continued persecution. They formed into three groups, "The Wandering Jews," "The Despairing," and "The Walkers," and traveled on foot from Moldavia to the port city of Hamburg. Aided by Jewish relief organizations they emigrated to the U.S. Their malnourished and ragged appearance aroused compassion and indignation wherever they went.[3]

1902

Against a background of widespread pogroms a unique event occurred in the Polish city of Chersteklov. Following an argument between a Jewish tradesman and a Polish woman a crowd of 15,000 Poles urged on by Catholic priests attacked Jewish shops

241

and houses. The pillage and assaults were accompanied by shouts of "Beat the Jews! Nothing will happen to us!" *The Russian authorities, however, reacted in an uncharacteristic manner. Soldiers fired a volley into the crowd and dispersed it. The public prosecutor urged severe punishment of the Poles. Many were sentenced to hard labor or prison terms and, in some cases, damages were awarded to the Jewish victims.* [4]

In New York City, during the funeral procession for Rabbi Jacob Joseph, the workers in a printing press factory threw hot metal, slag, and refuse down onto the marchers. A riot occurred and many Jews were injured by police clubs and the thrown metal. [5]

1902

In the White Russian town of Homel a pogrom followed a marketplace fight between Jews and Christians in which a peasant was killed. A crowd of 200 workmen began to demolish Jewish homes and synagogues. The crowd grew in size and was met in a square by several hundred Jews who were determined to stop the destruction. Soldiers arrived as the two groups faced each other and fired into the Jews killing three and wounding several more. The army protected the rioters against Jewish attacks for the rest of the pogrom. [8]

In Kiev, which was surrounded by a large Jewish population and had a number of "privileged" Jews in its permanent population, there was a great fear of invasion by "aliens" (Jews). In response to the fear, the police regularly raided hostelries to pick up Jews who were visiting Kiev to transact business. Those arrested were expelled from the city. This extra "night work" meant expanded police expenditures and an annual appropriation of 15,000 rubles was diverted from the Jewish meat tax. This tax was originally intended to maintain the charitable and educational institutions of the Jewish communities. [9]

1903

A shortened version of the *Protocols of the Learned Elders of Zion* was published by Pavolackai Krushevan in his St. Petersburg newspaper *Znamya* in August and September. [6]

The Czarist government, which interpreted the growing revolutionary movement in Russia as primarily a Jewish phenomena, organized the great pogrom at Kishinev. This pogrom surpassed previous pogroms in barbarism and lasted three days before orders came from St. Petersburg to end it. Forty-five Jews were murdered, hundreds were brutally beaten, and Jewish property and places of worship were pillaged.[7]

1904

The League of the Russian People (The Black Hundreds) was organized to combat constitutionalism and Jews. This group became synonomous with assassinations and pogroms and had the blessings and encouragement of Czar Nicholas II.[10]

1904

The regular pogroms of this year were complimented with the "mobilization" pogroms. Reserve troops mobilized for duty in Manchuria directed their hostility and anger at the Jews. Drunken soldiers accompanied by street mobs destroyed and looted Jewish homes and beat Jewish inhabitants. Many victims of these pogroms were families of Jewish reservists who had been activated.[11]

In the city of Alexandria in the province of Kherson, a mob invaded the synagogue on Yom Kippur and murdered 200 worshippers, wounded many others, and proceeded to loot and vandalize the Jewish quarter. The police made no attempt to interfere until the second day when the Cossacks summoned from an adjacent garrison restored order.[12]

Pogroms were carried out in Kiev and Volhynia.[13]

Jews were barred from resorts and spas within the Pale.[14]

1905

Following "Bloody Sunday" in January, widespread political strikes and demonstrations were called. Workingmen and students called for revolutionary action. The predominance of Jewish youth in the movement was seized by the Black Hundreds for their terroristic reactions.[15]

In the Volynian city of Zhitomir, the Black Hundreds rumored that Jews had been arming themselves and firing at the Czar's portrait in a field outside the city in preparation for the slaughtering of Christians. Between April 23-26, a battle between the Jews and the Black Hundreds assisted by soldiers and police occurred. Fifteen Jews were killed and hundreds were wounded. A Christian student who stood up for the Jews was beaten to death by the mob.[16]

Fourteen Jewish students from the town of Chudnov tried to go to the aid of the Jews of Zhitomir. As they passed through Troyanov, peasants and workers alerted by rumors that Jewish slaughterers were on the march, attacked the youths. Ten were savagely killed (disemboweled and beheaded) and the others were severely beaten.[17]

S. A. Nilus included the complete text of the *Protocols* as part of the third edition of his book *The Great in the Small* published at the imperial residence outside St. Petersburg, Tsarkow Selo.[18]

In Simferopol, the Black Hundreds spread a rumor that a Jewish boy had desecrated a Christian ikon. The pogrom that followed was checked by Jewish resistance and troops who acted to stop the violence.[19]

During the Passover season pogroms were openly organized by the Black Hundreds and occurred throughout the Pale. In the city of Bialystok the Cossacks openly participated. Homes, shops and synagogues were pillaged and looted. Jews were beaten and robbed.[20]

1905

After the defeat of the Russians by the Japanese in Manchuria the Black Hundreds convinced the soldiers that the cause of defeat was the enemy within, the Jews. Soldiers and Cossacks, bitter at their defeat, attacked the Jewish populations in the cities of Minsk, Brest-Litovsk, Syedletz, and Lodz and Bialystok. In Bialystok alone over 50 Jews were shot dead in the streets by the enraged soldiery.[21]

In the Crimean city of Kerch, a patriotic demonstration carrying a portrait of the Czar and singing the Russian national anthem sacked Jewish houses and stores and looted Jewish property. When armed Jews opposed the rioters, ten were killed on the spot by soldiers protecting the demonstrators.[22]

In one week in October, 670 pogroms were carried out; they were preceded by anti-Semitic pamphlets that were printed in government printing offices. Hundreds of Jews were murdered,

thousands were beaten, and tens of thousands were left homeless
by the destruction of the Jewish quarters.[23]

1906

The anti-Semitism in Czarist Russia reached a high point. The
Duma condemned the pogrom of 1906 and it was dissolved.
Pogroms continued and anti-Jewish restrictions were tightened.[24]

From October, 1905, to the end of 1906, pogroms were a
constant feature of the Russian Jews' existence. This period of
terror saw the Jewish quarters or settlements in 661 towns destroyed, 958 Jews murdered and thousands beaten, raped or
orphaned.[25]

1906

G. Butmi published his version of the *Protocols, The Enemies of
the Human Race* at St. Petersburg. Four editions were published in
two years.[26]

1908

The Pan-German League (Alldeutscher Verbund) openly embraced anti-Semitism and elected Heinrich Class, a leading anti-
Semite, as leader.[27]

New York City Police Commissioner Theodore A Bingham
published an article stating that Jews make up 50% of New York's
criminal class while only constituting 23% of the total population.
Commissioner Bingham later retracted his statement. (The actual
statistics show Jews comprising only 16% of convicted felons and
6% of "criminal class.")[28]

1911

The Jew and Modern Capitalism by Werner Sombart argued
that Judaism and capitalism were basically synonymous. In dealing with the "special" characteristics of the Jews that made this
possible, it stated:

> "Intellectual interests and intellectual skill are more strongly
> developed in him than physical (manual) powers. . . . The Jew
> lacks the quality of instinctive understanding; he responds less
> to feeling than to intellect. . . . Akin to this characteristic is that
> of a certain lack of impressionability, a certain lack of receptive

245

and creative genius . . . he has lost the true conception of the personal side of life . . . one finds among Jews an extraordinary knowledge of men . . . he will look at the world from the point of view of end, or goal, or purpose. . . . These four elements, intellectuality, teleology, energy, and mobility, are the corner-stones of Jewish character . . . two which are of special import in economic life—extreme activity and adaptability.''[29]

1911

The discovery of a murdered Russian boy in Kiev was seized by the League of the Russian People (The Black Hundreds) to organize pogroms against the Jews on the charge of ritual murder. Minister of the Interior Stolypin ordered the Kiev prosecutor to take the League's charges and make a case. Mendel Beilis, the manager of a brick factory and a Jew, was charged with ritual murder. This case became the Russian ''Dreyfus Affair.'' Despite threats and torture Beilis maintained his innocence. Leading jurists, newspapers and intellectuals came to his defense. The trial was accompanied by street demonstrations and repeated mob attacks on Jews and Jewish houses and establishments. After two years, Beilis was acquitted.[30]

1914

When Russia entered World War I, the ''Temporary Laws'' against the Jews were abolished. Many Jews enlisted to fight for Holy Mother Russia. Almost at once they were suspected of pro-German sentiments and accused of espionage and treachery. Consequently Jewish soldiers were systematically arrested and deported to Siberia. When the demoralized Russian forces retreated they vented their frustrations by pogroms against the Jewish settlements they passed through.[31]

1915

Leo Frank, a manager of the National Pencil Company in Georgia, was accused of murdering a 14-year-old girl. He pleaded innocent but was convicted and sentenced to hang. The trial caused high emotions pro and con throughout the country. During the trial populist leader, Tom Watson, in his publication the *Jeffersonian*

Magazine, called Frank the ''lecherous Jew . . ., the lascivious pervert guilty of the crime that caused the almighty to blast the Cities of the Plain.'' He also stated ''every student of sociology knows that the black man's lust after the white woman is not much fiercer than the lust of the licentious Jew for the Gentile.''[32]

When the Governor of Georgia on the last day of his term of office signed a commutation order changing Frank's sentence to life imprisonment he was attacked by a mob which threatened his life and forced him out of the state.[33]

After the commutation, Watson wrote: ''The next Leo Frank case in Georgia will never reach the court house. The next Jew who does what Frank did is going to get exactly the same thing that we give to Negro rapists.''[34]

On August 16, 25 men entered the State Prison Farm and lynched Leo Frank; no attempt was made to find the lynchers.[35]

Grand Duke Sergei, Commander-in-Chief of Russia's military, decreed Jews living in the Pale could not be trusted in territory occupied by the German army. As a result 600,000 Jews were forcibly relocated to interior Russia. Jewish homes and establishments were looted and burned while the inhabitants were rounded up and shipped to the interior. Approximately 100,000 Jews died from exposure or starvation during the relocation.[36]

1917

During the October Revolution in Russia, mass pogroms were organized and conducted by the Ukranians and the Whites. In the Ukraine 200,000 Jews were massacred; 300,000 children were left homeless and orphaned.[37]

During the Revolution and the ensuing civil war, pogroms were a continuous event in the life of Russian Jews.[38]

In the civil war, Jews were accused by each side as being members of the opposing forces. They suffered more from the Whites, however, who fought Jews as strenuously as they did Reds. Lenin outlawed pogroms, but there were instances of Red army pogroms. Lenin's policy and the generally good treatment Jews received from the Reds only further embittered the White forces and the anti-Semites had further ''proof'' of the ''Redness'' of the Jews. In the Ukraine, General Denikin put to the sword

247

orthodox Jews to whom Bolshevism was a godless abomination with the fervor he showed the Bolsheviks. In the massacre of the Jews, the White soldiers used swords and bayonets to conserve ammunition and literally butchered Jews in the street-by-street sweeps of the Jewish communities. It was considered a mercy to be killed outright instead of being gradually tortured to death. Parents were forced to watch the torture of the children and children the torture of their parents. Jewish women were subjected to gross obscenities and mutilation before they were killed.[39]

Protocols of the Learned Elders of Zion was published in England.[40]

1917-18
When Germany began to lose the war, anti-Semitic organizations terrorized the Jewish communities in Berlin and Munich.[41]

1918-1920
During World War I, the manual used by medical advisory boards in the U.S. contained the following statement concerning the selection of army personnel: ''The foreign born, especially the Jews, are more apt to malinger than the native born.''[42]

1919
A series of anti-Jewish riots occurred in Prague; Jewish stores and factories were looted and vandalized.[43]

Ukrainian guerrilla forces conducted over 493 pogroms and murdered over 70,000 Jews during the civil war in 1919. The Jewish populations in the towns of Novo Mirgorod, Ovruch, Berdichev, Zhitomir, Uman and Proscurov were particularly hard hit.[44]

When the White Russian forces under General Deniken defeated the Bolshevik and Petlurist armies in the last half of 1919 and occupied the Ukraine, Deniken's soldiers slaughtered at least 50,000 Jewish men, women and children.[45]

1919
Anti-Jewish riots occurred throughout Bavaria. When the Munich Soviet was crushed, all foreign-born Jews were expelled from Bavaria.[46]

In Poland, a major pogrom took place in Lemberg.[47]

1920

Anti-Semitic pogroms swept Hungary. Many Jews were killed or tortured. The bodies of the victims were thrown into the Danube.[48]

Gottfried zer Beek (Ludwig Muller) published the *Protocols* in Germany. There were six editions in 1920. Muller's version became the official Nazi version in 1929.[49]

Hungary established a quota system for universities. The "numerous clausus" law gave Magyar students from former Hungarian provinces priority over Jews in admission to universities.[50]

During the twenties there were 150 recorded pogroms in Poland. A speciality of the Polish pogroms was the forcible cutting off or pulling out of Jewish beards.[51]

In 1920, the Protocols were also published for the first time in France, the United States and Poland.[52]

In May, Henry Ford's Dearborn Independent began publication of a series of anti-Semitic articles mostly from *The Protocols of the Learned Elders of Zion* and *The International Jew.*[53]

1920

Widespread anti-Semitic sentiments found their expression in the "Return to Normalcy." The most obvious indication was the revived Ku Klux Klan that made anti-Semitism a major appeal. Less obvious but probably of greater consequence were the restrictive covenants among real estate owners and agencies that closed large areas of the cities and most suburbs to persons of "Hebrew descent."[54]

In the aftermath of the unsuccessful Kapp putsch, anti-Jewish riots occurred in Munich and Breslau.[55]

Articles IV of the 1920 Nazi programme guaranteed freedom of religion as long as it didn't threaten the morale of the German race or the existence of the state.[56]

The party also committed itself to combating Jewish materialism.[57]

On August 13th, Hitler made his first important speech against the Jews. In it he urged taking away all rights from the Jews and called on the German people to develop a mass instinct against the Jews.[58]

1921

The Story of the Ku Klux Klan, a pro-Klan book by Winfield Jones, quoted William J. Simmons (who revived the Klan in 1915) as saying, "We are not anti-Jewish; any Jew who can subscribe to the tenets of the Christian religion can get in."[59]

1921

It is estimated that over 250,000 Jewish civilians—men, women and children—died in Russia between 1915 and 1921. They were murdered in pogroms or died of starvation or exposure.[60]

Between 1881 and 1914, approximately 1,450,000 Jews had immigrated to the U. S. In an effort to stem Southern and Eastern European immigration to the United States, President Harding called a special session of Congress to rewrite the immigration laws. The resulting legislation limited immigration by nationality per year to 3 percent of the number of that nationality in the U. S. as of the 1910 census.[61]

1922

A. Lawrence Lowell, President of Harvard, called for a quota system of Jewish admission to relieve university overcrowding. The trustees defeated the quota plan but an unofficial quota was adopted and spread to many colleges, universities and professional schools.[62]

During the communization of the Soviet economy, 2,500,000 Russian Jews, mostly middlemen—a role mostly imposed upon them—were dislocated. Approximately 400,000 found employment in the Soviet Bureaucracy, and another 750,000 went to work in the factories. The rest suffered severe impoverishment and relocation difficulties.[63]

When the Soviet government attempted to expropriate the gold from churches, peasants, in the region of Smolensk, declared that if the gold were taken "not one Jew will survive, we will kill them during the night." Bands of women and youths roamed the streets

250

and beat any Jews they encountered. Their slogan was "Beat the Jews! Save Russia!"[64]

Walter Rathenau, Foreign Minister of the Weimar Republic was assassinated by an anti-Semitic gang.[65]

Many Jews moved into the semi-private enterprises that grew out of Lenin's New Economic Policy. In time they were branded as "NEP profiteers" and became the target of popular attacks. Jews were accused of invading the cities, monopolizing the "soft jobs," land speculation, taking over the Crimea, and infiltrating the government. In the factories the charges caused violence and indignities against the Jewish workers. The mood spread to the universities and even to government officials. Slogans such as "Kill the Kikes and save Russia" enjoyed wide popularity. Discrimination against Jews occurred in housing allocations and taxes.[66]

1923

The Christian League, a Rumanian anti-Semitic organization, and the Iron Guard, a right-wing terrorist organization, enjoyed the support and protection of the military and police forces in carrying out their pogroms against Rumanian Jews.[67]

1924

A KKK pamphlet was issued titled, "Christ and Other Klansmen," purporting that Jesus Christ embodied the true ideal of the Klan and should be counted as its first real member. It also blamed the Jews for the death of Christ and stated, "God is the author of Klanism."[68]

The increasing anti-Semitism in the United States that expressed itself in the strong rebirth of the Ku Klux Klan, employment and educational discrimination and quotas, restrictive practices in real estate, public accommodations and private associations, and a virulent anti-Semitic press, also gained expression in the revision of the immigration laws that occurred in 1924. The evidence of the hearing on the bill focused on Jewish immigration. The legislation was patterned on the 1921 act but limited annual migration quotas to 2 percent and used the census of 1890 as the base.[69]

1925

Mein Kampf by Adolph Hitler:

"Was there any form of filth or profligacy, particularly in cultural life, without at least one Jew involved in it?"[70]

"Slowly I had become an expert in their own doctrine and used it as a weapon in the struggle for my own profound conviction. Success almost always favored my side. The great masses could be saved, if only with the gravest sacrifice in time and patience. But a Jew could never be parted from his opinions."[71]

"I didn't know what to be more amazed at: the agility of their tongues or their virtuosity at lying. Gradually I began to hate them."[72]

"If, with the help of his Marxist creed, the Jew is victorious over the other peoples of the world, his crown will be the funeral wreath of humanity. . . ."[73]

"Hence today I believe that I am acting in accordance with the will of the Almighty Creator: *by defending myself against the Jew, I am fighting for the work of the Lord.*"[74]

1926

A ritual murder charge was accompanied by a pogrom against Jews in Uzbekistan (USSR).[75]

1927

Three Jewish interns were dragged from bed and doused with ice water in Kings County Hospital in New York.[76]

1928

In Yugoslavia, a ritual murder charge was made in Petrovo Selo.[77]

In Upper New York state, the disappearance of a four-year-old girl resulted in the state police summoning the rabbi of Massena for questioning by the mayor as to the custom among Jews of offering human sacrifice at Yom Kippur.[78]

During the twenties, Jewish medical students in Poland were required to furnish Jewish cadavers for their work in anatomy.[79]

Between 1922 and 1932, pogroms were a constant feature of Jewish life in Rumania.[80]

1928

Anti-Jewish riots occurred in most Hungarian universities.[81]

In December, a new ritual murder charge was made in Poland. Several synagogues were desecrated and looted.[82]

In the Lithuanian towns of Wilkowishki and Newl there were violent anti-Semitic riots.[83]

1929

In Lemberg, Poland, Jewish high school girls were accused of mocking a Catholic procession. On the basis of the rumor, bands of young Catholics and university students attacked the Jewish quarter and vandalized and desecrated ten synagogues and numerous homes and shops of the quarter.[84]

1930

On New Year's Day, eight Jews were killed in an anti-Jewish riot in Berlin. Jews' shops and homes were vandalized and many Jews were beaten.[85]

Anti-Jewish riots occurred in the Laguinilla Market in Mexico City.[86]

Following the elections in September, anti-Jewish riots occurred throughout Germany. Jews were beaten and Jewish homes and shops were vandalized in Wurzburg, Leipzig, Dusseldorf, Frankfort and Berlin.[87]

1931

On April 22, police supported by mobs expelled over 100 Jews from the public market places of Mexico City. They were further barred from conducting business in the markets. There was widespread newspaper and popular support for the action.[88]

In the Greek town of Salonika, a mob attacked and burned the Jewish quarter.[89]

Anti-Semitic student organizations attacked Jewish students in Polish universities.[90]

Between 1923 and 1932, 128 Jewish cemeteries and 50 synagogues were desecrated in Germany. The Weimar Republic was characterized as a Jew Republic by anti-Semites who blamed the Jews for all the problems of Weimar.[91]

1932

Jews were deliberately weeded out of German symphony orchestras and the opera. In addition, works of all Jewish composers were banned.[92]

The *Army and Navy Register* contained an article supposedly pointing out why there were not more Jews in the armed services: "the pay is poor, there is no profit in it, and more, they might be called upon to die for the country of their adoption."[93]

1933*

Anti-Jewish riots occurred in Bucharest.[94]

Thousands of Jews were robbed, beaten and murdered during the first months of 1933 in Germany. In March, S. S. troops in Braunschwieg were ordered to destroy two Jewish warehouses by S.S.-Fuhrer Alpers. Similar sabotage took place throughout Germany. In April, Hitler proclaimed a national boycott of Jewish shops. Jews were barred from civil service jobs, the legal professions, universities and from unpaid public service (jury duty). Public servants not of Aryan stock were removed from office and lost all pension rights. (Excombatants, those who had been in the civil service since 1914, and those whose fathers or sons had been killed fighting for Germany were exempted from the purge.) Many professions not directly state connected demanded "of their own volition" the expulsion of Jewish members. The medical profes-

*The comprehensive and overwhelming horror carried out by the Nazis and their collaborators defy the catalogue format. Any attempt to exhaustively list the Nazi-inspired atrocities would numb the mind and soul of any reader. Therefore, the anti-Semitic incidents that are included in the catalogue from 1933 are illustrative in nature and should not be taken as a complete or comprehensive listing. In addition, this period has been well documented and commented on by many scholars. Any attempt to duplicate this work would be arrogant and unnecessarily redundant.

sion, for example, declared that no Jew should treat German citizens.[95]

On April 8, the American Consul in Berlin declared that Jews had had two fundamental rights taken from them: free choice of profession and freedom of movement.[96]

1933
The Reich Press Law declared journalism a "public vocation" regulated by law and required all editors be German citizens, or Aryan descent and not married to a Jew. The same year, Jews were forbidden to teach in schools.[97]

1934
In Quebec, 75 French-Canadian interns at Notre Dame hospital and 44 in other hospitals went on strike when the directors of hospitals refused to dismiss Dr. C. Rabinovitch, who had been appointed as an intern. Dr. Rabinovitch resigned, and the striking interns were reinstated after they signed an apology.[98]

Throughout Canada in the early thirties anti-Jewish groups formed and urged boycotts of Jewish labor and stores. Many magazines expressed anti-Semitic sentiments.[99]

1935
Jews were excluded from the medical school of the University of Kounro in Lithuania.[100]

The Reich Citizenship Act, released at the Party rally in Nuremberg by Hitler, distinguished between persons subject to the state and those who were authentic Reich citizens with full political rights. Reich citizenship was restricted to nationals of German or racially-related blood who through their conduct proved their loyalty to the Reich.[101]

The law "For the Protection of German Blood and German Honor" released at the same time was designed to make the nation secure for the future by safeguarding the purity of German blood. It prohibited marriage and extra-marital relations between Jews and German subjects who were of German or racially-related blood. Marriages between such persons were declared void. This law also prohibited Jews employing as domestics any female of German or related blood less than 45 years old. They were also forbidden to fly the Reich or national flag or display the Reich colors. However, they were expressly permitted to display Jewish colors under the state's protection.[102]

On November 1, supplementary decrees to the Reich Citizenship Act were issued. Clause 4, Section 1 of the act was amended to explicitly state that no Jew could be a Reich citizen. Jews were denied the vote and could not be appointed to public office. A supplement to Clause 4, Section 2 revoked the Civil Service Act (see 1933) provisions exempting Jewish excombatants and those in public service since 1914.[103]

On November 14, a decree attached to the "Reich Citizenship Act" defined a Jewish Mischling (part-Jew) as one with no more than two full-Jewish grandparents. A person with more than two full-Jewish grandparents was a full Jew. Any grandparent who had belonged to the Jewish religion was considered a full Jew.[104]

1936

The Prussian law of the Secret State Police of February 10 stated: "The orders and affairs of the Secret State Police are not liable to investigation by administrative tribunal." Police detention of "enemies of the state" was thereby removed from judicial control and challenge.[105]

Widespread riots in Poland and Galicia, in April, killed 79 Jews and wounded over 500.[106]

In Bucharest, 210,000 marchers participated in the largest anti-Semitic demonstration in Romania's history.[107]

Anti-Jewish riots took place in the major Romanian cities.[108]

In the Stalin purges many Jews, such as Trotsky, Zinoviev, Radek, and Kamenev were denounced as traitors. The impression conveyed by the purge trials was that the Russian fatherland was being strangled by "Jewish internationalism." In addition to high ranking Jews, many of lesser rank within the party and state apparratchiki were liquidated. Others were removed from their positions and subjected to ostracism. Popular anti-Semitic incidents that followed went unpublicized and unpunished.[109]

• • •

Cardinal Hloud, the Primate of Poland, in a pastoral letter urged Polish Catholics to boycott Jewish businesses.[110]

1937

The Nazi propaganda organs actively and directly incited popular anti-Semitism.[111]

1937

In addition to the continuous theme of Jewish lasciviousness, Streicher's *Der Sturmer* regularly devoted issues to the theme of ritual murder illustrated in gory and pornographic detail. *Der Sturmer* was a graphic documentation of the sadistic element of anti-Semitism.[112]

In Poland, Jewish university students were required to sit in special segregated sections of classrooms.[113]

In May, the Gestapo ordered Jewish concentration camp inmates to wear a yellow triangle imposed over colored classification triangle to form Star of David.[114]

On August 3, the Italian government announced that foreign Jews would no longer be admitted to Italian universities.[115]

On August 4, a government order barred most Jews from teaching in Italian schools.[116]

The Sachsenhausen, Buchenwald and Lichtenburg concentration camps were established in Germany. They were modeled on the Dachau plan.[117]

A series of anti-Semitic decrees by the Rumanian government closed all Jewish newspapers, dismissed Jews from civil service, annulled liquor licenses held by Jews and prohibited Jewish commercial competition with Christians.[118]

In September, the Italian government ordered all foreign Jews and those who had acquired citizenship since 1919 to leave the country within six months. Jewish teachers at all schools and universities were dismissed and Jewish children were segregated in the schools.[119]

The *Protocols of the Learned Elders of Zion* was published and widely circulated in Italy in November.[120]

The Italian government issued a series of anti-Semitic decrees and moved to eliminate Jews from the economy.[121]

257

In Germany, at the end of 1937, the movement toward the Aryanization of the economy was speeded up.[122]

1938

As a prelude to the Nazi-Soviet pact, a number of Jewish cultural institutions, schools, newspapers, institutes, etc. were forcibly closed by the Soviet government and many of the Jewish communal leadership were executed.[123]

In April, the Hungarian government decreed that all cattle were to be stunned before slaughter. This was directed against the Jewish community. Shehital, ritual slaughtering, was thereby prevented.[124]

On April 7, a law was passed to reduce the number of Jews in the Hungarian business sector to 20% in five years. (Within six months, 5,000 Jews were unemployed.)[125]

After the annexation of Austria to the Reich, the SS set up a concentration camp at Mauthaussen. In Vienna, Jewish men and women were forced to scrub street gutters, public latrines, and the toilets of the SA and SS barracks. This work was performed with toothbrushes.[126]

In Vienna, a special organization under the SS set up by Reinhard Heydrich permitted 180,000 Austrian Jews to purchase their freedom by handing over all possessions to the Nazis. Called the "Office for Jewish Emigration" it became the sole agency for issuing permits to Jews to leave the country. (This office was headed by Karl Adolph Eichmann and soon became the agency for extermination, not emigration, of Jews.)[127]

. On June 1, Reinhard Heydrich ordered all male Jews with previous criminal records transferred to Buchenwald.[128]

On June 14, the Reich Citizenship Act was further amended to require that Jewish firms register as such and adopt a special identifying trademark. This was followed by other amendments barring Jews from the practice of medicine and law, even for other Jews.[129]

On July 6, the Nazi government passed orders requiring Jews to declare their assets and sell their businesses. They were also barred from engaging in caretaking, negotiating loans and real estate.[130]

258

On July 23, the Reich Gesetzblatt announced that all Jews had to carry identity cards.[131]

In the July 25 issue of *Social Justice,* Father Coughlin called for a Christian Front that would not fear being called anti-Semitic because it knows the term anti-Semitic is only a pat phrase in Communism's glossary of attacks. He also stated that the authenticity of the *Protocols* was irrelevant since "we cannot ignore the news value of their strongly prophetic nature."[132]

1938

On October 14, Goering demanded that all Jews be driven out of the economy.[133]

On November 7, a 17-year-old Jewish youth assassinated the Paris legation secretary, von Roth. This provided the excuse for the fulfillment of Goering's demand to remove the Jew completely from the economy. On November 9, at a party meeting in Munich, Reich Minister for Propaganda Goebbels gave a rabble rousing speech and unleashed the state sanctioned pogrom known as Reichskristallnacht. The S.S. was ordered not to interfere with the "spontaneous reaction of the German people." Synagogues throughout Germany were burned. Seven thousand Jewish shops were destroyed. A 1-1/4 billion mark fine was imposed on the Jews and all of their insurance was confiscated by the state. Ninety-one Jews were murdered and thousands were mercilessly beaten. The rioters were untouched unless they had committed race pollution.[134]

Following Reichskristallnacht the S.S. rounded up 30,000 wealthy Jews and sent them to concentration camps. Their wealth was appropriated by the state and they were then released and given permits to emigrate. This was followed by state orders barring Jews from schools, universities, theaters, concert halls, museums, sports stadiums, and swimming pools. Another order withdrew drivers' licenses, and another required Jews to surrender all gold and silver objects except wedding rings.[135]

In Italy, a decree was issued that barred Jews from all educational or cultural institutions. Jews were excluded from all grades and all schools and academies as students, teachers and directors. Books authored by Jews were also banned.[136]

In Hungary, a "Law for the More Efficient Protection of the Social and Economic Balance" limited Jewish participation in financial and productive employment and restricted Jews in the free professions.[137]

1939

On January 24, Goering issued an order to Heydrich that Jewish emigration should be promoted by all possible means and expropriation of Jewish property and expulsion of Jews should be continued. To implement this policy, Heydrich established a Reich Central Office for Jewish Emigration in Berlin. This office required that the Berlin Jewish Community submit a daily list of 70 families prepared to emigrate. (In 1939, 78,000 Jews left Berlin in contrast to 40,000 who emigrated in 1938.)[138]

The Zionist Immigration Bureau in the Palestine Mandate territory (Mossad de Aliyah Bet) and the S.S. and S.D. developed a working relationship as other emigration destinations began to refuse to accept more Jewish emigrees. The Foreign Ministry and the Party Foreign Organization opposed S.S. collaboration with the Zionists on the grounds that the effect was to help build a Jewish state. Instead of promoting an "internationally recognized increase of power, the object of Germany policy must be continued fragmentation of Jewry." Despite these rumblings of opposition, the Zionist cooperation enabled thousands of Jews to escape the Reich during 1939. This arrangement was abruptly shattered, however, with the beginning of World War II.[139]

In January, the Czechoslovakian government voted $2,500,000 to hasten the emigration of Jewish refugees.[140]

In February, the major synagogue in Budapest was bombed by anti-Semitic terrorists.[141]

Following the Nazi occupation of Czechoslovakia, Slovakia announced its independence and passed laws that stripped Jews of their civil rights.[142]

In May, the Dies Committee uncovered a fascist plan to seize power in the United States. The main members of the conspiracy were Major General George Van Horn Mosely (U.S.A. ret.); Dudley P. Gilbert, a wealthy New Yorker; and George Deatherage, head of the Knights of the White Camelia. During Committee hearings Mosely refused to drink water because he feared that it was poisoned by Jews.[143]

In April, Jews who could work were conscripted into forced labor under Goering's Four Year Plan.[144]

In June, in New York, a Jewish high school teacher was stabbed by a *Social Justice* vendor.[145]

1939

On the first of September with the invasion of Poland, the Einsatzgruppen der Sicherheitspolizei und des S.D. were created and entrusted with the duty of suppressing all elements hostile to the Reich and to Germany behind the fighting line.[146]

On September 21, Heydrich ordered the Einsatzgruppen to round up Jews in rural areas and concentrate them in a few of the larger towns with good railway facilities.[147]

Late in September, the Einsatzgruppen was organized into 15 Einsatzkommandos of 100 to 150 men. They were active in seizing and confiscating Jewish property and liquidating Jewish organizations. During this period an S.S. Totenkopf Standarte in Wloclowek arrested 800 Jews and shot many "while trying to escape."[148]

In the middle of October, the S.S. in occupied Poland began the systematic slaughter of Jews in the various localities annexed by the Reich.[149]

In December, the massive relocation of Jews in Poland began. The purpose was the establishment of a massive Jewish ghetto near Lublin.[150]

By the end of 1939, Rumania had removed Jews from economic participation. Jewish factory workers were discharged and Jewish doctors and lawyers were prohibited from practicing.[151]

In December, followers of Father Coughlin picketed radio station WMCA in New York because it would not broadcast the "radio priest." While picketing they attacked and beat Jewish passers-by.[152]

1940

The Gentile Co-Operative Association was organized by Eugene Filtcraft in Illinois. It published a Gentile Business Direc-

261

tory of Gentile merchants and urged subscribers to trade only with such merchants.[153]

In March, Hitler decided to abandon the creation of the Jewish state in Lublin as impractical and not solving the problem. Relocation to Lublin stopped in April.[154]

After the fall of France, the establishment of a Jewish ghetto in Madagascar was seriously considered. Four million European Jews were to be deported there and held as hostages to exact ''good behavior'' on the part of their ''racial brethren'' in America.[155]

Separate ghettoes were created one by one in the conquered territories. The first established in the former Polish areas was in Lodz-Litzmounstadt which was annexed to the Reich in April.[156]

In May, the Germans occupied the Netherlands. Concentration camps were established at Vught, Westerbork, Barneveld and Ellekon. The Jewish population suffered in sequence, economic and social discrimination, persecution and beatings, mass arrests, deportation and finally death.[157]

1940

On June 12, the Reich Citizenship Act was amended to disbar Jewish lawyers, and Jews were to be barred as defendants at the discretion of the courts.[158]

In July, shopping hours for Jews in Berlin were restricted to between 4 and 5 P.M.[159]

In August, the Madagascar Deportation Plan was affirmed by Hitler, approved by Himmler and given to Eichmann's department to work out the details. The objective was ''the collective evacuation of the Jews from Europe.''[160]

The first contingent of Polish Jews, more than 1,000, arrived at Buchenwald in August. Eleven were killed on arrival. After five months, only 300 were still alive.[161]

On September 13, the German General of Poland Hans Franck issued the general order for residence restrictions of the Jews, i.e., the creation of the ghettoes.[162]

Otto Thierach, National Socialist Minister of Justice, made arrangements with Himmler to hand over incarcerated Jews to the S.S. to be ''worked to death'' or exterminated.[163]

After Nazi occupation of France, alien and French Jews were arrested and sent to concentration camps established at Drancy, Pithimess, Beunela-Rolande, Gurs, Les Milles, and Rivesaltes.[164]

1940

In October, the first anti-Jewish decrees were promulgated in Nazi occupied Belgium. Breendonck was established as the chief concentration camp.[165]

On the 22nd and 23rd of October, 6,500 Jews in Gave of Baden and Saarpfalz had their property and possessions confiscated and were deported into unoccupied France on direct orders from Hitler.[166]

The Chelmno extermination camp was established near Kolo in Poznan province of Poland in November. Seven hundred Jews from Kolo were sent there on December 9. They were gassed in special trucks and buried in a mass grave in the nearby woods. The S.S. set up special workers brigades to make powder out of human bones that was used in the construction of walls in a nearby village.[167]

1941

"One of the most brutal pogroms in history" was carried out in Bucharest. The Jewish quarter and seven synagogues were destroyed. Some victims were slaughtered like animals; the headless corpses stamped "FIT FOR HUMAN CONSUMPTION".[168]

In February, 400 Dutch Jews arrived at Buchenwald; they were later transferred to Mauthausen in Austria where they were exterminated.[169]

During February and March, 5,000 Viennese Jews were deported to Poland.[170]

The Cracow ghetto was established in March.[171]

1941

In March, Hitler issued his secret decree that Jews in occupied areas of Russia should be eliminated. (This order accompanied the open order to shoot the political commissars of the Red Army.)[172]

This order was carried out by the S.S. Einsatzgruppen A, B, C, D which followed the conquering army. They were made up of Einsatzkommandos and Sonderkommandos who summarily shot the Jews as they were discovered.[173]

The Radom ghetto was established in April.[174]

When the Einsatzgruppen were organized in May, the liquidation order was given by word of mouth. All racial and political undesirables were to be put to death. The order extended to four main groups: communist officials, "second-class" Asiatics, Jews and Gypsies.[175]

In May, a decree issued by the RSHA (Reichssicharheitshauptamt—Central Security Department of the Reich) to Security Police operations in Belgium and France mentioned the "certain final solution of the Jewish problem" twice.[176]

On June 28, Jews and communist officials among the Soviet prisoners of war held in stalags were to be segregated for execution.[177]

In June, the Berlin Jews were issued ration cards stamped with a J to distinguish them from the rest of the population.[178]

1941

At Buchenwald during the summer, 104 Jewish prisoners were given experimental injections of *evipannatrium;* all died as a result.[179]

On July 2, Heydrich summarized the basic instructions already issued to the Einsatzgruppen and Einsatzkommandos in a written minute.[180]

On July 31, Goering sent an official memorandum to Heydrich ordering him to make "all necessary preparations in the organizational, technical, and material fields for a total solution of the Jewish problem."[181]

On September 18, Himmler in a memorandum to Gauleiter Greiser in Wartheland stated that "It is the Fuhrer's wish that the Altreich and the Protectorates should be cleaned of Jews from west to east."[182]

In 1941, an anti-Jewish persecution occurred in the Soviet

Union under the slogan that the Jews were deserting Moscow.[183]

In Germany during 1941, Jews were murdered at euthanasia stations set up under the Euthanasia Programme designed to eliminate the elderly, mentally ill and physically unfit.[184]

In the United States, Senator Benton K. Wheeler (Mon.), Congressman John Rankin (Mo.) and folkhero Charles A. Lindbergh accused the Jews of trying to force this country into war. Lindbergh warned of the Jewish danger growing out of their ownership and influence in motion pictures, the press, radio and government.[185]

On September 24, a landmine explosion wrecked the Nazi army rear area command post in Kiev. In retaliation, notices were posted throughout Kiev ordering all Jews in the province of Kiev to report to major road junctions at 8 A.M. on the 29th. Told they were to be resettled, they were advised to bring valuables, warm clothing and food for three days. Failure to report was punishable by death. They were rounded up and brought to the ravine Babi Yar. They were ordered to place their belongings in a neat pile and were marched in columns of 100 to the ravine edge where they were machine gunned. Children were simply thrown into the ravine alive. The extermination lasted two days and was carried out by Einsatzgruppen C—Extermination Command 4-A. German figures cite 33,771 victims. Soviet and Jewish figures place the total two to three times greater. (The generally accepted figure is 70,000.)[186]

On October 15, Einsatzgruppen A was ordered to solve the Jewish problem decisively and by all possible means.[187]

Birkenau concentration and extermination camp, the largest of all, was established in October.[188]

On October 23, all further Jewish emigration was barred by order of Reichsfuhrer S. S. Himmler.[189]

1941

The entire Jewish population of Moravia and Bohemia was transferred to Theresienstadt concentration camp in November, 1941.[190]

From November through June, 1942, Jews shipped from occupied territories to ghettos in Warsaw, Kovo, Mirsh and Riga were shot upon arrival by Einsatzgruppen waiting at railroad depots.[191]

On November 25, German national Jews were put under deportation regulations of the 11th order of the Reich Citizenship Act.[192]

Ghettos in occupied Russia were systematically eliminated by mass extermination by shooting in December.[193]

In December, at the extermination camp at Chelmo, the murder of Jews by mobile gas chambers using carbon monoxide began. By 1944, 152,000 had been murdered by this method at this camp.[194]

Himmler's records state that in 1941, 130,000 Jews were murdered in Lithuania and Latvia.[195]

In December, the penalties for assaults on German soldiers in occupied France were published. The measure included a one billion franc fine imposed on Jews of occupied territory, deportation to the east and immediate execution of 100 hostages.[196]

1941

The underground newspaper *France au Combat* reported that thirty-five Jewish refugees, old men and women, were thrown alive into three wells at Savignyen-Septaine and crushed to death by rocks thrown in to fill the wells.[197]

The Lemberg ghetto was established in December.[198]

1942

On January 10, the Jews living in Germany were ordered to hand in all fur and woolen articles.[199]

On January 20, Heydrich held the Wansee Conference at which the final solution to the Jewish problem was decided and all European Jews were ordered included in the murder program. Responsibility for carrying out the order was assigned to Gestapo Desk IV B4 headed by S.S. Obersturmbannfuhrer Adolf Eichmann.[200]

A report from Einsatzgruppen A on February 1 concerning executions carried out by November 25, 1941, listed the following:

Communists	1,064
Guerrillas	56
Mentally unsound	653
Poles	44
Russian POW	28
Gypsies	5
Armenians	1
Jews	136,421

This report was from a unit that had already executed 229,052 Jews.[201]

In March, the Belzec extermination camp was opened. It was the first camp equipped with permanent gas chambers. It exterminated Jews confined in the ghettos of Lublin, Galicia, Cracow and the Protectorate.[202]

On April 15, the Jews in Germany were ordered to paint the Star of David on their houses. In June, they were required to hand in to the state all unessential articles of clothing and any electrical or optical apparatus. In addition, all Jewish schools were closed and in July all forms of education for Jewish children were discontinued.[203]

1942

Medical experiments were carried out on human guinea pigs at Dachau, Ravensbrück, and Mauthausen.[204]

Beginning in June, S. D. Sonderkammando 1005 under S.S. Standartenfuhrer Blobel began the vain attempt to remove the evidence of the Einsatzgruppen mass murders in occupied territories. The Sonderkommando had the task of exhuming the mass graves and burning the bodies.[205]

Beginning the 22nd of July, a train carried 5,000 Jews daily from the Warsaw ghetto to Treblinka extermination camp. (The total from the Warsaw ghetto processed at Treblinka from 1942 to the end was 210,322.) Beginning the same date, a train carried 5,000 Jews twice weekly from Przemsyl to the Belzec extermination camp.[206]

In October, rations of eggs, meat products, cereals and milk were cancelled for German Jews. Himmler ordered all Jews removed from the labor force.[207]

1942
By November, the Einsatzgruppen had murdered by mass execution over 1,000,000 Jews in the occupied areas of Russia.[208]

1943
On January 20, in a communique to the Reich State Secretary for Transport, concerning deportation of state enemies from occupied territories, Himmler stated ". . . the deportation of the Jews is of the first importance."[209]

In March, the Reich Security Department and Minister of Justice instructed that Jews serving prison terms were to be sent to Auschwitz or Lublin on completion of sentence.[210]

On May 16, the Warsaw Ghetto rebellion, which began on April 19, was finally put down after thirty-three days of fighting. Some 7,000 Jews were killed in the fighting. Those who did not escape were transferred to Treblinka.[211]

Jews who were inmates of work camps and too weak or sick to work were murdered by S.S. doctors. The method of killing was injections of Phenol, Evipon or hydrocyanic acid.[212]

There were widespread acts of anti-Semitic vandalism against schools, synagogues, and individuals in the Washington Heights section of New York City in 1943 and 1944.[213]

In June, S.S. Sonderkommando 1005 began destroying evidence of mass murders in Lvov. The mass graves were dug up and the bodies burned in piles of 1,200 to 1,600 each. The ashes were then run through screens to recover gold. Large bones were crushed and ashes and bones turned into the fields. In a five-month period, this Sonderkommando sent 110 kilograms of gold to Germany.[214]

On June 21, Himmler ordered that all Jews in Ostland, Poland, be moved into concentration camps and the creation of a forced labor concentration camp near Riga.[215]

Through 1943 and 1944, medical experiments continued on inmate guinea pigs at Dachau, Buchenwald, and Auschwitz concentration camps.[216]

In August, a revolt by the prisoners of Treblinka, Poland, caused its closing. In its brief existence of slightly more than a year (July 23, 1942-August, 1943), 700,000 to 800,000 Jews were murdered.[217]

In October, the extermination camp at Sobibir Am Bug in the Lublin district began operations. The victims were mainly from east Poland, but Jews from the USSR, Czechoslovakia, Austria, Holland and France were also sent here. The method of extermination was exhaust gas. Over 250,000 were murdered here by the end of the war.[218]

When German troops entered Tatarsk, Russia, September 30, Jewish homes were systematically looted and burned. Every Jew in the town was hunted down. Children were killed in the streets either by bayoneting or bashing of the skulls. S.S. troops, using clubs and pipes, beat thirty to death. The rest were machinegunned.[219]

1943

In November and December, the mass graves around the Kounos area were exhumed and 12,000 corpses were burned in piles of 300. The remains were then crushed and turned into the soil.[220]

On November 3, Operation Erntefest was carried out. Over 17,000 Jews in labor camps and war industries in the Lublin area were herded into mass graves and machinegunned.[221]

1944

Medical experiments on concentration camp inmates continued through 1944. The press of the war and the need for workers spared some Jews from extermination. Beginning in 1944, Jews arriving at the concentration and extermination camps were separated as to fitness to work. Those who were well and healthy were used in the slave labor program. Those unfit to work were murdered.[222]

Following the liberation of Kiev from Nazi occupation, anti-Semitic sentiments on the part of the population resulted in a pogrom that killed 16 Jews.[223]

This year marks the destruction of Hungarian Jewry. Hoess, commandant of Auschwitz, boasts of the efficiency of Auschwitz in the "processing" of the Hungarian Jews. This year also marked a technological improvement in the extermination procedure, i.e., the use of Zyklon B (Prussic Acid) rather than the slower carbon monoxide method.[224]

1944

As Germans retreated, 3,000 Jews, Lithuanians, Poles, Estonians and Russians were executed and cremated at Klooga labor camp.[225]

Medical experiments continued at Buchenwald through 1944.[226]

American anti-Semitie Gerald L. K. Smith, speaking of World War II said: "This is an unnecessary war. . . . Nobody wanted it but the power mad internationalists operating under the direction of international Jewry."[227]

1945

The defeat of Germany was completed by the signing of the unconditional surrender by General Jodle on May 7.[228]

German records provide the ghastly record and effect of the "Final Solution."

Jews murdered in areas under S.S. control:

		%
Germany (includes Austria and Reich Protectorates of Bohemia and Moravia)	250,000	50
Slovakia	60,000	
Denmark	70	1
Norway	750	38
Holland, Belgium, Luxemburg	130,000	56
USSR	900,000	28
Poland	3,000,000	90
Yugoslavia	60,000	80
Greece	60,000	81
Rumania	270,000	34
Hungary	3,000,000	75
France and Italy	70,000	22
	5,100,000 [229]	
Jewish population of Germany in 1933	503,000	
Jewish population of Germany in 1945	23,000 [230]	

In April, Dr. Ernest M. Hopkins, President of Dartmouth College, strongly defended the quota system at Dartmouth. The quota was necessary, he said, to maintain Dartmouth's tradition of racial tolerance and to protect Jews from anti-Semitism. Without the quota system Dartmouth would be forced to exclude Jews altogether. "Dartmouth College is a Christian College founded for the Christianization of its students."[231]

1945-1970

All comprehensive studies of anti-Semitism are confounded by the Holocaust. The enormity of the Holocaust overwhelms, dwarfs and reduces to insignificance the anti-Semitism that precedes and follows it.

The magnitude of the Nazi atrocities portrayed in official documents, photographs, letters, diaries, testimony and autobiographies of the perpetrators, victims, witnesses and survivors destroys imagination and sensibility.

The Nazis showed clearly and unmistakably that anti-Semitism carried to its logical conclusion means, quite simply, nothing less than the extermination of Jews and all things Jewish. The evidence is available and unambiguous; anyone living since 1945 can verify the truth of this statement.

Incredibly, anti-Semitism survived the defeat of the Nazis and continues as part of the culture of the modern world. The following events are given only to illustrate the continued existence and the similarity of contemporary anti-Semitism with its past expressions. No attempt is made to be as inclusive as in the rest of the study and the format of the book to this point will not be used.

In the Soviet Union and Eastern Europe, anti-Semitism, in one form or another, has been an almost constant feature of state policy. As in the past under Czarist rule, when Jews were given two choices, conversion to Orthodox Christianity or elimination through expulsion or death, under Soviet rule Jews are given a similar choice* of conversion (total assimilation) or elimination (prison, exile to slave labor camps or execution). This choice,

*The alternative is a life of repression, restriction and second-class status with tremendous pressure to assimilate.

271

however, was not entirely genuine. Official Soviet condemnations of anti-Semitism notwithstanding, adoption of Marxism-Leninism, even party membership is no protection against the tradition of anti-Semitism. Jews who did embrace revolutionary scientific socialism are suspect, much in the same way that the Conversos in Spain were suspect under the Inquisition. In addition, anti-Semitic myths continued to be part of Soviet demonology; for example, Jewish conspiracy, Jewish cowardice, Jewish lack of patriotism, Jewish capitalism, etc.

In 1946, when the city of Lvov became Russian territory under the terms of the Teheran agreements, some 30,000 members of the Jewish community were deported to Poland. The same year, the Soviet press began a propaganda campaign that depicted Jews as speculators in gold and currency.[232] In 1948, a campaign to eliminate Jewish culture throughout the Communist bloc countries began. Jewish hospitals, homes for the aged, and schools were either closed or nationalized throughout the Soviet Union. Yiddish papers, publishing houses and theatres were closed. Jewish intellectuals, writers and artists were arrested and jailed. During the years from 1948 to 1953, persons "of Jewish origin" were systematically removed from high military and party positions throughout the Communist bloc.[233] Six thousand Jews were arrested in Hungary and deported to the Soviet Union for forced labor.[234] Thousands of Rumanian Jews were arrested and sentenced to forced labor.[235] Local anti-Semitic riots were frequent occurrences throughout this period in the Ukraine and in the satellite countries, especially Rumania.[236]

In 1953, the notorious "doctors plot" was publicized. The plot charged that Jewish doctors in league with British, American, and Zionist spies were involved in a systematic campaign to assassinate Soviet leadership. Shcharbakov and Zhdanov had already been murdered and Stalin was to be next. Massive deportation and relocation of Jews followed the announcement. Jews were summarily removed from industrial and civil service positions and Jewish doctors were deprived of state positions. The propaganda campaign that accompanied these actions used all the traditional anti-Semitic stereotypes.[237]

Some have sought to explain Soviet anti-Semitism as an aberration and a product of Stalin's paranoia. Evidence does not support this position. For example, Jewish nationality is recognized in the USSR and internal passports bear the designation of Jewish nationality. But there is no school in the Soviet Union that teaches Hebrew, Yiddish or any other Jewish dialect while fifty-eight languages in addition to Russian are used as languages of instruction. Additionally, Jewish history and literature are not taught in any language. With the largest Yiddish-speaking population in the Communist bloc, only thirteen books were published in Yiddish in the Soviet Union between 1959 and 1965. In 1966, there were only two Yiddish publications—a monthly the *Sovietish Heymland* and a three-times a week newspaper in Biro-Bidzhan. In 1935 there were ten Yiddish-language newspapers in the Ukraine alone.[238] In 1959, a Moscow synagogue was firebombed and the Jewish cemetery of Kiev was vandalized and desecrated.[239] In 1960, Jews were accused of ritual murder in a Soviet publication.[240] Between 1960 and 1963, fifty-five percent of those sentenced to death for economic crimes as a result of KGB prosecutions were Jews.[241] In 1963, making matzoh for sale to co-religionists to celebrate the Passover was an economic crime.[242] The same year, Khrushchev attacked the poet Yevtuschenko for his poem *Babi Yar*. The poem called attention to Soviet anti-Semitism.[243]

Official anti-Semitism in the Communist countries since 1945 has taken the form of attacks on religion, cosmopolitanism, Zionism, imperialism and reaction. In addition, Jews have experienced the surviving practices of private anti-Semitism that include continuance of sterotypes, hostility, prejudice and daily insults and indignities that are tolerated and sometimes encouraged by state and party officials at all levels of society.

Aside from the Communist bloc countries, the only other manifestations of anti-Semitism as official state policy since World War II have occurred in the Arab countries and some of the emerging nations in Africa. This is treated in a separate section of the study—Appendix I and II.

Similarly, in the West, anti-Semitism survived and flourished despite the disclosures of the Nazi horrors. Outside the Communist bloc and the Arab countries, the most virulent anti-Semitism is found in Latin America. Recent Spanish language editions of the

273

Protocols of the Learned Elders of Zion are available throughout Latin America in most bookstores and many newsstands. A wide variety of other anti-Semitic publications are also available. In addition to an active press and publishing enterprise, anti-Semitism in Central and South America finds expression in vandalism and desecration of synagogues and cemeteries, swastika and anti-Semitic slogans painted on Jewish homes, businesses and on public buildings and walls. More violent expressions include arson, bombings, kidnappings, beatings, torture and murder. Argentina has the dubious distinction of leading Latin countries in manifestations of anti-Semitism; however, incidents have occurred regularly throughout Latin America. Openly anti-Semitic and neo-Nazi organizations and movements are quite active in Argentina, Brazil, Paraguay and Chile.

Many factors contribute to the strength of this anti-Semitism including widespread ignorance, illiteracy and superstition, the closed system of social stratification, the dislocations and tensions of modernization and urbanization, and the exploitive and extractive nature of the economies. The two most important causes, however, are the religious tradition of the Latin countries and the presence of extensive pro-Nazi sympathies. Catholicism in Latin America is an outgrowth of Spanish Catholicism as a colonial and missionary force among an originally pagan indigenous population. It emphasizes the magical, ritualistic, fearful and superstitious aspects of Catholicism and is frozen in the Inquisitorial attitude toward Jews and Judaism. The pro-Nazi and neo-Nazi sentiments of the region reflect in part the German refugee population (many war criminals and former Nazis found sanctuary in the German immigrant centers in Latin America) and in part the flirtations of some political movements with the Axis powers during World War II.

In addition to those in South and Central America, countless other anti-Semitic incidents occurred in Europe and North America in the twenty-five years since 1945. The distinction between the Western variety and the Soviet and Arab variety of anti-Semitism is that the Western variety is not state policy. Nevertheless, anti-Semitism persists and remains an underlying theme and constant thread in the fabric of Western culture. It cannot be dismissed as a monopoly of the extreme rightwing or as simple vandalism or juvenile delinquency, even though these explanations have been given. Restrictive real estate covenants prevented Jews from living in certain communities and neighborhoods; Jews were barred from hotels and resorts; country clubs and other private clubs continued to deny Jews membership; employment quotas continued to restrict Jewish participation in the economic sectors.* Anti-Semitic beliefs, stereotypes and prejudices were still widely held. Surveys conducted in the 1960's showed widespread existence and acceptance of religious and racial anti-Semitic stereotypes and prejudice within the United States.[246] It is not unreasonable to infer that surveys in other countries would show more intense and extensive anti-Semitic attitudes.

These underlying attitudes are frequently translated into ugly actions. The West German government published a White Paper in 1960 that reported 685 anti-Semitic incidents had occurred during 1959.[247] In 1961, widespread anti-Semitic incidents occurred in West Germany, Great Britain, France, Latin America, South Africa and the United States. These ranged from painting swastikas and anti-Jewish slogans on homes and synagogues, to desecration and vandalism of synagogues and cemeteries, to bombing and arson of synagogues, to beating and killing of individuals.[248] In 1962, neo-Fascist gangs carried out numerous anti-Semitic attacks throughout Argentina, Brazil and Uruguay.[249] Sweden, West Germany, Great Britain, South Africa and the United States recorded numerous anti-Semitic incidents during 1965 and 1966. Among these is included the painting of swastikas and anti-Semitic slogans on the Jewish memorial at Dachau concentration camp.[250]

In the United States alone, the country which has historically had only a mild form of anti-Semitism, 165 temples and synagogues were vandalized and desecrated between 1965 and 1970.[251] Some of this anti-Semitic violence reflects a new dimension that has developed in anti-Semitism.

Traditionally, American anti-Semitism exhibited three dimensions: the genteel upper class ''gentleman's agreement'' variety that barred those of the ''Hebrew persuasion'' from resorts, clubs, neighborhoods, professions, and occupations; (2) nativist fears and prejudices against foreigners, carried out in hate campaigns

*In the U.S. obvious progress has been made in these areas.

275

and terror activities typified by groups like the Ku Klux Klan and other rightwing extremist groups; and (3) Christian variety both Protestant and Catholic typified by anti-Semitic stereotypes and taunts and insults and often took the form of revivalist preaching, passion plays, and mob or juvenile gang attacks against Jews and Jewish youths. These three dimensions or varieties often combined and complemented each other in some circumstances.

The new dimension present in America anti-Semitism, and in other parts of the West too, is the anti-Semitism of the New Left.[252] (The New Left is an umbrella term that includes the peace, civil rights, student, alternative life style, anti-capitalist, anti-materialist, pro-Third World, anti-imperialist, anti-colonial radicals and militants that expressed the mood of the politically engaged youth of the 1960's. The New Left is non-programmatic, non-doctrinaire, eclectic, ahistorical, and utopian in its approach to social, economic and political questions or issues.)

The anti-Semitism of the New Left is most developed in the Black Revolutionary and the anti-imperial, anti-colonial pro-Third World thrusts of the movement.[253] The conflict in New York City over the question of community control of the schools became a conflict between Black militants and the UFT (United Federation of Teachers) characterized as Jewish dominated and utilized typical anti-Semitic stereotypes. The New Left also tends to oppose establishment foreign policy and to support national liberation efforts. Consequently the Palestinian Liberation movement is supported and Israel is identified as imperialist, aggressive and undemocratic. In the latter case, efforts are made to distinguish between anti-Semitism and anti-Zionism. These efforts are unconvincing on two counts: (1) the charges and stereotypes used in the attacks on Zionism are the same as those historically associated with anti-Semitism; (2) the attacks are indiscriminate, the target or victim is Jewish, being an Israeli or a Zionist is irrelevant.

Considering the New Left's professed sympathy with and commitment to the struggle of oppressed peoples to gain their independence, it is peculiar that Jewish nationalism—Zionism—is the only independence or nationalist movement the New Left does not recognize but instead, actively attacks. The distinction between anti-Zionism and anti-Semitism is not plausible or convincing.

Rather, the New Left, in its search for an explanation for the social evils it correctly perceives, had adopted the conventional explanation of an international Jewish conspiracy.

The anti-Semitism of the New Left is not confined to the movement in the United States. Similar manifestations of anti-Semitism have occurred in the New Left in France, Japan, Great Britain, West Germany, Italy and throughout Latin America and the Third World. In this sense, the radical left and the radical right have another common ground. New Leftists and neo-Nazis agree on the common enemy. Whether this will lead to a further blurring of the distinction between left and right is not clear. Nevertheless, it is unnerving to hear spokesmen for the Ku Klux Klan and some Black Power advocates agreeing that the enemy is the Jew.

In short, the truth revealed by the Nazis did not free modern civilization of anti-Semitism. From 1945 to 1970, virtually every historic anti-Semitic belief and tactic, either religious, or racist, can be found. The tragedy of 1939 to 1945 has been blotted out of memory. dismissed as the work of madmen or explained away as an aberration. (Although it should be noted that every anti-Semitic act, except the ultimate extermination, carried out by the Nazis had precedent in Canon Law.) The beliefs that the Jew is variously, serially, or collectively, the Christ-killer, the consort of the Devil, the Devil, the anti-Christ, the usurer, the parasite, the ritual murderer, the lecher, the international conspirator, the subversive, the exploiter, the culture destroyer, the coward, the cheat, the cursed of God, the shylock, the shyster, and the kike are accepted and shared by significant numbers of people. These beliefs are all too often acted upon and produce state policy, mob attacks or private actions that add up to the continued hatred and persecution of the Jews.

CONTINUUM:

Anti-Semitism, in the twentieth century, includes virtually all the beliefs, attitudes, and tactics that have developed from the first century. The only anti-Semitic practices that do not occur are compulsory baptism and forced attendance at conversion sermons.

There are, however, ritual murder charges, discriminatory taxation, restrictions on religious practice, confiscation of property, expulsion, denial of civil and political rights, attacks, slaughter and pillage carried out by mobs or by the state. Anti-Semitic stereotypes and attitudes permeate the arts and communication media. This does not mean, however, that there were no innovations.

A major factor that influenced and intensified anti-Semitism throughout the world was *The Protocols of the Learned Elders of Zion.* Though actually fabricated in the last years of the nineteenth century, the *Protocols* were not publicly circulated until the twentieth century. This libel that describes an international Jewish conspiracy directed to Jewish world control became a best seller wherever it appeared. Despite its patent absurdity and the fact that it was proved a fraud and forgery in a court case, *The Protocols* are widely distributed and believed even today.

The other major innovations involve the Nazis and the systematic efficiency they brought to the practice of anti-Semitism. The Nazi contributions include medical experimentation, mass production methods of slaughter, and specialized training in murder and torture. The most dramatic Nazi contributions were the stated national goal of the elimination of the Jews as a people and the psychological terror of the swastika.

The anti-Semitism of the twentieth century, though including beliefs, attitudes and practices rooted in religious anti-Semitism, is tied to nationalism, racism and ideology. And as if to underline the irrational quality of political and social behavior, anti-Semitism survives with vitality.

PART X—THE 20TH CENTURY

1. Massing, op. cit., p. 108.
2. Dubnow, op. cit., III, 37-38.
3. Ausubel, op. cit., p. 205.
4. Dubnow, op. cit., III, 36-37.
5. Morris Schappes, *Jews in the U.S.* (New York: The Citadel Press, 1951), p. 149.

6. Cohn, op. cit., pp. 65-66.
7. Dubnow, op. cit., III, 71-72.
8. Ibid., pp. 87-89.
9. Ibid., p. 20.
10. Flannery, op. cit., pp. 190-91.
11. Dubnow, op. cit., III, 100.
12. Ibid.
13. Ibid., pp. 99-100.
14. Ibid., p. 18.
15. Ibid., pp. 115-16.
16. Ibid.
17. Ibid., pp. 116-118.
18. Cohn, op. cit., pp. 66-67.
19. Dubnow, op. cit., III, 115.
20. Ibid., pp. 114-15.
21. Ibid., pp. 119-20.
22. Ibid., p. 120.
23. Flannery, op. cit., pp. 190-91.
24. Ibid.
25. Elbogen, op. cit., pp. 392-402.
26. Cohn, op. cit., p. 66.
27. Massing, op. cit., pp. 142-43.
28. Isaac Landman (ed.), *Universal Jewish Encyclopedia* (New York: Universal Jewish Encyclopedia, Inc., 1939), p. 296.
29. Werner Sombart, *The Jews and Modern Capitalism* (Glencoe, Ill.: The Free Press, 1951), pp. 252-68.
30. Lionel Kochan, *Jews in Soviet Russia Since Nineteen-Seventeen* (New York: Oxford University Press, 1970), p. 163.
31. Flannery, op. cit., pp. 196-97.
32. Carey McWilliams, *A Mask for Privilege* (Boston: Little, Brown and Company, 1948), pp. 31-32.
33. Ibid.
34. Ibid.
35. Ibid.
36. Sachar, op. cit., p. 297.
37. Kochan, op. cit., pp. 64, 298.
38. Hugo Mauritz Valentin, *Antisemitism Historically and Critically Examined,* (trans. A. G. Chater; New York: The Viking Press, 1936), pp. 94-95; Flannery, op. cit., pp. 196-98.
39. Ibid.
40. Landman, op. cit., p. 361.

41. Elbogen, op. cit., pp. 487-88.
42. McWilliams, op. cit., p.
43. Landman, op. cit., p. 359.
44. Sachar, op. cit., pp. 302-303.
45. Sachar, op. cit., pp. 302-303; Salo W. Baron, *The Russian Jew Under Tsars and Soviets* (New York: The MacMillan Company, 1964), pp. 217-22.
46. Elbogen, op. cit., pp. 487-89.
47. Landman, op. cit., p. 380.
48. Ibid., p. 375.
49. Cohn, op. cit., pp. 128-37.
50. Landman, op. cit., p. 375.
51. Ibid., p. 380.
52. Cohn, op. cit., pp. 146-67.
53. Landman, op. cit., p. 396.
54. McWilliams, op. cit., p. 37.
55. Marvin Lowenthal, *The Jews of Germany* (New York: Longmans Green and Co., 1936), p. 344.
56. Landman, op. cit., p. 137.
57. Ibid.
58. Martin Broszat, et al., *Anatomy of the SS State* (Cambridge: William Collins Sons and Co., 1968), p. 21.
59. Jones, Winfield. *Story of the Ku Klux Klan.* (Washington: American Newspaper Syndicate, no date), p. 90.
60. Israel Pocket Library, *Anti-Semitism.*, p. 134.
61. Sachar, op. cit., pp. 313-15.
62. Flannery, op. cit., p. 258.
63. Ibid., p. 236.
64. Lionel Kochan (ed.), *The Jews in Soviet Russia Since 1917* (New York: Oxford University Press, 1970), pp. 299-300.
65. Sachar, op. cit., p. 425.
66. Flannery, op. cit., pp. 236-37.
67. Elbogen, op. cit., pp. 539-43; Sachar, op. cit., pp. 361-67.
68.
69. Elgogen, op. cit., pp. 559-70.
70. Adolph Hitler, *Mein Kampf* (trans. Ralph Manheim; Boston: Houghton Mifflin Company, 1972), p. 57.
71. Ibid., p. 62.
72. Ibid., p. 63.
73. Ibid., p. 65.
74. Ibid.
75. Kochan, op. cit., pp. 299-300.

280

76. Flannery, op. cit., p. 258.
77. Landman, op. cit., p. 388.
78. Ibid., p. 398.
79. Ibid., p. 380.
80. Ibid., p. 382.
81. Ibid., p. 374.
82. Ibid., p. 380.
83. Ibid., p. 377.
84. Ibid., p. 381.
85. Marvin Lowenthal, *The Jews of Germany* (New York: Longmans, Green & Co., 1936), p. 375.
86. Landman, op. cit., p. 392.
87. Lowenthal, op. cit., pp. 375-76.
88. Landman, op. cit., p. 392.
89. Ibid., p. 373.
90. Elbogen, op. cit., pp. 535-36.
91. Lowenthal, op. cit., pp. 368-80.
92. William Lawrence Shirer, *The Rise and Fall of the Third Reich* (Greenwich, Conn.: Fawcett, 1960), p. 334.
93. McWilliams, op. cit., p. 126.
94. Landman, op. cit., p. 382.
95. Broszat, op. cit., pp. 23-24, 27; Shirer, op. cit., pp. 283, 358.
96. Broszat, op. cit., p. 25.
97. Shirer, op. cit., p. 338.
98. Landman, op. cit., pp. 390-91.
99. Ibid.
100. Ibid., p. 378.
101. Borszat, op. cit., p. 32.
102. Ibid., pp. 32-33.
103. Ibid.
104. Lucy S. Dawidowicz, *The War Against the Jews, 1933-1945* (New York: Bantam Books, 1976), p. 91.
105. Broszat, op. cit., p. 426.
106. Landman, op. cit., p. 382.
107. Sachar, op. cit., p. 363.
108. Landman, op. cit., p. 382.
109. Flannery, op. cit., pp. 237-38.
110. Sachar, op. cit., p. 360.
111. Shirer, op. cit., pp. 244-48.
112. Ibid., p. 80.
113. Sachar, op. cit., p. 360.

114. Broszat, op. cit., p. 451.
115. Landman, op. cit., p. 377.
116. Ibid.
117. Broszat, op. cit., p. 445.
118. Sachar, op. cit., p. 364.
119. Landman, op. cit., p. 377.
120. Ibid., p. 376.
121. Ibid., p. 377.
122. Broszat, p. 38.
123. Jacob Freid (ed.), *Jews in the Modern World* (New York: Twayne Publishers, Inc., 1962), p. 111.
124. Landman, op. cit., p. 376.
125. Ibid.
126. Shirer, op. cit., p. 477.
127. Ibid.
128. Broszat, op. cit., p. 455.
129. Ibid., p. 36.
130. Ibid., p. 39.
131. Ibid., p. 37.
132. Flannery, op. cit., p. 261.
133. Broszat, op. cit., p. 39.
134. Ibid., pp. 40-41.
135. Ibid., pp. 41-42.
136. Elbogen, op. cit., pp. 669-70.
137. Sachar, op. cit., pp. 366-67.
138. Heinz Hohne, *The Order of the Death's Head* (New York: Ballantine Books, 1971), pp. 391-92.
139. Ibid., pp. 392-95.
140. Landman, op. cit., p. 360.
141. Ibid., p. 376.
142. Sachar, op. cit., p. 436; Flannery, op. cit., pp. 216-17; Shirer, op. cit., pp. 428-54.
143. Landman, op. cit., p. 404.
144. Ibid.
145. Ibid.
146. Broszat, op. cit., pp. 50-51.
147. Ibid., p. 52.
148. Ibid., pp. 51-52.
149. Ibid.
150. Ibid., pp. 53-54.
151. Elbogen, op. cit., p. 672.

282

152. Landman, op. cit., p. 402.
153. Harold Braverman, "Combatting Anti-Semitism by Exposing Anti-semites," *Jewish Social Service Quarterly*, Vol. 23.
154. Broszat, op. cit., p. 55.
155. Ibid.
156. Ibid., p. 58.
157. Dawidowicz, op. cit., pp. 495-98.
158. Broszat, op. cit., p. 80.
159. Ibid., p. 78.
160. Ibid., pp. 56-57.
161. Jewish Black Book Committee, *The Black Book: The Nazi Crime Against the Jewish People* (New York: Suell, Sloan and Pearce, 1946), p. 253.
162. Broszat, op. cit., p. 58.
163. Ibid., p. 81.
164. *The Black Book*, p. 276.
165. Ibid., p. 268.
166. Broszat, op. cit., p. 57.
167. *The Black Book*, pp. 377-78.
168. St. John, Robert. *Foreign Correspondent*, (Garden City, New York: Doubleday & Company, Inc., 1957) pp. 214-20.
169. *The Black Book*, p. 253.
170. Broszat, op. cit., p. 57.
171. Ibid., p. 58.
172. Ibid., pp. 65-66.
173. Ibid., pp. 57-78.
174. Ibid., p. 58.
175. Ibid., p. 64.
176. Ibid., p. 67.
177. Ibid., p. 63.
178. Ibid., p. 78.
179. *The Black Book*, p. 253.
180. Broszat, op. cit., pp. 62-63.
181. Ibid., p. 68.
182. Ibid., p. 69.
183. Kochan, op. cit., pp. 304-307; Baron, *The Russian Jew*, pp. 301-308.
184. Broszat, p. 95.
185. Flannery, op. cit., pp. 261-62.
186. Ronald I. Rubin (ed.), *The Unredeemed: Anti-Semitism in the Soviet Union* (Chicago: Quadrangle Books, 1968), pp. 127-29.
187. Broszat, op. cit., p. 63.
188. Ibid., p. 475.

189. Ibid., p. 69.
190. Ibid., p. 87.
191. Ibid., p. 75.
192. Ibid.
193. Ibid., p. 73.
194. Ibid., p. 76.
195. Lord Russell of Liverpool, *The Scourge of the Swastika*, (New York: Ballantine Books, 1961), p. 220.
196. The Black Book, pp. 276-77.
197. Ibid., p. 277.
198. Broszat, op. cit., p. 58.
199. Ibid., p. 78.
200. Ibid., p. 83.
201. Ibid., p. 64.
202. Ibid., pp. 98-99.
203. Ibid., pp. 78-79.
204. Ibid., p. 480.
205. Ibid., p. 74.
206. Ibid., pp. 100-104.
207. Ibid., p. 78.
208. Ibid., pp. 74-122.
209. Ibid., p. 66.
210. Ibid., p. 82.
211. Ibid., p. 122.
212. *The Black Book*, p. 248.
213. Jewish Black Book Committee, op. cit., p. 311.
214. The New York Times, 1943-44
215. Broszat, op. cit., p. 73.
216. Shirer, op. cit., pp. 979-91.
217. Broszat, op. cit., p. 99.
218. Ibid., p. 99.
219. *The Black Book,* pp. 338-40.
220. Ibid., pp. 327-28.
221. Broszat, op. cit., p. 122.
222. Ibid., p. 100.
223. Kochan, op. cit., p. 306.
224. Ibid., pp. 100; 124.
225. *The Black Book,* p. 317.
226. Ibid., pp. 248-49.
227. David H. Bennett, *Demagogues in the Depression* (New Brunswick, New Jersey: Rutgers University Press, 1969).

228. T. L. Jarman, *The Rise and Fall of Nazi Germany* (New York: The New American Library, 1961), p. 307.

229. Heinz Hohne, *The Order of the Death's Head* (trans. Richard Barry; New York: Ballantine Books, Inc., 1971), p. 749.

230. Ibid., p. 346.

231. McWilliams, op. cit., pp. 31-32.

232. Simon Federbash (ed.), *World Jewry Today* (new York: T. Yoselaff, 1959), col. 361.

233. Freid, op. cit., pp. 109-11; Federbush, op. cit., col. 628; Ronald Rubin, *The Unredeemed: Anti-Semitism in the Soviet Union* (Chicago: Quadrangle Books, 1968), pp. 153-54.

234. Federbush, op. cit., col. 586.

235. Ibid., cols. 628-29.

236. Flannery, op. cit., pp. 239-43; Kochan, op. cit., 309-10; Baron, *The Russian Jew*, pp. 310-26.

237. Flannery, op. cit., p. 242; Kocahn, op. cit., pp. 310-19; Baron, *The Russian Jew*, pp. 323-26.

238. Kochan, op. cit., pp. 232-68.

239. Kochan, op. cit., p. 315.

240. B. Z. Goldberg, *The Jewish Problem in the Soviet Union*, p. 311.

241. Kochan, op. cit., p. 12.

242. Rubin, op. cit., p. 118.

243. *New York Times*, March 11, 1963, p. 9.

244. Arnold Forster and Benjamin Epstein, *The New Anti-Semitism* (New York: McGraw-Hill Book Company, 1974), pp. 221-54.

245. Ibid., pp. 268-84.

246. Charles Y. Clock and Rodney Stark, *Christian Beliefs and Anti-Semitism* (New York: Harper & Row, Publishers, 1966).

247. *New York Times*, March 26, 1960, p. 1.

248. *New York Times*

249. *New York Times*, January 18, 1962, April 4, 1962, April 13, 1962; July 18, 1962; August 10, 1962.

250. Saul Carson, *One Hundred and Sixty-five Temples Desecrated* (New York: Popular Library, 1971); *New York Times*, May 13, 14; July 10; October 28; November 30.

251. Carson, op. cit.

252. See Arnold Forster and Benjamin Epstein, op. cit., *The New Anti-Semitism* (New York: McGraw-Hill Book Co., 1974).

253. Ibid., pp. 125-221.

CAUSES OF ANTI-SEMITISM: WHY THE JEW?

CAUSES OF ANTI-SEMITISM:
WHY THE JEW?

INTRODUCTION

Why anti-Semitism? Why is the Jew so consistently persecuted through most of Western history? Certain points must be omitted in any synthesis especially in one covering such a broad and complex topic, but we believe there are comprehensible causes forming an observable core:

1. Background and Culture
2. Religious Conflict and Attitudes
3. Psycho-Christian Demands
4. Perpetual Strangers in Conflict Through Social and Economic Roles
5. Psychological Demands
6. Exploitation and Utilization
7. Conspicuousness and Vulnerability
8. Environment
9. Resistance to Solution
10. A Life of Its Own

The ten basic factors listed do not necessarily apply to all situations; they overlap a great deal (repetitions are not avoided—each unit is, to some extent, self-contained); their complex interaction cannot be adequately presented; and some are technically sub-topics but deserve and receive major listing.

289

CAUSES

1. Background and Culture

The Jews—evicted from their homeland because of their strategic geographical position and refusal to submit to their conquerors—found themselves in Western countries as a foreign, cohesive, powerless, landless, unique, despised "nation." They were generally industrious, resourceful, independent, jealous of their freedom, literate, secularly righteous, religiously intransigent, and often culturally defensive—qualities that helped sustain their identity.

The maintenance of the distinctive Jewish culture and traditions contributed to the Jewish experience in the following ways:

1. Their religious values sometimes conflicted with Western and Christian values inside the social sphere. For instance, the Jewish religion demanded more literacy (and generally stressed education) which, when obeyed, gave its adherents an advantage over their neighbors. Also, by concentrating on the here and now, it stressed social justice while Christianity, with its emphasis on an after-life—and on faith which led to that after-life—stressed eternal salvation;

2. Their culture was different. At times they chose to remain separatists,[1] wear different clothing and observe different customs (although when accepted fully, they usually tended to assimilate). Like the Phoenicians, they were more sophisticated in trade;

3. They were the only non-Christians in a world where Christianity pervasively and profoundly affected all levels of life;

4. As a part of Jewish tradition but also in reaction to the persecutions they suffered, inclinations to enter a country's mainstream and pursue social contact were dampened; isolation and inward-looking religious tendencies were periodically increased;

5. Defensive measures, in the form of isolationism and cohesion, were encouraged;[2]

290

6. Tendencies toward achievement were reinforced by the will to endure and survive. Restrictions that barred Jews from many roles and activities or prohibited Christians from certain roles and activities resulted in concentrating Jews in disproportionate numbers in certain roles and occupations. Economic success was frequently one of the few successes Jews were permitted and one of the few that afforded protection (by buying their way out of persecution).[3]

2. Religious Conflict and Attitudes

The theological and proselytizing competition[4] between Jews and Christians in the Roman Empire during the early Christian centuries and the consequent de-Judaizing of Christianity[5] created antagonisms between the two faiths. When Christianity became the state religion, the Jews found themselves ostracized, despised, and powerless, under a militant church that preached damnation outside the church. They were trapped in the theological role of God-killer, God-blasphemer, and devil: doomed to eternal punishment without conversion, probably without grace.

This role was sustained by the following religious factors:

1. The continued de-Judaizing of Christ and Christianity and the distorting of Jewish secular and religious history[6] in order to fit historical and theological misconceptions both in the Gospels and in their interpretations and to fill the needs of a church militant to explain the failure of Jews to accept Christianity. This was brought on in part by the church's ancient but continuing fear of Judaism as a religious competitor and fifth column corrupter of the Christian faith;

2. The merging of Christian anti-Jewish attitudes into religio-secular attitudes and legislation (generally, beginning with Constantine);

3. The depth and fanaticism of religious feeling during the next 19 centuries (reinforced by the stress of Christ's terrible suffering and the abomination and cruelty of the Crucifixion—displayed and expressed daily, reenacted annually);

4. Church legislation and official and unofficial pronounce-

ments castigating and slandering Jews as cultural and religious pariahs and restricting them to despised occupations, dress, etc.;[7]

5. The maintenance, through continual reinforcement of anti-Semitic attitudes, of an almost indispensable theological role (based on the divine destiny of Jews[8]) of damned infidel, and representative of the anti-Christ devil (Christ the new "human" God needed a new "human" Satan, and Satan himself, playing an important role in the Gospels, helped provide one; the purpose of Christian anti-Semitism is to "render the Jews hateful");[9]

6. Christianity's growing dogma and the tradition of indirect and direct anti-Semitism which made it increasingly difficult for it to deny anti-Semitism's validity (church and clerical pronouncements often placed the believer in the position of rejecting certain anti-Semitic traditions at the risk of infidelity to the church);[10]

7. The conflicts arising from the church's sporadic attempts to convert the Jews; and the unwillingness of the Jews to convert, thus proving "their damnable state";[11]

8. Christian resentment over the secret practice of Judaism by some Jews who had been compelled or encouraged by force or conditions to convert—or who had inherited the new religious mask of their parents;

9. Hellenized Christianity—patron of the arts, intellectual, sophisticated in the ways of power and cautious progress—conflicted in mind and emotion with those parts and times of Judaism which were puritanical and tradition-bound;

10. Sophisticated Judaism which was frequently rationalistic, inventive and socially righteous, conflicted in mind and emotion with those parts and times of Christianity which were guilt-ridden, superstitious and conservative;

11. Heresy controversies within the major faiths sometimes included anti-Semitism as Jews were accused of supporting or aiding the heresy or simply because Jews were caught in the middle between the conflicting factions. (Cf. the Albigensian and Waldensian heresies and the Sabbatarian sect.)

3. Psycho-Christian Demands

Christianity grew directly out of Judaism, and at one time was considered only one of many competing Jewish sects. For Christianity, however, the Second Coming was imminent and required a rebirth of spirit and morality of saintly dimensions. When Jews rejected the Christian message and Judaism continued to survive, even threatening the faith of new Christian converts (the Judaizing tendency), the Christian mission was redefined and directed to the Gentile and Pagan world. Christianity, therefore, had to distinguish itself from Judaism and at the same time discredit the parent faith. The mutual rejection and recriminations of this period and the central role the Jew played in basic Christian theology—as Christianity's discarded father and villainous brother—set the tone and content of future Christian-Jewish relations. The Christian, guilt-ridden through theological dictate, sought to alleviate this guilt by nurturing Christianity's anti-Semitism and justifying its past, present and future by finding fault with the Jews. He was thus able to accuse them of his own condemned emotions and to resist any realization that his anti-Semitism was unjustified. The more the Christian persecuted Jews or felt hostility towards them, the more he found it necessary to concoct, create, and exaggerate Jewish sins, and maintain his anti-Semitic attitudes.

These psycho-Christian demands are expanded on in the following:

1. As the father of Christianity (the begetters of Christ, "the old man,"[12])[13] and, in a manner of speaking, the Christ himself, and as the legal villains of Christianity, the Jews were a natural, permissible, recipient of the Christian's suppressed, rebellious anger against the moral strictures of Christ (hatred of Judaism = hatred of Christianity?);[14]

2. As the Christian's theological, psychological other self, the incarnation of his subconscious guilt-ridden wish to have "also" killed his father (a wish subconsciously regarded as a deed, an awesome source of self-hate), the Jews again served as an object for the Christian's projection and displacement—a substitute target;

3. As the rebellious son of Christ or the rebellious brother of

Christians the Jews became the hated, envied symbol of the Christian's subconscious rebellion against his new father;

4. As a group disassociating themselves from the rebellious Son, Christianity,* the Jews engendered in the Christian subconscious feelings of inferiority and sin. He purged himself of these feelings by projection (The Jews were inferior, not the Christians);

5. The emphasis on social justice found in Judaism and practiced by many Jews was to some Christians (subconsciously regarded as an unwanted conscience) a disturbing neighbor;

6. Subconsciously the Christian may have resented Jesus for being Jewish. The resulting feeling of guilt and inferiority (the Christian was not a member of the original in-group) encouraged further anti-Semitism;

7. The *sudden* morality demanded of the pagan by Christianity increased his subconscious obsessive anxiety; the myth of the villainous Jew was created and continued as one explanation for the anxiety;

8. Jews were the only outlet for man's superstitions, fears, insecurity, anger, perversity and barbarity that was morally sanctioned by the very tradition of the church;

9. The Christian, as guilt-ridden persecutor, subconsciously feared Jews as instruments of retribution against him and as living reminders of his guilt (the latter was especially true when Jews verbally called attention to his anti-Semitic sins); so the more the Christian persecuted Jews, the more he found it necessary to "protect" himself by continuing that persecution;[15]

10. The desire of religious men to explain life through the existence of good and evil supernaturals and the strong expression of this in the New Testament encouraged the Christian to deify enemies, opponents, and disbelievers of his God (thus his ability to believe in exaggerated slanders regarding the Jews). Since the closest thing to a devil (or anti-Christ) in the New Testament were the frequently-mentioned Jews,[16] they alone filled the roles;

11. The faith in supernatural claims required by Christianity—coupled with man's insecurity—made easy the belief in slanders against those considered its villain.

*Against the old covenant.

4. Perpetual Strangers in Conflict Through Social, Economic and Religious Roles

In contrast to other ancient cultures and peoples, such as the Assyrians, the Babylonians, the Carthaginians, the Egyptians, the Cretans, the Greeks and the Romans, the Jews did not follow the pattern of disappearing from history. Neither dispersion, conquest nor systematic attempts at obliteration destroyed the Jews as a conscious cultural and national group as well as the carriers of a distinctive religion. The Roman destruction of the Jewish state begun in 70 A.D. and completed in 135 A.D. did not result in the assimilation and disappearance of Jews without a homeland. Jewish survival as a unique and distinctive cultural, "national" and religious minority made them permanent aliens, perpetual strangers within a hostile larger culture. Indeed, some argue that this continuous persecution is one of the major forces that not only shaped the stance and content of Judaism but made Jewish survival possible. They suggest that without persecution Jews would have assimilated and disappeared as a people, a religion and an ethos.

The condition of permanent alien as a cause of anti-Semitism is clear in the following:

1. The Jews, owing to their dispersion and distinct customs and beliefs, were foreigners throughout a world that was xenophobic, insecure and, at times, swept by religious and national fanaticism, a world that was often ruled by governments that either sought, for their own security, a homogeneous populace or, for their own solidarity, "an animosity against an outside minority";[17]

2. The Jews constituted a foreign, "international," talented competing body (often high achievers, in spite of and because of persecution),[18] and were persecuted, segregated and maligned by countries steeped in distrust and status anxiety, by a citizenry anxious to thwart competition ("the Jew succeeds because he cheats") and by a populace—especially those at the bottom of the social and economic ladder—often subjugated, economically deprived and prone to visit their frustrated wrath and insecurity on the helpless—on "safe" targets;[19]

3. The Jews were often relegated to unpopular and insecure occupations that distinguished them from the populace, demanded a high level of achievement and consequently created more suspicion and resentment on the part of non-Jews;

4. They stubbornly defied oppression and in most cases, religious assimilation. They refused to be exterminated, physically or spiritually. Thus they became eternal strangers;

5. Their exiles, of course, caused them to burst unwanted into countries, often carrying with them a threatening sophistication enhanced by their enforced travel and travail;

6. Their religious and cultural emphasis on freedom and social justice[20] was shown justified by continual persecution and was therefore reinforced;

7. The Jews were the only lasting infidels and theological villains in Western culture;

8. Most governments with strong ties to the state religion desired to rule over a populace that was religiously homogeneous;

9. Because of all or parts of the above factors Jews were rarely accepted as citizens of a country. (If they were, it was usually with restrictions and in an environment of anti-Semitic attitudes.)

5. Psychological Demands

Man has a psychological need to rationalize his fears, shut out inconvenient truths, release, act out and justify his repressed hostilities and dreams. Prejudice against Jews helped fill this need.

The following indicate the ways in which anti-Semitism satisfied psychological needs:

1. The Jews provided the Gentile with a tangible, isolated, simply defined evil, a thing that made injustice understandable (e.g., the "Jewish conspiracy");

2. Hatred and condemnation of the Jew was a *popular* outlet—one that promised rare unity and a kind of security

among the Gentiles, that was sanctioned by his fellow man and his religion, that could be practiced with impunity,[21] and that grew because of its bandwagon appeal;

3. The Jews were the victims of the persecutors' projection, accused of harboring his own hate (toward the Jew) and his own taboo feelings and characteristics;

4. They were the objects of transference, the recipient of subconscious and conscious anger, hate, envy,[22] etc., emotions actually arrayed against government, class, intellectual or economic superiors and God;

5. The Jews as subhuman or devil-like victims capable of taking on any form provided release for numerous natural and neurotic pressures: guilt, anxiety, alienation, self-hate, barbarousness and perversity;[23]

6. The Jews provided an outlet for repressed barbarity, hostility, frustration, and fear caused largely by the West's exploitation and/or natural calamity. Jewish culpability became the great superstition—"the Great Hate";

7. The Jews, fingered by God himself as a threat, provided man with an object for that innate fear which he cannot identify;

8. The paranoia of man could utilize with ease the disreputable Jew, who, in turn, could encourage its localization;

9. Man's fear of "the old man," of death, of sex and the devil created the iniquitous and/or licentious Jew for a visible target (the latter two were topics often interwoven through slanders directed against Jews);

10. Circumcision might have evoked fears of castration in the subconscious of the uncircumcized West;

11. Group hate, which supports the antagonistic group's self-group concept, found the Jew its natural prey;

12. Man's appetite to slander, which in part evolved as a means to satisfy his hunger for tangible evils and provide answers to life's mysteries, directed itself at the nearest and choicest victim;

13. The non-Jew experienced purification and was entertained by the persecutions and sufferings of the Jews;

297

14. The Jews providing the weak with an object of hate, lent him strength and superiority;

15. The Jew could satisfy easily man's subconscious needs for status and feelings of moral superiority;

16. The non-Jew had a reason to fear Jews as a result of his own guilt over his role as persecutor;

17. He feared Jews as potential tempting victims for his guilt-ridden potential hostilities;

18. To avoid recognizing his own guilt or the guilt of his fellow persecutors he was motivated to find culpability and complicity on the part of his victim and to perpetuate past actions in order to justify them;[24]

19. To avoid guilt he frequently avoided asking *why* Jews suffered in order to avoid answers that might incriminate him, his institutions, peers, leaders, family and father figures. Instead he asked *who*—other than himself and his culture—was responsible. The Jew was a convenient answer;[25]

20. To the above must be added the general psychological inclinations towards hate and oppression and their manifestations analyzed with great thoroughness in the great body of work found on the subject of prejudice.

6. *Exploitation and Utilization*
Because of their disproportionate cosmopolitan background and/or the West's economic needs (some owing to religious strictures) the Jews were often encouraged or forced to practice trade, become merchants, middlemen, and financiers. For the same reason their relative sophistication was often utilized by leaders to strengthen their countries.[26]

The ways anti-Semitism served economic and political needs follow:

1. The Jews were utilized and exploited by secular rulers; as buffers between them and the masses (e.g., tax collectors); as scapegoats for the masses' anger at their lot and their government; as a means to mobilize the masses (through anti-Semitism); and as potential sources of emergency capital through cancellation of debts, expropriation, blackmail, and

enforced exile (Jews were sometimes given a choice between cancellation of their credits, or misfortune such as imprisonment, torture, death, or exile);

2. Frequently, their property was simply expropriated—occasionally allowed to build up and then expropriated again;

3. Often Jews were imprisoned or threatened with death for concocted crimes or because of a false conviction for real crimes and were then released for a ransom;

4. Expulsion was at times followed by an invitation to return if payment for the privilege was made;

5. They could be and were heavily taxed, exploited and exiled;

6. They could be and were blamed for misfortunes, and so slandered, terrorized and slaughtered;

7. They could be and were used as a focus for aggression, as an enemy for national cohesion;

8. They were used by the church as an agent of cohesion;

9. They were also utilized and exploited by competing political, economic or religious factions; thus, caught in-between and torn apart.

As a result of the above, and religious prejudice and psychological needs, governments helped to keep the Jews defined as a special people.

7. *Conspicuousness and Vulnerability*
The Jews were ubiquitous and international through dispersion, exile, expulsion and migration. In the Christian West, Jews were theological freaks and villains forced into unpopular, exposed occupations. They were easily identified by required modes of dress (often degrading), residence restrictions and restrictions on movement. In reaction and also by their own religio-cultural traditions, Jews were cohesive, sometimes possessed their own language and dress and were frequently exposed through disproportionate achievement. With the exception of the Khazak Kingdom, Jewish existence in the West from 70 A.D. to the 19th century was by permission not a matter of right. Jews, in every country until the establishment of Israel, were a minority popula-

tion, without country, nation, numbers, durable power or natural allies. Therefore, the Jews were constant, conspicuous, and vulnerable.

Conspicuousness and vulnerability resulted from and added to anti-Semitism in the following ways:

1. In all manner of things, Jews were restricted; they were, in most cases, kept from the political mainstream and from social contact; they were kept in questionable social status—even when in "status" positions; they were exploited and humiliated into despised "types" by religious and secular law and custom;

2. From the consequent isolation and conspicuousness, Jews appeared mysterious, fascinating and were believed capable of any sinister crime and wonderment—therefore easily suspected by a religious, superstitious, fearful and ignorant public;

3. As a visible foreign element, without political power or allies, Jews could be persecuted with impunity and with success. Close at hand and surrounded by those who found persecution of the Jews morally sanctioned by culture, by large segments of religion, and by many of religious and political leaders—the Jews were especially vulnerable to the weapons of prejudice.

Anti-Semitism caused Jewish conspicuousness and vulnerability and these encouraged anti-Semitism. The Jews were a durable, identifiable scapegoat.

8. *Environment*

Anti-Semitic expressions in art, literature, language, education, history, sermons, religious writings (especially lectures and textbooks),[27] traditional conversations and folk myth became ubiquitous, insidious, and profound. And anti-Semitic customs, conventions, and laws continually reinforced existing anti-Semitic attitudes and activities—and bore them anew.

The inculcation and pervasiveness of anti-Semitism in Western culture is illustrated by the following:

1. The portrait of the Jews presented in the New Testament,

the charge of Deicide, rejection of the Messiah, the trial of Jesus, the story of Judas, were elaborated on in the writings and preachings of the early Church. Jewish history was rewritten to fit Christian theology;

2. In the effort to attract Gentiles, Christianity made great efforts to disassociate itself from Judaism and to discredit Judaism. The intemperate charges and slanders against Judaism of this early period found their way into the writings of the greatest of Churchmen—St. Augustine, St. Ambrose, St. Jerome, St. Thomas Aquinas, Innocent III, etc.;

3. The Church Councils and Synods constantly issued anti-Jewish decrees;

4. The Canon Law of the Church included many anti-Jewish provisions;

5. Canon Law, Conciliar and Papal decrees and Christian doctrine became state and secular law when Christianity became the official state religion;

6. Sermons, hymns, plays, church feasts celebrations and ritual incorporated anti-Jewish slanders and myths, and became part of the Christian tradition;

7. The above religious anti-Semitic attitudes and their secular offshoots were absorbed by the books, beliefs, traditions and art growing up around them;

8. Vulgar and morbid slander developed charging Jews with all manner of heinous crimes against Christians and Christianity—including ritual murder, host desecration, the use of Christian blood in Passover matzoh, and devil worship;

9. The myth of the Jewish conspiracy first in well poisoning, later in economic roles and as corruptors of Christian civilization and culture developed. The blame for natural, economic or political disasters and crises was placed on the Jews;

10. Jewish stereotypes grew from anti-Semitic tradition, the lascivious seducer, sexual pervert, dishonest businessman, money grubber, international banker, unpatriotic coward, loud-mouthed and pushy interloper, subversive, pornographer and were utilized and preserved by transmitting agencies (e.g. the arts, tribal wisdom). They took on a life of their own.

*   *   *

301

The following is addressed to the artistic expressions that have unknowingly added to the anti-Semitic environment. It does not apply to blatantly anti-Semitic manifestations in art or the work of conscious or committed anti-Semites.

11. Unflattering descriptions of Jews and Jewish life in literature or other artistic creations, although not the work of anti-Semites and possibly accurate concerning the authors' experiences, might reflect an acceptance of anti-Semitic stereotypes and thinking common to the day, and in any case, serve to reinforce them. The criteria for determining anti-Semitic intent in a work of art have not been established. The valid arguments justifying all such characters or commentary revolve around the fact that there are scoundrels among all peoples. The valid arguments against including this material could be presented as follows:

1. When the only Jews portrayed—or the vast majority of them—are villains or unappealing, the direct communication of anti-Semitic "evidence," intended or not, takes place, and the book or parts of it can justifiably be labeled anti-Semitic.

2. When a Jewish character is portrayed (if only fleetingly) with anti-Semitic stereotypical characteristics, the result is the reinforcement of anti-Semitic attitudes.

3. When the general tone and viewpoint of a book expresses disapproval or disdain for Jews or Jewish life, the impression usually left with the Western reader who has been exposed to the general anti-Semitic stereotypes, is that the author is alluding to *all* Jews.

The above points derive their strength from the assumption that anti-Semitism is prejudice and that prejudice by definition is not true. Art should attempt to reveal truth not perpetuate falsehood. The weakness of these arguments is the assumption that the artist defines his role in a moral context.

This leads to a fourth point that belongs in another category: art does not exist in a vacuum. From an artistic viewpoint each of the three points above can be refuted. The inclusion of Jewish

302

villains, stereotyped Jews, or unflattering portraits of Jewish life in novels or works of art can be justified because they can and do exist or are the artists' vision of truth. But from a moral perspective—given the background of anti-Semitism and its consequent latent potential and accepting the premise that the inclusion of such portraits will, however indirectly, add to that potential—justification should rest on a broader base.

This argument admittedly demands much of the artist. It necessarily limits the range of creative definition. It does, however, also expand the role of the creative person. It challenges the writer to consider the impact of the written word. In short it demands the artist be a whole person with social as well as artistic integrity.

12. The Jew is blamed for (never praised for) the rise of capitalism, the democratic revolutions, socialism, communism, and pacifism;

13. The Jew is portrayed as the supreme manipulator and conspirator. Great power and evil intent are ascribed to him regardless of facts to the contrary;

14. The consequent development of an academic and folk-loric tradition of anti-Semitism provided a growing foundation of "proof" for anti-Semitic beliefs (tainted sources);

15. The consequent unearthing of new "proofs" of Jewish wickedness: ritual murder, host desecration, etc.;

16. The churches' relative toleration of contempt and lack of motivation to counter its anti-Semitism;[28]

17. When Jews had the opportunity to no longer be foreign—through choice or Christian encouragement, intimidation or torture—the consequent substantial assimilation did not necessarily eliminate future anti-Semitism. And when they were not achievers, when they were out of sight, "minding their own business," quiescent—even absent—static, provincial, simple, poor, etc. [which was not infrequent],[29] the prejudice against them, nourished by Christian anti-Semitic myth, remained;[30]

18. In recent times when Jews attempted to assimilate in one sphere without assimilating in another (e.g., striving for social acceptance in Christian circles while maintaining their own

religion) they were often regarded as interlopers and therefore as "pushy";

19. They were forced into ghettos, compelled to wear distinctive, unbecoming, humiliating dress, excluded from and forced into certain unappealing—yet envied—occupations. Among these were buffer occupations;[31]

20. The often wretched state of the Jews which resulted from anti-Semitism (a state advocated by Gregory IX, Innocent III, St. Augustine, St. Thomas Aquinas, Martin Luther and numerous others)[32] was utilized and encouraged as proof of the Jew's damnation (self-fulfilling prophecy);[33]

21. Even when Jews were not present in the population anti-Semitism was. An example of this is England from the end of the 13th to the 17th centuries. No Jews, to speak of, lived in the country. Yet England, during this period was most prolific in anti-Semitic literature and references. This was the case in other areas as well.[34]

Anti-Semitism has been an international unifying factor in a factious world, a rare common denominator for Western man. Where there were no Jews, they had to be invented, and could be with ease owing to the inherited environment.

9. *Resistance to Solution*
The mass complexity, resilience, ubiquity, horror and banal evil found in anti-Semitism and its tenacious hold on Western history discouraged an understanding of its dynamics and a confronting of its force.
Reasons for this include:

1. The great ignorance among Jews and Christians alike concerning its nature prevents the recognition of anti-Semitism and its perniciousness and potential for destruction;
2. It is a complex, lengthy, depressing and "minor" subject that discourages study. (And the past generally, especially if unpleasant and not playing a major historical role, is quick to

304

be minimized and forgotten both by educators and the populace);

3. The desire of Jews not to face their historical isolation and uniqueness, the surrounding nightmare implied at times by anti-Semitism, and the responsibility it dictates, causes them to avoid confronting its reality—often by belittling its extent or denying or justifying its existence (the latter manifestation signals one of the birthplaces of the Jewish anti-Semite);[35]

4. Anti-Semitism serves as a source of guilt for the Christian;[36] therefore he is often unwilling to face the evil extent of anti-Semitism, tending to deny, justify or belittle it and frequently responding to Jewish charges of anti-Semitism with renewed defensive hostility, dismissing them as outpourings of hysteria, paranoia, and self-pity.[37] And to avoid his own culpability he is continually motivated to find evidence of the Jews' culpability and to ignore evidence of their innocence. For the same reason, he has the tendency to accuse the Jews of bringing anti-Semitism on themselves (or imagining it) not necessarily through evil deeds but through overreaction and clannishness;[38]

5. An acceptance by Christians of Christian culpability in historical anti-Semitism would place on them either the difficult and irritating responsibilities found in combating future anti-Semitism (not excluding their own); or the guilt unearthed by ignoring it;

6. If a Christian chooses not to be an anti-Semite but, at the same time, chooses not to deal with such an unpleasant force, he can find relief from this dilemma in the simple refuge of convenient insensitivity and indifference;

7. Non-Jews often attempt to minimize the magnitude of anti-Semitism—and their responsbility for it—by equating the Jew with other ethnic groups, thus negating the uniqueness of his suffering and their special relationship to it. They find it difficult to see that special concern over Jewish survival should exist not because of any mistaken notions that Jews are more deserving of survival or at every moment they are more threatened than other groups, but because their 3,000-year-old complex history as victim (in Diaspora) and its potential fertility

for further persecution requires it. Thus, non-Jews are not especially concerned with anti-Semitism;

8. Non-anti-Semitic Christians, in trying to absolve Christianity from guilt in the development of anti-Semitism, often find themselves with little else or not enough, to cogently blame—except the victim;[39]

9. Once anti-Semitism or indifference to anti-Semitism became "universal" in the Western world, opposition to it would often be opposition to the overwhelming attitudes and activities of one's neighbors;

10. Once anti-Semitism became an apparent part of Christianity, opposition to it would often be considered opposition to the true and surrounding faith;

11. If the non-Jew no longer maintained anti-Semitic attitudes and ceased seeing evidence for anti-Semitism he would undermine the economic and social restrictions on Jews which were to his benefit;

12. The motivation of righteous indignation to fight anti-Semitism is sparse (and consequently the sins of omission are numerous—e.g., world response during the Nazi persecutions). Obviously, few people identify enough with their tribal neighbors to become aware of and work for them. This lack of identification is not only based on dissimilarity but encouraged by man's unwillingness to accept identification's demands: sacrifice, time, responsibility and unpleasant knowledge (such indifference to others is often justified or camouflaged by the resources of prejudice);

13. There has been no need for the non-Jew to resist anti-Semitism. It is a prejudice that apparently he can tolerate and practice with impunity;

14. There is a tendency on the part of those who do combat it to respond primarily to its current motivations and problems often at the expense of those historical elements less apparent but as relevant and as demanding of attention;

15. People do not normally wish to remember any unpleasant past unless it is in their interest to do so;

16. For the paranoid bigot, at least, "erroneous judgments (are) not subject to correction by experience."[40]

10. *A Life of Its Own (Anti-Semitism*
Causes Anti-Semitism)
Western history created and nurtured a symbiotic, interacting
prejudice against the Jews—deep-rooted, obsessive, cumulative,
self-perpetuating, the old sustaining the new, and effect often
becoming new cause.
The interrelatedness and rejuvenating and reinforcing nature of
anti-Semitism can be seen in:

1. The religiously sanctioned damnation of the Jews and
their consequent negative role, their exploitation, ubiquity,
isolation, conspicuousness, vulnerability and enforced voca-
tions caused them to become the natural villains of Western
society. This was reinforced by the frequent manifestations of
Jewish culture and Western prejudice such as Jewish cohesiveness, vitality, achievement, prominence and strangerhood;
2. Most tendencies in society to identify evil and blame the
stranger were directed at them. Stereotypes and negative images
of the Jews had to be maintained and developed by society to
alleviate guilt and justify socio-economic restrictions, religiously dictated anti-Semitism, past anti-Semitism and comfortable
attitudes;
3. Evidence of culpability and complicity was found by the
persecutor, the fellow traveler, the low-key conventional anti-
Semite, and the passive onlooker, not only in slanders but in the
Jews' natural acts, in their natural sins, or in reactions caused by
the prejudice in the first place.[41] (A latent, volatile anti-
Semitism was established. Normal sins or activities of Jews
which otherwise would have been hardly noticed exploded in
the inflammable fantasy world of anti-Semitism);
4. Such "evidence" lent credibility to the Jews' villainy
and increased suspicion of and belief in their hidden villainy
which in turn offered more corroboration—and the cycle continued. (At the same time, of course, evidence of the Jews'
innocence was ignored—for instance, their existence outside of
stereotype. With so much riding on the prejudice, it had to be);
5. The persistence of anti-Semitism through so many ages

307

and countries became proof itself of Jewish culpability.[42] The big lie—a lie repeated enough—is believed;

6. The self-fulfilling prophecy took root: the Jews are damned, persecute them; their (consequent) wretched state is proof of their moral inferiority; because of their moral inferiority they must be persecuted; etc.

7. All of this, of course, built up a tradition (based on tainted sources) of anti-Semitism which, with its development by and its absorption into Christian tradition, became necessary to sustain (and increasingly difficult to refute—especially in light of what such refutation might do to the church's credibility and its own faith in itself);

8. During this process anti-Semitism became so intertwined and dependent on irrational beliefs—and so successful and safe in reflecting them—it became almost as durable. So belief in the "despicable" Jew as a source of sustenance for and protection from man's neurotic and primitive drives (in so many spheres—economic, political, psychological and social) was instinctively maintained by society. It provided one of the few structured homes and fortresses for irrationality, the one most *easily* maintained (irrationality's path of least resistance) and shared (a collective psychosis);

9. The resultant guilt rather than acting as a restraint often acted as a provocation for the anti-Semite to avoid his guilt by justifying and perpetuating his past sins. The more he persecuted the Jews the more he felt guilty, and the more he was encouraged to deny that guilt by justifying his persecutions and therefore perpetuating them. And the more he justified and perpetuated his persecutions the more he had to project and transfer his feelings on those he had been guilty of persecuting, deny the reality of their innocence, "perceive" their guilt, and, consequently, continue his persecutions.

10. The more the self hater hated himself the more he hated his scapegoat; the more he hated his scapegoat the less sure he was of his own innocence and logic and the more guilt he had to project onto his scapegoat. (Allport)

11. Guilt also caused the anti-Semite to fear Jews, so the more he hated and persecuted them, the more he felt it necessary

to protect himself from retribution by persecuting them (which necessitated justifying that persecution). All of this, of course, prevented or discouraged Jewish participation in the mainstream of non-Jewish everyday activities, thus increasing Jewish isolation, thus strengthening a condition which supported the non-Jew's stereotypes of Jews, which in turn continued to inhibit Jewish participation in the country's mainstream.

12. And as the history of anti-Semitism, feeding on itself, grew longer and more complex, the chance, ability and motivation of Christians to understand (or even be aware of) its historical nature diminished. This set the stage for an increasing number of players who innocently made remarks and took actions which out of historical context did not strike them or their ever-expanding equally ignorant audience as reflecting or aggravating anti-Semitism—though they might have been perceived by some as inaccurate or unethical. It also set the stage for those who consciously or subconsciously might or might not be quite so innocent and who could give expression to anti-Semitism without seeming to do so (e.g., General Brown's statements regarding Jewish "control" over the American economy and mass media).[43]

MODERN ANTI-SEMITISM

With the decline of religious faith and its partial replacement by secular reason, certain emphases in anti-Semitism underwent a change. Supernatural damnation was not cited as often or as vehemently as justification. However, it continued to thrive more than is commonly accepted. (A 1960 survey of the United States—one of the most liberal of Western countries—showed that "over 1/3 of Protestant and nearly 1/4 of Catholic respondents did not repudiate the notion that 'the reason that the Jews have so much trouble is because God is punishing them for rejecting Jesus.' ")[44]

And where religious prejudice did not motivate anti-Semitism directly, it functioned indirectly:

1. As that which bore secular anti-Semitism. When the man of reason could no longer cite supernatural causes to explain his

309

antipathy toward the Jew (which his parents and his society had transmitted to him on the basis of theology, and which they in turn had previously accepted on the same basis), he had to find other basic reasons to justify his inherited prejudice. These took the form of cultural prejudice ('the Jews have always been a despicable, ignorant, superstitious people' whose "God" was a God of hate; or, 'anti-Semitism has turned them into a despicable people'); racial ('they are genetically inferior'); ideological ('they are a constant, the cause of all or much that is bad within our system').[45]

2. As a demifaith fed by a latent 2,000 years of tradition not often directly cited by the individual as the reason for his anti-Semitism but vaguely utilized by his conscious and martialed by his subconscious, both as justification of feelings already felt and as a force with which to release his natural inclinations to blame and hate.

3. As the progenitors of stereotypes and reputations. In many cases these latter remained as real and as powerful as when the religious prejudice created them. (Prime examples are those found in literature, history and art.) The Jew as greedy, dishonest, conspiratorial, crude and troublesome could be believed if one simply was on the lookout for these traits. For since these traits existed in humans and since the Jews were human, the rationale held.[46]

4. As something which could be utilized by ambitious leaders (if Nazi persecutions were not as "Christian" as those perpetrated in the past, there was, certainly, an "historic complicity." For instance, the historic Jewish stereotypes utilized by Hitler).

But it must be emphasized here that by the time religious motivation and justification for anti-Semitism declined, the offshoots of that particular prejudice had already taken on a life of its own. "Modern" anti-Semitism did not merely spring from religious anti-Semitism (and strangerhood). It also sprang from the burgeoning *offshoots* of religious anti-Semitism, new trees seeded by the old—which would mature by the time the first trees began to age. (An example of this is the Jews' reputation vis-à-vis money:

The story of Judas, church-enforced money lending, enforced middlemanship and defensive achievement, all surrounded by envy and resentment, established an independent reputation.)

In other words, religious anti-Semitism so pervasively and widely formulated and maligned the reputation of the Jews that even later, when the original "proof" was at times lost (and then often at the conscious level only), the original bad reputation and its ramifications—new bad reputations—continued and so encouraged the understandably suspicious to see and seek out new "proof."[47]

As a result, the Jews became the best targeted prey for man's propensity to slander (providing as it does a salutary and safe outlet for frustrations and hostility). And the more widely the slanders were believed, the more nourishment they provided for additional similar beliefs, and the more easily and innocuously they were passed on through non-anti-Semitic processes (means which only incidentally presented the odious Jew—e.g., novels, plays, etc.). The Jew's bad reputation has, in effect, taken on a nearly autonomous existence.

Add to this the following, and anti-Semitism's life of its own comes into focus: in modern times the Jews were still strangers, powerless (in the Diaspora) and conspicuous, as such they still served psychological needs, provided simple answers to complex questions, continued to unify those around them by being a common object of hate (to some extent still morally sanctioned); they were still disproportionately successful; they were still spread throughout nations and so suspect; they still agitated for their and others' freedoms.

REACTIONS

During both ancient and modern times there were numerous reactions of the Jews to anti-Semitism which "justified" or encouraged more anti-Semitism and which, in turn, caused more reaction, setting in motion a vicious circle. Although these reactions are not prime causes of anti-Semitism and in fact are quite

311

minimal, they are still contributing factors. The reactions fall under three categories: defenses, attitudes, and characteristics and customs.

Defenses: Some Jews adopted the attainment of success and position to counter the insecurity resulting from persecution. Numerous times Jews in trouble could extricate themselves only by influence, by being a contributing minority or by buying themselves out. As mentioned, this condition was often created by the nobility to increase their power and income. This achievement caused envy and resentment which caused more persecution which prompted more achievement. . . .

Another protective reaction was a further strengthening of the family[48] and community (occasionally, inter-communal as well as local), which caused more distrust and resentment which engendered more persecution which further strengthened the family. . . .

Still another defense of some Jews grew out of acceptances of stereotypes imposed on them by their Christian neighbor. For instance, bolstered by the facts that they and their ancestors had survived and in some cases were even successful under persecution, and that many of them had revered and sought education, some Jews and non-Jews began to translate the epithet "shrewd" as "intelligent." The translation accomplished two things: It provided the Jews with a pride direly needed in view of their denigrating environment; if absorbed by their subconscious, it diluted subconscious self-hate. Other Jews accepted an unambiguous stereotyping. The prejudice encouraged them to agree with their persecutors, to take over from them their persecution in order to win their approval, and to acquire, through identification with the majority, a sense of security. (Occasionally, as a result, they literally fled their original identity.) All of this often impaired them psychologically and socially. Ironically, the reaction of their hosts was often negative.

Still other Jews out of fear and a desire to escape the stigma placed on them by society sought to respect and join that society although they rejected the validity of the stigma. But this response was often met with distrust.

Infrequently the Jews counter-attacked, joined together and

312

fought their persecutors. They were then accused of being vicious, or clannish.

Many of these and other defenses, often strengthened by a variety of reactions to anti-Semitism, tended to strengthen Jewish life. This helped Judaism to endure which permitted anti-Semitism to endure as well.

Attitudes: The attitudes of some Jews toward Christians were, of course, affected by anti-Semitism. These, however, were mostly defensive and seldom manifested themselves in revenge or hate. Over-reaction and over-sensitivity, although appearing in Jewish life, were quite minimal. In fact, the lack of Jewish antipathy towards Christians which is found in Jewish religion, culture and tradition is, considering the circumstances, somewhat remarkable.[49]

Among these attitudes are the following:

1. Fear of Christianity owing to the villainous roles into which it had cast them and the offensive characteristics it had assigned to them.

2. Resentment against the Christian for his persistent efforts to convert them.

3. Over-reaction, over-sensitivity, and paranoia. All these were encouraged not only by persecutions, the Western tendency to minimize it, to attribute its cause to Jewish character, to ignore its danger signals and to fail to acknowledge it in history,[50] but also by the subtle ubiquity of anti-Semitic attitudes in Western culture, seen even in its models and heroes, in its literature and saints.

4. Dual-loyalty. At times the Jews' alien status and persecution generated a lack of patriotism, but throughout history, in spite of persecution, the Jews, when given the chance, were usually, excellent patriots, not only through conscience and identification but also to prove their reliability, improve their security, and instill in themselves a sense of belonging. Still, a surrounding suspicion of disloyalty was prevalent, provoked, in part, by the host's guilt over his treatment of the Jew.

5. Social righteousness. Already emphasized in Judaism,

this was increased by the injustice directed at its people. The consequent "arrogance," added to the Jews' other "failings," only exacerbated the Christian's guilt and resentment and provided "justification" for his prejudice.

6. Jewish feelings against the injustice perpetrated against them had to be repressed. This at times caused Jews to feel more resentment and become more isolated—both of which provoked Christian mistrust.

Characteristics and Customs: Jewish "characteristics" and customs were affected to some degree by anti-Semitism. Some Jews walking outside of the ghetto no doubt did so in a fear, resembling furtiveness. If they were clothed in identifiable "religious" or imposed dress they might have presented a picture ludicrous, offensive and threatening to their neighbors. Contrary to some anti-Semitic theories these "characteristics" seldom took the form of bad traits which then "justifiably" created anti-Semitic reactions. Such theories do not hold up under investigation. However, the "thinking" anti-Semite claims the exception as the rule. He adds it to his exaggerations of the Jews' natural human failing and his denigrations of Jewish "characteristics" or customs—that is, those which differ from his own—and then presents the new conglomerate as further evidence of Jewish despicability.

All of the above defenses, attitudes and "characteristics" and customs were exaggerated by the non-Jew and many of them were presented as "further" proof of the ancient theological slander that Jews hated Christians.

SYNOPTIC EXPLANATIONS

There are several symbolic and analogical approaches to anti-Semitism that might offer a more succinct, comprehensible explanation of its lasting strength:

One regards anti-Semitism as an infectious disease—multifaceted, widespread and reinfecting. Western man is the patient whose background, environment and culture give him a low resistance to this particular strain of perniciousness. The organ it attacks, Jewry, necessary or not, will not go away. (One sure cure of anti-Semitism is to destroy the Jews.)

Another appreciates the unfortunate chemistry of all the aforementioned factors of anti-Semitism (not all of them in and of themselves negative). Something formed in the universe of the Western world, a new living entity, that perpetuates itself (anti-Semitism causes anti-Semitism) and is poisonous and difficult to break down.

A different explanation allows man to see the Jew in the Western world as one sees the Black in the American South. History, accident, economics, politics, etc., turned the Black into a slave and second-class citizen for 300 years. Generally, the religion of the Jew was to Western history what the Black's skin and background was to his exploiter.

Another defines Anti-Semitism as a religion or as an ideology (something to believe in) with all its faith and superstition and potential for growth, and its ability to assuage man's insecurities, justify his evil and perversities, and satisfy his everyday psychological demands.

One approach studies the Jews as a weak but resilient nation next to a strong one, a small nation that plays the part of villain in the religion and myth of its neighbor, a nation that practices "strange customs," both envied and resented for its successes. A nation that can be continually exploited with impunity. Would not such a nation invite continual attack?

Another approach pictures the Jews as a punching-man given to a species that retains its "immature" desire to vent its hostility. The "toy" is durable and no matter how—or how often—it is beaten manages to right itself. When attempts are made to take it away to safety the child grasps it with an affectionate ferocity and possessiveness born of primitive need.

Still another explanation sees the Jew as the perennial innocent victim of rape, the body most inviting to attack, most attractive and vulnerable to its peers, most sanctioned as an object of ravishment.[51]

The latter is perhaps the most telling analogy. Without recognizing that man creates suffering through his needs and that he has a

315

natural inclination to become obsessed with particular outlets to satisfy those needs, it is almost impossible to accept the overwhelming innocence of the Jews in on-going anti-Semitism. It is impossible to see that culpability is not necessary to a victim's longevity as a victim—that only his survival, his availability to his attacker, his attractiveness to his attacker and an environment which encourages and sanctions the victimization are needed.

CONCLUSION TO CAUSES

Without an awareness and an understanding of these points the question "why anti-Semitism?" will carry with it a question with an ugly implication: Why the Jew? They themselves must in some form be responsible, for they appear at first glance to be the only constant in the long story of anti-Semitism. The persecutors and persecutions appear too varied to be culpable.[52]

Certainly there is a tendency by some (even among Jews) to feel that so many ages, nations, and political movements cannot be wrong, that certain elements of Christianity in all its power and success cannot be wrong, that numerous great thinkers, artists, statesmen and saints cannot be wrong. All these factors—by their very number and power, by the recurring patterns they have created over 2,000 years, by their loose consensus, though they are often separated by time, conditions, occupation, temperament, politics, religion, class and culture—must attest to the need for anti-Semitic actions and the truth of anti-Semitic allegations. Indeed the Jews must be wicked, lowly, and in some sense deserving of damnation.

Certainly the error of this assumption must be made manifest. The unhappy logic of anti-Semitism—that it sprang in all its variety from understandable causes not at all related to godly sanctions or culpable victims—must be understood.

Finally, this irony: As the reader notes, the prime purpose of this effort and any such effort is to help provide the knowledge necessary to combat anti-Semitism. An indispensable part of that knowledge is Christianity's role in the birth and nursing of anti-

Semitism. But it is quite possible that such a conclusion, in spite of the fact that it is based on our honest interpretation of our research, will negatively affect some sincere Christians. Those who honestly believe Christianity is unable to contain in its body the seeds of anything so evil as anti-Semitism may attack the analysis in a way that will unintentionally contribute to and encourage anti-Semitism. Others may feel compelled to further justify anti-Semitism rather than work to remove this element of hate from what is essentially a message of love.[53]

NOTES TO CAUSES

1. The attack against Jews as stiff-necked and unassimilable contains an irony. If they had assimilated before the first century, what would have borne Christianity? In any case, the position is incorrect. When there was an open society, assimilation occurred and does occur (vide the U.S.). Furthermore the "lost" ten tribes obviously assimilated.

2. To a great extent "Jewish Family" and the role it played in the Diaspora sustained Jewish life. Its strength came from two sources: the Jewish religion and the Jewish experience.

Jewish myth and/or history depicted a religion born through family and tribe, God the Father, the patriarchs and their sons. Family trees are carefully traced. (God made His covenant with a family. Only later, under the Prophets, did He become universal.) With little or no emphasis on after-life in Judaism, the family was its immortality.

The experience of the Jews before and in the Diaspora made the family indispensable for survival. In Biblical times during the Jews' nomadic years, the family was a shelter against unfriendly deserts. During their years as a nation, occupying and holding strategic and fertile lands, the family formed a unit of defense (and a company for campaigns). During the Diaspora the family was forged by and became a shield—however limited—against anti-Semitism and pressures for conversion.

3. Jews living elsewhere (without the stigma of Christian persecution) did not play a role disproportionate to their numbers. (Cf. Islam, China and India.)

4. There is disagreement as to the division and priority of blame regarding unfair tactics in the theological fight between Jews and Christians during the first centuries after Christ. Some scholars maintain that the Jews began the bad feelings, citing Jewish anti-Christian writings and participation in the persecution

317

of Christians. Others maintain that the source for the allegations of persecutions are all Christian anti-Jewish and that the anti-Semitic, anti-Jewish theological writings and allegations of early Christian leaders were prompted primarily by competition and religious proselytizing fervor not revenge and reaction.

A consideration of both positions might yield the following: at first, the competition between two sects, Christian and Jewish, was "normal." But then feelings grew bitter, the former accusing the Jews, who at the time had the upper hand in the competition, of rejecting the Messiah and cooperating in the pagan persecutions, the latter accusing the Christians of castigating them as Christ-killers and infidels, and of breaking the faith. The anger of the underdog Christians grew as did their rhetoric. Also to proselytize more successfully, it was necessary for them to de-Judaize Christianity in order to universalize it, to concoct the guilt of the Jews in order to play down the guilt of the Romans. The battle grew more heated with action and counteraction. The Christians gained the upper hand and found themselves left with an anti-Semitic, anti-Jewish mythology sanctioned by their most sacred writings, their early Saints and teachers. The consequences are a matter of history.

What percentage of early Christian anti-Semitic activity resulted from Jewish anti-Christian activity is hard to determine. Considering the type and quantity of evidence regarding the anti-Christian activity, the other motivating factors behind Christian anti-Semitism, and the continued growth of anti-Semitism after Jewish opposition ceased to be measurable, it is difficult to regard the percentage as high. Certainly, Christian anti-Semitism grew so great, distant and durable that any attempt to explain Christian anti-Semitism by citing early Jewish anti-Christianity, even if it were substantial and not provoked, would be unconvincing.

5. Modern church scholarship, especially since the discovery of the Dead Sea Scrolls, has recognized the distortions and countered some of the interpretations of Christ's teachings that had supported anti-Semitism. This, of course, does not obviate a faith in the New Testament's spiritual veracity. It is increasingly recognized that the writers of the Gospels were quite human and affected to no small extent by their environment, specifically the surrounding struggle of Christianity to convert and integrate into a pagan world and to compete with and disassociate itself from Judaism.

6. Three primary historical distortions are: (a) the role of the Jews and Romans in Christ's death; (b) the Diaspora as punishment for the killing of Christ; and (c) the degeneracy of Judaism at the time of Christ (see *The Teaching of Contempt*).

A. The Romans and Pilate, rather than innocent bystanders drawn into action by the evil Jews (in Augustine's version of The Passion, the Romans do not even appear), were bloody suppressors of all those suspected of revolution—and Christ was so suspected, especially in a country that at the time was a hotbed of rebellion. (Philo tells of Pilate's "crimes, his rages, his greed, his injustices, his

abuses, the citizens he had put to death without trial, his intolerable cruelty."
Josephus tells of massacres under Pilate and Luke [13:1] mentions Pilate ordering
a massacre of Galileans.) Also only a tiny segment of the Jews were agitating
against Christ. These were made up of a small oligarchy totally subservient to
Rome "which appointed or dismissed them at will." The true spiritual leader of
the Pharisees, as defined in Acts 5:35-39, took a cautious position based on
the possibility that Jesus might indeed be representing God's will [see *The
Teaching of Contempt,* pp. 125 and 139].

At the same time, although the majority of the multitudes who followed Christ
were Jews, the "theys" and other references of Christ and the Evangelists to
those Jews opposing Him or those living "ungodly" lives have traditionally been
interpreted as applying to the Jews as a monolithic enemy.

Much of this tradition stems from the Evangelists themselves. Although the
first three often refer specifically to the leaders of the Pharisees and the rulers of
the Jews as Christ's antagonists, the writers and Jesus in their Gospels, in varying
degrees, also preach or suggest the collective guilt of the Jews and their progeny
for their denial of Jesus as the Messiah and their role in Christ's death. The fourth
Evangelist is the most supportive of this tradition. Almost all distinction between
the Jews as a people and some of their leaders is ignored. It is "the Jews" that
occur throughout John as the arch-villains. They are continually spelled out as
those responsible for His death and incapable of accepting Jesus as the Messiah
and damned for both. (John's change of emphasis can be explained, in part, by the
fact that he was writing later than the other Evangelists, when the need to separate
Christianity from Judaism was more apparent and when the Pharisees and the
Christians were especially bitter enemies.)

These are but two of other inaccuracies found in the role played by the Jews in
Christ's death (e.g., present day knowledge of Jewish life and tradition during
Christ's time throws serious doubts on parts of the Gospel's story [the times of the
purported Sanhedrin meeting, etc.]).

Two articles pertaining to this subject are worth quoting. One is from *The
Ecumenist, A Journal For Promoting Christian Unity,* "The Jews, Faith and
Ideology" by Father Gregory Baum in July-August, 1972:

"The anti-Jewish trends present in Christian preaching have been discovered
only fairly recently. It was only when Christians were confronted by Hitler's
violent anti-Semitism that they were driven to examine their own teachings on
Jews and Jewish religion and found the courage to face up to an enormously
destructive aspect of their own past. In the Catholic Church, Petersen, Maritain
and Journet led the way in this self-examination. At first it was held that the
anti-Jewish trends present in the Church's preaching were distortions belonging
only to certain periods of its history; more detailed scholarship and a more
fearless look at the past, however, revealed that these trends were present in the
Church almost from the beginning and pervaded its entire life. Even the New

Testament contains passages of anti-Jewish bias. The Christian Church, understanding itself as the true and authentic Israel, tried from the very beginning to make credible, and give reasons for, the substitution of one people by another.''

The same problem was covered in a more popular manner (presentation and publication) in the Easter 1975 issue of *Newsweek Magazine* (April 23, 1973). The article discussed the concerns shared by Christian and Jewish scholars of the possible anti-Semitic impact of traditional Easter services. The common concern was ''*how* the Easter story is told and, more precisely, *who* is blamed for the death of Jesus.'' Quoting Rosemary Reuther, a Roman Catholic theologian: ''Christians have been willing to acknowledge an element of anti-Semitism as accidental to Christianity. But they have yet to admit that it is deeply rooted in the Gospel itself.'' The article examines the controversy of Biblical anti-Semitism. There is no general agreement on this question and scholars, in the area, are deeply divided. However, there is general agreement that the Gospel passages most susceptible to anti-Semitic interpretation and manipulation are those dealing with the trial and crucifixion of Jesus. In contrast to the impression given in the New Testament (almost exonerating the Roman authority and placing almost total blame on the Jews), the scholars mentioned in the article are generally in agreement that, in reality, the Roman role was considerably larger and the Jewish role considerably smaller.

In essence theGospel accounts include distortions and contradictions that many scholars have questioned. Eduard Lohse, a Lutheran theologian, has found 27 violations of Jewish law governing procedures of the Sanhedrin in the accounts of Jesus' trial presented in the Gospels of Matthew and Mark. Father Jeffrey Sobosan (Notre Dame University) has written on the progression of anti-Jewish bias found in the succeeding Gospels. Concerning the last Gospel (St. John), ''Sobosan notes that it is simply 'the Jews' in general who take Jesus out and lead Him to be crucified.''

The article pointed out that Father Raymond Brown of Union Theological Seminary, while generally agreeing with Fr. Sobosan, argues that the Gospel of St. John has to be considered within the context of its origins. The Fourth Gospel was written at a time when Judaism and Christianity were enmeshed in a bitter struggle and the conversion of all Jews to Christianity was hopeless. Brown argues that ''John's polemics were theological thrusts against Judaism not ethnic slurs. 'Bad as it is, anti-Judaism is not the same as anti-Semitism.' '' Father Sobosan does not think such distinctions are particularly meaningful. ''He is convinced that scriptural anti-Judaism is largely responsible for Christian anti-Semitism and that the two are often indistinguishable in practice.'' The article states that Fr. Sobosan believes the Churches must go further than Vatican II which proscribed anti-Semitism on theological grounds, and take the necessary steps to ''set the Gospel record straight.''

320

The article noted that Philosophical Library Publishers has published a version of St. John's Gospel without anti-Semitic language and phrasing. Father Brown argues that tampering with the language of the Gospels would be a disservice to history. Instead he believes Christians should be forced to come to grips with the Gospels. "People in the pew ought to know that they cannot adopt every attitude in the Bible just because it appears there."

B. The Diaspora of the Jews did not begin after the killing of Christ in 70 A.D., (the myth that helps bear out the damnation theory—the Jews were dispersed because they killed Christ), but in 721 B.C. with the fall of Israel and 586 B.C. with the fall of Judea. From these times forward the Jew's place of residence was no longer Palestine alone. (In the Roman Empire, at the time of Christ, approximately 2 million Jews were in Palestine, 5 million outside of it.)

C. The degeneracy of Judaism at the time of Christ is simply not sustained by historical records. It was a vital religon at the time, with right, center, and left, conservative and revolutionary factions, fighting for the mind of the public. Indeed, the Dead Sea Scrolls indicate that Christ was influenced by one of the more revolutionary sects.

7. The Church at times acted as protector of the Jews but, on balance, its role was more often instigator of anti-Semitism rather than adversary of anti-Semitism. Indeed, even in its role of adversary, in most cases it merely underlined the Jews' alienation. In other words, to quote Jules Isaacs in *The Teaching of Contempt:*

It should be said in the defense of the Roman Catholic Church that at least it has never gone as far as genocide, that it has always recognized the right of the Jews to exist as "living testimony," and that on occasion it has endeavored to curb the hatred of the people—after its own teachings had helped to unleash it.

8. The concept of the divine destiny of the Jews is common to both Jewish and Christian theology.

9. In the Old Testament there is little mention of the Devil, and when he appears it is generally in a role written by God. But in the New Testament and in Christian writings and literature he plays an independent major part (e.g. John 12:31 "the Prince of this world"; *The Divine Comedy; Paradise Lost;* etc.).

It was certainly the Old Testament's concept of sin (and its early walk on-slither-off Devil) that bore and reinforced Christian belief in Satan. But while the generators and interpreters of the Old Testament, under unspoken orders from an omnipotent abstract God, sentenced the Devil to near oblivion—with a few exceptions, primarily some of those living during late pre-Christian times—the

321

generators and interpreters of the New Testament with a God of flesh and blood in mind, resurrected the Devil as being able to get to an everyman, infected with original sin, immediately and genetically—matching God talent for talent. (In the Gospels, Christ performs numerous exorcisms and the powers of the Devil play a continuing role.) This explains, in part, why Paul, Augustine, Calvin, and Luther were all obsessed with man's wickedness, an obsession which in turn guaranteed the continual incarnating of its source. The Jew, in many instances, became the Devil—the anti-Christ—the source of evil, wickedness and human suffering.

10. A few modern scholars ignore or minimize the durable and fertile soil laid down by religious anti-Semitism—and with it the complex anti-Semitic jungle it produced—as a cause of modern anti-Semitism. Their argument usually consists of quickly dismissing religious causes because they were not as readily visible, proximate, definitive, directive or dogmatic as they were, and blaming, instead, new causes exposed by their own perceptiveness and modern scholarship.

11. Why should God permit the Jews to exist unconverted if not to confirm the wretched consequences of not accepting Christ? The condition of the Jew had to reflect his rejection of Jesus. Good Christians, therefore, aided God when mistreating Jews or acting to assure their subordinate position.

12. One theory holds that the fear of "the old man"—of the primitives' dead father or tribal leader—was a primary source of religion.

13. See the writings of the Catholic philosopher, Jacques Martain.

14. Some writers urging that modern anti-Semitism is also anti-Christian maintain that persecution of Jews is an acceptable substitute for persecuting Christ. This argument holds that fear of Christ (Christophobia) or rejection of the burden of Christian teaching is at the root of anti-Semitism. Therefore the hating of Jews is really the hating of Christ.

15. And if a Christian, encouraged by his belief that his faith alone entitled him to salvation, took on the attitude of the paranoid, he could victimize his "paternal persecutor," and then blame his victim.

16. And Satan—in the Bible and in Western literature—had also been a *favorite* (the chosen?) of God (e.g. "most dearly loved of God"—Marlowe's *Doctor Faustus*).

17. See Cause 1. Background and Culture (pp. 290-91), and Notes 1 and 2 to Causes.

18. The Jews were not always "successful." During various periods, whole Jewish "nations" were "unsuccessful," unsophisticated, uneducated and poor. Although in certain periods of history, Jews were quite productive (because of or in spite of persecution), this phenomena should not be equated with the Jewish talents. education. and thirst for opportunity and freedom accumulating for centuries behind the constraining ghetto walls and prejudices of Europe. This dormant force was suddenly released with tremendous energy and visibility upon the modern Western world by the French Revolution.

19. Some writers have drawn the parallel between anti-Semitic attacks on Jews and lynch mob attacks on Negroes in the U.S. The literature on the authoritarian personality suggest that the outlet for aggression is usually weaker than the aggressor. The brutalized worker who beats his wife or the henpecked husband who beats his kids or kicks the cat are homely examples of this tendency.

20. This is not to suggest that the attitudes of Jewish communities were without intolerance. When orthodox, their religion demanded vigilance against heresies among their own, although this vigilance (with some exceptions) was not implemented with the brutality frequently employed by their neighbors.

21. Up until the eighteenth century man's psychological need to prejudge some group was directed at the Jews primarily by religion, but when religion diminished as a motivator and catalyst (diminished, but by no means eliminated) the non-Jew's *successful* experience with his victim still remained, thus making it his most reliable and justifiable source of satisfaction.

22. Jews were sometimes feared by the Christian because they often came to symbolize a certain superiority, especially beginning with the 19th century emancipation of the Jews. (The origins of the reputation of superiority are complex and touched on repeatedly in these pages. To mention a few: literacy, defensive achievement, a reputation as the instruments of the "superior" Devil, existing as the people of God, the father of God, God Himself, etc.) This symbolism was translated clearly in the writings of Wilhelm Marr who helped modernize anti-Semitism into the racial version that gave it the new strength necessary to thrive in a new, less religious society.

23. "Cursed by the parents that engendered me!
No, Faustus, curse thyself, curse Lucifer"
—Marlowe's *Doctor Faustus*

People who feel alien to themselves and, therefore, a threat to themselves, because of repression, look for alien victims. The greater the underlying anxiety of an individual, the more prejudiced he is because the pressure of the anxiety weakens his personal controls. Thus weakened, he seeks release through prejudice which serves to reduce his anxiety because prejudice facilitates the discharge of hostility.
(Peter Lowenber, *Psychology of Racism,* p. 197.)
(Also see Psycho-Christian Demands, first point)

24. Recently, Soviet writers have accused the Zionists of plotting the Holocaust. This was based partially on political considerations (Arab-Israel-USSR relations and criticism of Soviet treatment of minorities) and no doubt also grew from age-old Russian anti-Semitism. But other versions of this canard have surfaced frequently in anti-Semitic circles, fed by factual incidents of betrayal or cooperation by some Jews during the Nazi period. (See Arendt, *Eichmann in Jerusalem.*) These arguments have been used to shift the blame for anti-Semitism to the victim.

25. The enemy becomes the carrier of traits or elements we repress in ourselves. (See Rollo May-*Love and Will*).

26. The anti-Semitic tradition of the Jew as money-hungry and dishonest stretches from Judas to enforced usury, middlemen roles, merchant and international "banker" (of which it took only a few examples to corroborate a stereotype) to the modern middle-class Western Jew.

In modern times it is one of the more tenacious of the ancient stereotypes owing to many factors: the heavy middle-class role the Jew finds himself in, as a result of his history; the tremendous literature and folk myths which continually reinforce the characterization; and the sudden release of his talents—manifested in all fields—triggered by the French Revolution and the new Western freedom. So the Jew was fed into the modern era as a natural choice for economic villain.

A theory of Hannah Arendt maintains that Jews in the nineteenth and twentieth centuries became the object of universal hate *primarily* because their power and wealth became unnecessary (previously those Jews who could contribute to the country's power or economic strength were frequently utilized either because there were not enough sophisticated Christians to contribute adequately or because they were not allowed to contribute for political or social reasons). No doubt the loss of power and specific function as a cause of anti-Semitism is a distinct possibility—but that it is the great cause of modern anti-Semitism is not likely, especially as the theory is now presented, severed from any causes of anti-Semitism promulgated by the past.

27. Anti-Semitic myths and allegations in religious schools (in lectures and textbooks) were especially harmful to the Jew. They were numerous and can easily be considered a fabric of Christian religious education rather than stray threads. Fortunately, during the past decades some measurable progress has been made within religious institutions to re-educate the teachers and to make the textbooks more accurate.

28. See Causes Two and Three, pp. 291-94.

29. In Russia, Jews were by state policy isolated and powerless. They were, nevertheless, victims of vicious anti-Semitism. In 19th century Russia, Czar Nicholas I developed anti-Semitic policies because Jews were too little in the mainstream, too clannish, too aloof.

30. Anti-Semitism has flourished where there were no Jews, e.g. in England, France and Spain after Jews had been expelled.

31. See Cause Six, pp. 298-99 and Note 25.

32. Cf. statements of religious leaders and theologians in Catalogue.

33. See Cause Two, pp. 291-92 and Notes. One of the clearest examples is Pope Gregory IX who complained that the Jews in Germany were not living "in the state of utter wretchedness to which God had condemned them." (Heer, *God's First Love*, p. 74.)

34. This underscores the importance of Christian teaching and the Christian tradition with its unflattering portrait of Jews and Judaism and the Jew as theological villain. Areas and peoples not directly or indirectly influenced by this religious factor did not develop anti-Semitism. (See Glossman, *Anti-Semitic Stereotypes Without Jews*.)

35. The other major birthplace is Freudian in concept: The Jew can react to his greater society, which is not Jewish, as the child can react to his mother and father, taking on his self-concept from the anti-child attitudes of his parents—and identifying with them to lessen his fear of them.

36. Anti-Semitism has caused the death, terrorization, humiliation and isolation of the majority of Jews who have lived in the Christian world.

37. Infrequently, over-reaction does occur, but it is too often labeled as the rule rather than the exception. (This to refute the magnitude of anti-Semitism and thus the guilt of those who allow or practice it.)

38. In the same light some have tried to dismiss the Holocaust as merely another calamity, if anything, "dwarfed" by other calamities such as the killing of millions of Russians during World War II. They feel the Holocaust was a terrible but an isolated tragedy. They feel the Jews are mesmerized by the six million (and was it really six?) into a state of paranoia that alienates them through attitude and their consequent defensive organizations and cohesiveness which only aggravate, not help their future security.

To answer point by point: The Holocaust certainly was another calamity in the terrible history of man's inhuman treatment of man. But it was a unique one demanding unique considerations and reactions. It was not the widely practiced and age-old slaughter of civilians by armies caught up in the fever and brutalizing psychology of war, but the calculated policy of a modern civilized nation. It was not an explosion of horror, the sudden murder of innocents, but a slow carefully written nightmare: persecution, terror, the stripping of clothing and dignity, the ripping apart of frightened children from frightened parents, their abuse and torture by banal bullies and sadistic scientists, the exposure of a people to a life stretching from days to years under the control of the conscienceless, the vicious, and even the Everyman.

Of course, the leveling and slaughter of a village and the genocide practiced by Hitler are both horrible. A family of civilians destroyed by a bomb or shot by a patrol and the terrorization, torture and eventual elimination of civilians have the same end. But the means and motivations are not comparable. They evoke different emotions, as they should. The conscious slaughter of civilians by clashing armies and the planned genocide of a people by a national government do not cancel each other out. The uniqueness of the latter with its strange means seen against the background of historical anti-Semitism which, however indirectly, motivated it (again, the Holocaust was not an isolated tragedy but part of an historical progression) should indeed provide the Jews with a special concern and a justification for demanding that the Holocaust not be lumped together with other tragedies. If it is, it will not be seen as it existed and therefore will not communicate its lesson.

This need for the defining of tragedies and a recognition of the lessons they teach are not confined to the Jews but are shared by all victims. As the Russians are concerned over their borders so should the Jews be concerned over their survival. And if we hear more about the slaughter of Jews from the Jews than about the slaughter of Russians from the Russians, it is because, first, the former are in a less secure position by virtue of size, dispersement, power, historical precedent and present-day realities (among them the persistence of a 2,000-year-old anti-Semitism); and second because of the indelible uniqueness of Hitler's horror show.

To accuse the Jews of fostering anti-Semitism by attempting to defend themselves (to prevent future threats to their freedom and survival) through organizations, is simply to ignore history. Granted, at times, the consequent appearance of a fortress clan adds to the "evidence" of anti-Semites and those who blame the Jews for their own misfortune ("if they just weren't so clannish . . ."); and granted, at times, defense encourages some isolation, and mutual mistrust—but what is the Jew to do? When he has not helped his fellow Jews he and they have still been attacked, and when he has tried to help them he has at least met with some success. When he has forgotten past anti-Semitic acts, future ones did not go away. When he has remembered them—and acted accordingly—he has at least dulled some of those in store for him or destroyed the conditions which would have created them.

Anti-Semitism emanates from a Christian West, not from Jewish defense organizations. Nor, as we have stated, from Jewish cohesiveness, etc. Again, when the latter was not a matter of fact, when the Jew was especially busy assimilating, the roof often caved in (e.g. Spain, 1492, Germany 1930's).

This is not to argue against assimilation. Successfully executed over a long enough period of time, it no doubt would put an end to anti-Semitism. But the Jews, as all others, have a right to maintain their identity.

39. One of the most difficult resistances to the recognition of the perniciousness of anti-Semitism and, therefore, to the awareness necessary for its effective opposition is the inability of some non-Jews who are infected by anti-Semitism to accept the fact that they themselves suffer from that particular disease. This type of resistance might be seen in the natural hostility man can feel towards loved ones but which he cannot face. The more it is called to his attention the more he rejects it, espcially if the accuser is his victim. In fact, not only does he reject it but to defend against it, he finds reasons in the victim to justify his actions, reasons outside his darker self.

40. Kraeplaen as quoted in Gordon Allport, *Nature of Prejudice,* p. 394.

41. Thus he has to be accused of being Christian-hating, predatory, a ritual-murderer, clannish, cheap, etc.; and thus his innocence or non-stereotypical existence had to be ignored or refuted.

42. The theme of co-responsibility between victim and criminal deserves mention. First, pertaining to definition: Co-responsibility does not always imply sins on the part of the victim, sometimes it merely connotes some function of the victim that could have been avoided,* that helped bring on anti-Semitism. But usually sin is the implication. (A distinction is made on these pages between co-responsibility and complicity. The former suggests the Jews asking for it; the latter, the Jews helping their persecutors.)

That the Jews, being human, were not without guilt is obvious. But any reading of the history of anti-Semitism shows their moral conduct to be normal compared to that of other groups. (If anything, it was better, if not because of their culture, at least because of their powerless status, which permitted less latitude for persecution, or because of their sensitivity through constant intensified exposure to life's tragedies and the need to counter them with virtue.) And a mere glance at history shows their sins to be infinitesimal compared to the excesses of anti-Semitism. In no way could their common failings, so held in common with other groups, be considered a basic cause of anti-Semitism. They might have set or helped set off excessive anti-Semitic response, but only because they acted in an anti-Semitic atmosphere.

The charge that the Jews shared some responsibility for their destruction with the Nazis should not go unanswered in this discussion. We are not referring here to the charge made by propaganda machines but that which Arendt** and a few others have presented.

That some Jews cooperated in the deportation of Jews to the concentration camps is not disputed. Some did it out of cowardice, fear, and total selfishness. But they were few in number, and in all groups turncoats have been and can be found. Others cooperated out of a belief that by administering the deportations themselves they could save some of their people and ameliorate the cruelty that

*Father Edward Flannery (one of those scholars and activists in the forefront of exposing the causes and history of anti-Semitism) who utilized the term "co-responsibility" has explained that the term was not meant to imply equal responsibility or even co-responsibility according to its popular definition; but rather to indicate that the Jew was not an arbitrary scapegoat, that he was persecuted because of his unique role in Christian Western history—a role not created by culpability.

**Many of Hannah Arendt's opinions pertaining to modern Jews and modern anti-Semitism are considered in these pages because—interwoven as they are with provocative and revolutionary ideas (e.g. the banality of evil) that add much to man's understanding of man—they demand examination.

might have occurred under direct Nazi administration. Still others did it because of a combination of the two motivations.

That, except in a few cases (but in more than is generally realized), the Jews reacted to their destruction passively is again indisputable. But it is amazing that this should seem odd to anyone familiar with the history of anti-Semitism and the conditions of the Jews and their surroundings in the twentieth century:

—Whenever the Jews had resisted physically in the past, the result had not only been futile but had often made the situation worse for other Jews;

—Some did not know the true nature of the camps;

—Others "knew" but grasping at the straws of hope chose to be unsure;

—Some were unsure;

—Deportations were nothing new to their history;

—Nothing like Hitler's program had taken place in their historical experience;

—They were without arms or allies and strategically were at the mercy of the Nazi government;

—The various pockets of Jews and the partially and completely assimilated Jews (demographically, socially and religiously) were not united. They were not a geographical-cultural group, like the Irish, capable of mounting a revolution. With few exceptions, they had always been foreigners with a history of chronic exile;

—The Nazis' computer-like totalitarian rule—built by national fervor and terror—made the Jews' identification easy, their hiding difficult, and any organized mobility nearly impossible.

—The Jews through 2,000 years had learned that survival in Europe could not be attained through arms but only through tenacity and resilience. This experience had pervaded their religion and culture. They were primarily thinkers and believers, not revolutionaries and soldiers.

Given the above it is little wonder that the majority of Jews chose hope, however slim, over suicide—"allowed" themselves to be herded to trains, rather than attacking their captors, which would have assured their own and their families' immediate death.

Resistance was not only practically untenable but historically impossible. The lack of resistance—given past and present conditions—was a normal understandable and predictable reaction based not on the willingness of victims to be slaughtered but on a persecuted people's will to live, not on co-responsibility but on an historical experience that did not permit its people to envision the evil magnitude and organization of Hitler's dream. That the Jews were damned if they resisted or damned if they did not and so should have resisted—is only apparent in the aftermath of the nightmare.

Why a fair-minded Jew or Christian would attempt to stretch the theory of co-responsibility between Jew and persecutor beyond what appears endurable in the domain of evidence and reason is an interesting point and one that must lie within the realm of psychological speculation. A few thoughts might be considered: First, the Christian, as mentioned, might be subconsciously attempting to minimize the mistakes of his religion and culture. This could come quite naturally since Jewish culpability was not only conventional wisdom but elitist wisdom as well. It was one of the few truths that could be accepted without question while searching for those more elusive. Second, a Jew might subconsciously wish to find reasons for anti-Semitism outside of his persecutors so that he may not resent or fear them as such: so that he may have more hope for the cessation of his persecution and his chances for dealing with the majority about him—the Christians; so that, without the burden of fear, he may like them and/or identify with them more easily; so that getting them off the hook of his resentment, he might win their approval. Third, the Christian (and, to a lesser extent, the Jew) would be tempted to find reasons that would refute the presence of an evil inherent in Western man's moral order, in his way of life, from which he gathers his faith, if not in God, at least, in his society and his society's just and secure future. Certainly, to any man, the realization that such evil can flourish in such goodness must be disturbing.

43. See *New York Times,* Jan. 31, 1975; *Time Magazine,* March 10, 1975.

44. A 1963 survey of white church members showed that 33% of Protestants and 29% of Catholics felt that Jews—more than Christians—are likely to cheat in business. *(Kike,* edited by Michael Selzer. Straight Arrow/World.)

45. The fact that anti-Semitism easily made the jump from the conservative clergy to the liberal secularists did not prevent anti-Semites from fighting in the front ranks of the former against the latter.

46. E.G., Hannah Arendt, the scholar who so brilliantly exposed the banality of evil, almost discounts the past in assessing modern anti-Semitism. Her justifications for doing so are interesting. She, herself, admits that the fact that anti-Semitic provocations can be successful is more important than the provocation itself. But then she goes on to dismiss all past (as opposed to modern) reasons for this success with several arguments.

She refutes two theories cited by many as historical reasons for anti-Semitism: scapegoatism and eternal anti-Semitism. The first she correctly undermines by pointing out that this theory would not explain why the *Jews* were chosen as scapegoats. The second she again correctly dismisses, but this time she falsely attributes the whole life of the theory to anti-Semites and those Jews who used it to

329

keep their people together; and to the contention that it was a mere "secularized travesty of the idea of eternity inherent in a faith and chosenness and a Messianic hope." She ignores the real possibility that the theory sprung in large part from a simplistic, short-sighted view of anti-Semitism's long history.

Both theories she then attributes to an escapism based on the persecutor's and the victim's desire to avoid responsibility (See preceding Note Forty Two for a discussion for the motivation to believe in co-responsibility.) Thus with a reasoning that mixes hard arguments into specious approaches, she dismisses two theories—rooted in the past—that attempted to explain anti-Semitism utilizing a reasoning that is largely simplistic. (Undermining an opinion by delimiting its arguments and then attacking the motivation of some of its proponents is not especially cogent, nor is generalizing about such unsubstantiated motivations in so complex a situation.) But the dismissals themselves are correct. To explain anti-Semitism by invoking man's need for a scapegoat ignores its particular victim. To believe that anti-Semitism is an eternal phenomena is an article of blind and bad faith.

But then she jumps to the conclusion that all traditional causes of anti-Semitism are inadequate to explain modern political anti-Semitism—as if the debunking of two historical theories justifies dismissing them all.

She does pause briefly to acknowledge Christian anti-Semitism, but only as a dead issue (*The Origins of Totalitarianism*):

> This superstition (that eternal anti-Semitism implies an eternal guarantee of Jewish existence) . . . has been strengthened through the fact that for many centuries the Jews experienced the Christian brand of hostility which was indeed a powerful agent of preservation, spiritually as well as politically. The Jews mistook modern anti-Christian anti-Semitism for the old religious Jew hatred—and this all the more innocently because their assimilation had bypassed Christianity in its religious and cultural aspect. Confronted with an obvious symptom of the decline of Christianity they could therefore imagine in all ignorance that this was some revival of the so-called dark ages (pp. 7-8.)

So the Christian past is neatly dismissed but not—given other research—realistically: Christian anti-Semitism and its profound effects through 2,000 years could not in one century suddenly drop off the ends of the earth. And clear evidence shows it to be far from the edges.

This is not to leave unexamined her points that:

"Ignorance or misunderstanding of their (the Jews') own past were partly responsible for their fatal underestimation of the actual and unprecedented dangers which lay ahead. . . .Jewish history offers the extraordinary spectacle of a people unique in this respect [without government, without country and without language] which began its history with a well-defined concept of history and an almost conscious resolution to achieve a well-circumscribed plan on earth and then without giving up this concept avoided all political action for 2,000 years. The result was that the political history of the Jewish people became even more dependent upon unforeseen accidental factors than the history of other nations, so that the Jews stumbled from one role to the other and accepted responsibility for none.'' (Origins, p. 8.) The above factors or some variation of them certainly contributed—but only that—to anti-Semitism's Life of Its Own.

47. See Cause 10. Life of Its Own, and Catalogue for further elaboration and illustration.

48. See Cause One, pp. 290-91 and Note 2.

49. Some might ascribe this lack of antipathy to religious or cultural factors; others to a repressive environment which ordered potential hate into a philosophy of acceptance. Both theories probably contain a measure of truth.

50. This helps explain some Jewish reaction to things the non-Jew does not see at all or sees as unimportant or meaningless. If the name of a villain in a television plot happens to be Jewish, (and certainly if he displays some Jewish stereotypical traits) a Jew with a realistic or unrealistic viewpoint, with a profound or sparce knowledge of Jewish history might involuntarily wonder, consciously or subconsciously, if this reflects accidental or intentional artistic license or anti-Semitism—might wonder if this incident (if an ''incident'' at all) is an innocuous and sporadic manifestation of anti-Semitism or is part of a pattern or part of the beginning of one—might wonder whether this symptom (if a symptom at all) is caused by a benign growth or signals a small infection that exists throughout the body politic where it can remain a mere irritant or grow in strength.

In most incidents such as these (in the United States), certainly the chances are that any reaction is wasted or is a show of undue concern. The possibility that a villain's Jewish name is a harbinger of evil times is small. But irrespective of the odds, concern is understandable and an awareness unburdened by oversensitivity is not unwarranted. After all, anti-Semitic incidents have appeared and burgeoned in the United States. They have often lost their strength precisely because of the active responses of Jews. (And little incidents have multiplied into anti-Semitic movements abroad.)

Related, if not similar, sets of ''Jewish'' conjectures might surface in response to a variety of *potential warning signals* invisible to the average Christian, to the Jew not educated or sensitized to the early symptoms of anti-Semitism, to one not convinced of their potential or one not concerned with Jewish life:

—The questioning of anti-Semitism's virulence—such as doubting the accuracy of the *six* million (a valid challenge; or an attempt to create a rationale for

331

a lack of sympathy based on anti-Semitic feelings, for the abrogation of responsibility, or for the suggestion of Jewish self-pity?);

—The application of certain words which are common in the lexicon of anti-Semitism to a man who incidentally or not is Jewish—"haggling," "arrogant," "tight" (words born of observation and opinion; or reflecting the speaker's prejudice?);

—The mention of a Jew's sins or complicity in an act against his own people (a simple report; or a suggestion of Jewish co-responsibility in Western anti-Semitism or of a racial propensity towards betrayal—inherited from Judas?);

—An accusation of militarism against Israel (an honest assessment; or a distortion of beleaguered self-defense which would not have been formulated if the nation were not Jewish?); etc.

Past and present experience contrives to provoke the question: Are the above normal outgrowths of human curiosity, communication, opinion, creativeness, etc. or reflections—conscious or not—of long-lived bigotry?

To separate disguised expression of anti-Semitic attitudes from honest observations and opinions is not easy—especially in the context of blatant anti-Semitism, old and new. Jews can both over-react and under-react, but in most cases throughout history, the majority (perhaps to lighten its load) has under-reacted.

More difficult still is the separation of acknowledged anti-Semitic expressions into categories that deserve different degrees of response. Here, again there is no doubt that at times some Jews over-react—especially emotionally—to certain anti-Semitic manifestations, and thus exaggerate their importance. But as mentioned—and it bears repeating—more frequently the wary response of alert or "instinctively" defensive Jews to small signs of anti-Semitism is all too realistic. The incidents that have so frequently followed them in the past lend them unseen weight. Only to non-Jews—and to many Jews as well—who are not aware, or refuse to be aware of anti-Semitism's history and potential, does the response seem out of keeping—to be dismissed as the consequence of paranoia.

51. The Jew has been compared to the woman raped. If she is raped more than twice her innocence is seriously called into question. The possibility that her continual rape is sanctioned and encouraged by those about her is not considered.

52. See the Catalogue of Incidents, Conclusions (pp. 337-64), and Causes One, Eight and Ten.

53. It should be mentioned here that the nature of this book excludes frequent mention of actions that countered anti-Semitism. Therefore, the role Christianity and its churches played in protecting the Jews is not adequately presented.

332

(Incidentally, it is not uncommon for the same forces that persecuted the Jews to aid them. The nobility is another prime example.)

Of course, many pious Christians accept the primary role of Christianity in anti-Semitism and do not regard this responsibility as a phenomena incompatible with their faith. They regard the role as a perversion of Christian spirit. (See Note 6 to Causes.)

CONCLUSION

VI. CONCLUSION

Four cautionary points about the study are necessary before moving to the conclusions. First, the catalogue is, of course, incomplete. The best that can be done in any historical work is a partial reconstruction of past reality. Many incidents have been lost, many were never recorded, and much has been distorted. The researcher investigating anti-Semitism is faced with the same problems of one investigating the history of the American Indians or the history of the Negro in America. The histories, documents and other materials and evidence that do exist are typically works of the dominant cultural group. The existence of strong historical tradition in the Jewish culture does offset the obvious bias of the non-Jewish historical works, but the problem is still a serious one. Certainly the minor, everyday indignities, insults, fears and little terrors are not presented.*

Second, the catalogue is detached. The emotional component is muted. The study has avoided the twin dangers of a topic of this nature—sentimentality and romanticization. The cries, screams and whimpers, the tears and heartaches, the anger, frustration, rage and despair that accompanied the incidents are left out. The human and personal effects and costs of anti-Semitism cannot be measured. These dimensions are better handled by poets, prophets, storytellers and novelists.

*These are in addition to the limitations stated in the Introduction and Preface.

337

Third, the number of people affected and of victims throughout the catalogue with the exception of the Nazi period (the Nazis were compulsive and accurate bookkeepers) are probably exaggerated. This is particularly true for the figures up to the 17th and 18th centuries. The early historians and chroniclers up through the Middle Ages are notorious for overestimation of populations and the number of people involved in events. And, as every attorney knows, eyewitness accounts are rarely reliable. This kind of inaccuracy, however, does not negate the catalogue or challenge its purpose. If one were to over correct for this inaccuracy, and assume the actual victims of anti-Semitism were only ten percent of the recorded victims, there would remain an astonishing history of hatred, persecution, injustice and suffering.

Fourth, the study presents nineteen centuries of history through the lens of anti-Semitism. It is an ugly story. It necessarily paints a distorted portrait of that history. Any history focusing on one dimension over such a time span is distorted. No doubt there were periods, places and communities with good Jewish/non-Jewish relations. There were throughout, as there are today, individuals and groups free of anti-Semitism. Nevertheless, such a presentation of this history has a valuable purpose. It provides a view of history that allows the non-Jewish reader to understand his history from the point of view of one of its major victims, and to begin to appreciate the historic role of anti-Semitism and its continuity.

The study has led to a number of clear and unambiguous conclusions about anti-Semitism that are disturbing but inescapable. Some are and will seem obvious and trite; others are less transparent and more complex. For most, these conclusions will be uncomfortable, for some irritable, but they are unavoidable and undeniable. A common reaction to uncomfortable or disturbing information or experiences is denial or avoidance. This has been the usual response to mental illness, leprosy, child beating, poverty, injustice, crime, perversion and prejudice. It has certainly been the reaction to anti-Semitism. Until it is faced squarely and recognized in all its dimensions and then action taken to counteract and eliminate it, anti-Semitism will continue. (Indeed denial and avoidance and their more passive counterparts, indifference and insensitivity are often masks for anti-Semitism—especially in the United States.)

338

No people in history has been hated, maligned and persecuted so continuously and systematically as the Jews. In light of the history of anti-Semitism, the continued survival of the Jew and Judaism is a major historical triumph. They did not, however, merely survive. Jewish survival included the growth and development of a dynamic religio-cultural tradition. There were, certainly, periods and places of stagnation, but the overall thrust of the Jewish historical experience has been one that included not only integral development and growth but also major contributions to the larger and hostile environment and culture in which Jews survived.

The one over-arching conclusion of this study is that anti-Semitism has been a continuous and pervasive element of Western history and culture. The extreme anti-Semitic behavior during the Crusades, the Black Death, and the 17th and 20th centuries were not unrelated episodic aberrations or random violence directed at a convenient minority. These outbursts have to be recognized as reflections of a theme of contempt and hatred for Jews that permeated the culture, and a tradition that permitted, tolerated, encouraged and rewarded anti-Semitic actions.

Anti-Semitism as a theme and tradition of Western culture and history developed and grew over a period of centuries. It did not suddenly appear fully developed, nor was it accepted or embraced immediately by all segments of the population. The content, dimensions and variety of anti-Semitism and its manifold expressions developed and expanded as its influence and pervasiveness grew through history. However, it can be traced to two interrelated and mutually supporting factors that form its base. One is the religious belief and teaching that was formative and dominant in the West—Christianity. The other is the condition in which the Jew survived after the destruction of the Judean state—permanent alien. The latter is partially an effect of the first in that the statelessness of the Jew became a supporting element of Christian teaching and was perpetuated by that teaching.

The origins of anti-Semitism can be traced, simply enough, to a sectarian conflict. In the tradition of the prophets, Jesus' teachings were a challenge to the conventional morality, orthodox theology, and religious and political hierarchy of his time. Some of his teachings reported in the Gospels, the accounts of the Crucifixion and the activities and experiences of some of his early followers laid the basis for the split from Judaism and are the foundation of the anti-Semitism that developed over the following centuries.

During the first century, Christianity had not yet distinguished itself as a separate religion. It was for the most part still one of the many sects of Judaism. The conflict within the early Church between the Jerusalem-based Apostolic faction and the faction led by St. Paul resulted finally in the triumph of the Pauline faction and the separation of Christianity from Judaism. This internal conflict of Christianity was part of a larger conflict within Judaism. Typical of all internecine conflicts the mutual antagonism and bitterness was extreme and uncompromising.

The dominant Sadducee faction of Judaism saw the Christian sect as (1) an absurd blasphemy and (2) a political threat. On the first point, the Hellenistic strain in Christianity, involving the belief in the resurrection, the deification of Jesus, and the incorporation of elements of the mystery cults, was, from a strict Judaic view, heresy and evidence of the influence of Greek paganism. This kind of blasphemy could not be tolerated by the Sadducees and indeed, was a source of conflict between Christians themselves; the Hellenized Christians led by Paul vs. the Hebrew Christians led by Peter and James.

On the second point, the political threat was two-pronged. The Sadducees were the priestly class of the Sanhedrin and had worked out a *modus vivendi* with the Roman authorities. They were, in effect, the privileged ruling class within the Jewish protectorate. They saw any tampering with the status quo not only a threat to their position but a danger to the survival of Judaism. Christians, with their messianic and millennial fervor, were lumped together with the Zealots as threats that had to be eliminated. The charges and counter-charges between Christians and Jewish orthodoxy in this setting became more extreme and acrimonious.

Christianity, at this time, had to cope with serious problems of internal dissension and theological controversy, uncertainty, heresy and leadership rivalries. The historical setting was not favorable to a tranquil working out of the differences. The political upheavals, the imminence of the Second Coming and the usual fanaticism of religions in the formative stage pressured the early Church to get about its business. The decimation of the Hebrew

340

Christians that accompanied the Roman suppression of the Judean revolts eased the triumph of the Hellenized faction. And the attacks by the Jewish orthodoxy on Christianity strengthened Paul's argument that the mission of the Church should be to the Gentiles. This made the effort to distinguish Christianity from Judaism and the struggle against the Judaizing tendency a paramount concern of the Reorganized Church.

It is within this historical setting that anti-Semitism developed and bitter feelings and high emotions of this situation were incorporated in Christian doctrine and teaching. As Christianity rose to a dominant position, anti-Semitism became a Western tradition and ultimately developed in numerous areas a life and existence almost totally independent of its religious base. As Western culture achieved a dominant place in world civilization and influenced the non-Western world, the Western tradition of anti-Semitism has achieved almost universal acceptance.

While the religious base and justification of anti-Semitism is ostensibly irrelevant in some areas e.g., the Soviet Union, and less important generally than in the past, it is misleading and dangerous to underestimate its overall importance. Even racial atheistic anti-Semitism relies on anti-Jewish stereotypes and attitudes that were created by religion. In addition, the underlying cultural predisposition and bias to anti-Semitism was created and cultivated throughout the religious period. Without this, the non-religious variety, if developing at all, would not have enjoyed such complete success or as long a life.

Christianity has played a central role in creating, sustaining and encouraging anti-Semitism. For a number of reasons indicated in the catalogue and in the section on causes and discussed above, Christian belief and teaching has included a portrait of Jews and Judaism that has had a horrible impact on Jewish existence. The most important is the role assigned the Jews, by Christian teaching, in the crucifixion and death of Jesus.* Jews are, in this tradition, guilty of deicide and the guilt applies not just to those who made up the mob described in the Gospels, but all Jews who have lived since that time. This is a terrible type of guilt. It is a new original sin and has justified Jewish persecutions and suffering

*Within the setting of the Jews' rejection of Jesus as the Messiah—a rejection which exposed them as men condemned.

since then. The problem is that crucifixion was a peculiarly Roman form of execution. The first Christian martyr, St. Stephen, who was executed by Jews, was killed in the prescribed manner: by stoning.

Taking the Gospel accounts at face value (and there is considerable disagreement among Biblical scholars as to their accuracy), it is difficult to understand how the Romans escaped any charge of guilt for the crucifixion. Indeed, the Gospels seem to exonerate the Romans of any complicity in the execution. The portrait of Pontius Pilate, who made a career of slaughtering Jews, as a seeker of justice and truth and a fair and impartial (though possibly too weak), administrator strains the most credulous imagination. (Some later Christian writers would have Pilate a secret Christian and a saint.) Furthermore, the Gospel accounts minimizing the obvious Roman role and portraying the crucifixion as a Jewish act, are incredible, given the nature of Roman rule, and also in light of what the Jewish revolts tell us of Roman reactions to such challenges.

The other important element in the deicide charge is the transcendent and universal Jewish guilt attached to the act. This is based in part on some sayings attributed to Jesus, but most directly on the account of the crucifixion found in St. Matthew which has the mob shout "His blood be on us and on our children . . ." in response to Pilate's protestation of innocence after symbolically washing his hands. It is not an improbable story. Mobs have been known to do and say stranger things. The problem lies in the implication that a mob, which had to be an infinitesimal portion of the Jewish population at the time, can force God's hand and condemn an entire people for centuries. Nevertheless, Churchmen throughout history have held this position and have justified and explained persecution of Jews and Jewish misfortunes on this basis. The siege of Jerusalem and the destruction of the Temple were the first to be so explained. On this point a serious distortion of history developed. Christian writers, who certainly knew better, redated the Diaspora (the dispersion of the Jews which occurred seven centuries earlier with the conquest of Israel by Babylonia) with the Roman siege and attributed it to God's punishment for the crucifixion.

While deicide and the transcendent Jewish guilt are the most important Christian elements in the development of anti-Semitism, there are other features of the Gospels that have had great significance. The generalized portrait and overall impression of Judaism and the Jews is quite negative and distorted. Judaism appears as a hollow, rigid, knit-picking, overly ritualized, legalistic sham dominated by the high priests and the scribes and pharisees oppressing and exploiting the people. Judaism, as portrayed in the New Testament, has little to recommend it. There is none of the vitality and force or complexity indicated in other histories of the period in the Gospel's version of Judaism.

The Gospel portrait of the Jewish people is dominated by Judas Iscariot, the money-grubbing traitor, the hypocritical Scribes and Pharisees and the conniving murdering High Priests and Sadducees. There is a tendency to forget that Joseph and Mary, John the Baptist, Jesus, Peter and Paul, the Apostles, and all the other personalities in the New Testament excepting the Romans and Samaritans were Jews. Instead, Judas Iscariot came to be the stereotype of the Jew, not only in the period of struggle between Judaism and Christianity, but historically and is even found in the writings of the racial anti-Semites. The anti-Jewish bias of the New Testament is, of course, strongest in the writings of St. John where the very word Jew has the quality of an epithet. In this Gospel, Jesus almost appears to be non-Jewish. It portrays the ministry of Jesus as one of Jesus versus the Jews.

The other important early Christian contribution to anti-Semitism is the association of Judaism and the Jews with the Devil, as handmaids or tools of Satan, and the anti-Christ that is found in the Epistles and the Book of Revelations.

The importance of these anti-Semitic charges, stereotypes and images cannot be overstressed. They are found in the fundamental theological and doctrinal source of Christianity. The New Testament, as the whole Bible, is considered the revealed word of God. It is a divinely inspired document for the believer. The charges and images of the Gospels and the New Testament were further developed and elaborated on over the succeeding centuries in the Christian theological tradition. As such, their irrationality and inaccuracy is difficult to combat. The recent efforts by Catholic and Protestant leaders to soften and modify the anti-Semitism of the Christian tradition have concentrated on fairly minor manifestations that grow from the New Testament basis. The efforts have all stopped short of any consideration to modify the Biblical source. Even these minor adjustments have been met with strong opposition. (See Footnote 6 to Causes, Appendix 4.)

By the time Christianity achieved its dominant position and official religion status in the fourth century, these Biblical charges and stereotypes had been amplified and expanded by some of the most important Christian writers and Churchmen and anti-Semitism began to have a life of its own. Despite these vicious attacks, the common people of both religions seemed to have gotten along quite well. In spite of the thunderings and anathemas hurled about, there is little evidence of popular attacks by either Jews on Christians or Christians on Jews. The efforts by the Church to insulate and protect its adherents from contact or interaction with Jews was not successful. The ineffectiveness of the exhortations, sermons, homilies and Church decrees and threats was recognized and the Church turned to the power of the state to achieve these objectives. From this grew a whole body of Canon and secular law affecting the Jews, and regulating the relations and interactions of Christians with Jews. The laws and regulations reflected Church teachings about the Jews and further increased anti-Semitism by creating new roles and attitudes that were eventually reflected in new anti-Semitic stereotypes. The motivations and intentions underlying this development were complex and require some discussion.

Christianity saw itself as the one true faith, as the only way to salvation. Much of its claim was based not on the teachings of Jesus but on his mystification as the Son of God. The Crucifixion and Resurrection became central to the faith, and consequently the role ascribed to the Jews was also of central importance. Christianity was also the New Covenant, the coming, death and resurrection of Jesus and his message superceded the older Jewish Covenant embodied in the Mosaic Law. Christianity was therefore doctrinally put forth as superior to Judaism.

One of the early difficulties the Church faced was the Judaizing tendency. There were many instances of converts to Christianity in turn converting to Judaism. This occurred because Judaism was also an aggressive proselytizing religion at the time and because Jews and Jewish communities were present throughout the Empire. New converts sometimes unsure of their new faith and interacting on friendly terms with Jews often turned to Judaism. The influence of Judaism was also a factor in some of the theological disputes that arose within Christianity at this time. An obvious solution to the Judaizing tendency was to forbid interaction by Christians with Jews and restrict the activities, occupations and movements of Jews to make contact with Christians more difficult.

Another source of this body of anti-Semitic law and practice is the theological relationship of the two faiths: Judaism is the source of Christianity. The Old Testament is accepted by Christians and a direct line of growth from Abraham through Moses and the Prophets to Jesus is part of Christian doctrine. Christianity claims to be a fulfillment of God's promise in the Old Testament. It is a clear and unmistakable fulfillment. Therefore the continued existence of Judaism and the refusal of Jews to convert to Christianity is an embarrassment and difficult to explain. For early Christian leaders, the Jewish failure to recognize the obvious truth of Christianity was inexplicable and could only be the result of hardness of heart, wrongheadedness and stubbornness or the work of some evil force. The insults of the Epistles and the Apocalypse therefore took on a new meaning and a new existence. The equation of the Devil with the Jew helped to explain Jewish aversion and refusal to accept Christianity. The high content of the mystical and magical in Christian belief, teaching and practice made demonic influence quite credible. Whatever the source of the Jewish refusal to convert, the Church had to assure the dominance of Christianity. Continued wrongheadedness or demonic influence could not enjoy success or prosperity as it might cast doubts on Christian claims. Therefore in addition to minimizing the danger of the Judaizing tendency, the Church had to place the Jew and Judaism in a subordinant social and civil position.

Three factors combined to create the religious base of anti-Semitism: (1) the need of Christianity to distinguish and disassociate itself from Judaism, (2) the role of Christ-killer and rejector and the transcendent guilt placed on Jews by the Gospels; and (3) the rise of Christianity to the status of official state religion and dominant belief system. A complimentary factor that made it possible for anti-Semitism to have the impact it has had up to the present time is the condition in which Judaism and Jews survived until 1948. When Rome put down the Jewish revolts of the first and second century, the Jewish state and homeland in Palestine was destroyed. The siege of Jerusalem and the destruction of the Temple by Titus was followed after later revolts by the destruction of Jerusalem. In the second century after the third Jewish revolt, Jerusalem was rebuilt as a pagan city and Jews forbidden residence. Indeed, the revolts and the Roman justice carried out after the revolts resulted in the slaughter of most of the Jews living in the area. The overwhelming majority of the surviving Jewish population lived scattered in communities throughout the empire. Judea and the Temple had served as a unifying force and a homeland for these dispersed Jews. As a result the Jews now found themselves as permanent aliens, a homeless people within a larger and often hostile population due to the force of religious belief.

Other peoples and civilizations subjected to the same conditions disappeared from history. The Jewish religion, culture and tradition, however, proved more durable and adaptable, and *Judaism* and Jews continued to survive. A major development in Judaism that made this survival possible was the Talmud. The emphasis of Judaism shifted from the priests and the Temple to the rabbi and the Talmud. The Talmud provided a portable and living religion unencumbered by physical structures and allowed for flexibility in responding to change. The persecutions and martyrdom suffered by Jews in this role of permanent alien also contributed a will to survive that fit into the new role for Jews as God's witnesses. (See Dimont, *The Indestructable Jews*.)

A reading of the history of anti-Semitism leads to a conclusion based on this survival. The major offense (aside from the theological charge of deicide) committed by Jews during the last 1600 years of Christian dominance has been their refusal to become non-Jews, to disappear as a people, a culture, a tradition, a religious group. Jews were the one conspicuous minority group where ever they resided, the one heretical presence, the one religious deviation, the one barrier to a uniform society. They insisted on surviving as Jews despite restriction, disadvantages, harassment, prejudice, the hatred of their neightbors, the disapproval of the major social institutions and despite threats, penalties and persecutions. Such a feat of survival and such a survival urge is a behavior that, with this exception, is universally admired and respected. In the case of Judaism and the Jews, however, it has elicited contempt, suspicion and hate.

Jews were the distinctive minority wherever they lived. Unlike other foreigners, Jews could not return to their native land; did not have a haven to flee to when persecuted; could not appeal to their homeland for protection; had no allies to come to their aid. They were singularly exposed and vulnerable. They could be mistreated by authorities and mobs with impugnity.

In spite of the Christian image of the Jew, the Church's initial efforts to restrict Jewish/Christian interactions and the position of the Jew as a contemptible distinctive minority, the members of both faiths lived together in a fairly amicable manner. This compelled the Church to apply state sanctions to achieve its objectives. Out of this a web of laws and regulations and stereotypes developed that expanded anti-Semitism.

Laws were made and enforced that severely limited the occupations open to Jews. In long term effect, the most devastating were the provisions that drove Jews out of agriculture and made landownership and successful farming virtually impossible for Jews. Within societies that were primarily agricultural, this had the effect of further isolating and stereotyping the Jews. As a result of these provisions, and the insulated and self sufficient nature of the feudal manor, at one stage, the term Jew and merchant were synonomous. The other effect was to concentrate Jews in urban settings. Other laws imposed additional occupational restrictions. Jews frequently were barred from civil, political, and military positions of authority. Jewish professionals were not to serve Christians and Christians were barred from using the services of Jews. For example, Jewish physicians and midwives were forbidden to attend Christians, and Christians were not to use such services when performed by Jews. Similarly Christian physicians and midwives were forbidden to treat Jewish patients.

As guilds came to control the crafts, Jews were barred from

347

many occupations as artisans. The guilds were religiously based and to learn a craft one had to be a Christian. Other legal provisions barred Christians from certain economic activities. Money lending is the most obvious illustration, and it became identified as a Jewish activity. The stereotype of the Jew as usurer clearly grew from these earlier anti-Semitic economic restrictions. This development is particularly interesting because of its impact in furthering anti-Semitism. It has two important causes.

In the 11th century, international trade was almost a Jewish monopoly. In addition to the religious motivations, one of the causes of the Crusades was to open the trade of the Middle-East to the rising Christian merchant class. The First Crusade while slaughtering thousands of Jews that were encountered on the way to the Holy Land also extorted Jewish communities. Jewish communities and merchants were unwilling, but major, financial backers of various Crusading armies. This tendency to blackmail and ransom required Jews to have wealth in more liquid, easier negotiated form than barrels of spices and bolts of silk. Money lending as a Jewish occupation grew from this experience and developed between the First and Second Crusades. In the exhortations, preachings and appeals for the First Crusade no mention is made of Jewish usury. A major incentive for the Second Crusade, however, was the annulling of debts owed to Jews. Crusaders who participated in the Second Crusade could consider their obligations to Jewish creditors non-binding.

The effect of this body of law was to close many occupations to Jews and to place Jews in a decidedly inferior and insecure economic position. At the same time it created new negative stereotypes of Jews that furthered and increased the attitudinal basis and predisposition for anti-Semitism. While motivated from religious considerations, these new elements took on an existence that continued in the economic life and culture of the society when the theological justifications dimmed in memory.

Other provisions of law designed to protect the faithful from Jewish contamination and to subordinate the Jew included regulations broader than the economic restrictions. Residential restrictions required Jews to live in certain areas and closed other areas to Jewish residence. The requirements that Jews wear distinguishing and often ridiculous modes of dress further singled out Jews as a conspicuous group. Some sumptuary laws forbade Jews to wear certain styles of clothing. Jews were restricted in travel and sometimes forbidden to appear in public during Easter Week. Jewish religious practice was restricted to prevent proselytizing and also to denigrate Judaism or to make being a Jew less attractive. The number of synagogues was limited. In efforts to convert Jews, but also to underscore the inferior status of Jews and Judaism, Jews were required to listen to conversion sermons preached in their own synagogues, to maintain houses of conversion, and to conform to Christian religious observances and dietary practices.

Despite these anti-Semitic efforts, with a few exceptions of isolated mob attacks, the average man for centuries went about his day-to-day activities either ignorant of the laws and pronouncements or simply ignoring them. Regular church services and religious observations were late in being institutionalized and the number of clergy available to serve the faithful was limited. It was not until the founding and growth of the mendicant preaching orders that the average Christian had regular contact with the Church and was regularly exposed to religious and spiritual teaching.

In the 10th and 11th centuries, the nature and impact of anti-Semitism changed dramatically as the anti-Semitic teachings that were part of the Christian message seeped down into the consciousness of the average Christian. This period of spiritual renewal and revitalization, sparked by the activities and zeal of the Franciscans and the Dominicans also marked the beginning of mass anti-Semitism. The Jews found themselves subjected not only to a more systematic enforcement of the anti-Semitic provisions of state and Canon Law but henceforth, the victims of mob attacks and brutality as well. Some of these anti-Semitic attacks by the masses were so extreme that even the elite, who had encouraged them, felt compelled to intervene and give protection to the very Jews they had been attacking and condemning on a more intellectual level.

The next six centuries (the 11th through the 16th) set the pattern and tradition of anti-Semitism that infected and pervaded all strata of society. The distinction of earlier centuries between elite anti-

Semitism and mass indifference to the anti-Jewish preachings, decrees, and laws disappeared. Where Jewish existence was tranquil and tolerated, it was always a matter of privilege, never a right, and consequently always uncertain. The privilege could be revoked at and time and often was. The systematic enforcement of Canon Law provisions resulted in the establishment of the ghetto system throughout Europe and in turn produced a new anti-Semitic stereotype. The anti-Semitic teachings and beliefs and the stereotypes growing from anti-Semitic practices and restrictions created a mindset disposed to believe the most incredible nonsense about Jews. Jews were the subject of preposterous accusations and victimized on the basis of such charges. This indicates the depth and pervasiveness of anti-Semitism in the culture and consciousness of the non-Jewish population.

From the 17th through the early 20th centuries, anti-Semitic incidents as a pervasive and constant feature of social behavior showed a marked decrease. There were fewer outbursts of this type and those that did occur were concentrated in particular regions and countries. The increasing tolerance accompanying the scientific, economic and political revolutions that undercut the old order and transformed civilization is the usual explanation offered for this decline in anti-Semitism. This was a period in which the role of religion in society became more narrowly defined. During this period, Jews were granted increased freedom and in some cases full equality and citizenship. Many countries repealed laws discriminating against Jews or restricting their activities. This breakthrough was not universal, however, and Roman Catholic countries and Orthodox Russia continued their usual anti-Semitic policies.

Jews living in the countries where these changes occurred experienced real improvements in their lives and status. One of the side effects was a major voluntary migration of Jews to the countries that had granted freedom and equality to Jews. However, these laws only removed the legal and official barriers to Jewish participation in the fuller society. For while energies and talents that had been suppressed now benefited the whole society, the attitudinal and cultural structure that had supported and enforced the anti-Semitic laws and regulations remained. These found new expression in the practice of private prejudice. The decline of theology and religion in the life of Western man was not accompanied by a decline in hatred for the Jew. The cultural anti-Semitism continued to be transmitted and therefore the attitudinal predisposition to anti-Semitism continued to exist.

The development of racial theories of history and racial interpretations of society provided a perfect vehicle for the manifestation of this suppressed anti-Semitic tradition. The concept of racial superiority included racial inferiority and who better fit the mold than the Jew as his image and sterotype had been passed from generation to generation. The irrationality and absurdity of these theories did not prevent their widespread acceptance. At a time when the more optimistic scholars were anticipating the natural death of anti-Semitism (due to the decline of religion and the rise of science), the racial theories gave it new life and a veneer of scientific respectability. The modern variety contained most of the elements of the traditional and religiously based anti-Semitism and gained adherents who scoffed at Medieval superstition.

The widespread acceptance and intensity of modern anti-Semitism (in addition to the continuation of religiously based anti-Semitism) would not have been possible without the existence of the underlying attitudinal predisposition and cultural stereotypes that had been nourished throughout Western history. Contemporary and racial anti-Semitism has to be seen as an extension of this older form and not a new phenomena. The beliefs, accusations, stereotypes and practices are the same. The same language of hate voiced by Sts. Eusebius, Origen, Augustine, John Chrysostrom, John Capistrano and Martin Luther is spoken by the Nazis, the Ku Klux Klan and some Arab militants.

The willingness to believe Jews responsible for or capable of inhuman, subhuman, superhuman or demonic activities or possessing powers with these characteristics grew from the Christian teachings and deliberate casting of contempt on Jews and urging hatred as the proper reaction toward the Christ killer. These were actualized in anti-Semitic behaviors that were tolerated, encouraged and rewarded. Thus was set the attitudinal structure formed in a period of great ignorance and superstition that has survived to the present.

351

A listing of the absurd charges made against Jews and widely believed throughout Western history staggers the imagination and challenges assumptions about man's rationality: The killing of God and its attendant transcendent guilt was the basis for many atrocities and extrapolations. The Wandering Jew is one of the more harmless and quaint. In addition, Jews have worshipped the Devil, worshipped goats and snakes and engaged in sexual orgies, infanticide and cannibalism in religious rites. Jews reenact the Crucifixion annually with a fresh Christian victim. Christian blood is a necessary ingredient for the Seder matzoh. Jewish physicians are sworn to murder Christian patients (usually by poisoning). Jews cause earthquakes, hurricanes and military defeats. Jews caused the bubonic plague through an international conspiracy that poisoned the wells of Christians. Jews steal consecrated hosts in order to desecrate them and again torture Jesus. Jews are committed to the death of all Christians. Jews are the anti-Christ and in league with the Devil. Jews are the Devil. The horned hats required as Jewish dress in some places during the Middle Ages actually covered real horns. Michaelangelo's Moses is further proof of Jewish horns. Jews are oversexed and licentious perverts committed to seducing Christian women and reducing them to white slavery.

In addition to these wondrous and perverse activities Jews are blamed (never praised) for such things as capitalism, democracy, especially the French Revolution, Free Masonry, Liberalism, Socialism, Communism, Modernism, Abstract art, and World Wars I and II. They compose an international conspiracy dedicated to Jewish world domination, the enslavement of Christians and the destruction of culture. Mao Tse-tung was once described as the Trotskyite tool of Wall Street Jews. Some have argued that the Nazi exterminations were a hoax created by the Jewish press. More recently, Jews have been blamed for civil rights and the energy crisis.

When these beliefs and accusations are contrasted with the Jewish historical experience of persecution and oppression the psychotic and pathological nature of anti-Semitism is clearly evident. Anti-Semitic beliefs and attitudes are not susceptible to reality testing. This is to be expected in ages dominated by religion

352

or superstition, but, in the modern age, the age of science, empiricism and analysis, the continued acceptance of the all powerful international Jewish conspiracy in the face of the Nazi atrocities is proof of the basic madness that infuses all of anti-Semitism.

Further indications of the perverse and pervasive quality and depth of anti-Semitism in Western and modern man are the portraits of Jews and the reactions to portraits of Jews in literature.* Beginning with the New Testament, Judas Iscariot, of all the Jews presented, is taken as the typical Jew. Whatever Judas was, then or now, he has to have been a most atypical personality. Of all the heroes, villains and fools that people the works of Shakespeare, the only one to become a national or cultural stereotype is Shylock. Shylock's eloquent speech about the experience of being a Jew is rarely heard and less remembered. It adds a dimension to his character that does not fit anti-Semitic expectations. Similarly, among the many characters of Dickens, Fagin has become the typical Jew. Scrooge to be sure is a typical tightwad, but, not a typical businessman, or a typical Englishman in the perceptions of readers. In contemporary literature, Hemingway portrays a bastard in *The Sun Also Rises* and the character is identified as a typical Jew, not a typical bastard or even as a typical Jewish bastard.**

The continuity and persistence of anti-Semitism over the past nineteen centuries indicates that it is an integral part of Western culture. It has existed in slave, feudal, capitalist and socialist economic systems. It has existed in monarchies, aristocracies, theocracies, democracies, dictatorships, police states, and authoritarian and totalitarian regimes. It has existed in religious, secular and atheistic societies. It has existed in rural and urban populations, in small towns and suburbs. It has even existed in places where there were no Jews. No matter what the Jews did there has been no sure escape. Even in countries or periods in which Jews had achieved power, position, and privilege, the foundation was never secure. The Jews in Spain in the 15th century, in Poland in the 17th century, in Germany in the early

---

*And in most other transmitting agencies in cultures.

**These are only prominent examples of anti-Semitic stereotypes in literature, the number is legion.

20th century seemed secure until the outburst of anti-Semitism devastated and destroyed them.

There have been periods and places that saw a relaxation and decline of anti-Semitism. Certainly, progress has been made over the centuries. Since World War II, anti-Semitism as state policy is no longer a universal condition. The clearest example of anti-Semitism as state policy is the Soviet Union. The centuries old Russian anti-Semitic tradition and practices (despite Marxist theory) are still a feature of government dealings with its Jewish population. (see 1945-70 of Catalogue). Outside those countries with anti-Semitism as state policy, violent manifestations of anti-Semitism that have included bombings, arson, beatings, desecration, psychological terror such as swastika daubings and sometimes kidnapping and murder have been the work of extremist gangs—neo Nazi, neo-Fascist or racists. Widespread popular attacks on Jews have been relatively rare and concentrated in particular countries. Since 1945, the only mob attacks on Jews have been in the Arab countries at the time of the First and Second Israeli/Arab wars, and in some South American countries most recently and notably Argentina.

The exposure of the Nazi horrors stripped anti-Semitism of the fashionable and respectable qualities enjoyed from the latter 19th century through World War II. This is not to say the attitudinal base and cultural tradition of this hatred has been expunged, but rather, that few but crackpots openly proclaim or admit to being anti-Semitic. In addition, some Catholic and Protestant leaders have been making serious efforts to eliminate the anti-Semitic elements in worship services. There is a belated and partial recognition of the Christian role in anti-Semitism and anti-Jewish doctrine and symbols have been de-emphasized. The most significant recent development is the recognition that anti-Semitism is an evil and has been condemned and denounced by responsible religious and political leaders.

A knowledge of the history of anti-Semitism, however, cautions against any undue optimism. Similar periods of decline occurred throughout history. In the past, great popes, saints and various secular leaders condemned anti-Semitic actions. Some gave protection to persecuted Jews. Others provided haven and refuge from

354

persecutions elsewhere. In the middle of the 19th century, many shared the hope that anti-Semitism was being eliminated. In every case succeeding events proved the hope false and the decline of anti-Semitism only a lull in its history.

The catalogue and the historical overview chart clearly show that the violent outbursts of anti-Semitism have occurred at times of tension and social dislocation and that periods of security and prosperity correlate with a decline in overt and violent anti-Semitism. The similarity of the attacks and the accusations on which they are based indicate that the underlying continuity and predisposition was a constant in the culture. Nothing has transpired in the last thirty years to have changed this dimension. Indeed, the available evidence based on attitude surveys shows this predisposition still survives. Recent statements by prominent Americans during and in the aftermath of the energy crisis are evidence of the pervasiveness of anti-Semitic myths and attitudes. If a really serious economic or political emergency occurred, it is likely that anti-Semitism would again emerge in its uglier manifestations.

The conclusions discussed to this point—the religious origins, the continuity, persistence and pervasiveness of anti-Semitism and the supporting role of the Jewish status as permanent alien are fairly obvious. There is another, less obvious, conclusion revealed in the study. This relates to the development of anti-Semitism. The focus and technique used in the study abstracts and isolates anti-Semitism and provides a view of the subject unencumbered by distracting factors. A result is the clear definition of the progressive dimension in anti-Semitism and its inexorable push to totalism.

The objectives of anti-Semitism have advanced overtime from segregation to apartheid through conversion and expulsion to acculturation and assimilation and finally extermination. Early anti-Semitism was primarily intended to protect the faithful from the Judaizing tendency and Jews had to be insulated and cut off from contact with Christians. As Christianity became more secure and powerful, anti-Semitism was directed to the conversion of Jews to Christianity, refusal to convert usually meant death or expulsion. The decline of religion and religious motivations

355

brought about a change in the emphasis and direction of anti-Semitism. Its target became Jewish distinctiveness and the Jew who acculturated and was assimilated escaped. The final stage of anti-Semitism, that developed out of racial ideology, is total in its objective and effect; it requires the extermination of all Jews and things Jewish.

This progression of savagery in terms of the objectives and intent of anti-Semitism has been accompanied by a progression in application. The number of Jews affected and the size of areas affected expanded progressively with the progression of anti-Semitic intent and objectives. Early anti-Semitism had few victims. Later expressions affected specific communities in a random and episodic manner. The anti-Semitism of the Crusade and Black Death periods victimized Jews living in particular regions and countries. The Spanish Inquisition focused primarily on Jews who had converted to Christianity. The ghetto experience was restricted to Catholic countries. The victims of anti-Semitism in the 17th and 18th centuries were concentrated in East Europe and Russia. Modern racial anti-Semitism in the 19th and 20th centuries had all Jews as its targets and most horribly the Jews of continental Europe during the Nazi period. Until this latest stage, Jews had a number of escapes from anti-Semitism available to them: conversion, migration, and acculturation and assimilation. The opportunity or possibility of escape was removed in the latest form of anti-Semitism. Regardless of religion, nationality, citizenship, status, success or wealth, all Jews were to be eliminated.

Another element of the progression of anti-Semitism is the increasingly efficient and bureaucratized methodology. The lynch mob approach of the earliest attacks, where Christian commoners led by fanatical monks or preachers attacked, plundered and slaughtered Jewish communities gave way to the more military and organized slaughter and persecutions of the Crusades. The crusading period of soldiers running amok was replaced by the ritualized and legalistic murder during the Black Death and the Inquisition. This in turn was superceded by the state planned and orchestrated violence of the pogroms. The ultimate progression on this dimension is seen in the Nazi application of industrial mass

356

production techniques to the systematic murder of a people. The triumph of bureaucracy can be seen in the Nazi bureaucratization of death. The most dreadful acts of recorded history were carried out by insignificant moral cripples typified by Eichmann, Speer and Rudolph Hoess; people so shallow and so lacking in imagination that they were capable of evil on an unprecedented level but, in terms of their reaction, may just as well have been counting the grains of sand on a beath. The religious fanatic and the plague-crazed villager acting out of passion, revenge or fear gain a dimension of nobility when contrasted to the bloodless, detached and faceless bureaucrats of the Third Reich.

In the 1900 years covered by the study, the only development that justifies any long term optimism is the creation of the state of Israel. This conclusion runs counter to some assessments of the Middle East situation. Superficially, the existence of Israel seems to have caused an increase in anti-Semitism. This point of view argues that Arab anti-Semitism expressed by various nationalist leaders and manifested in many popular and state actions was created by Israel. The argument further states that Israeli policies have caused an increase in anti-Semitism throughout the world and has the potential of instigating anti-Semitic outbursts against Jews residing outside of Israel. In addition, the conflict between Israel and the Arab nation has led to the spread of anti-Semitism to people and countries previously unaffected as they make common cause with Arab nationalism against ''Jewish imperialism.''

This position has some merit. A considerable amount of contemporary anti-Semitism justifies itself on these grounds. Communists and Trotskyists repeatedly make the point that Israeli policies encourage anti-Semitic reactions. The rise of anti-Semitism in sub-Saharan Africa appears to grow out of a feeling of Third World-Non-white solidarity against Western-White encroachment. In many cases opposition to Israel or anti-Zionism is only historical anti-Semitism in disguise. Anti-Zionism provides an acceptable vehicle for hating the Jew.

This is not to imply that anti-Zionism is necessarily anti-Semitism or that all anti-Zionists are anti-Semitic. Many anti-Zionists are truly free of anti-Semitic attitudes or intentions. How-

357

ever, it is an easy disguise and much anti-Zionism includes beliefs, myths and stereotypes that have been the historical stock in trade of the anti-Semite.

These arguments cannot be dismissed out of hand, but there is a stronger case that can be made. The existence of Israel has eliminated one of the major historical causes and supportive elements of anti-Semitism. Since the second century until 1948, Jewish identity and nationalism has existed without a nation. Until the 19th century, Jewish existence was generally a question of privilege not a right. Jews during this period were permanent aliens wherever they resided. They were identified and recognized as a peculiar foreign element everywhere. This status as permanent alien meant more and had greater consequence than that of foreigners. Other foreigners living in a host country had a homeland, some place to return to, a refuge and a haven. Foreign nationals had a government they could call on for protection and frequently allies who would also provide protection. Discrimination or attacks on these nationals could cause diplomatic repercussions or retaliation and reprisal. This gave some security to the national away from the homeland. (This was less than adequate but however weak it offered some confidence and safety when outside the native land.)

Jews had none of these protections. Their alien role was complete and their positions considerably more precarious than other foreigners. Lacking a guaranteed place of refuge and having no outside political force to rely on or appeal to for protection, they were especially vulnerable to any xenophobic tendencies of the host population. In the case of the Jews, anti-foreigner feelings could be vented without fear of reprisal. The isolated alien status was in a sense a form of double jeopardy for Jews. They were aliens because they were Jews and because they were Jews they were aliens. This existence was further complicated because Jews were not simply aliens or foreigners. They were also Jews. The cultural environment in which they existed included anti-Semitism. Alien status coupled with identity as Jews encouraged more than simple xenophobic reactions. While the natural hostility toward the outgroup was certainly part of the hostility experienced by Jews, it was intensified and overshadowed by anti-Semitism. Anti-Semitism and permanent alien status originated independently and have different basis but developed a mutually reinforcing relationship.

Until the 19th century, the only way a Jew could escape the permanent alien role was by converting to Christianity, and as the Spanish experience indicated, even this step which required in effect the Jew to become a non-Jew, was an uncertain escape.* Later, as society became secularized, national identity was no longer tied to religious belief and Jews were granted equality and full citizenship. Under this arrangement, Jews became citizens of the countries in which they resided and could remain Jews. The formal and legal barriers to Jewish participation in the full life of society was struck down. However, the removal of these formal barriers did not remove the underlying anti-Semitic attitudes in the dominant population, and, as is common to every minority or immigrant groups, Jews found that acculturation was a condition for assimilation; the more similar a Jew in appearance and behavior to the dominant culture, the greater his chance of acceptance and full participation. Conversely, Jews who were or remained distinctive, in contrast to the dominant culture, were less likely to gain acceptance and enjoy full participation.

The emancipation of the Jews, therefore, was not a total emancipation. To choose to be distinctively Jewish, while no longer encumbered by formal and legal restrictions and penalties, still entailed disadvantages. In this sense, the Jewish historical experience and especially the history of anti-Semitism clearly illustrates the common pattern of bicultural or multicultural societies. In populations or societies that are not ethnically, racially or culturally homogeneous, the patterns of dominance and subordination tend to cut along ethnic, racial or cultural lines. The perceived minority has been historically placed in a subordinate relation to the ethnic, racial or cultural majority. No nation or society with a

---

*NOTE: The one exception was the Khazar kingdom that emerged in south Russia in the 7th century and disappeared in the 10th century. The Khazars were a Turkish people whose king and aristocracy converted to Judaism but permitted full religious freedom. Khazar was a major trading center and, in this remarkably tolerant state, Jews, Moslems, Christians and heathens lived and mingled in peace and prosperity.

heterogeneous population has been able to resolve this problem. The most powerful evidence of this is the Jewish experience as expressed in anti-Semitism.

This subordination is the experience of all minority and immigrant groups. The sociological pattern is acculturation before assimilation. However, acculturation is no guarantee of assimilation, but rather, a necessary condition if assimilation is to occur. In the case of the Jews, the problem of achieving assimilation or full acceptance and participation in the society which they live, has been exaggerated and intensified by the existence of anti-Semitism. In the period following emancipation, even those Jews who totally acculturated, to the point of abandoning Judaism as well as the Jewish cultural tradition, still found full acceptance difficult to achieve. Part of this difficulty arose from the development of racial anti-Semitism that occurred almost in tandem with Jewish emancipation. The most emancipated Jews, those non-Jewish Jews who had totally accepted the dominant culture suddenly found themselves again subjected to the penalities of anti-Semitism.

It was a realization that emancipation, acculturation, and even total rejection of the Jewish heritage offered no protection against anti-Semitism that brought the Jewish nationalist movement—Zionism—into existence. The goal was the establishment of a Jewish homeland, a Jewish state where Jews can, with security, live a Jewish life. Without getting into the question of what a Jew is, a question that has been discussed and argued by many and from various points of view but is still unresolved, the importance of Israel cannot be ignored. The positive potential and necessity of a Jewish state is clearly revealed in the study.

The Israeli Law of Return guarantees a haven and refuge of Jews throughout the world. In the past, whenever anti-Semitic persecutions victimized Jews in particular communities, regions or countries, they could only escape if another community, region or country permitted their immigration. Whenever Jews were expelled from an area, their resettlement depended on the good will and the permission of the area to which they moved. This permission was sometimes not granted, sometimes entailed many conditions, and was often arbitrarily and suddenly revoked. The tragedy of the 1930's, when Jews trying to leave Nazi Germany were refused admission wherever they tried to disembark and were forced to return to Germany and the concentration camps, will never occur so long as Israel exists.

In addition to the passive role as haven from persecution and as a state where Jews are free to live as Jews, Israel has an active role to play in eliminating anti-Semitism. Most obviously, diplomatic channels, trade, foreign aid and the structure of alliances can be used to persuade other governments to modify or suppress anti-Semitic practices. Presently, a major concern of Israel is the condition of Soviet Jewry and is a clear example of the use of diplomacy to aid Jews suffering from anti-Semitism.

Less obviously, the existence of Israel should contribute to the modification, if not elimination, of stereotypical thinking that has been part of anti-Semitism for centuries. These stereotypes often were the basis and justification for anti-Semitic beliefs and practices. Aside from the earlier and exclusively religiously based beliefs and stereotypes, much of contemporary anti-Semitism is based on stereotypes that grew out of various restrictions. Israel is a nation free of these restrictions and disabilities. Consequently, Jews in Israel are found in every occupation and walk of life that are found in any nation. With a population of farmers, skilled and unskilled workers, craftsmen, artisans, professionals, engineers, scientists, soldiers, sailors, merchants, dock workers, factory workers, school teachers, students, artists, musicians, writers, upper class, middle class and lower class, wealthy and poor, police and criminals—Ashkenaz, Sephardic, Hassidic and Oriental, immigrant, pioneer, native-born, Orthodox, Conservative and Reformed, rulers and the ruled, what is the stereotype of the Israeli? Israel in this way destroys the basis of the stereotype and underscores that anti-Semitic practices created some stereotyping which in turn created more anti-Semitism. When free of restrictions, regulations and disadvantages, Jews have not concentrated in particular occupations or avoided others.

A more subtle factor in the fight against anti-Semitism is the effect of Israel on Jewish and non-Jewish attitudes. Israel gives Jews, wherever they live, a new source of pride, confidence and sense of purpose. The role of pariah and the mindset that this

361

stigma created has been reduced by Israel's existence. Hope and cautious optimism has a concrete and nonmetaphysical basis in the Jewish homeland. The "miracle of Israel" has affected the attitudes of non-Jews as well. While anti-Semitism has continued to survive and spread, another and new dimension has been added to the popular attitudinal structure in Western countries. This is the admiration and respect (sometimes grudging) that many feel toward Israel. This was not a feature before Israel was established.

On this point, a consequence of Israel, that is not often recognized, is the contribution it has made to the normalization of the role and identity of the Jew. Simply put, in addition to the problems peculiar to its geographic position and its struggle for existence, Israel faces the same difficulties and challenges common to all modern societies. As a sovereign state, it has a record of domestic politics and international relations that encompasses more than particular Jewish concerns. Furthermore, as a member of the international community Israel's voice and vote reveal a record equally addressed to the common problems of mankind. In short, Israel as a nation has had successes and failures, and continues to work out the problems of modern civilization.

These developments have not been an unmixed blessing. Along with the respect and admiration there is often an expectation of perfection. Israel is expected to act differently from any other nation. Activities and policies taken for granted or excused in others are often condemned when found in Israel. Democratic Israel has been romanticized into a "City of God" type of society and is assumed to be: (1) above acting in self-interest, and (2) free of stupidity. Israeli actions, counter to these expectations, are disappointing and intemperately condemned. This is similar to the romantic view of workers held by intellectuals and radicals in the 1930's. When workers acted against expectations—less heroically or didn't appreciate classical music—there was bitter disappointment.

This is not to imply that Israel and a Jewish homeland is in any sense a panacea. Anti-Semitism still exists on an almost world wide basis and still embraces religious and racial beliefs. Anti-Semitism has increased in the Arab world and among Third World

Nations, and the continued survival of Israel cannot be taken for granted. Most Arab nations have not yet recognized the right of Israel to exist. Those that have moved in this direction have usually attached conditions that preclude a secure and stable existence. Until genuine peace is achieved in the Middle East, all projections about anti-Semitism based on a Jewish homeland must be tentative.

Nevertheless, Israel's existence is crucial for the humane survival of Jews. This lesson is the clearest conclusion of the study. Anti-Semitism is an integral part of the Western tradition, possibly indestructable and not to be expunged. This fact, coupled with the sociological pattern that demands acculturation as a condition for full participation means that the survival of Jews as Jews requires a separate Jewish state. Without a Jewish state, the historical lesson drawn from the study indicates the most probable futures for the Jews are: (1) disappearance as a distinctive group through acculturation and assimilation; (2) complete disappearance through a more horrible and more efficient and complete final solution; or (3) the continuation of diaspora along the pattern of the last two centuries with its outbursts of terror and continuous anxiety.

Presently, the Arab-Israeli conflict tends to encourage a pessimistic view of the viability of Israel. But there are some factors in the situation that are grounds for a long-term sense of optimism. Serious efforts to destroy Israel have failed and its success and survival in this hostile environment indicate a basic strength and vitality. Much of Arab hostility to Israel was tied to internal political and social conditions that have been, in some cases, drastically modified. Some of the hostility was part of the leadership style of particular leaders. Hopefully, a more moderate group of leaders will emerge making way for the resolution of the territorial and national-population disputes. If this occurs the major "real" (as distinct from ideological, historical and religious) cause of Arab-Israel conflict will be diminished.

Furthermore, the anti-Semitism found in the Arab world does not have the historical roots or the basis of that found in the West. While Judeo-Islamic relations were not as amicable as some historians portray, historically the Islamic-Arabic brand was not as continuous, pervasive or virulent as in the West. The contemporary Arab anti-Semitism contains much of the transplanted Nazi brand and that is not part of the cultural and historic tradition. In short, the anti-Semitic element of Arab hostility to Israel is likely to disappear or become minimal if peaceful relations and normal interaction between the Arabs and Israeli occur.

Finally it is probable that many of the present conflicts between Israel and the Arab countries are the natural consequences or birth-pangs of their realization of national aspirations. Both seek identity and legitimacy out of an immediate past that shared oppression and exploitation. Objectively the mutual benefits from cooperation far outweigh any gains from continued conflict.

ISLAM

INTRODUCTION

The study has shown the historic continuity and pervasiveness of anti-Semitism in Christian and Western culture. The only reasonable expectation for Jews is a continuation of various degrees of prejudice, hostility, discrimination and persecution within that setting. All attempts to modify or minimize this syndrome have proved futile. If Jews wish to continue as Jews, any historical judgment has to favor the establishment of a Jewish state. It was the recognition of this historical fact that, in part, led to the creation of Israel.

However, some have argued that the Zionist movement and the founding of Israel has increased rather than diminished the problem of anti-Semitism and that Israel as presently organized has not brought security to Jews, but instead, greater danger of extermination. This argument states that the Jewish colonizing of Palestine spread anti-Semitism to the Arab and Moslem countries. The Moslem world is portrayed as being free of anti-Semitism prior to the colonizing efforts. It is further argued that Jews and Arabs are fellow Semites and anti-Semitism is unnatural to the Arab and a reaction to the "Jewish invasion." This point of view holds that the insistence on a Jewish state is a reactionary impulse and its failure is inevitable. The solution proposed in this argument is the reorganization of the boundaries and politics of the area to establish a secular pluralist Palestinian state as an alternative to Israel.

The idea of s secular pluralist Palestinian state is, on the surface, an attractive one. It eliminates many of the uncomfortable consequences of Israel's presence. Without specifying how justice will be served, the whole problem of the Palestine refugee magically disappears. The unfashionable and supposedly unmodern phenomena of a religiously influenced state* is removed from our secular vision. Finally, a major source of Middle East conflict and a major cause of world tension is eliminated.

The scheme appears workable because it is based on two misreadings of history and one unwarranted sociological assumption. The historical errors are: (1) the definition of anti-Semitism as a purely European and Western problem, and (2) the portrait of Judeo-Islamic historical relations as cooperative and cordial.

This point of view has considerable currency and prominent spokesmen. It cannot be dismissed out of hand. As with every political or intellectual controversy, it has a factual basis. In terms of anti-Semitism, there is no question that the Western and European record overshadows all others in terms of continuity, persistence and intensity. Similarly, the religious base of Western anti-Semitism and one of its major causes is obviously not a central factor in non-Christian societies. Additionally, in contrast to the Christian/Western, the Islamic/Arabic record of anti-Semitism is much better. The Islamic/Arabic pattern does not include continuous and systematic persecution and slaughter. However, to say that Islamic and Arabic societies have been free of anti-Semitism or to maintain that Judeo/Islamic relations were cordial, cooperative and based on mutual respect is a considerable distortion of history. Jews, while classified as "people of the book" and officially protected under Islam, were subject to extensive discrimination and relegated to an inferior status under Moslem law and rule. One of the most odious anti-Semitic practices—the Jew badge—was invented by the Moslems 500 years before it was incorporated in Christian anti-Semitism. Jews were also subject to other social, political and religious disabilities in Moslem countries. In addition, there were episodic violent attacks on Jews

---

*The religious component of Israeli public policy reflects an adjustment of secular pluralist democratic politics to the interests of the Orthodox interests. It does not enjoy constitutional permanence.

periods of religious fanaticism on the part of Moslem rulers.

The misrepresentation of Arabic/Jewish relations is partially due to the generalized ignorance about the Islamic/Arab world. (The conventional focus of history has been the West and Europe. The non-European/non-Western world has been relegated to footnote status due partially to linguistic and cultural barriers and partially to the ethnocentrism and stance of superiority of the West toward other civilizations. This is the case with Arabic civilization despite its proximity, contact, and great contributions.) The jihad (holy war) against Jews has only occurred a few times widely separated in time. These are recorded. What is ignored is the pattern of subject and inferior status that made up the nature of Jewish existence under Moslem rule. These factors combine to give the inaccurate impression of mutual respect, equality, tolerance and cooperation.

The sociological assumption deals with the pattern of dominance and subordination within heterogeneous populations. Bicultural and biracial societies have always reflected the pattern of dominance and subordination along cultural or racial lines. Even societies founded in heterogeneity, such as the United States, or those committed to revolutionary egalitarianism, such as the Soviet Union, have not been able to overcome this tendency. To assert that Jews and Arabs are different than other peoples and have reached a level of enlightenment and civility not known in the species is wildly optimistic. Furthermore, the recent experience of the Middle-East provides overwhelming evidence against this assumption.

As a final point, the use of Semite in the term anti-Semitism does not include any group but Jews. This is so obvious that we are hesitant to state it. However, the frequent assertion that Arabs are Semites and therefore cannot be anti-Semitic requires some comment. The term itself is a psuedo-scientific outcropping of the racial ideologies. Just as racial theories attempted to give some respectability to persecutions of Jews, anti-Semitism is simply a code word for hatred of the Jew that is more palatable in a secular, non-religiously dominated world. A reading of anti-Semitic literature clearly indicates the target is the Jew, not all Semites. Asser-

369

tions to the contrary are either semantic gamesmanship or simple intellectual dishonesty or ignorance.

The following catalogue dealing with the experience of Jews under Islamic or Arabic rule is intended to clarify some of the misconceptions on this point and provide a better understanding of the role of anti-Semitism in the formation of Israel and the necessity of Israel's continued existence as a Jewish state.

THE ISLAMIC CATALOGUE, 600-1970 A.D.

BACKGROUND:

The rise and spread of Islam is one of the most remarkable religious and political events in history. The conversion of the bedouin, merchant Arab from polytheistic paganism to the monotheistic Moslem faith transformed the politics and civilization of the Near East. The weakness and decay of the Roman Empire and neighboring kingdoms to the East made them no match for the vitality and force of the Arab warriors armed with the sword and the Moslem faith. In less than a century the Islamic Empire gained control of the Mediterranean world from Spain through North Africa, Syria, and Persia to India.

As was the case with Christianity, Islam had a world-wide mission of salvation but in contrast to Christianity was armed with the sword of the state at its inception. Infidels were given the choice of Islam, the sword, or tribute. The Moslem religion made two exceptions to its quest for converts, Judaism and Christianity. Jews and Christians, while urged to recognize the truth and convert, were permitted to continue their religious beliefs. This unusual tolerance (especially for a monotheistic faith) is usually attributed to the great debt Mohammed felt to those two faiths. Islam borrows heavily from Judaism and Christianity and proclaims itself the more perfect version of God's covenant. The Koran recognizes and honors the great Jewish religious leaders and patriarchs, Mary and Jesus, and the Old and New Testament. Islam, however, rejects the idea of Jesus' divinity and sees him as a

371

great teacher, prophet and holy man. Because of this lineage, Jews and Christians have a special status in Islam as "people of the book." They have the right to practice their religion and have the protection of the state.

In this regard, there is a closer link between Islam and Judaism than between Islam and Christianity. The Judaic influence is stronger and more direct than the Christian influence. In addition, the core beliefs of Islam and Judaism are more similar and compatible. In contrast to Christianity, which also drew heavily from Judaism, Islam does not include the fundamental antagonistic elements toward Judaism found in Christianity. Jews are not the central theological villains in Islam as they are in Christian teaching.

Mohammed's first objective was to convert the Arab population from paganism to Islam. After a series of setbacks he was successful. The Jewish communities in the Arabian peninsula were the next targets. The Jews in and around Medina were of particular concern because this was Mohammed's adopted home. The Jews not only refused to convert but ridiculed his claims and interpretations of Scripture, characterizing him as an "illiterate uneducated madman." In response the Jewish communities in the area of Medina were attacked and either slaughtered or forced to migrate. Various explanations have been offered for these attacks and the truth is probably a combination. Mohammed certainly was disappointed and no doubt insulted by the Jewish rebuff. The Judaic sources in original Islam were minimized and anti-Semitic remarks added to the Koran after the failure to convert the Jews. So the impulse to redress insult and regain honor was present. Furthermore the continued existence of a rival monotheistic faith in the Prophet's backyard was not only an embarrassment but was a threat to unity that had to be removed. On the more mundane level, since most of Mohammed's followers in Medina were emigres and without property or wealth, the displacement of the Jewish owners of the agricultural developments enabled the Prophet to reward his followers and give them permanent settlement.

The early Moslem fury against the Jews living around Medina was quickly changed to a more tolerant attitude toward Jews further removed from Mohammed's home base. The Jews living north of Kaibhar were besieged by the Army of Islam but the siege was lifted in exchange for tribute. Shortly after Mohammed's death the Kaibhar Jewish settlement was expelled and the northern Arabian peninsula was purged of all infidels. Jewish settlements continued in Yemen however and with the exception of a short term expulsion in the 17th century continued to exist in Yemen until 1948.

Jews and Christians as "people of the book" enjoyed religious freedom and state protection under Islamic rule. There were episodic outbreaks of persecution, but they were rare and usually followed efforts at reform or revitalization of the Islamic faith that unleashed feelings of religious fervor and fanaticism. Other persecutions followed the pattern found elsewhere and are associated with crises or dislocations in the society.

It is important to understand that this tolerance and relative freedom from persecution did not follow from a societal structure where all groups had equal status. Islamic society was distinctively hierarchical in nature. The adherents of Islam were the clearly dominant group. There was also a hierarchy within the dominant group. The ruling group of Moslems consisted of the Caliphate kinship group and the Arabian Moslems that made up the aristocracy. Neo-Moslems or non-Arabic peoples who converted to Islam in the wake of the Arab conquests formed a subordinate class within this dominant group.

Members of tolerated religious Jews and Christians (but later Zoroastrians, Harrans and Berbers) "people of the book" occupied a distinctly subordinate position in relation to the Moslem population. These groups were known as Dhimmis, members of revealed religions with whom the Moslem leadership had made covenants granting religious freedom and state protection. Below the Dhimmis were the pagans whose choice in contact with the Armies of Islam was Islam or the sword. At the bottom of the social order were the slaves. Originally slaves were as in other societies of the time prisoners of war. Later the lucrative nature of the slave trade resulted in slaves being gathered through raiding parties which was not exactly the same as prisoners of war or conquest.

The status of the Dhimmis in Islamic society was clearly that of

373

subject. The tolerance and state protection was in exchange for payment of tribute and included other requirements by which the superior status of the Moslem population was assured. In addition to the tribute, taxes discriminated against the non-Moslem. They were forbidden to carry arms or ride horses and barred from civil positions of authority over Moslems. Sumptuary laws required them to appear less prosperous than the Moslems. Their houses and places of worship could not be higher than Moslem houses or places of worship. Non-Moslems were required to wear distinctive clothing or badges indicating their infidel status. Houses of worship were restricted and religious services were to be conducted in such a way as to not disturb or offend their Moslem neighbors. The inferior position of the Dhimmis vis-à-vis the Moslem population was clearly prescribed in Moslem law.

It should be noted that enforcement of the law was haphazard and inconsistent. Generally the more orthodox Moslem countries such as Yemen were more systematic and thorough going in enforcing these provisions. The more lax countries were less so. Periods of spiritual renewal or reform saw a more systematic enforcement outside the more orthodox countries.

With the exception of very early Islam when religious fanaticism was at its peak and a few isolated periods of persecution under some Moslem rulers, the relations between Jews and Moslem-Arabs had been generally nonviolent until the 20th century. The Jewish colonization of Palestine* and the rise of Zionism coincided with the birth of Arab nationalism. The rival claims over the area and the clash of the national interests of both groups changed the nature of Jewish/Arab relations. (It should be noted that the deceit and deviousness of the British on the Palestinian question added to the antagonisms in the region.)

The relative tolerance toward Jews of the previous 12 centuries in the Moslem countries was displaced by open hostility and violent persecutions. In addition, racial anti-Semitism intruded

---

*It should be noted that much of the Arab population of Palestine migrated to the area as a result of improvements that were made by the Jewish immigration.

into the area and was embraced by many Arab leaders. Arabic editions of *The Protocols of the Learned Elders of Zion* became quite popular. Many Arab leaders flirted with the Nazis, some actively supported the Nazis and applauded their approach to the Jewish question. The establishment of Israel intensified Arab hostility. Jews living in Arab countries were subjected to intense persecution and were forced to flee and had their property confiscated. Most migrated to Israel as refugees in the wake of persecutions that followed the first Israel/Arab war.

Anti-Semitic propaganda became a common feature of the mass media and educational systems of the Arab countries. Anti-Semitism has been a tool of domestic politics in the Arab world since Israeli independence and remains a major barrier to peace in the Middle East.

Many have argued that the only solution to the Middle-East crisis is the elimination of Isarel as a Jewish state and the establishment of a Palestinian state of Jews and Arabs—secular, democratic, pluralistic. Such a state would grant full citizenship and equality to all residents regardless of religion, race, or nationality. This position maintains that Arab hostility toward Isarel is directed not at Jews but at Zionism. If the Jewish political expression of Israel were removed, Arab/Jewish relations would return to the normalcy of mutual cooperation, tolerance and respect that existed in the past.

Even if the rhetoric of militant Arabs on the topic is dismissed as only rhetoric, the materials here indicate that the only accepted relation of Jew to Moslem is that of subject and inferior status. The problem of subordination and dominance in bicultural societies has not been resolved by Moslems any more successfully than other cultures (cf. Lebanon). From a Jewish perspective and for anyone who views Judaism and the Jewish cultural tradition of value and worth preserving the only acceptable position is the insistence on an independent and Jewish Israel.

The *Koran,* the sacred book of Islam, contains many favorable comments about Judaism. The influence of Judaism and Christianity on the Moslem faith is quite clear and acknowledged by Mohammed. There are, however, also a number of negative comments about Jews. The sura of the Cow has been characterized as a

375

polemic against Jews. This is assumed to reflect Mohammed's disappointment that Jews did not convert to Islam.

"And when a book came unto them from God, confirming the scriptures which were with them, although they had prayed for assistance against those who believed not, yet when that came unto them which they knew to be from God, they would not belief therein: therefore the curse of God shall be on the infidels."[1]

. . . they brought on themselves indignation on indignation; and the unbelievers shall suffer an ignominous punishment.[2]

Moreover, as for infidels, I will punish them with a grievous punishment in this world, and in that which is to come; and there shall be none to help them.[3]

They are smitten with vileness wheresoever they are found; unless they obtain security by entering into a treaty with God, and a treaty with men: and they draw on themselves indignation from God, and they are afflicted with poverty. This they suffer, because they disbelieved the signs of God, and slew the prophets unjustly; this because they are rebellious, and transgressed.[4]

Thou shall surely find the most violent of all men in enmity against the true believers to be the Jews, and the idolaters:[5]

Fight against them who believe not in God, nor the last day, and forbid not that which God and his apostle have forbidden, and profess not the true religion, of those unto whom the scriptures have been delivered, until they pay tribute by right of subjection, and they be reduced low.[6]

INCIDENTS:
624 A.D.

The Jewish communities around Medina had sided with the forces opposing Mohammed. In retaliation, Mohammed led his forces against these settlements. The settlement of Banu Quinaqua was the first attacked and after fifteen days was defeated. Mohammed intended to execute the survivors but an Arab chieftain Abdellah Ubn-Ubey intervened on their behalf and pleaded for mercy. Mohammed relented and banished the survivors from Arabia. Their property was confiscated, but they were permitted to take movable possessions.[7]

376

In Badr (Syria) a Jew played a prank on a Moslem woman that caused her humiliation (immodest exposure). A Moslem killed the Jew and was himself killed. Following the incident, a Moslem mob attacked the Jewish quarter and the Jews were forced to flee Syria. Their property and possessions were confiscated.[8]

626

The Jewish settlement at Banu-Modhir was attacked by Mohammed's army. Those not killed were forced to flee. Their property and possessions were confiscated.[9]

627

Mohammed led his forces against the Jewish settlement at Banu-Quaraiza. After the battle, a mock trial was held and all male Jews were condemned to death unless they converted to Islam. Between 650 and 700 were beheaded and thrown into a common grave. The women and children were enslaved.[10]

628

After the conquest of the area around Medina, Mohammed turned his attention to the north. The Jewish settlement at the Khaibar oasis was the next attacked. After resisting for two weeks a negotiated surrender provided that the Jews could maintain their settlement but had to pay a tribute of half of their annual produce.[11]

Following Khaibar, Mohammed concluded similar treaties with the Jews of Fodak, Teima, Maqnu, and other communities from the Red Sea to the Persian Gulf.[12]

634

Omar (Umar) I, Mohammed's successor, expelled his Jews from Khaibar two years after the Prophet's death.*[13]

638

During the siege of Jerusalem, Omar I accepted the conditions for surrender made by the Patriarch Sophronius. When the Chris-

*After unifying the Arabian peninsula under the Moslem faith, Omar I embarked on a career of world conquest unprecedented since Alexander the Great, and established Arabic hegemony throughout the Mediterranean.

tians surrendered, Omar expelled the Jewish community and forbade Jews to live in Jerusalem.[14]

As the Islamic empire expanded, Omar dealt with the problem of dealing with the increasing number of "people of the book" now under Islam rule. Expulsion was no longer a practical solution. As a solution, the Covenant of Omar was established. However, no new synagogues were to be built nor were existing ones to be repaired. Co-religionists were not to be hindered in converting to Islam. Religious services has to be performed in subdued tones and prayers for the dead had to be silent. Moslems had to be shown great respect whenever encountered. The "people of the book"— the Dhimmis—paid a tribute to Islam and were granted state protection and religious toleration. Jews were not to ride horses. They were required to wear clothing that indicated they were not Moslems and they were not permitted to use signet rings.*[15]

650

Every non-Moslem adult male living under Islamic Rule had to pay a special tax (the Jizyah). This was the tribute required of the dhimmis (protected people) in exchange for state protection and religious toleration. (See Covenant of Omar and Introduction and Background paper to Islam Catalogue.) Flogging, imprisonment and torture were sometimes used to collect the tax. In Iraq, the tax receipt was branded on the neck. Any non-Moslem not bearing the brand was liable to the death penalty.[16]

717-720

Omar II** formalized the Covenant of Omar by promulgating the Code of Omar. Jews were required to wear distinctive clothing or badges and were forbidden to ride horses or own weapons. The

*The Covenant of Omar applied to all "people of the book." Jews and Christians. Christians had to follow similar requirements.

**The Code was motivated by Omar's concern over the laxity and worldliness of the Umayed court in Damascus. It was an attempt to purify Islam and assure greater segregation of infidels from the faithful. With the exception of periods of religious reform and some of the more orthodox countries such as Yeman, the Code was not strictly enforced.

Code prohibited building any new places of worship. Jewish religious buildings and private homes were not to be higher than Moslem structures. Religious services had to be conducted in a subdued tone so as not to disturb or give offense to Moslems.[17]

807

Abassid Caliph Haroun Al Rashid enforced the Code of Omar with considerable security. Jews were required to wear a yellow badge and a rope in place of a girdle (belt).[18]

849-856

Arabian Caliph Al-Matavaklid renewed the enforcement of the Code of Omar. He also siezed a number of synagogues and converted them into mosques.[19]

850

Al-Jahiz (a Moslem scholar) wrote that Jews were unfit for abstract thinking because of continuous inbreeding.[20]

997

The Caliph Ibn Ali Amir (Al-Mansur) enforced the Code of Omar on Jews living under his rule in Spain. They were required to wear dark blue garments with sleeves that reached to the ground and wide skull caps that covered their ears.[21]

996-1021

The third Fatimid Caliph Al-Hakim went insane midway through his reign and embarked on a program of fanatical religious persecutions. His attacks on Christians included the destruction of the Church of the Holy Sepulchre and were a major cause of the Crusades.[22]

1008

Al-Hakim enforced the Code of Omar and attempted to force Jews to convert to Islam. Those who refused to convert were required to wear a picture of a calf around their necks. Jews who did violate the Code were exiled and had their property confiscated.[23]

1010

Jews under Al-Hakim's rule accommodated to the calf badge by transforming the requirement into a piece of decorative jewelry. Al-Hakim, in turn, required Jews to wear a six-pound wooden yoke around their necks, shaped like a calf's head with bells attached to warn Moslems of a Jew's approach.[24]

1014

Al-Hakim intensified his persecution of Jews. Synagogues were attacked and demolished. He ordered the Jewish quarter of Cairo burned with its inhabitants and all remaining Jews were expelled from his jurisdiction.[25]

1032-33

Moslem mobs attacked Jews living in Fez (Morocco). Six thousand Jews were slaughtered.[26]

1066

Moslems and Berbers massacred 4,000 Jews in Granada. Surviving Jews were expelled and their property was confiscated.[27]

1148

The rise of the Almohad caliphate in Morocco and Spain was accompanied by new persecutions. Jews in Spain and Morocco were given the choice of conversion to Islam or expulsion.[28]

1290

Following the Mongol conquest of Persia, Moslem mobs attacked and slaughtered Jewish communities throughout Persia.[29]

1438

The first ghetto was established in Morocco. Jews living in Fez were required to move into a walled area south of the city. These ghetto-like quarters were called mellahs in the Islamic countries.*[30]

---

*The establishment of the mellahs were a departure from Moslem practice and theology. Previously, non-Moslems were not required to live in segregated areas. Integrated communities were seen as an aid to proselytizing by the Moslems.

15th Century
The Jews in Persia and Afghanistan were forced into mellahs (walled off areas). They were not permitted to have any businesses outside the walls of the mellah.[31]

1493-1497
Many Jews expelled from Spain and Portugal migrated to Moslem countries. In most cases they found refuge. However, those who landed at Oran and Algiers were attacked by the Moslem population, locked out of the towns and left to starve.[32]

1535
The Jews in Tunisia were attacked by Moslem mobs; those not killed were expelled.[33]

1557
The Jews in Marrakesh were forced to move into a mellah (ghetto).[34]

1625-27
Moslem mobs regularly attacked Jews living in Jerusalem.[35]

1650
The Jews living in Tunisia were required to move into mellahs.[36]

1655
The synagogues in Palestine were closed to force payment of special taxes.[37]

1679
Jews were expelled from Yemen. The synagogue of San'a was converted into a mosque. (They were readmitted the next year but were required to live in mellahs outside the towns.)[38]

1790-1792
Jewish communities throughout Morocco were regularly attacked by Moslem mobs. Jewish property was destroyed or plundered and thousands were beaten and murdered.[39]

1805
Moslem mobs attacked and massacred Jewish communities in Algeria.[40]

1831
Jewish communities in Persia were attacked by Moslem mobs.[41]

1834
The Jewish community in Safaud (Palestine) was attacked by a Moslem mob.[42]

Moslem mobs attacked Jewish communities throughout Persia.[43]

1838
Mobs attacked the Jewish community in Safaud (Palestine).[44]

1840
A ritual murder accusation in Damascus was followed by persecution and massacre of the Jewish community.[45]

1848
Forced conversion to Islam took place throughout Persia.[46]

1859
In Morocco, mob attacks killed 400 of the Jewish community at Tetum.[47]

1869
Destruction of the Jewish Religion, an anti-Semitic tract, was published in Arabic in Beirut.[48]

1878
Moslem mobs attacked the Jewish communities in Arzela and Laraiche (Morocco).[49]

1891
Jewish communities throughout Persia were attacked by Moslem mobs.[50]

1899
An Arabic translation of August Rohling's *The Talmud Jew* was published in Cairo.[51]

1912
Moslem mobs attacked the Jewish mellah in Fez, Morocco.[52]

1920-21
Anti-Jewish riots occurred throughout the Arab world. Moslem mobs attacked Jewish settlements throughout Palestine. Forty-three Jews were killed and 134 wounded by mobs in Jaffa.[53]

1929
Anti-Jewish riots occurred throughout Palestine. Arab mobs killed 150 and wounded over 350 Jews in Jerusalem, Hebron, Safed and other communities.[54]

1934
Anti-Jewish riots occurred in Algeria; Arab mobs killed over 100 Jews and hundreds were injured.[55]

1935
Anti-Semitic legislation was passed in Iraq. The teaching of Hebrew was prohibited. Jews were barred from public employment.[56]

1936
Anti-Jewish riots occurred in Palestine.[57]

1941
Anti-Jewish riots in Iraq killed 150 Jews. Jewish homes and businesses were vandalized.[58]

1945
Anti-Jewish riots occurred in Egypt and Lybia. In Tripoli, 130 Jews were killed.[59]

1947

In Syria, Jews were forced to proclaim their opposition to Zionism. Mass arrests of Jews were carried out. Twelve synagogues were burned. The death penalty was imposed on Jews who attempted illegal emigration to Palestine.[60]

1947

Anti-Jewish riots occurred in Aden. The Jewish quarter was burned.[61]

1948

Anti-Jewish riots occurred in Lybia.[62]

Anti-Jewish riots occurred in Lebanon. Jewish homes and institutions were bombed.[63]

First Israel/Arab War

Anti-Jewish riots and attacks on Jews occurred throughout the Arab world. The governments of Egypt, Lebanon, Syria, Iraq imposed severe restrictions on Jews under their jurisdiction.[64]

In Egypt, Jews suspected of Zionist activities were imprisoned, their property was confiscated and assets were frozen. Widespread mob attacks on Jewish communities with beatings, killings and looting occurred.[65]

In Iraq, thousands of Jews were imprisoned or taken into protective custody on charges of Zionism. Laws were passed that limited the movement of Jews, barred them from schools and hospitals and severely restricted all business activity.[66]

In Lebanon, Jews ''under suspicion'' were confined in a prison camp.[67]

In Syria, Jews were forbidden to buy or sell property, bank accounts were frozen.[68]

First Israel/Arab War

In order to escape anti-Jewish persecutions and restrictions approximately 500,000 Jewish refugees migrated to Israel from Arab countries. Their property and possessions were confiscated by the Arab countries. Iraq alone gained property and assets valued at $200 million when 120,000 Jews fled to Israel.[69]

1951
A synagogue in Alexandria was bombed.[70]

1952
Anti-Jewish riots occurred in Tunisia; Jewish shops and commercial centers were looted.[71]

Jewish establishments in Cairo were attacked.[72]

1953
Two Jewish youth groups, the Maccabbi and the Boy Scouts, were ordered to disband by the Lebanon government. The groups were charged with carrying out military training.[73]

Libya ordered the Jewish youth group—the Maccabbi—to disband.[74]

1954
Egyptian government arrested 150 Jews on charges of Zionist activities. Thirteen were convicted as Zionist spies. Two were executed.[75]

1956
Egypt carried out program to remove Jews from economy. Bank accounts were frozen. Businesses were closed and confiscated. Jews were barred from professions. Synagogues were closed. Jews were declared enemies. Thirty-six thousand Jews were forced to migrate. Most of the refugees went to Israel.[76]

United Arab Republic Information Services published an Arabic translation of *The Protocols of the Elders of Zion.*[77]

1959
Jews were not permitted to emigrate from Syria.[78]

In Lybia, Jews were not permitted to vote or hold public office and were barred from serving in military or police forces. Special restrictions were applied to foreign Jews residing in Lybia and Jewish travel outside the country was restricted.[79]

1961
Anti-Jewish riots occurred in Algeria. Rebel forces destroyed a synagogue.[80]

1962
Three Jews were killed in anti-Jewish riots in Algeria.[81]

1963
Iraqi government required all Jews to register.[82]

1965
Anti-Semitic propaganda embracing racial and conspiratorial myths including *The Protocols* were present in mass media and education programs throughout the Arab world.[83]

1967
Arabic translation of *The Protocols of the Elders of Zion* was published in Cairo.[84]

1970
Libyan government issued decrees confiscating the property of all Jews living in the country.[85]

CONTINUUM:

Under Moslem/Arab rule Jews were subject to religious, civil, and political restrictions, discriminatory taxation, economic limitations, confiscation of property, forced conversion, expulsions, mob attacks and mass murder. Virtually every type of anti-Semitic behavior and action found in the Christian/Western world has occurred in the Moslem/Arab world. In some instances Islam has been the innovator and later copied by the West (most notably by the Jew badge). As infidels, Jews were formally placed in a subordinant and inferior social position *vis à vis* the Moslem.

However, in contrast to the Christian/Western experience anti-Semitism in the Islamic/Arab world was extremely mild and episodic until the 20th century. Restrictions were haphazardly enforced and a condition of religious toleration existed that was unknown in Christian society. And the Jews were not central villains in Moslem theology.

The 20th century, however, saw a change in the nature of anti-Semitism in Arab countries. Racial anti-Semitism made its appearance and the antagonism growing out of the establishment of Israel brought a pervasive anti-Semitism whose goal seems to be making the Middle East *Judenrein.* This has practically been achieved in the Arab countries as a result of state policies following the first Israeli/Arab war.

Unless permanent peace including the recognition of the legitimacy and sovereignty of Israel is achieved, further conflict between Israel and the Arab countries seems inevitable. In the event of Israel's defeat the probable result will be the total elimination of Jewish populations in the area.

NOTES TO THE ISLAMIC CATALOGUE, 600-1970 A.D.

1. *The Koran* (5th ed.; trans. and with explanatory notes and preliminary discourse by George Sale; Philadelphia: J. B. Lippincott & Co. 1864), p. 12.

2. Ibid.

3. Ibid., p. 43.

4. Ibid., p. 49.

5. Ibid., p. 92

6. Ibid., p. 151.

7. Graetz, op. cit., III, 77-78; Durant, *The Story of Civilization, Part IV The Age of Faith,* pp. 168-70.

8. Graetz, op. cit., III, 75-76.

9. Graetz, op. cit., III, 78-79; Phillip K. Hitti, *History of the Arabs* (New York: Macmillan & Co., Ltd., 1956), p. 117.

10. Graetz, op. cit., III, 79-81; Hitti, loc. cit.

11. Graetz, op. cit., pp. 81-83.

12. Ibid., pp. 82-83.

13. Graetz, op. cit., III, 84-85; Hitti, op. cit., pp. 140-42, 169.

14. Graetz, op. cit., III, 87-88.

15. Graetz, op. cit., III, 87-89; Hitti, op. cit., pp. 169-72.

16. S. D. Goitein, *Jews and Arabs* (New York: Schocken Books Inc., 1955), pp. 96-98; Hitti, op. cit., pp. 169-72.

17. Hitti, op. cit., pp. 231-36; Gil Carl Alroy, *Behind the Middle East Conflict* (New York: C. P. Putnam's Sons, 1975), pp. 183-84; Amir Hussar Siddiqi, *Non-Muslims Under Muslim Rule and Muslims Under Non-Muslim Rule* (Karachi: The Janiyatal Falah Publications, 1969), pp. 1-62.

18. Graetz, op. cit., III, 145; Alroy, op. cit., p. 184.

19. Graetz, op. cit., III, 176-77.

20. Goitein, op. cit., p. 100.

21. Graetz, op. cit., III, 511-12.

22. Goitein, op. cit., pp. 83-84; Hitti, op. cit., pp. 620-21.

23. Graetz, op. cit., III, 247.

24. Ibid., p. 248.

25. Goitein, op. cit., p. 84.

26. Alroy, op. cit., p. 185.

27. Graetz, op. cit., III, 275-79.

28. Graetz, op. cit., III, 357-62; Durant, *The Story of Civilization, Part IV The Age of Faith*, p. 372.

29. Graetz, op. cit., III, 648-50.

30. Israel Pocket Library, *Anti-Semitism,* p. 117.

31. Ibid., pp. 116-17.

32. Graetz, op. cit., IV, 361-62.

33. Israel Pocket Library, *Anti-Semitism,* p. 206.

34. Ibid., p. 117.

35. Alroy, op. cit., p. 187.

36. Israel Pocket Library, *Anti-Semitism,* p. 207.

37. Alroy, op. cit., p. 187.

38. Goitein, op. cit., pp. 74-76.

39. Israel Pocket Library, *Anti-Semitism,* p. 208.

40. Ibid., p. 208.

41. Flannery, op. cit., p. 194.

42. Alroy, op. cit., p. 187.

43. Flannery, op. cit., p. 194.

44. Alroy, op. cit., 187.

45. Graetz, op. cit., V, 632-41.

46. Elbogen, op. cit., p. 77.

47. Ibid., p. 75.

48. Israel Pocket Library, *Anti-Semitism,* p. 53.

49. Alroy, op. cit., p. 186.

50. Flannery, op. cit., p. 194.

51. Israel Pocket Library, *Anti-Semitism,* p. 53.

52. Ibid., p. 209; Flannery, op. cit., p. 194.

53. Elbogen, op. cit., pp. 589-99; Frank Gervasi, *The Case for Israel* (New York: The Viking Press, 1967), pp. 36-41.

54. Elbogen, op. cit., pp. 616-24; Gervasi, op. cit., pp. 45-51; Aharon Cohen, *Israel and the Arab World* (Boston: Beacon Press, 1976), p. 32.

55. Feberbush, op. cit., col. 666.

56. Ibid., col. 35.

57. Elbogen, op. cit., pp. 628-32; Cohen, op. cit., pp. 42-43.

58. Alroy, op. cit., p. 186.
59. Gervasi, op. cit., pp. 119-20.
60. Federbush, op. cit., col. 361.
61. Gervasi, op. cit., p. 119.
62. Israel Pocket Library, Anti-Semitism, p. 212.
63. Federbush, op. cit., col. 357.
64. Gervasi, op. cit., pp. 118-21.
65. Ibid., p. 120.
66. Ibid., p. 118; Forster & Epstein, op. cit., p. 157.
67. Federbush, op. cit., col. 357.
68. Gervasi, op. cit., p. 119.
69. Federbush, op. cit., col. 352.
70. Ibid., col. 676.
71. Ibid., col. 711.
72. Ibid., col. 675.
73. Ibid., col. 357.
74. Ibid., col. 685.
75. Ibid., col. 676.
76. Gervasi, op. cit., p. 120.
77. Y. Hurkabi, *Arab Attitudes To Israel* (Jerusalem, Israll: Israel Universities Press, 1972), p. 231.
78. Federbush, op. cit., col. 361.
79. Ibid., cols 684-85.
80. *New York Times,* September 12, 13, 1961; January 12, 1962.
81. *New York Times,* May 6, 1962.
82. *New York Times,* April 3, 1963.
83. Forster & Epstein, op. cit., pp. 162-63.
84. Israel Pocket Library, *Anti-Semitism,* p. 212.
85. *New York Times,* July 22, 1970.

BIBLIOGRAPHY

BIBLIOGRAPHY OF WORKS CONSULTED

Abboushi, W. F. *The Angry Arabs.* Philadelphia: The Westminster Press, 1974.

Abel, Ernest L. *The Roots of Anti-Semitism.* Cranberry, N. J.: Associated University Presses, Inc., 1975.

Abramovitch, R., et al. (ed.). *The Jewish People, Past and Present.* New York: Jewish Encyclopedia Inc., 1946.

Ackerman, Nathan, and Marie Sahoda. *Anti-Semitism and Emotional Disorder, A Psychoanalytic Interpretation.* New York: Harper, 1950.

Adler, H. G. *The Jews in Germany.* Notre Dame: Notre Dame University Press, 1961.

Agar, Herbert. *The Saving Remnant: An Account of Jewish Survival.* London: Rupert Hart-Davis, 1960.

Agus, Jacob Berhard. *The Meaning of Jewish History.* New York: Abelard-Schman, 1963.

Allport, Gordon. *The Nature of Prejudice.* Garden City, N.Y.: Doubleday Anchor, 1958.

Alroy, Gil Carl. *Behind the Middle East Conflict.* New York: G. P. Putnam's Sons, 1975.

Altman, Alexander (ed.). *Jewish Medieval and Renaissance Studies.* Cambridge, Mass.: Harvard University Press, 1967.

Anti-Semitism. Israel Pocket Library, Jerusalem: Keter Publishing House Jerusalem Ltd., 1974.

Arendt, Hannah. *The Burden of Our Time.* London: Secker and Warburg, 1951.

―――. *Eichmann in Jerusalem.* New York: Viking Press, 1963.

―――. *The Origins of Totalitarianism.* 2nd ed. New York: Meridian Books, 1958.

Arnold, T. W. *The Preaching of Islam.* Lahore, Pakistan: S. H. Muhummad Ashraf, 1961.

Arthur, Gilbert. *A Jew in Christian America.* New York: Sheed and Ward, 1966.

Askowith, Dora. *The Toleration and Persecution of the Jews in the Roman Empire.* New York: 1915.

Atkinson, S. L. Bopne. *The Development of the Inquestorial Precedure in the Pontificate of Innocent III.* Baton Rouge: L. S. U., 1941.

Ausubel, Nathan. *The Book of Jewish Knowledge.* New York: Crown Publishers, Inc., 1964.

―――. *Pictorial History of the Jewish People.* New York: Crown Publishing Company, 1953.

Baer, Yitzhak. *History of the Jews in Christian Spain.* Vols. I and II. Trans. from Hebrew—Louis Schoffman. Philadelphia: Jewish Publication Society of America, 1961.

Baily, Albert Edward, and Charles Foster Kent. *History of Hebrew Commonwealth.* New York: G. Scribner's Sons, 1920.

Bakan, David. *Sigmund Freud and the Jewish Mystical Tradition.* Princeton, N. J.: Van Nostrand Co., Inc., 1958.

Baldwin, James and Others. *Black Anti-Semitism and Jewish Racism.* New York: R. W. Baron, 1969.

Barkai, Meyer (trans. and ed.). *Fighting Ghettos.* New York: Tower Publications, Inc., 1962.

Baron, Salo Wittmayer. *The· Russian Jew Under Tsars and Soviets.* New York: Macmillan Company, 1964.

―――. *A Social and Religious History of the Jews.* 14 vols. New York: Columbia University Press, 1958-69.

Barrett, W. D. *The Trial of Jeanne d'Arc; A Complete Transla-*

tion of the Text of the Original Documents. London: G. Routledge and Sons Ltd., 1931.

Ben-Guiron, David. *The Jews in Their Land.* Trans. Misha Louvish. Garden City, New York: Doubleday, 1966.

Bennett, David H. *Demagogues in the Depression.* New Brunswick, New Jersey: Rutgers University Press, 1969.

Berdyaev, Nikolai Alekandrovich. *Christianity and Anti-Semitism, With Commentary and Notes* by Alan A. Spears. Trans. Spears, Alan, and Kanter, Victor B. Great Britain: Ditchling Press Sussex, 1952.

Bevan, Edwyn, and Sir George Adam Smith, and Others. *The Legacy of Israel; Essays.* Oxford: Clarendon Press, 1927.

Biberfield, Phillip Leon. *Universal Jewish History.* New York: Spero Foundation, 1948.

Bloch, Joshua. *The People and the Book: the Background of Three Hundred Years of Jewish Life in America.* New York: Bloch Publishing Company, 1954.

Bloch, Joseph S. *Israel and the Nations.* Berlin: Benjamin Harz, 1927.

Borchsenius, Poal. *The History of the Jews.* New York: Simon and Schuster, 1965.

Bottomore, T. B. trans. & ed. *Karl Marx: Early Writings.* New York: McGraw-Hill Book Company, 1964.

Bradford, Ernle. *The Sundred Cross: The Story of the Fourth Crusade.* Englewood Cliffs, N. J.: Prentice-Hall, 1967.

Braverman, H. "Combatting Anti-Semitism by Exposing Anti-Semites," *Jewish Social Service Quarterly,* Vol. 23.

Bright, John. *Early Israel in Recent History.* Chicago: A. R. Allenson, 1956.

Broszat, Martin, et al. *Anatomy of the SS State.* Cambridge: William Collins Sons & Company Limited, 1968.

Browne, Lewis. *Stranger than Fiction, Short History of the Jews from Earliest Times to Present.* New York: Macmillan Company, 1927.

Buchler, Adolf. *Studies in Jewish History.* London & New York: Oxford University Press, 1956.

Byrnes, Robert F. *Antisemitism in Modern France.* New Brunswick, N.S.: Rutgers University Press, 1950.

Cadoux, Cecil John. *Phillip of Spain and the Netherlands: An Essay on Moral Judgment in History.* London: Lutterworth Press, 1947.

Calisch, Rabbi Edward. *The Jew in English Literature.* Port Washington, New York: Kennikat Press, 1969.

Carson, Saul. *One Hundred Sixty-Five Temples Desecrated.* Ed. Norman Hill. New York: Popular Library, 1971.

Chapman, A. B. *English Merchants and the Spanish Inquisition in the Canaries of Marquess of Bute Archives.* London: Offices of the Society, 1912.

Cohen, Aharon, *Israel and the Arab World* (abridged ed.). Boston: Beacon Press, 1976.

Cohn, Norman. *Warrant for Genocide.* New York: Harper & Row Publishers, 1966.

Coulton, G. G. *Inquisition and Liberty.* Boston: Beacon Press, 1959.

———. *Inquisition in the Spanish Dependencies.* New York: MacMillan Company, 1908.

Daniel-Rops, H. *History of the Christian Church.*

Davies, J. C. *The Early Christian Church.* New York: Holt Rinehart & Winston, 1965.

Davis, Israel. *The Jews in Roumania; A Short Statement of Their Recent History and Present Situation.* London: Trubner and Company, 1872.

Dawidowicz, Lucy S. *The War Against Jews.* New York: Bantum Books, 1975.

Dellon, C. *An Account of the Inquisition at Goa, in India.* Boston: Samuel T. Armstrong, 1815.

Dimont, Max I. *The Indestructible Jews.* New York: New American Library, 1971.

———. *Jews, God and History.* New York: Simon and Schuster, 1962.

Divine, R. *American Immigration Policy.* New Haven: Yale University Press, 1957.

Dubnov, S. M. *History of the Jews in Russia and Poland: From the Earliest Times Until the Present Day*. 2 vols. Trans. from Russian by I. Friedlaender. Philadelphia: The Jewish Publication Society of America, 1920.

Durant, Will. *The Story of Civilization*. 8 vols. New York: Simon and Schuster, 1963.

Eban, Abba. *My People: The Story of the Jews*. New York: Berham House, 1968.

————. *Voices of Israel*. New York: Horizon Press, 1957.

Elbogen, Ismar. *A Century of Jewish Life*. Trans. Moses Hados. Philadelphia: Jewish Publications Society of America, 1945.

Elkins, Michael. *Forged in Fury*. New York: Ballantine Books, Inc., 1971.

Epstein, Benjamin R., and Arnold Forster. *Cross-Currents*. Garden City, New York: Doubleday, 1956.

————. *Some of My Best Friends . . . "* New York: Farrer, Straus and Cudahy, 1962.

Federbush, Simon (ed.) *World Jewry Today*. New York: T. Yoseloff, 1959.

Finkelstein, Louis. *Jewish Self-Government in the Middle Ages*. New York: P. Feldheim, 1964.

————. *The Jews: Their History, Culture and Religion*. New York: Harper, 1955.

Flannery, Edward H. *The Anguish of the Jews: Twenty-Three Centuries of Anti-Semitism*. New York: MacMillan, 1965.

Fleetwood, John. *The Life of Our Lord and Savior Jesus Christ*. Boston: Wentworth and Company, 1856.

Foerster, Friedrich Wilhelm. *The Jews*. Trans. Robert McAfee Brown. New York: Farrar, Straus and Cudahy, 1961.

Forster, Arnold. *A Measure of Freedom*. Garden City, N.Y.: Doubleday and Company, Inc., 1950.

————, and Benjamin Epstein. *The New Anti-Semitism*. New York: McGraw Hill Book Company, 1974.

Freid, Jacob (ed.). *Jews in the Modern World*. New York: Twayne Publishers, Inc., 1962.

Freud, Sigmund. *Moses and Monotheism*. New York: Vintage Books, 1939.

Fulton, John. *Index Canonum*. New York: Pott, Young & Co., 1872.

Gay, Ruth. *Jews in America.* New York: Basic Books, 1965.

Gervasi, Frank. *The Case for Israel.* New York: Viking Press, 1967.

Glanz, Rudolph. *The Jews in American Alaska.* New York: H. H. Glanz, 1953.

Glassman, Bernard. *Anti-Semitic Stereotypes Without Jews.* Detroit: Wayne State University Press, 1975.

Glazer, Nathan. *The Many Faces of Anti-Semitism.* New York: American Jewish Committee, Institute of Human Relations, 1967.

Glock, Charles Y., and Rodney Stark. *Christian Beliefs and Anti-Semitism.* New York: Harper and Row, 1955.

Godby, Allen H. *The Lost Tribes a Myth: Suggestions Toward Rewriting Hewbrew History.* Durham, N. C.: Duke University Press, 1930.

Goitein, Soloman. *Jews and Arabs, Their Contact Through the Ages.* New York: Schoken Book, 1955.

Goldman, Eva, and Zeeu. *A Land That I Will Show Thee: The Jewish People Through the Ages.* New York: Putnam, 1968.

Goodman, Paul. *History of the Jews.* New York: Dutton, 1951.

Gottheil, Richard. *Fragments from the Cairo Genizah in the Freer Collection.* New York: The MacMillan Company, 1927.

Government of the Federal Republic of Germany. *The Anti-Semitic and Nazi Incidents, From Twenty-Five December 1959 until Twenty-Eight January 1960.* White Paper of the Government of the Federal Republic of Germany. Bonn: 1960.

Graber, Isaque. *Jews in a Gentile World: Problem of Anti-Semitism.* New York: MacMillan, 1942.

Graetz, Heinrich Hirsh. *History of the Jews.* 5 vols. Philadelphia: The Jewish Publication Society of America, 1898.

Grayzel, Soloman. *A History of the Jews from Babylonian Exile to the Present.* Philadelphia: Jewish Publication Society of America, 1968.

Grayzel, Soloman. *The Church and the Jews of the Thirteenth Century.* Philadelphia: The Dropsie College for Hebrew and Cognate Learning, 1933.

Greenberg, Louis. *The Jews in Russia.* London: H. Milford, Oxford University Press, 1944.

Guignebert, Charles. *The Jewish World in the Time of Jesus.* London: K. Paul Trench, Trubner and Company, Ltd., 1939.

Hay, Malcolm. *Europe and the Jews.* Boston: Beacon Press, 1950.

Harkabi, Y. *Arab Attitudes to Israel.* Trans. Misha Louvish. Jerusalem: Israel University Press, 1972.

Harris, Maurice. *Medieval Jews From the Moslem Conquest of Spain to the Discovery of America.* New York: Bloch Publishing Company, 1958.

Heer, Friedrich. *God's First Love.* Trans. Geoffrey Skelton. New York: Weybright and Tulley, 1967.

————. *The Medieval World.* Trans. Janet Sondheimer. New York: New American Library, 1961.

Hilbery, Raul. *The Destruction of the European Jews.* Chicago: Quadrangle Books, 1961.

Hitti, Phillip. *History of the Arabs.* New York: St. Martin's Press, 1956.

Hitti, Phillip. *Makers of Arab History.* New York: St. Martin's Press, 1968.

Hochhuth, Rolf. *The Deputy.* New York: Grove Press, 1964.

Hohne, Heinz. *The Order of the Death's Head.* (trans. Richard Barry;) New York: Ballantine Books, Inc., 1971.

Hosmer, James Kendall. *The Jews, in Ancient, Medieval and Modern Times.* New York: G. P. Putnam, 1889.

Howe, Irving, and Carl Gershman. *Israel, The Arabs and the Middle East.* New York: Bantam Books, 1972.

Huebener, Theodore, and Carl Voss. *This is Israel; Palestine: Yesterday, Today and Tomorrow.* New York: Philosophical Library, 1956.

Hyamson, A. M. *A History of the Jews in England.* London: Chatto and Windus, 1908.

Ingrahm, Reverend Joseph Holt. *The Pillar of Fire; or Israel in Bondage.* New York: Pudney and Russell, 1859.

Isaac, Jules. *The Teaching of Contempt.* New York: McGraw-Hill Book Company, Isaac, 1965.

Rael Jean. *Israel Divided.* Baltimore: Johns Hopkins University Press, 1976.

Ives, I. M. *Lectures on the Inquisition.* Milwaukee: Rufus King and Company, 1853.

Jarman, T. L. *The Rise and Fall of Nazi Germany.* New York: The New American Library, 1961.

Jewish Black Book Committee. *The Black Book, the Nazi Crime Against the Jewish People.* New York: Duell, Sloan and Pearce, 1946.

Jones, Winfield. *Story of the Ku Klux Klan.* Washington: American Newspaper Syndicate, no date.

Jonker, Abraham. *The Scapegoat of History.* Capetown: Central News Agency Limited, 1941.

Josephus, Flavius. *The Wars of the Jews.* London: John Harris, 1832.

Kahler, Erich. *The Jews Among the Nations.* New York: F. Unger Publishing Company, 1967.

Kahn, Roger. *The Passionate People.* New York: William Morrow and Company, Inc., 1968.

Kamm, Josephine. *The Hebrew People: A History of the Jews From Biblical Times to the Present Day.* London: Gollancz, 1967.

Kane, William T., and John J. O'Brien. *History of Education.* Chicago: Loyola University Press, 1954.

Kaplan, Mordecai M. *Judaism as a Civilization.* New York: Thomas Yoseloff, Inc., 1957.

Katz, Jacob. *Out of the Ghetto.* Cambridge, Mass.: Harvard University Press, 1973.

———. *Tradition and Crisis: Jewish Society at the End of the Middle Ages.* New York: Free Press of Glencoe, 1961.

Katz, Shlomo (ed.). *Negro and Jew: An Encounter in America; A Symposium Compiled by Midstream Magazine.* New York: MacMillan, 1967.

Katzenstein, Julius. *History and Destiny of the Jews.* Trans. Paterson. New York: The Viking Press, 1933.

Kennedy, John. *On Israel, Zionism and Jewish Issues.* New York: Theodor Herzl Foundation, Inc., 1965.

Kent, Charles Foster. *The Heroes and Crisis of Early Hebrew History From the Creation to the Death of Moses.* New York: Scribner's Sons, 1908.

Khouri, Fred J. *The Arab-Israeli Dilemma.* Syracuse, N.Y.: The Syracuse University Press, 1968.

Kisch, G. *The Jews in Medieval Germany.* Chicago: University of Chicago Press, 1949.

Kochan, Lionel. *Jews in Soviet Russia Since Nineteen-Seventeen.* London, New York: Oxford University Press, 1970.

The Koran (trans. George Sale). Philadelphia: J. B. Lippincott & Co., 1864.

Krey, August. *The First Crusade: The Accounts of Eye-Witnesses and Participants.* Glovester, Mass.: Princeton University Press, 1921.

Lacquer, Walter. *Confrontation: The Middle East and World Politics.* New York: New York Times Book Co., 1974.

————. *A History of Zionism.* New York: Holt Rinehart and Winston, 1972.

Lamb, Harold. *The Crusades.* London: Garden City Publishing Co., 1930.

Landman, Isaac (ed.). *Universal Jewish Encyclopedia.* New York: Universal Jewish Encyclopedia Inc., 1939.

Lapide, Pinchas. *Three Popes and the Jews.* New York: Hawthorn Books, Inc., 1967.

Lea, Henry Charles. *A History of the Inquisition of the Middle Ages.* New York: Harper and Brothers, 1888.

————. *The Inquisition in the Spanish Dependencies.* New York: MacMillan Company, 1908.

Learsi, Rufus. *Israel: A History of the Jewish People.* Cleveland: World Publishing Company, 1949.

Van Leeuwen, Arend Theodor. *Christianity in World History.* New York: Charles Scribner's Sons, 1964.

Leon, Abram. *The Jewish Question: A Maryist Interpretation.* New York: Pathfinder Press, Inc., 1960.

Leroy-Beaulieu, Anatole. *Israel Among the Nations A Study of the Jews and Antisemitism.* Trans. Frances Hellman. New York: Putnam Sons, 1895.

Leschnitzer, Adolf. *The Magic Background of Modern Anti-Semitism: An Analysis of the German Jewish Relationship.* New York: International University Press, 1956.

Levinger, Lee Joseph. *Anti-Semitism Yesterday and Tomorrow.* New York: The MacMillan Company, 1936.

Lewy, Guenter. *The Catholic Church and Nazi Germany.* New York: McGraw-Hill Book Company, 1964.

Lieberman, Saul. *Hellenism in Jewish Palestine.* New York: Jewish Theological Seminary of America, 1962.

Liptzin, Soloman. *The Jews in American Literature.* New York: Block Publishing Company, 1966.

Littell, Franklin. *The Crucifixion of the Jews.* New York: Harper Row, 1975.

———. *German Phoenix: Men and Movements in the Church in Germany.* Garden City, N.Y.: Doubleday, 1960.

Litvinoff, Barnet. *A History of Zionism.* New York: Frederick Praeger, Publishers, 1965.

Loewenstein, Rudolph Maurice. *Christians and Jews, A Psychoanalytic Study.* Trans. Vera Damman. New York: International Press, 1959.

Long, Emil. *Two Thousand Years: A History of Anti-Semitism.* New York: Exposition Press, 1953.

Lowenthal, Marvin. *The Jews of Germany: A Story of Sixteen Centuries.* Philadelphia: Jewish Publishing Society of America, 1936.

McKenzie, John L., S.J. *The Power and the Wisdom.* Milwaukee: The Bruce Publishing Co., 1965.

McWilliams, Carey. *A Mask for Privilege.* Boston: Little, Brown and Company, 1948.

Manners, Andre. *Poor Cousins.* Greenwich, Conn.: Fawcett Publications, Inc., 1972.

Marcus, Jacob R. *The Jew in the Medieval World.* New York: Atheneum, 1969.

Maritian, Jacques. *Antisemitism.* London: G. Bles, Century Press, 1939.

Massing, Paul W. *Rehearsal for Destruction.* New York: Harper Brothers, 1949.

402

Mayar, Benjamin, and Moshe Davis. *The Illustrated History of the Jews.* New York: Harper & Row Publishers, 1963.

Maycock, Alan Lawson. *The Inquisition From Its Establishment to the Great Schism.* New York: Harper, 1927.

Miller, Leonard Martin. *Outgroup Rejection and Hostility in a College Population.* Baton Rouge: Louisiana State University Press, 1960.

Mocha, Frederic David. *The Jews of Spain and Portugal and the Inquisition.* New York: George Dob Sevage, 1933.

Modder, Montagu Frank. *The Jew in the Literature of England.* New York: Meridian Books, Inc., 1960.

Morris, Terry. *Better Than You.* New York: Institute of Human Relations Press, 1971.

Nasser, Gamal. *The Philosophy of the Revolution.* Buffalo: Smith, Keynes and Marshall, Publishers, 1959.

The New Testament (Trans. from the Latin Vulgate; a Revision of the Challoner-Rheims Version). Patterson, N.J.: St. Anthony Guild Press, 1951.

New York Times. March, 1960-July, 1970.

Niewyk, Donald L. *Socialist, Anti-Semite and Jew: German Social Democracy Contfronts the Problem of Anti-Semitism.* Baton Rouge: Louisiana State Univeristy Press, 1971.

Olson, Bernhard Emmanuel. *Faith and Prejudice: Intergroup Problems in Protestant's Curricula.* New Haven: Yale University Press, 1963.

Ostrowski, Wiktor. *Anti-Semitism in Byelorussia and Its Origin: Material for Historic Research and Study of the Subject.* London: Byelorussia Central Council, 1960.

Paetow, Louis J. (ed.). *The Crusades and Other Historical Essays: Presented to Dana Munro by his Former Students.* New York: F. S. Crofts and Company, 1928.

Parkes, James William. *Antisemitism.* London: Vallentine, 1963.

Peloulet, D. D., And Alice Adams. *Peloulet's Bible Dictionary.* Philadelphia: John C. Winston, Company, 1947.

Pharr, Clyde. *The Theodosian Code.* Princeton: Princeton University Press, 1952.

Philipson, David. *The Jew in English Fiction.* Cincinnati: R. Clarke and Company, 1889.

Pichon, Charles. *The Vatican and its Role in World Affairs.* Trans. Jean Misrahi. New York: E. P. Dutton & Company, Inc., 1950.

Poliakov, Leon. *The History of Anti-Semitism.* Trans. Richard Howard. New York: Vanguard Press, 1965.

Pulzer, Peter G. *The Rise of Political Anti-Semitism in Germany.* New York: John Wiley & Sons, Inc., 1964.

Ruddock, Charles. *Portrait of a People.* 3 vols. New York: Judaica Press, 1965.

Raisin, Max. *A History of the Jews in Modern Times.* Rev. ed. New York: Hebrew Publishing Company, 1949.

Randel, William Pierce. *The Ku Klux Klan: A Century of Infamy.* Philadelphia: Chilton Books, 1965.

Reichman, Eva Gabriele. *Hostages of Civilization, the Social Sources of National Socialist Anti-Semitism.* Boston: Beacon Press, 1951.

Resner, Lawrence. *Eternal Stranger: The Plight of the Modern Jew.* Garden City, N. Y.: Doubleday, 1951.

Rice, Edward. *A Young Peoples Pictoral History of the Church.* New York: Farrar Straus and Company, 1963.

Robb, James H. *Working-Class Anti-Semite; A psychological Study in a London Borough.* London: Tavistock Publications, 1954.

Robinson, T. H. *A History of Israel.* Oxford: The Clarendon Press, 1951.

Rogge, Oetje John. *The Official German Report: Nazi-Penetration 1924-42 Pan-Arabism 1939-Today.* New York: T. Yoseloff, 1961.

Rogow, A. *The Jews in a Gentile World.* New York: MacMillan, 1961.

Rosenstock, Morton. *Louis Marshall, Defender of Jewish Rights.* Detroit: Wayne State University Press, 1965.

Roth, Cecil. *A History of the Jews in England.* Oxford: Clarendon Press, 1965.

Roth, Cecil. *A Short History of the Jewish People.* London: East and West Library, 1959.

————, and Max Wurmbrand. *The Jewish People Four Thousand Years of Survival.* Jerusalem: Massadah P. E. C. Press, 1960.

————. *The Jews in the Renaissance.* Philadelphia: Jewish Publication Society of America, 1930.

————(ed.). *The Standard Jewish Encyclopedia.* Garden City, New York: Doubleday, 1959.

————. *Venice, Jewish Community Studies.* Philadelphia: Jewish Publication Society of America, 1930.

————. *World History of the Jewish People.* Vol. XI: *Dark Ages.* New Brunswick, N. J.: Rutgers Viking Press, 1963.

Rubenstein, Richard L. *After Auschwitz.* New York: Bobbs-Merrill Company, Inc., 1966.

Rubin, Ronald. *The Unredeemed; Anti-Semitism in the Soviet Union.* Chicago: Quadrangle Books, 1968.

Runciman, Steve. *A History of the Crusades.* Vol. I: *The First Crusade.* Vol. II: *The Kingdom of Jerusalem.* London: Cambridge University Press, 1953, 1957.

Runes, Dagobert. *The Jew and the Cross.* New York: Philosophical Library, 1966.

Runes, Dagobert. *The War Against the Jews.* New York: Philosophical Library, 1968.

Lord Russell of Liverpool. *The Scourge of the Swastika.* New York: Ballantine Books, 1961.

Sachar, Abram. *A History of the Jews.* New York: Knopf, 1969.

Sachar, Howard. *The Courses of Modern Jewish History.* Cleveland: World Publishing Company, 1958.

St. John, Robert. *Foreign Correspondent.* Garden City, N.Y.: Doubleday, 1957.

————. *Roll, Jordan, Roll.* Garden City, N. Y.: Doubleday, 1965.

————. *Shalom Means Peace.* Garden City, N. Y.: Doubleday, 1949.

Sandars, Thomas Collett. *The Institutes of Justinian.* Chicago: Calloghan and Company, 1876.

Saretsky, Augusta. *A Guide to Jewish Juvenile Literature.* New York: Jewish Education Committee Press, 1968.

Saron, Gustav (ed.). *The Jews in South Africa.* New York: Oxford University Press, 1955.

Sartre, Jean Paul. *Anti-Semite and Jew.* Trans. Geo. S. Becker. New York: Schoken Books, 1908.

Schappes, Morris U. *The Jews in the United States.* New York: The Citadel Press, 1958.

Schonfield, Hugh J. *The Passover Plot.* New York: Bernard Geis Associates, 1965.

Selzer, Michael. *"Kike!"* New York: World Publishing Company, 1972.

Selznick, Gertrude S., and Stephen Steinberg. *The Tenacity of Prejudice: Anti-Semitism in Contemporary America.* New York: Harper and Row, 1969.

Seuver, James Everett. *Persecution of the Jews in the Roman Empire.* Kansas: Lawrence University of Kansas Publications, 1952.

Sevenster, Jan Nicholas. *The Roots of Anti-Semitism in the Ancient World.* Leiden: Brill, 1975.

Sharf, Andrew. *The British Press and Jews Under Nazi Rule.* New York: Oxford University Press, 1964.

Shirer, William Lawrence. *Rise and Fall of the Third Reich.* Greenwich, Conn.: Fawcett, 1950.

Siddiqi, Amir Hasan. *Non-Muslims Under Muslim Rule and Muslims Under Non-Muslim Rule.* Karachi: The Jamiyatul Falah Publications, 1964.

Simonhoff, Harry. *Saga of American Jewry.* New York: Arco Publishing Company, Inc., 1959.

Sleeper, A. James, and Alan L. Minly. *The New Jews.* New York: Random House, Inc., 1971.

Smith, Lacey Baldwin, and Jean Reeder Smith. *World History.* Woodbury, N.Y.: Barron's Educational Series, Inc., 1966.

Smolar, Boris. *Soviet Jewry: Today and Tomorrow.* New York: The Macmillan Company, 1971.

Snoek, Johan M. *The Grey Book: A Collection of Protest Against Anti-semitism and the Persecution of Jews by Non-Roman Catholic Churches and Church Leaders.* New York: Humanities Press, 1970.

Steinber, Herbert and Others. *Jews in the Mind of America.* New York: Basic Books, 1966.

Stromberg, Ronald N. *A History of Western Civilization.* Homewood, Ill.: Dorsey Press, 1969.

Strong, Donald. *Organized Anti-Semitism in America.* Washington, D. C.: American Council on Public Affairs, 1941.

Synan, Edward A. *The Popes and the Jews in the Middle Ages.* New York: Macmillan Company, 1965.

Theme, R. B., Jr. *Anti-Semitism.* Houston: Berachah Tapes and Publications, 1974.

Trachtenberg, Joshua. *The Devil and the Jews.* New Haven: Yale University Press, 1943.

Tumin, Melvin Marvin. *An Inventory and Appraisal on American Anti-Semitism.* New York: Freedom Books, 1961.

Turberville, A. S. *Medieval Heresy and the Inquisition.* London: C. Lockwood and Sons, 1920.

Vacandard, E. *The Inquisition: A Critical and Historical Study of the Coercive Power of the Church.* New York: Longman and Green Company, 1908.

Valentin, Hugo Mauritz. *Antisemitism Historically and Critically Examined.* Trans. A. G. Chater. New York: The Viking Press, 1936.

Verrill, A. Hyah. *The Inquisition.* New York: D. Appleton and Company, 1931.

Walker, Brooks R. *The Christian Fright Peddlers.* Garden City, N. Y.: Doubleday and Company, 1964.

Walsh, William Thomas. *Characters of the Inquisition.* New York: P. S. Kennedy and Sons, 1940.

Weinryb, Bernard D. *The Jews of Poland.* Philadelphia: The Jewish Publication Society of America, 1972.

Weintraub, Ruth. *How Secure These Rights? Anti-Semitism in the United States in 1948; An Anti-Defamation League Survey.* Garden City, New York: Doubleday, 1949.

Weyl, Nathaniel. *The Jew in American Politics.* New York: Arlington House, 1968.

Wollmantsamir, Pinchas. *The Graphic History of the Jewish Heritage.* New York: Shengold Publishers, 1963.

Works Progress Administration Personnel. *Pamphlets Relating to the Jews in England During Seventeenth and Eighteenth Centuries.* San Francisco: California State Library, 1939.

Yinger, John Milton. *Anti-Semitism: A Case Study in Prejudice and Discrimination.* New York: Anti-Defamation League of B'Nai and B'rith, 1964.

OTHER SOURCES

Encyclopaedia Judaica. 16 v. New York: Macmillan Company, 1971.

Gilbert, Martin. *The Jewish History Atlas.* New York: MacMillan, 1969.

The Jewish Encyclopedia. 12 v. New York: Funk and Wagnalls, Co., 1906.

The Jewish Social Science Quarterly.

The New York Times.

Newsweek Magazine.